HISTORY OF EUROPE
(1492–1815)

BY

CHESTER PENN HIGBY, Ph.D.

Professor of History in the University of North Carolina

UNDER THE EDITORSHIP OF
JAMES T. SHOTWELL, LL.D.
Professor of History in Columbia University

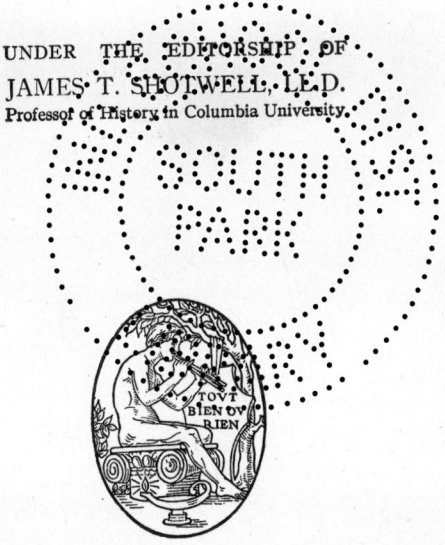

HOUGHTON MIFFLIN COMPANY

BOSTON   NEW YORK   CHICAGO   DALLAS   SAN FRANCISCO

The Riverside Press Cambridge

COPYRIGHT, 1927
BY CHESTER PENN HIGBY

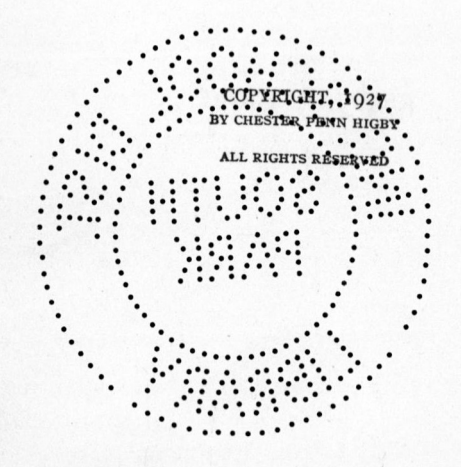

ALL RIGHTS RESERVED

The Riverside Press
CAMBRIDGE · MASSACHUSETTS
PRINTED IN THE U.S.A.

Lamar College

TO
REV. J. H. HIGBY.

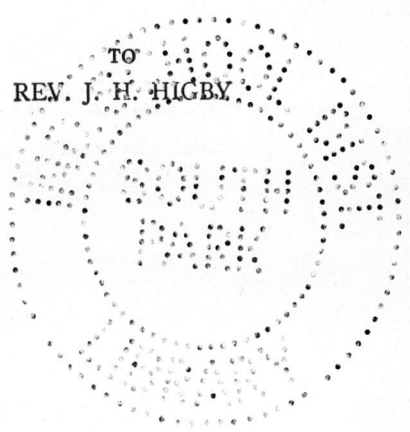

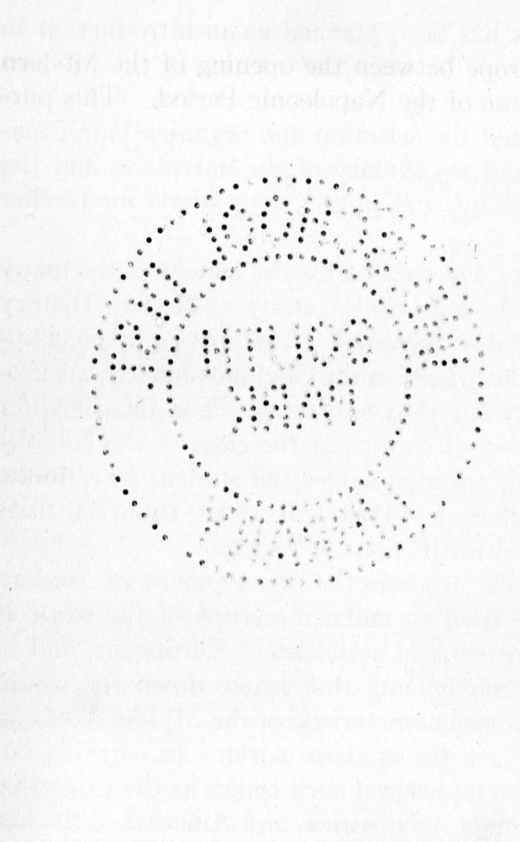

PREFACE

THE present work has been planned as an introduction to the history of Europe between the opening of the Modern Period and the close of the Napoleonic Period. This purpose has determined the selection and organization of material, the style and vocabulary of the narrative, and the character of the maps and of the suggestions for further reading.

The first chapter was written for the benefit of the many college students who take up the study of Modern History with little historical background. The next eighteen chapters narrate in orderly fashion the chief movements of European History between 1492 and 1815. The final chapter gives a cross-section of Europe at the close of the Napoleonic Period. This survey enables the student to estimate the permanent influence of the events of the three centuries on the peoples and institutions of Europe.

The theme of the work is the development of Modern Europe. I have tried to make the scope of the work as broad as the interests and activities of Europeans, and to emphasize those movements that broke down the conditions and institutions characteristic of the Middle Ages and so helped to produce the modern world. In carrying out these aims I have emphasized such topics as the expansion of Europe — through Asia, Africa, and America — the history of Russia and the Balkans as well as that of Western Europe, the growth of Protestantism, the reform of the Roman Catholic Church, the development of modern science and thought, the evolution of parliamentary institutions, the rise of the middle class, the Industrial Revolution, and the abolition of feudalism. In short, I have attempted to interweave in the narrative the economic, social, religious, and intellectual threads with the political and military.

I am not consciously a disciple of any particular school

of History. I have honestly tried to keep an open mind amid the clashing claims of rival interpretations. I have, I hope, included the important economic and social movements of European History without feeling forced to consider the Protestant Revolt and the Catholic Reformation merely as economic phenomena; and I have endeavored to avoid writing a "battle history" without, on the other hand, passing in silence the hard fact of war. My endeavor has been to show that history is the product of many forces.

C. P. HIGBY

CHAPEL HILL
NORTH CAROLINA

ACKNOWLEDGMENTS

The author would feel guilty of ingratitude if he did not acknowledge his great indebtedness to the teachers, historians, friends and colleagues, who contributed directly or indirectly to the making of the present volume. From the lectures and seminar discussions of Professors Shotwell, Robinson, Shepherd, Hayes, and Sloane came many of the specific facts and the generalizations to be found in the chapters on "Beginnings of Overseas Expansion," "The Intellectual Revolt against Authority," "England in the Latter Half of the Eighteenth Century," "The French Revolution," and the Napoleonic Period. From a host of monographs, biographies, histories of countries, periods and movements, and general works came much of the other material, the references at the end of each chapter being merely designed as an aid to the student and not as an indication of the scope of the author's own reading. Finally, many friends and academic colleagues put at the author's service their rich, special stores of knowledge.

A more detailed acknowledgment is due these friends and colleagues: Professor J. G. de Roulhac Hamilton, of the history department of the University of North Carolina, suggested the writing of the book, gave freely of his advice and encouragement, and read much of the manuscript. Professor R. D. W. Connor, of the same department, read the entire manuscript in a most painstaking manner. Professor Harry Elmer Barnes, of Smith College, read the first five chapters and made important suggestions concerning the organization of the book and the themes it should emphasize. Professor J. Fred Rippy, of Duke University, read the chapter on "Beginnings of Overseas Expansion" and several other chapters. Professors W. E. Caldwell, of the Department of History of the University of North Carolina, and Oliver Towles, of the Department of Romance Languages of New York University, made important contributions to the sections on the Renaissance. Professor R. J. Kerner, of the University of Missouri, criticized the two chapters dealing with Slavic Europe. Professors R. E. Coker, of the Department of Zoölogy of the University of North Carolina, J. A. Eiesland, of the Mathematics Department of West Virginia University, and W. W. Pierson, Jr., of the Department of History of the University of North Carolina, made invaluable criticisms of the chapter on "The Intellectual Revolt against Authority." Professor C. C. Tansill, of the Department of History of the American University, Washington, D.C., read the chapters dealing with the Roman Catholic Church. Professor H. M. Wagstaff, of the Department of History of the University of North Carolina, read the two chapters dealing with England and a number of other chapters. Professor Henry E. Bourne, of Western Reserve University, gave a most careful criticism of the four chapters treating the French Revolution and the Napoleonic Period. Professors Carl Becker, of Cornell University, and Preston W. Slosson, of the University of Michigan, gave indispensable criticisms on the entire manuscript. Mr. R. A. Newsome, Secretary of the North Carolina Historical Commission, read nearly the whole work. The style profited much from the criticisms of Professor H. R. Warfel, of the Department of English of Bucknell University. The work has had the editorial supervision of Professor James T. Shotwell, of Columbia University, who made important contributions to the organization, the content and the style of the book. Professor W. E. Caldwell and the author's wife read both the manuscript and the proof with the most exacting care.

CONTENTS

I. EUROPE AT THE OPENING OF THE SIXTEENTH CENTURY . 1
    The Great Estates — The Cities: Industry and Commerce — Social Organization — Religious and Ecclesiastical Conditions — The Cultural Heritage from the Middle Ages — Political Conditions.

II. BEGINNINGS OF OVERSEAS EXPANSION 47
    Commerce in the Later Middle Ages — The Portuguese Explorations — Spanish Explorations — The Results of Overseas Expansion.

III. THE PROTESTANT REVOLT IN GERMANY AND INTERNATIONAL RIVALRIES 64
    The Lutheran Revolt — International Rivalries — The Anabaptist Revolt.

IV. THE PROTESTANT REVOLT IN OTHER LANDS . . . 87
    The Work of Zwingli — The Calvinist Revolt — The Anglican Revolt — Results of the Protestant Revolt.

V. THE CATHOLIC REFORMATION AND THE ASCENDANCY OF SPAIN UNDER PHILIP II 115
    The Catholic Reformation — Philip II — The Revolt of The Netherlands — The War between England and Spain — The Wars of Religion in France — Position of Spain at the Close of the Sixteenth Century.

VI. DUTCH COLONIAL AND COMMERCIAL SUPREMACY, THE THIRTY YEARS' WAR, AND THE BEGINNING OF FRENCH ASCENDANCY 140
    The Period of Dutch Colonial and Commercial Supremacy — Henry IV and Richelieu — The Thirty Years' War — Mazarin and the War with Spain.

VII. THE DEVELOPMENT OF PARLIAMENTARY GOVERNMENT IN ENGLAND 168
    The Quarrels of the Early Stuarts with their Parliaments — The Period of Personal Rule — The Long Parliament — The Civil War — The Commonwealth and the Protectorate — The Restoration — The Revolution of 1688 — The Results of the Revolution.

CONTENTS

VIII. Ascendancy of France under Louis XIV . . . 186
    The Work of Colbert — The War of Devolution — The Dutch War — The Revocation of the Edict of Nantes — The "Reunions" — The War of the League of Augsburg — The War of the Spanish Succession — The Results of the Reign of Louis XIV.

IX. The Rise of Russia and Prussia 201
    Russia in the Early Modern Period — The Work of Peter the Great — The Work of the Great Elector.

X. The Struggle for Colonial and Commercial Supremacy in the Eighteenth Century 220
    The Colonial Situation in 1689 — The Early Struggles of the English, French, and Spanish — The Work of Dupleix — The Seven Years' War.

XI. Austria and Prussia in the Eighteenth Century . 235
    Austria in 1740 — Prussia under Frederick William I — The Wars of Frederick the Great — Frederick the Great as an Enlightened Despot — Joseph II as an Enlightened Despot.

XII. Slavic Europe and the Ottoman Empire in the Eighteenth Century 258
    The Immediate Successors of Peter the Great — Catherine II as an Enlightened Despot — Poland on the Eve of the First Partition — The Partition of Poland and the Dismemberment of Turkey — The Southern Slavs and the Ottoman Turks.

XIII. The Intellectual Revolt against Authority . 274
    The Medieval World Scheme — The New Astronomy — Progress in the other Sciences — Progress in Philosophy — Development of Skepticism — Development of Political Theory — The French Philosophers.

XIV. The British Empire in the Latter Half of the Eighteenth Century 301
    England in 1750 — The Industrial Revolution — The Agricultural Revolution — The Wesleyan Revival — Attempts to Modify the English Constitution — The American Revolution — The Extension of the Empire in the Far East.

XV. France on the Eve of the French Revolution . 325
    The *Ancien Régime* — Economic Conditions — Social Organization — Religious Conditions — Political Conditions — The Decline of the Absolute Monarchy.

XVI. The French Revolution 350
    The Struggle for the Control of the Government — The Reforms of the National Assembly — Decline and Fall of the Monarchy — The National Convention — Reforms of the Legislative Assembly and the National Convention.

CONTENTS

XVII. CONSOLIDATION AND EXTENSION OF THE FRENCH REVOLUTION 391

Europe on the Eve of the Wars of the French Revolution — The War of the First Coalition — The Struggle with England — The Directory — The Establishment of Napoleon Bonaparte in Power — The Beneficent Dictatorship — Consular Imperialism.

XVIII. NAPOLEONIC EUROPE 420

England during the Revolutionary Period — The War of the Third Coalition and its Results — The War of the Fourth Coalition and its Results — The Continental System — The National Uprising in Spain — The War of 1809 with Austria and its Results — The Partial Reorganization of Prussia — Extension of French Influence in Europe — France under the Empire — The Defeat of Napoleon.

XIX. THE RECONSTRUCTION OF EUROPE 448

Restoration and Reaction — The Congress of Vienna — The Hundred Days — Permanent Result of the French Revolution and the Napoleonic Period.

XX. EUROPE IN 1815 463

Political Organization — Cultural Conditions — Religious and Ecclesiastical Conditions — The Cities: Industry and Commerce — Rural Organization.

INDEX i

LIST OF MAPS

EUROPE AT THE OPENING OF THE SIXTEENTH CENTURY (*colored*)	between 28–29
MEDIÆVAL TRADE ROUTES	48, 49
THE PRINCIPAL VOYAGES OF DISCOVERY (*colored*)	between 50–51
EMPIRE OF CHARLES V (*colored*)	facing 80
THE RELIGIOUS SITUATION IN EUROPE ABOUT 1560 (*colored*)	facing 110
EUROPE AT THE TREATY OF WESTPHALIA (1648) (*colored*)	between 160–161
EXTENSION OF THE FRENCH FRONTIERS, 1552–1766 (*colored*)	facing 188
GROWTH OF RUSSIA TO 1725	213
THE GROWTH OF PRUSSIA TO 1713	217
THE COLONIAL SITUATION ABOUT 1689 (*colored*)	between 220–221
INDIA IN THE TIME OF CLIVE AND DUPLEIX	227
EXPANSION OF PRUSSIA UNDER FREDERICK THE GREAT	243
PARTITION OF THE KINGDOM OF POLAND (*colored*)	facing 264
INDUSTRIAL ENGLAND	305
NAPOLEONIC EMPIRE AT ITS HEIGHT (*colored*)	between 436–437
EUROPE IN 1815 (*colored*)	between 456–457

HISTORY OF EUROPE
(1492–1815)

. .

CHAPTER I

EUROPE AT THE OPENING OF THE SIXTEENTH CENTURY

THE three centuries and more between the first westward voyage of Columbus and the final defeat of Napoleon at Waterloo profoundly modified the institutions, the habits, and the ideas of Europeans. In the year 1492 Europe was just emerging from the medieval period. By 1815 it had witnessed the discovery and exploitation of the non-European world, the conquest of new realms in the field of science and thought, the rise of the concepts of religious toleration and freedom, veritable revolutions in commerce, agriculture, and industry, and the growth of the principles of democracy and nationalism in politics. A careful survey of Europe at the opening of the sixteenth century will give us a basis for judging the importance and significance of the forces and movements which gradually transformed it into the Europe of the opening of the nineteenth century.

THE GREAT ESTATES

Far the larger part of the people lived on great estates [1] and supported by their daily labor, not only themselves and their families, but the great proprietors, the clergy, and the kings and their courts. Consequently these great estates with their clumsy, ignorant, hard-working peasant tenants formed the economic base on which European society, in the main, was built.

As is still the case, most of the rural population lived in little villages instead of in scattered farmhouses. The arrange-

[1] Known in England as manors.

ment of these villages showed no common plan, but often all the houses faced a single street. Above the low habitations of the ordinary peasants a mill, a church, and a dwelling somewhat better than the rest, might stand out conspicuously. In the mill the landlord compelled his peasants to grind their grain. Around the church centered the social and religious life of the villagers. In the house, more commodious than the huts of the peasants, lived the lord of the estate or his representative. A village might consist of only a dozen or of several hundred hearths; and the lord or his representative might live in an extensive château or castle, or in a house hardly distinguishable from the cottages of the peasants.

Every district of Europe had a distinctive type of peasant architecture. The chalet of the Swiss mountaineer differed greatly from the hut of the miserable East Prussian serf, as did the stone dwelling of the French villager from the adobe habitation of the Spanish peasant; but practically everywhere the lower classes lived in poor and dingy quarters. Frequently a peasant and his family occupied a single room and shared the shelter of their roof with the cattle and the poultry. The windows of his house contained no glass and the hard-packed earth often served as a floor. A few pots and pans, a chest and a bed many times constituted the sole furnishings of his hut.

The habitation of the peasant usually stood huddled in friendly intimacy with the barns and sheds which housed his hay and stock, his grain and his few tools. In some parts of Europe a single roof covered the whole group of farm buildings, but more often each stood separate, and opened off a central courtyard in which was to be found the malodorous manure pile that furnished the peasant with his all too scanty supply of fertilizer.

From the village stretched away on all sides arable fields and meadow and pasture land. Save for temporary hedges the fields were unenclosed. Fences were unknown on the Continent, and hedges were not yet a characteristic feature of the English landscape.

The arable land, the land which was plowed and sowed, was divided into a few — more often than not, into three — large fields, which were subdivided into long, narrow strips of varying size, called acres, separated from each other by a line of unplowed turf, a row of stones, or merely a furrow. These acres varied in length, width, and direction as the contour of the land or mere chance happened to dictate, and gave the landscape an appearance similar to that of an old-fashioned, patchwork crazy quilt. The meadows, which were also divided into acres, developed naturally along the banks of the streams. Beyond the arable fields lay the common pasture, the waste land, and the woodland of the estate.

Everywhere the peasants used the most primitive agricultural methods. They transported burdens on the backs of their farm animals or in two-wheeled carts. They broke up the arable land with rude plows drawn by four, eight, and even twelve horses or oxen, and harrowed it by striking the larger clods a blow with a heavy club or by dragging a tree over the recently plowed fields. They sowed the grain by hand, as in Biblical times, and cut it at harvest time with a sickle or a scythe, as is still done in parts of Europe. They threshed the grain by scattering it over a hard, smooth area and driving horses, oxen, or other farm animals over it to loosen the kernels from the stalks and husks. Finally, they winnowed the grain by throwing it into the air to let the wind carry away the lighter chaff while the heavier kernels fell to the ground. To plow, to harvest, and to thresh by these methods required much coöperation among the peasants. A half-dozen villagers would join together to provide twelve oxen for plowing. A dozen or more would work together, sickle in hand, to harvest the grain of a single field. Partly as a result of this need for coöperation, the custom of the manor, and not the wish or fancy of the individual peasant, dictated what should be planted and when it should be put into the ground. This prevented experimentation by adventurous individuals and made agricultural progress almost impossible. In obedience to custom the peasants usually planted a fall crop, like wheat or rye, in one field; a spring crop, like oats, barley, or peas, in another; and left a third fallow. The cattle, sheep, and pigs of every one living on the estate were herded together by one or more watchmen on the stubble of the fallow land, in the common pasture, or in the woodland. This way of handling stock prevented any selection or breeding of better farm animals. Methods of farming were everywhere wasteful, unscientific, and consequently unprogressive.

The villagers held a peculiar relation to the estate and its lord. If the villager were a serf, as was usually the case, he was bound to the soil and could never leave the estate on which he lived. In theory, at least, his lord could not drive him from it. The typical peasant had a hut of his own, the use of some acres in the arable fields, and rights in the meadow, the common pasture, and the woodland of the estate. His acres were scattered in such a way that he had an equal number in each arable field, no two of his acres even in the same field ever being adjacent. The land assigned to the parish priest and even that held by the lord of the estate, was usually arranged in the same fashion, although the latter might have a particularly choice piece of land enclosed and set apart for his exclusive use. The peasant turned his stock out with the cattle of the other villagers to graze in the common pasture or in the fallow fields, gathered fallen branches in the common woodland for fuel, and occasionally cut down a tree in order to repair his barn or his hut.

The obligations of the peasant were more numerous than his rights. If he were a serf he commonly gave his lord three or more days of labor each week, and extra days of work at certain times of the year in plowing, harvesting, threshing, hauling, hedging, and carrying messages. Often the state as well as the lord demanded the time and services of the serf and his cart. Besides his labor the serf usually owed his lord at certain fixed times in the year payments in produce and in money. He also had to grind his grain in the mill, bake his bread in the oven, and press out his grapes in the winepress provided by the lord, and he had to pay the latter well for these privileges. While the lord hunted and rode over all the land of the estate at will, and often half ruined the growing grain, the serf did not dare to kill the game which ate his crops. He was subject to restrictions even more galling than these. He could not marry without the consent of his lord, and had to pay for the privilege of selling his own cattle. When he died the lord might seize his best beast or his most valuable bit of movable property.[1] If the peasant were fortunate enough to be a freeman, his obligations were somewhat lighter. His services and payments were always more definite and often smaller than those of the serf. He owed no work each week to the lord; he could marry whom he pleased; and, in theory at least, he could leave the estate if he wished to do so. Both serfs and freemen were subject to the court of the lord, a tribunal which had jurisdiction over cases of inheritance, the transfer or grant of lands belonging to the estate, the fining of tenants for breaches of custom or for failure to fulfill their obligations to the lord, and over petty crimes and misdemeanors, if not capital offenses. In fact, the lords frequently retained their rights of jurisdiction after they had disposed of their other rights over a piece of land. As a result of these restrictions all the peasants, and particularly the serfs, lacked much of the freedom enjoyed by the humblest laborer to-day.

Life was thus hard and bare for the ordinary villager. Most of the year he ate a fare that was often scanty and always monotonous. He was poorly sheltered and was provided with few or no comforts. He worked with rude tools of his own making, and wore coarse clothing made in his own household. He suffered from famine and pestilence, from marauding invaders, and from the fears born of his ignorance and superstition. His landlord, his parish priest, and his king often exploited him. He knew little of the past or of the world beyond the boundaries of his own estate. Finally, worn out by toil and misery, he sank prematurely into the grave.

THE CITIES; INDUSTRY AND COMMERCE

In the year 1500 cities were relatively few in number and

[1] This was known as the right of heriot.

small in area and population. If not examined too closely they were often picturesque in appearance. For the sake of protection they frequently were built on the top of a hill or by a diked water-course and were surrounded by deep moats and battlemented walls. In many cities a castle both overawed the citizens and offered a final place of refuge for the defenders of the city in case the outer walls were carried by storm. High over the tiled roofs of the houses rose the belfry or watchtower of the city and the steeples of the important churches. Within the city walls twisted and turned narrow, crooked streets, named usually after the chief industry carried on in them, of the sort still seen in the older parts of Chester, Bruges, Carcassonne, Toledo, and Florence. There were Milk streets, Candle streets, and Money streets, streets named after the furriers, armorers, joiners, cordwainers, writers, potters, fullers, and other craftsmen who plied their trade in them, and market places for the sale of grain, poultry, vegetables, eggs, and fish. In the better quarters timbered gables, overhanging stories, and bits of woodcarving over doorways and at house-corners, gave the city a touch of quaintness and color. At the center of the city was the public square, the scene of much petty trading on market days and still oftener the meeting place for idle, animated groups of citizens. Around it stood the chief edifices of the city: the cathedral or principal church, the belfry, the municipal building, some of the gild halls, and possibly a few fine private houses.

In such a city the individual counted for little. He could reside there only after he had obtained the consent of the municipal authorities. He had to be a citizen before he could enjoy many political and economic privileges, and he had to belong to the proper gild before he could work at a craft. Even if he belonged to a gild he was greatly restricted by regulations concerning the hours of work, the number of apprentices and journeymen that could be employed, the raw materials that might be used, and the quality, weight, and size of the goods that might be manufactured. As a rule, too, he did not obtain these various privileges easily nor quickly.

Those engaged in each branch of industry or commerce in a city were organized into a gild. Originally these organizations had received charters from the king or the town government, which authorized their formation and regulated, often quite minutely, the rights and obligations of their members. Persons who wished to engage in any branch of trade or industry first served an apprenticeship, which might last as long as seven years. During this time an apprentice was almost the slave of the man from whom he was learning the craft or trade. Instead of receiving wages he sometimes even paid for the opportunity to learn. After he had learned his trade or craft he became a journeyman and received full wages for his work. When a journeyman received permission from the gild to set up an establishment of his own he became a master. The masters of any particular craft controlled the gild and made it difficult for an apprentice to become a journeyman, or for a journeyman to become a master. The gild was usually a social and beneficial as well as an economic organization. Its members dined together at stated intervals and aided each other in case of sickness or death. The gilds were, therefore, very important organizations in the life of most European cities.

Trade and industry were on an incredibly small scale. Such trades as existed were carried on in tiny shops situated at the front of the houses occupied by the masters. At most a master employed only a few journeymen and apprentices. There was little need for the exchange of commodities between town and country, for the townsmen frequently had their own acres in the arable fields surrounding the town and the peasants of the great estates supplied most of their own wants. Such exchanges as took place were carried on through the public markets held on market days in the open squares of the cities. For the same reason only a few rare necessities such as salt and iron and a few luxuries for the upper classes such as wine, armor, fine stuffs, and spices, figured in the commerce between different countries and provinces. These were supplied through the fair, a temporary institution authorized by the king, a lord, or an abbot, where once a year or oftener traders came, paid for the privilege of setting up booths, and traded for a week or so with the people who flocked to the fair from the surrounding country. After the fair came to an end the traders moved on to another part of the country. Even this small trade was hampered by innumerable restrictions. The lords of the great estates collected countless tolls from the merchants passing along the roads and rivers. Often the petty lords, known as robber barons, robbed the merchants outright instead of merely levying from them extortionate tolls. Barbarous laws also gave the lord the right to any object which fell on his land from a passing cart or which was washed up on the shore by a storm at sea. In spite of these conditions, however, commerce was slowly increasing and the merchant class was growing in wealth.

Most cities enjoyed some degree of self-government. Venice, Genoa, and a few other cities in Italy and several scores of places in Germany were independent of practically all outside control, and were known as city-states, because they included just a single city and a little of the country surrounding it. Numerous cities in every country possessed more limited rights of self-government. In the Middle Ages every city of Europe had cherished the ambition of obtaining a charter which would grant the citizens such privileges as the right to pay their taxes in a lump sum collected by their own officials and the right to be governed and judged by officials of their own choosing. Naturally the cities had met with varying success in their efforts to obtain these privileges. In all classes of the cities the control was in the hands of a limited number of persons.

On the whole life was freer and more joyous in the cities than on the great estates. Though the urban centers were crowded, dirty, unsanitary, malodorous, and subject to pestilence and sickness, they were full of life and movement. In the city one had always contact with one's fellows. A member of a gild might participate in pageants and celebrations in honor of kings and saints. If he were so fortunate as to become a master he might even hope to become a man of some importance in the government of the city, to provide himself with some of the luxuries of the time, and to give his children at least the rudiments of an education.

SOCIAL ORGANIZATION

At the opening of the sixteenth century feudalism still shaped, for the most part, the social organization of European society. In the early Middle Ages government had broken down and individuals and institutions made whatever arrangements they could to protect their lives and property. The peasants put themselves under the protection of a near-by monastery or of a powerful landlord of the neighborhood and the weaker lords sought the protection of the stronger. In return for protection the peasant gave up much of his freedom and assumed, or had forced upon him, the irksome obligations that have already been described, and the lesser lords took upon themselves the duty of homage and fealty, military and court service, and the payments known as feudal aids and incidents,[1] the lord who granted the protection being known as the lord or suzerain, and the one who received it as a vassal. The vassal usually performed his feudal obligations in return for the fief [2] which he held from this suzerain. The relation existing between a vassal and his suzerain was considered an entirely honorable one; that between lord and peasant an ignoble one. This whole complicated network of relationships, based on land and personal ties between holders of great estates, is known as the feudal system. In time practically all relations in Western Europe became feudalized. Abbots, abbesses, bishops, archbishops, and other higher officials of the Church assumed feudal relations, and even the rising cities, which contained the germ of modern democracy, were imperfectly fitted into the medieval system. Individuals ceased to regard themselves as citizens with obligations to some particular state but fought, paid taxes,

---

[1] For definitions of these terms consult the chapter on feudalism in any standard textbook on medieval history.

[2] The fief was usually an estate large enough to support a vassal without work.

and submitted to the jurisdiction of some particular court because of the feudal bonds uniting vassals to suzerains.

The natural result of the feudal system was to separate society into privileged and unprivileged classes. At the top of the social scale were the nobles and the clergy, whose position will be explained in the description of the Church. At the bottom were the unprivileged peasants. Occupying a position between these two extremes was the rising middle class of the cities.

The nobles controlled most of the great estates and enjoyed many special privileges. They paid few of the taxes being imposed by the new central governments and received most of the lucrative posts in State and Church. Over their estates they exercised the rights of petty sovereigns. They lived lives of rude leisure in their châteaux or manor houses. Troops of servants waited on them and the countryside paid them special marks of respect. The peasant paid his lord the same deference that the negro in the southern part of the United States often pays his white neighbors. During his lifetime the lord occupied a special seat in the parish church and after his death his bones rested within the walls of the church instead of in the churchyard with those of his humbler tenants. When a vacancy occurred he appointed the parish priest, and once a year the parishioners celebrated the name day of the lord (the day of the saint whose name he bore), as a holiday. When he wished recreation the lord hunted at will over the land of his peasants and even demanded their assistance in beating up the game. In short, the lord was the great man of the rural community, whose character and conduct affected the ordinary peasant vastly more than the acts and policies of the distant sovereign.

During the early Middle Ages most of the peasants of Western, Central, and Southeastern Europe had been serfs. By the year 1500 other classes of peasants had made their appearance. Most of the rural population in England, France, and Spain, and a small minority in various other parts of Europe had become free through emancipation at the hands of their lords, or through the purchase of exemption from many of their former obligations. In England and France, too, a class known as leaseholders or metayers had begun to appear, as a result of a lord's surrendering to one or more peasants his arable acres and supplying them with the necessary tools, seed, and stock in return for a share of the crop. When this took place the lords ceased to farm on their own account and became merely rent-collecting landlords. About the same time a class of hired laborers, recruited from runaway serfs, from peasants who held no land at all, and from those whose holdings were too small to support them, arose to provide the labor formerly supplied by the serfs.

Protected by the privileges of their cities and their gilds, the merchants and master artisans of the rising cities, known as burgesses in England, burghers in Germany, and bourgeoisie in France, were much better off than the peasants of the open country. Their city walls and their collective power and wealth protected them fairly well from grasping lords and avaricious kings. They had more wealth, more comforts, and more education than most of the nobles. Beneath them in the cities was a motley collection of artisans, domestics, and beggars.

RELIGIOUS AND ECCLESIASTICAL CONDITIONS

At the beginning of the modern period everybody in western Europe, except the Jews, had to belong to the Catholic Church. An individual then was born a member of the Church, just as to-day he is born a citizen of some country. Instead of contributing to the support of the Church when he felt like doing so, he had to pay regular taxes called tithes, and to give certain fees. As the Church compelled every one to believe unquestioningly its pronouncements concerning matters of faith, neither religious freedom nor religious toleration existed. Religion was thus a compulsory matter.

The Church had many more privileges and powers than it has to-day. During the Middle Ages the State had let both the clergy and the property of the Church almost slip from its control. As it was expressed at the time, the Church was a state within a state. The Church and its clergy paid the secular authorities little in the way of taxes and often hardly recognized the jurisdiction of the courts of the State in civil or criminal cases. On the contrary, the Church maintained courts of its own, which judged all cases touching the Church and its clergy and cases concerning tithes, marriage, wills, contracts, legitimacy of children, and Church discipline which involved persons belonging to the laity. In addition to performing these political functions the Church looked after such education as there was, and in some places even cared for travelers. The Church thus touched the life of the people daily at every turn, and was, in consequence, the most important institution of Western Europe.

ORGANIZATION OF THE CHURCH

The Church needed an unusual organization to carry on these varied activities throughout Central and Western Europe. In many ways it resembled a state. It exercised executive, legislative, and judicial functions and possessed a regular hierarchy of administrative districts and officials.

The smallest of these administrative districts was the parish. In rural districts it might include the people of a single village or the inhabitants of a number of villages. In urban centers it might include the whole, or merely a part of a city. In both city and country its boundaries depended largely on chance or local history.

A parish priest was in charge of each parish. He said masses for funerals and marriages, and on Sundays and saints' days, baptized the newly born, catechized the children, heard confessions, supervised the faith and morals of those under his charge, cared for the sick, administered the last rites to the dying, and on rare occasions preached to his parishioners. For performing these various duties the parish priest received an income and other perquisites. In most cases he had the use of a house or rectory. In rural districts, he had his own acres in the arable fields and in the meadow land, and rights in the woodland and the common pasture.[1] He also received fees for administering the sacraments and a

[1] In England the land of the parish priest was known as the glebe.

share of the tithes. He obtained his position in the first place through presentation to the "living" by a patron — the chief proprietor of the parish, a neighboring bishop or abbot, or even the king — who held the right to make the appointment. He formed the best element in the clergy. Contemporary satirists made much of his ignorance but said less against his morals. Although he usually came of peasant stock he stood next to the lord in the estimation of the rural community.

A group of parishes formed a diocese, or bishopric, an administrative district, which varied greatly in area and population. In charge of a diocese was a bishop, an official with great powers and an extensive range of duties. He supervised the education of candidates for the priesthood, ordained them, gave or withheld his consent for their appointment as parish priests, and disciplined and admonished them after they were installed in office. He saw to it that the religious edifices of his diocese were kept in repair and that all the Church property was devoted to its proper uses. Save where they had received exemption from his jurisdiction from the Pope, he inspected all the monasteries and nunneries of his bishopric, under the seal of secrecy heard the complaints of each inmate, and inspected the business accounts of each institution. His court exercised the jurisdiction claimed by the Church over ecclesiastical property, the clergy, and the laity. At the principal city of his diocese he had a palace and a cathedral church.

Upon the latter edifice the successive bishops and their fellow citizens had lavished their wealth and attention. For centuries, perhaps, architects, sculptors, wood-carvers, painters, and glass-makers, had employed all their knowledge and skill to make the cathedral a masterpiece for the glory and honor of God and the fame of the city. The main altar, the choir, and the chapels became veritable museums of painting, sculpture, wood-carving, and the art of the gold and silver smiths. The treasury of the Cathedral amassed not only the relics of saints, but jewels, chalices, crucifixes, and priceless vestments. All over Europe rose these incomparable cathedrals.

In addition to his religious functions, the bishop performed many duties which made him a great figure in the State. Over the extensive lands which were always attached to a bishopric he exercised the same powers and enjoyed the same privileges as a lay landlord. In countries like England, France, and Spain, he usually served as a member of Parliament, of the Estates General, or the Cortes. As his education made him superior as an official to the unlettered members of the nobility, who were often unable to read or write, he might occupy one of the highest offices in the State. In the Holy Roman Empire especially he might be at the same time a great landed proprietor, an important Church dignitary and the sovereign of a little state. In consequence of his extensive powers and privileges, he usually enjoyed a great revenue and lived like a prince. For these reasons the nobles eagerly sought these positions for members of their families with the result that the bishoprics were sometimes entrusted to men lacking in religious zeal, education, and morality.

A group of bishoprics constituted an administrative district known as an archbishopric, archdiocese, or province, which was under an archbishop. The archbishop did not control and supervise the bishops in the same way that the latter controlled and supervised their parish priests. He had rank and prestige rather than power and authority over the bishops of his province. He had special insignia to distinguish him and he took precedence over the other clergy of the province on all ceremonial occasions. In one of the dioceses of his province he really performed all the duties of a bishop. Like the bishop, furthermore, he might be a member of Parliament, a high officer in the State, a great landholder, or a petty sovereign. One archbishop in each country outranked the others and was known as the primate.

Over the whole Church was a central government with a capital at Rome and with the Pope as its sovereign. The latter was assisted in the task of governing the Church by tribunals and officers of various grades and by an army of officials. The whole body of officials was known as the Papal Curia. Highest in rank were the cardinals. As individuals

THE OPENING OF THE SIXTEENTH CENTURY 15

they filled the great administrative offices of the Papal Government. Collectively they were known as the College of Cardinals and elected the popes, usually choosing an Italian and a member of their own body. Their own ranks were kept filled, in turn, by papal appointment.

The Pope resembled the secular monarchs in many respects. In a way Western Europe was his empire. He issued decrees for the guidance of both the clergy and the laity. His curia was the final court of appeal in all matters over which the Church claimed jurisdiction. His Government had its own revenues, receiving a payment known as Peter's Pence from the faithful in many countries, a payment from papal appointees known as first fruits or annates,[1] and various fees in return for its judicial and administrative services. He was represented at the courts of most of the other European sovereigns by legates, officials who were likely to exercise at the court to which they were accredited both the functions of an intimate adviser and the duties of a foreign ambassador. Like other European monarchs he had fine palaces like the Vatican and the Quirinal to live in and a large court which was governed by its own rules of etiquette. Over the laity in his empire, however, his authority extended only to such matters as faith and morals, wills, tithes, marriage, and legitimacy of children.

The parish priests, the bishops, and the archbishops usually belonged to the branch of the clergy known as the secular clergy from the fact that they lived in the world (*in seculo*) like most other people. In certain ways, however, they were differentiated from the laymen among whom they lived and worked. They never married. They wore a closely shaved circular spot on the backs of their heads, known as the tonsure, and a distinctive garb consisting of the flat, round hat and the long black robe still worn by the clergy of Southern Europe.

Besides the secular clergy, there were the men and women called monks and nuns, who lived apart from ordinary men in monasteries and nunneries, and were known as regular

[1] A sum equivalent to the first year's revenue from an ecclesiastical office.

clergy, because they lived according to rules (*regula*). They were separated into orders, each of which had its distinctive dress, its own regulations, and its own origin and history. Sometimes the rules of an order bound its members to the simplest fare, to the wearing of uncomfortable clothing, to fasting, prayer, and absolute silence, and, in general, to lives of great hardship and discomfort. Other orders permitted an easy-going life that differed little from that led by ordinary men. In theory the monks and nuns were supposed to abandon all thought of the world and to concentrate their attention on God and his service. They took vows never to marry, to have no property, and to obey their superiors, and they were supposed to devote their time largely to such pious acts as fasting, prayer, and the hearing and singing of mass. In practice they were likely to be interested, like other people, in what they ate and drank and in hearing and repeating the petty gossip of the monastery. For, shut off as it usually was, the monastery was a little world in itself.

The monastic institutions varied greatly in size, power, wealth, and number of inmates. A monastery might house a mere handful of individuals, or scores of monks. It might draw its support from only a few or from many rural estates, which had been acquired at some time through pious gifts. Its inmates might occupy a single shabby building or an imposing group of edifices. In the latter case it might include, like the medieval monastery of St. Gall, a large church or chapel, a chapter house where the brethren met to transact the business of their order, a dormitory in which to sleep, a refectory in which to eat, a house in which to lodge guests, a school building, a bakery, a wine-press, a brewery, cellars in which to store beer and wine, and the barns, stables, and outbuildings needed by a large rural estate. On its church or chapel the religious community always lavished the same kind of care and attention that the bishops and their fellow citizens poured out on the great cathedrals. As a result, the monasteries, like the cathedrals, became veritable museums of art. Around the whole monastic establishment was likely to be a wall, which shut in the brethren and excluded the world.

An official known as an abbot or prior ruled over a monastery, and an abbess or prioress over a nunnery. The head of an important monastery was a person with great prestige and authority, often vying with the bishops in dignity. He controlled the religious life of the community under his authority, governed wide estates and a large population as a landlord, belonged to the central parliament or the local diet of his state or province, and, in Germany, sometimes ruled a small, independent state of his own. Since he was supposed to represent the power and wealth of his institution, he lived apart from the other members of the community, maintained a large establishment, and entertained lavishly the passing notables. As in the case of the bishoprics the nobles sought for members of their families the offices of abbot and abbess, with most unfortunate results for the spiritual life of the Church.

An important branch of the regular clergy was the friars. They resembled the regular clergy in some respects and the secular clergy in others. They dressed like the monks and took the same three vows of chastity, poverty, and obedience, but they worked in the world like the secular clergy and built their houses in the crowded quarters of the towns instead of in solitary places. The two oldest and most famous orders of the friars, the Franciscans and the Dominicans, had been organized early in the thirteenth century. Later the Carmelites and the Augustinians had been established. At first the friars lived lives of great usefulness and performed for the poor services similar to those now rendered by the Salvation Army, but, in time, their zeal began to wane and the cunning and greed of some made all the friars objects of suspicion.

The semi-religious military orders were numbered among the regular clergy. The Teutonic Knights and the Knights of Malta had been organized during the crusading period to fight the infidels; the three powerful Spanish orders to fight the Moslems of Spain. These orders had retained their wealth and their privileges but they had outlived their usefulness.

PURPOSE, DOCTRINES, AND SERVICES OF THE CHURCH

The avowed purpose of this elaborate organization was the salvation of souls. The Church was the sole agent of God in the all-important task of saving men from everlasting punishment for their sins. It guarded and interpreted the two great sources of religious truth, the Bible and the unrecorded traditions of Christianity. Through its theology it pointed out the way of salvation. Through its clergy it mediated between God and sinful man. Through its sacraments it started the individual in the way of salvation and increased his righteousness. Its services, its ceremonies, and its various institutions all contributed to this same end. Salvation was the chief end of the Church.

In this work the seven sacraments of baptism, confirmation, the eucharist, penance, extreme unction, marriage, and holy orders played a part of vital importance. They kept the individual reconciled to God. Baptism freed the child from the portion of original sin with which he was born. Confirmation conferred on the boy or girl receiving it full membership in the religious community. The sacrament of the eucharist (communion) identified the individual for the moment with the person of Christ, for, according to the accepted doctrine of transubstantiation, the officiating priest performed the miracle of transforming the bread and wine into the body and blood of Christ. Contrition, confession, and penance removed the guilt of the penitent sinner. Extreme unction put the sick or dying soul in harmony with God. The sacrament of marriage gave a religious character to the family tie. Ordination or holy orders endowed the priest with power to mediate between God and man. The bishop administered confirmation and ordination; the parish priest administered the five remaining sacraments.

The sacrament of penance calls for a somewhat fuller explanation. According to the doctrine of the Church the sinner could scarcely hope for salvation unless he received absolution from a priest endowed through the sacrament of ordination with the unique power of forgiving sins. To obtain forgiveness the sinner must feel truly sorry for his sins and confess them openly to the priest, for the priest could not pass judgment on sins about which he knew nothing. Absolution, however, only freed the sinner from the danger of everlasting punishment. It did not exempt him from temporal penalties. The sinner might expiate these in this world through such acts of penance as fasting, repeating prayers, making pilgrimages to holy places, and by making gifts of money to pious causes, or in the next world by suffering for a time the cleansing fires of purgatory. The priest imposed the penance. In performing this important function the Church was soon to encounter the criticism of Luther.

Around the sacrament of the eucharist developed the Mass — the central ceremony of the Church. According to the doctrine of transubstantiation Christ was believed to be sacrificed anew in each celebration of the Mass. This service, consequently, aroused the holiest emotions of the communicants of the Church. They assumed an attitude of the greatest reverence during the ceremony, bent the knee upon passing the altar, and housed the service in magnificent churches and cathedrals. Masses were said at weddings, at funerals, for the souls of the dead, on Sundays and saints' days, and, in the larger churches, daily and even hourly. Instead of merely starting the week by attending divine service on Sunday the more zealous Catholic was likely to begin each day by attending Mass. On its celebration the Church lavished a wealth of incense, candles, vestments, and ritual that stirred the emotions and appealed to the senses of the worshiper.

CRITICISMS OF THE CHURCH

At the opening of the sixteenth century this Church, which was the historic embodiment of the religious life of Europe, was increasingly subjected to both criticism and attack — criticism from those who held that it was not sufficiently spiritually minded, attack from those who challenged its political claims. This movement was destined to develop into the Protestant Revolt or Reformation, which split the unity of the Church; but at first it was directed against alleged evils within the Church rather than against the institution itself. The new centralized states of Europe resented the wide powers still exercised by the Church. Since the opening of the fourteenth century the kings of France and England had been waging a determined struggle against the appointive power of the Pope in respect to bishoprics, archbishoprics, and monasteries, the extensive jurisdiction of the Church courts, the interference of the Pope in internal affairs, and the exemptions enjoyed by the clergy in the matter of taxation. By the year 1500 many of the other sovereigns of Europe were striving to free themselves from these same limitations on their power.

The spiritually minded were shocked at abuses within the Church. Some of the popes and higher clergy, as well as parish priests, at times led lives that exposed the whole Church to criticism. Pope Nicholas V surrounded himself with skeptics and scoffers who mocked the Papacy, poked fun at the monks, attacked the Bible, and exalted the antique pagan spirit. Sixtus IV nearly exterminated the family of Colonna by a series of judicial murders in order to advance his own family. Innocent VIII obtained the Papacy through the payment of enormous bribes, sold the offices of the Church to the highest bidder, and stopped a crusade in return for the payment of tribute by the Sultan. Alexander VI, the reigning Pope in 1500, surpassed even these men in evil reputation by reason of his own crimes and vices and those of his children. Not infrequently the clergy kept unmarried wives in spite of their vows of chastity or led lives of utter worldliness. Priests were at times so ignorant that they were unable to repeat correctly the creed or the Lord's Prayer or to understand the words that they used in the service. In the monasteries many men and in the nunneries some women failed to keep the vow of chastity. In spite of these conditions the clergy undoubtedly had higher standards of conduct than most of the men of their age and included many men of saintly character.

Opposition to these conditions within the Church developed into a revolt for different reasons. The kings and the nobles coveted the large amounts of property which it had accumulated through the centuries as the result of pious gifts. The commercial classes objected to the immobilization of capital sorely needed by the rising commerce and industry. The devout and spiritually minded, particularly in Germany, cried out against the greedy officials who were accused of selling, for the sake of financial gain, the offices of the Church, pardons for all sorts of offenses, dispensations from the laws of the Church, and the indulgences which remitted the temporal penalties of sin. The scholars and men of letters were shocked at the attitude of the Church toward the new learning.[1] The failure of the Church to meet these criticisms is one of the causes of the revolt against the Church commonly called the Reformation or the Protestant Revolt.

RELIGIOUS ORGANIZATION OF EASTERN EUROPE

In Eastern Europe the Catholic Church had little or no hold. In the Balkan Peninsula and around the Black Sea, where the Turks had established their rule, Islam (commonly called Mohammedanism) was the dominant religion. The Russians and the various Christian peoples subject to the Turks belonged to the Eastern Church.

Under the Roman Empire and in the early Middle Ages most Christians had been united in a single Church. In the year 1054, however, they split into the Eastern and the Roman Catholic Churches over the question of the relation of the Father, Son, and Holy Spirit. Through the years the two churches have come to differ on many other points. The Eastern Church, for example, rejects the headship of the Pope, denies the doctrines of Purgatory, and the immaculate conception, conducts its services in either Greek or old Slavonic instead of Latin, baptizes by immersion, and rarely hears confessions. In the Catholic Church the laity partake only of the bread during the communion service, while the priest partakes of both the bread and the wine. The Eastern Church makes no such distinction between the clergy and the laymen. In the Roman Church the clergy take vows of celibacy and in consequence, never marry. In the Eastern Church the ordinary clergy, but not the bishops, marry. In

---

[1] The new learning is discussed later in this chapter.

most other respects the two churches closely resemble each other.

The "Christendom" of Western Europe was shut in on the south and southeast by a different civilization, equally vast and in some ways equally enlightened. Islam is the religion preached by the prophet Mohammed, who died in 632 A.D. After his death his sayings were compiled and preserved in the Koran, which then became the sacred book of his followers. Its fundamental tenet is belief in one God. Its simple creed asserts, "There is no God but God, and Mohammed is the apostle of God." The Koran strictly enjoins prayer, cleanliness and abstinence from wine. It sets forth four supreme laws. The good Moslem prays five times a day with his face toward Mecca, fasts from sunrise to sunset during one month of the year, goes to Mecca at least once in his life on a pilgrimage, and gives alms to the poor. Mohammed, however, assigned a very low place to women with the unfortunate result that he debased marriage and family life. Though he tried to combine the Christianity, the Judaism, and the heathenism which he found in his country, the Moslems and the Christians have nearly always hated and despised each other.

THE CULTURAL HERITAGE FROM THE MIDDLE AGES

At the opening of the sixteenth century educated men were just beginning to escape from a system and method of thought known as Scholasticism. The Scholastic philosophers gave an exaggerated deference to a few books which they considered authoritative and attempted to widen the boundaries of knowledge by deductive reasoning alone instead of by observation and experiment. From the Bible, the works of Aristotle, the writings of the early leaders of the Church, and a few other books they gradually evolved principles which dominated their thinking just as completely as the idea of evolution influences the thought of intelligent men to-day.

Although Scholasticism has now become almost a term of reproach, the Scholastic philosophers made an important

THE OPENING OF THE SIXTEENTH CENTURY

contribution to the history of thought. They had been preceded by a barren period in which much of ancient civilization had disappeared. The barbarian invasions had caused the destruction of villas, the disappearance or decline of towns, the burning or neglect of libraries, and the closing of schools. In consequence, knowledge was reduced to the compass of small compendiums; correct scientific, literary, and historical information was scarcely to be had, and life, in general, became a struggle for mere existence.

About the middle of the eleventh century this situation began to change. Conditions became more settled and intellectual ambition slowly revived. Enterprising monasteries and an occasional bishop opened schools. The teachers in these schools possessed few books but sharp wits. From the meager supply of books at their command they spun out elaborate systems of thought, in which they tried to give a reasonable answer to the doctrines of the Church. They taught their ideas by taking one of the accepted texts and commenting upon it, the comments of the more famous teachers becoming, in time, texts to be commented on by succeeding teachers. Few persons ever thought of conducting scientific experiments or of observing nature at first hand. As a result of the decisions given from time to time by the Church the fields open to the free play of the medieval mind gradually became more circumscribed.

Authoritative pronouncements had already been made concerning such questions as the method of creation, the origin and destiny of man, and the nature of the universe. According to the Scholastic philosophers, the sun, the moon, and the planets moved around the earth as a center; God created the world in exactly six days; man suffered throughout his temporal existence because of the sins of Adam; and man's life on this earth determined his future existence. These and other accepted ideas of the time obtained a sort of unofficial sanction from the leaders of the Church. Thus arose many of the strongly rooted traditions against which science is still struggling.

By the end of the Middle Ages such consecrated traditions had begun to lose their universal dominion. Bold thinkers arose who challenged the accepted beliefs and evolved a new philosophy of life. They concerned themselves less with life in the hereafter and turned their attention more to life in this world. They became filled with the joy of living and interested in all that contributed to a full life. They found, pictured in the writings of the Roman and later the Greek authors, the kind of life to which they themselves aspired, and consequently turned with enthusiasm to antiquity for their ideals. From their interest in humanity, they are known as "Humanists" and their philosophy of life as "Humanism." At the beginning of the sixteenth century they were engaged in a bitter struggle in Italy, France, Germany, and England, with the supporters of the old traditions.

The new intellectual movement began in Provence and Italy. Petrarch began to collect libraries of ancient authors, to search the monasteries for manuscripts of classical works, to imitate the style of writers like Seneca, Livy, Virgil, and Cicero, and to hunt for ancient coins. Boccaccio and other writers continued his work, and wandering teachers arose, who went from city to city communicating an interest in Latin literature. The chief result of the work of Petrarch and the early Humanists was to bring the Italians of their generation into contact with antiquity.

Later the Humanists became interested in Greek literature. From time to time Greeks came to Italy bringing a knowledge of their ancient literature. Particularly they introduced the work of Plato and his method of looking at all sides of a question. In the Greek authors the Humanists found their ideals expressed even more fully than in the Latin.

Groups of Humanists soon sprang up everywhere in Italy, but Florence always remained the real center of the movement. Often the Humanists organized academies for the promotion of the new learning, which met in the villas or the palaces of powerful patrons like the Medici at Florence or some of the later popes. Cosimo de Medici (1389–1464), for example, employed agents to collect ancient coins, inscriptions, and manuscripts, accumulated and housed libraries which he put at the disposal of the people of Florence, gathered an important group of Humanists around him, and organized a Platonic academy. His grandson, Lorenzo the Magnificent, wrote poetry, generously patronized scholars, architects, sculptors, and painters, and also associated himself with the famous Humanists of the time. After the middle of the fifteenth century most of the popes were Humanists. They began the extraordinary collections of books, manuscripts, and objects of art which are now housed in the Vatican. They devoted their attention to Humanism and neglected the real interests of the Church.

Long before Humanism reached its final stages of development in Italy, it began to spread to the countries north of the Alps. It followed the retreating army of Charles VIII into France,[1] and found its way into England and Germany with returning scholars and students. On the whole, the northern Humanists were more serious-minded than the Italian. In their reaction against the asceticism of the Middle Ages the Italians often become sensual pagans. The northern Humanists made use of the new learning to solve the serious problems of life and to throw light on religion.

The ideals of the northern Humanists are well illustrated by the career of Erasmus (1466–1536), their acknowledged leader and master. He learned to love the ancient classics, while at school at Deventer in his native Holland. Then he entered a monastery and lived as a monk until a powerful friend and patron obtained permission for him to abandon the monastic life. For the remaining two thirds of his life Erasmus lived as a scholar, wandering from place to place and eking out a precarious existence from the fees of students, the pensions given him by wealthy patrons, and gifts made to him by those to whom he dedicated his writings or for whose writings he wrote introductions. He preferred to live in this way because it gave him his freedom. He first attracted favorable attention through his "Adages," a collection of familiar quotations from the classics, which long

[1] The Italian expedition of Charles VIII is described briefly in Chapter III.

served to embellish the speech and writings of those who wished to use classical quotations. A few years later he established his international reputation as a man of letters through the publication of his *Praise of Folly*, a work which spared no class and showed that every one was in bondage to folly.

Erasmus, however, was a Christian as well as a Humanist. He worked throughout his life to establish a "simple, rational, and classical Christianity," through the publication and thorough study of the early Christian texts. His Greek New Testament with its copious notes appeared in 1516. In this work he applied to the study of the Bible, for the first time in centuries, the methods now regularly employed in studying any work of literature. In preparing his work he made use of ten different manuscript versions of the New Testament in an effort to establish a correct text. His work greatly influenced Luther and became the source for the translations of the Bible into the language of the common people which began to appear in the various countries of Europe. From 1521 until his death, fifteen years later, he made his headquarters at Basel, where he was associated with Froben, one of the early publishers, as a sort of literary editor for new editions of the Church fathers. His consistent application of common sense and reason to religion and life undoubtedly shook the ecclesiastical edifice which the more violent Luther later split asunder and partially demolished.

Humanism gained general adherence only after the lapse of centuries. In the year 1500 the ideas and methods of the schoolmen still dominated the thinking of both the universities and the clergy. Even down to our own day many earnest, honest people have maintained their allegiance to the beliefs attacked by the Humanists.

The new spirit of curiosity and inquiry fostered by the new learning did not confine itself wholly to literature. The works of learned Moslems in Spain and the study of the classical authors revealed a new world of scientific knowledge not known to medieval man and stimulated a search for new information. This revival of science began in the thirteenth century with the work of Roger Bacon and a number of other remarkable men. Roger Bacon made important discoveries in physics and chemistry, substituted observation and experiment for the deductive methods of his contemporaries, and anticipated the achievements of modern science by a number of brilliant guesses. The next two centuries witnessed a revival of algebra, geometry, and trigonometry, progress in the real sciences of astronomy and chemistry through the investigations of the practitioners of the false sciences of astrology and alchemy, a beginning in human dissection, and the coming into general use of the compass, the astrolabe, and better methods of calculating the position of ships. These contributions constitute the foundation on which later scientists built.

The diffusion of the new learning was greatly facilitated by the new invention of printing from movable type. While there is some dispute as to its inventor, John Gutenberg certainly established a successful printing house at Mainz as early as 1448. At first the new art of printing was a carefully guarded secret, but the sacking of Mainz in 1462 scattered the pupils and workers of Gutenberg, and widely diffused the new art. From the excellent presses of Germany, Italy, France, Spain, and England, cheap editions of the classics and new books and pamphlets began to make their appearance.

The new interest in living also had an important effect on art. In the Middle Ages art had been extremely formal and conventional, and almost exclusively the handmaid of religion. Its subjects came from well-known incidents of the Bible and of the lives of the saints. Its figures, its poses, and its colors were stereotyped. Most medieval pictures were painted on wood or plaster. With the revival of individuality painters began again to express themselves through their pictures. They made use of classical and contemporary models, adopted oil and canvas as a medium, and chose secular as well as religious subjects. In the sixteenth century they began to work mainly for royal patrons, and used their art to glorify national life.

POLITICAL CONDITIONS

Throughout the early Middle Ages Europe was in political chaos. During the fourth and fifth centuries the declining Roman Empire had gradually succumbed to the vigorous blows dealt it by the invading Germans until all central authority had gone to pieces. In spite of various efforts to maintain some sort of central government in Western Europe political power fell more and more into the hands of the Church, the clergy, and local lords. This anarchy culminated in the feudalism of the ninth and tenth centuries.

In this period of disorder the Church assumed many political functions. Under the later Roman Emperors the Church and its clergy had been exempted from certain onerous offices and taxes and had been permitted to receive bequests. During the disorders following the German invasions the Church and the clergy had increased their privileges and their wealth. As a result of these developments the clergy formed by the end of the Middle Ages a semi-independent state within the State and stood in the road of the new tendencies toward political centralization. The clergy and the extensive lands of the Church paid few of the taxes imposed on the laity and the Church courts exercised jurisdiction over many cases now decided in the courts of the State.

During the same period the local lords became almost independent rulers of the petty feudal districts which they controlled. They raised little feudal armies among their vassals, carried on almost constant warfare with their neighbors, maintained courts for their vassals and their serfs, drew an independent revenue from dues, tolls, and fines, and exercised most of the powers of the sovereign within their fiefs. Intrenched behind their feudal privileges, they resisted, during the latter half of the Middle Ages and the early years of the modern period every attempt of the rising central governments to destroy their independent position. At the opening of the sixteenth century the Church and the feudal nobility were the chief obstacles to the rise of absolute monarchies in most of Western Europe.

EUROPE
at the opening of THE SIXTEENTH CENTURY

THE OPENING OF THE SIXTEENTH CENTURY

The idea of having some central authority lived on, however, in spite of the disorganization of the early Middle Ages. Men looked back to the supposed order and peace of the Roman Empire as an ideal. The Church, too, fostered the idea of a universal monarchy as the complement and defender of the universal church and threw its powerful influence on the side of the central government in most of the contests between monarchy and feudalism. In response to this idea the Holy Roman Empire arose in Germany and in Italy, national monarchies in France, Spain, Portugal, and England, and semi-feudal monarchies in other parts of Western Europe.

THE HOLY ROMAN EMPIRE

The Holy Roman Empire included over three hundred German states differing greatly in size, power, population, and organization, and had shadowy claims to the Swiss cantons and Northern Italy. No ordinary map of the Holy Roman Empire could show all of its subdivisions. The aggregation of provinces ruled by the Habsburgs counted as a great power in the diplomacy of the time. Brandenburg, Electoral and Ducal Saxony, Bavaria, Württemberg, and Hesse were large enough to have considerable political influence. Many of the ecclesiastical states, ruled by archbishops, bishops, abbots, or abbesses, the city-states, controlled by little oligarchies of well-to-do merchants and gild masters, and the smaller states of the secular princes were too small to have any political significance. Although none of the ecclesiastical states were of any great size, the archbishops of Cologne, Trier, and Mainz were numbered among the seven electors who chose the emperors. The city-states of Hamburg, Bremen, and Lübeck still survive and form part of the present German Empire. Some of the smaller states were less than a square mile in area and were inhabited by only a few miserable serfs. Located for the most part in the valleys of the Rhine and the Upper Danube and too weak to defend themselves, these petty states of the Empire invited the encroachment of France.

Regardless of their size, all the states of the Empire exercised most of the powers of independent states. They maintained separate military forces, taxed their subjects, and possessed the executive, legislative, and judicial powers of any ordinary state. Their subjects often suffered from tyranny and injustice. Frequently the smaller the state the more tyrannical was its government.

The Empire had a central government, consisting of an emperor, a diet, and an imperial court, which exercised little real authority. The seven electors of the Empire — the Archbishops of Cologne, Trier, and Mainz, the Count Palatine of the Rhine,[1] the Elector of Saxony, the Margrave of Brandenburg, and the King of Bohemia — chose the emperor and had come to choose him regularly from the Habsburg family. The diet consisted of three houses, a house of electors, a house of princes, and a house composed of the representatives of the free imperial cities (the city-states) which was considered quite inferior to the other two houses. The diet met from time to time in solemn session, but exercised no real power. The emperor had neither an army nor an independent revenue at his command. In consequence, the central government was at the mercy of the individual states.

The real situation of the Empire contrasted strangely with its pretensions. The emperors considered themselves the successors of the old Roman emperors and of Charlemagne and claimed all Western Christendom for their empire. They really enjoyed, however, only an empty precedence over the other rulers of Western Europe on ceremonial occasions.

The weakness of the Empire was the result of its history. As a result of their efforts to achieve the ideal of universal monarchy the medieval emperors had grasped at power in all directions and had ended by letting their real powers slip through their fingers. While they wasted men and money on repeated expeditions to Italy, which gave them no permanent authority in the peninsula, the German nobles usurped the powers that the emperors had once exercised north of

[1] The ruler of the Upper and the Lower Palatinate.

THE OPENING OF THE SIXTEENTH CENTURY

the Alps. Their policies thus left both Germany and Italy without strong central governments.

THE HABSBURG AND BURGUNDIAN STATES

The largest and most important state of the Holy Roman Empire had gradually been put together by the Habsburg Emperors. After their first elevation to the imperial office in 1273, the various emperors of the family neglected the interests of their empire and used their newly acquired power and prestige to advance the interests of their house by building up an hereditary state of their own. In 1278 they obtained possession of Austria proper, Styria, and part of Carniola as a result of the important battle of Marchfeld. During the following century they conquered Tyrol, Carinthia, and the remaining portion of Carniola. In 1477 they gained control of the greater part of the possessions of the Dukes of Burgundy. These acquisitions gave the Habsburgs control of a loosely connected, widely scattered collection of counties and duchies, situated in the Valley of the Danube, The Netherlands, and the Upper Valley of the Rhone.

The Burgundian state had been built up in a somewhat similar manner. Starting with the French Duchy of Burgundy in the Upper Valley of the Rhone, the Dukes of Burgundy had gradually acquired the adjoining Free County of Burgundy (Franche Comté) and the greater part of the seventeen provinces of The Netherlands and had become vassals both of the kings of France and of the Holy Roman Emperors. Upon his succession to the Burgundian throne in 1467 Charles the Bold, the most famous member of the house, began a struggle for the acquisition of the royal title and for possession of the province of Lorraine which separated the Burgundian possessions into two parts. After the death of the Duke upon the battlefield of Nancy (1477) Louis XI of France seized the Duchy of Burgundy and some districts north of the Somme river and Maximilian of the Habsburg family married Mary of Burgundy, the daughter of Charles the Bold, and gained possession of most of the other provinces of her rich inheritance.

A state composed of such scattered provinces as the Habsburg state naturally included a great variety of peoples. Frenchmen lived in the Free County of Burgundy; Dutch, Flemish, and Walloons in The Netherlands; Germans in Austria, Styria, and Tyrol; and many Slavs, a few Germans, and a considerable number of Italians in the other districts. The whole group of provinces ruled by the Habsburgs had a population of over four millions.

The diversity in economic conditions was equally striking. The inhabitants of the hereditary Habsburg possessions carried on mining and agriculture as their chief occupations. There was almost no manufacturing. The mountains of Tyrol contained salt and metal mines and the other regions produced an abundance of wine and grain. Commerce consisted mainly in the exchange of these raw materials for fine manufactures and articles of luxury. Agriculture was almost the sole occupation of the 300,000 inhabitants of the Free County of Burgundy. The provinces of The Netherlands, in contrast, contained some of the chief manufacturing and commercial centers of Europe. Flanders and Brabant had long been famous for their textiles and Bruges and Antwerp were in succession the great commercial centers of Europe.

The Habsburgs held their scattered provinces and diverse nationalities together mainly by the tie of a common sovereign. The various rulers of the family had made only a beginning toward the creation of a modern centralized state. Each of their counties, duchies, and provinces had its separate semi-feudal machinery of government and the different provincial estates often prevented the Habsburgs from carrying out their policies. In spite of its defects of organization their state ranked next to France and Spain among the states of Europe.

The geography of their state greatly influenced the foreign relations of the Habsburgs. Their widely scattered possessions prevented them from concentrating on a single objective. They strove to conquer the lands of Charles the Bold seized by Louis XI of France, to obtain a foothold on

THE OPENING OF THE SIXTEENTH CENTURY

the Adriatic, to extend their hegemony in Germany, and to ward off the attacks of the Turks. These aims involved the Habsburgs in diplomatic and military struggles with France, Venice, the German princes, and the Turks. The lack of natural boundaries for their provinces both invited invasion and opened a prospect of unlimited expansion in Germany, Italy, and the Slavic lands to the east. The Habsburg policy of expansion finally proved the undoing of the house.

The size of their state also exerted an influence on the foreign relations of the Habsburgs. Like the rulers of Spain they felt the need of allies to cope with the superior forces of France. This situation had just caused the marriage of Philip the Handsome, heir to the Habsburg and Burgundian lands, to Joanna, heiress of Ferdinand and Isabella of Spain, and paved the way for the union of Castile, Aragon, the hereditary lands of the Habsburgs, and the possessions of Mary of Burgundy under the rule of Charles V, their son and heir.

ITALY

Italy lacked even the shadowy central government possessed by Germany. The peninsula was divided among a number of states too weak and too disunited to protect themselves from foreign invaders. Off the coast, Sicily and Sardinia were already dependencies of Spain, and Naples in the southern part of the peninsula had become a bone of contention between the sovereigns of France and Spain. In Central Italy were the Papal States, the principalities of Ferrara, Mantua, and Modena, the Republic of Florence, and the city-state of Siena, which Florence was about to absorb. In the Po Valley lay the Republic of Venice, the Duchy of Milan, and the province of Piedmont, a possession of the House of Savoy. Between the Alps and the Mediterranean in Northwestern Italy was the Republic of Genoa and south of Lake Geneva, on the French side of the Alps, nestled the ancestral Duchy of the Dukes of Savoy. In the year 1500 France and Spain had already begun a struggle for control of the peninsula.

Venice was the only state of Italy that even approached the status of a Great Power. Though unable to contend on equal terms with France, Spain, and the Habsburgs, it defended itself and carried on an independent policy. It owed its prestige and power to its population of one million seven hundred thousand, its protected position off the Adriatic coast, its powerful navy, its flourishing trade and manufactures, the foresight of its ruling aristocracy, and its extensive possessions in Dalmatia, Albania, and the Greek Islands. At Venice converged the sea routes from the East and the land routes from Central and Northern Europe. Venetian fleets brought the luxuries of the East to the warehouses of the city to be reëxported to the countries north of the Alps. The artisans of Venice manufactured silk goods, gold brocade, and gold and silver ware for exportation. The Venetian diplomats accredited to the various courts of Europe kept their Government informed about everything that might contribute in any way to the commercial and political success of the state. The ruling aristocracy sought particularly to assure the city an adequate supply of grain and raw material and to avoid conflicts with the Great Powers. The expansion of Venice on the Italian mainland, however, had aroused the fears of the other states of the peninsula and had just led to the intervention of France and Spain in the affairs of Italy.

The Duchy of Milan had a population of a million and a quarter and was an important manufacturing and commercial center. It manufactured gold brocades and silk, wool, and velvet goods, and almost monopolized the making of arms. Its proximity to Genoa gave Milan great influence over the government and powerful navy of the little Genoese city-state. By the opening of the sixteenth century France, Spain, and the Habsburgs had already begun a struggle for possession of the Duchy of Milan, because of its wealth, the technical skill of its artisans and its control of Genoa.

The Kingdom of Naples, with a population of over two millions, was one of the largest and the most populous states of the peninsula, but it possessed neither the resources nor the power of Venice and Milan. Its revenues hardly met the expenses of the government and its great landholders with their little armies and their fortified strongholds were just as likely to join forces with an invader as to aid their legal sovereign. In the year 1504 Naples came definitely into the possession of Spain.

Sicily, which was already under the rule of Spain, was of more political importance than Naples. Although it had a population of only seven hundred thousand it was easily defended and yielded a rich revenue. Its great surplus of grain furnished Spain a valuable means for bringing diplomatic pressure on the other states.

The remaining states of Italy were of much less importance. The Papal States were larger in area and about equal in population to Naples but the time and attention of the Pope were largely taken up with vain efforts to exercise real control over his various vassals. Florence, with a population of seven or eight hundred thousand, was on the decline. It was torn by internal feuds and its commerce and industry were being destroyed by the new commercial policies adopted by England and France in the interest of their domestic industries. Genoa lacked the strategic position of Venice and was dependent on Sicily for grain and on Savoy and France for wood.

FRANCE

At the opening of the sixteenth century France was the most important single state of Europe. At that date it did not embrace all the territory within its present boundaries. Since that time it has acquired considerable territory on the northeast; the greater part of the region between the Rhone and the Saône Rivers, and the Alps and Jura Mountains on the east; the province of Roussillon and the portion of the little Kingdom of Navarre on the French side of the Pyrenees on the south; and on the north many famous cities like Lille, Arras, Sedan, Metz, Verdun, and Strassburg, which were then a part of the Empire or of The Netherlands. The conquest of these lands was to be one of the chief aims of French policy during the modern period of history.

France was in a very satisfactory economic position. With a population of sixteen millions, it had more inhabitants than any state in Europe save the Empire, and was twice as populous as Spain, its strongest rival. Its soil produced grain and wine and was capable of supporting even a larger population. Its commerce, which was still largely in the hands of foreigners, was confined to the exportation of the surplus of wine, grain, and salt, and the importation of a few commodities like metals, silk goods, brocade, glassware, and jewelry, the articles of luxury coming largely from Italy.

The firm control which the French kings had gained over the military, political, and financial resources of their kingdom, made France the most powerful state in Europe. In the year 987 the French kings had actual rule of only a very small district around Paris. Over the remainder of the kingdom the great feudal lords really held power. The extension of the royal authority over all France, at the expense of that of the nobles, had been the principal task of the French kings during the Middle Ages. By the opening of the sixteenth century neither the parlements (the principal courts of France), the provincial estates, the Estates General (a sort of national parliament), nor even the turbulent nobles who had begun to look to the king for positions in the army and the Church for their younger sons, acted as an effective check on the king. As a result, the French kings were free to tax their subjects and able to maintain an army.

In the art of fortification, in artillery, and in the heavy cavalry, which was recruited among the sons of the nobility, the French army was superior to those of the surrounding states. On the sea and in infantry it was inferior to its rivals. The labor of the French peasants was needed in agriculture and the infantry, consequently, had to be hired for the most part in Germany and Switzerland.

France had really serious differences only with the Habsburgs. Upon the death of Charles the Bold, Duke of Burgundy, in 1477, Louis XI of France and Maximilian, ruler of Habsburg lands, began a struggle for the hand and the territories of Mary of Burgundy, the daughter of Charles the Bold.

THE OPENING OF THE SIXTEENTH CENTURY 37

Maximilian obtained the heiress, the Free County of Burgundy (Franche Comté), and the greater part of the Netherlands, but the wily Louis XI seized for France the Duchy of Burgundy, a slice of Flanders, and the valley of the Somme. Naturally neither was satisfied with only a part of the Burgundian lands.

The relations of France with the remaining powers of Europe were on the whole amicable. England had just lost all its possessions in France save Calais, and was on the point of turning its attention mainly to the New World. With both the Swiss cantons and the German princes, France regularly cultivated good relations in order to insure a supply of mercenaries. With Spain its relations were not quite so favorable, since the Spanish province of Roussillon lay in the path of the natural expansion of France and the portion of Navarre[1] on the Spanish side of the Pyrenees in that of Spain. The greatest danger from French expansion lay in the new spirit animating the French sovereigns. Having consolidated fairly well their power at home, they were beginning to look towards Naples and Milan as regions offering a favorable opening for conquest.

SPAIN AND PORTUGAL

South of the Pyrenees lay Spain and Portugal, the greater part of the Iberian peninsula being occupied by Spain. Besides Spain proper, its sovereigns possessed Roussillon, the islands of Sicily and Sardinia, a few posts in Northwestern Africa, and the islands just discovered in America by Columbus. Ferdinand, one of the joint sovereigns of Spain, was on the point of conquering Naples in Italy and Spanish Navarre in the Spanish peninsula.

At the beginning of the sixteenth century the political unity of Spain was not yet assured. In the early Middle Ages Moslem invaders had forced their way into the peninsula and overrun all the country save a few strongholds on the southern slope of the Pyrenees, which the Christians succeeded in defending. Around these as centers there devel-

[1] Finally acquired by Spain in 1512.

oped a number of little Christian states. The last five hundred years of the Middle Ages saw the gradual expansion of these states over the greater part of the peninsula, and the slow development of political unity. By the year 1500 only the small states of Portugal and Navarre were independent of the Kingdoms of Castile and Aragon, which had been united in 1469 by a personal union through the marriage of Ferdinand of Aragon to Isabella of Castile. Though the two sovereigns followed thenceforth a common policy, their states were not yet fused into a single organic union.

Spain proper was neither as populous nor as prosperous as France. About six million of its seven million inhabitants lived in Castile. The unity of the population was seriously broken by religious, racial, and geographic differences. While the nobles owed much of their prosperity to their Moslem tenants, the middle and lower classes found it difficult to compete with the Jews in the cities and the Moslem peasants of the rural districts, and hated them bitterly. This situation later resulted in the expulsion of the Jews and Moriscos from Spain.[1] The mountains of Spain, furthermore, divided the population into Galicians, Andalusians, Catalans, Castilians, and Aragonese, groups which were markedly unlike one another in origin, dress, speech, customs, and point of view.

The economic situation of Spain differed considerably from that of France. Trade was in the hands of foreigners and small in bulk. Grain was brought in from Sicily and The Netherlands. Industry was so slightly developed that the commonest cloth had to be imported from The Netherlands. The chief exports were wool and minerals. Agriculture was on the decline but cattle and sheep raising were developing. The lack of rain and the resulting barrenness of the soil largely explain the inferior economic conditions in the peninsula.

As a result of its history Spain was less centralized than France. Castile and Aragon still retained their own cortes or parliaments, their historic constitutions, and their jeal-

[1] The Moriscos were Christianized Moslems.

ously guarded rights. To make matters still worse, the historic divisions of Aragon and its dependencies — Catalonia, Aragon, Valencia, Sicily, and Sardinia — had their distinct institutions. The carefully guarded local privileges of Aragon made it a real obstacle in the way of the development of absolutism in Spain. Consequently, Castile, which was more docile, paid most of the taxes and furnished more than its quota of the troops required by the kings of Spain in their wars.

The Spanish sovereigns had at their disposal a fairly satisfactory army. The long wars with the Moslems had created a military spirit among the people, and the economic situation made possible an abundant supply of cheap and trustworthy infantry, since sheep and cattle raising require a smaller labor force than agriculture. In the Mediterranean, Spain was stronger in naval power than France, but supremacy there really depended on the terms that could be made with Genoa.

In foreign relations the sovereigns of Spain were confronted by a variety of problems. The inferiority of Spain to France in respect to population and power caused its rulers to maintain diplomatic representatives in England, at Vienna, at Rome, and at Venice, and to be on the lookout for allies. The corsairs of Northern Africa continually harassed the Mediterranean coasts of Spain. The Spanish sovereigns also steadily aimed at a peaceful absorption of Portugal. The protection of Naples and the conquest of Milan, however, proved to be the chief problems of Spanish foreign policy between 1494 and 1559.

Portugal occupied only a small part of the Iberian peninsula. In the year 1500 it had just started on the great colonial career that was to make it a state of the greatest importance for a century.

ENGLAND, SCOTLAND, AND IRELAND

England was inferior to the Great Powers of the Continent in area, population, and military power. Its sovereign ruled England and Wales, and the city of Calais in France, and laid claim to all of Ireland. His control, as yet, did not extend over the weak, sparsely settled, badly organized state of Scotland, and his rule in Ireland did not extend beyond a small region around Dublin known as the Pale. The four million inhabitants of England proper were engaged mainly in agriculture. The political importance of England in the sixteenth century arose from the fact that its sovereigns held for a long time the balance of power between France on one side and Spain and the Habsburgs on the other.

For later generations, but not for the men of the sixteenth century, the English Government was a matter of especial interest. By the close of the Middle Ages England had already laid the foundation for its subsequent parliamentary government. It had a parliament of two houses, the upper house being composed of hereditary nobles and great dignitaries of the Church and the lower house of elected members representing the towns and counties. Parliament had already exercised on rare occasions the powers which it later regularly enjoyed, but it lacked the democratic basis of the modern English parliament.

BOHEMIA

The Kingdom of Bohemia included Bohemia proper, the Duchy of Silesia, and the Margraviate of Moravia. In the latter province lived the Moravians, a people of Slavic stock, in Bohemia proper the kindred Czechs and large numbers of Germans, and in Silesia Germans and Poles. This mixed population numbered all told about three and one half millions. Manufactures were being developed on a considerable scale, the soil was fertile, and the mountains were rich in minerals. Up to 1526 the kingship was elective — but by choosing Ferdinand, the younger brother of Charles V and his regent for the hereditary Habsburg lands, as King of Bohemia in that year, the Bohemians paved the way for the total loss of their independence.

HUNGARY

The Kingdom of Hungary lay just east of the hereditary lands of the Habsburgs in the rich Hungarian plain of the

THE OPENING OF THE SIXTEENTH CENTURY

Lower Danube Valley. In the ninth century the still heathen Magyars had pressed into this region and established their rule over its Slavic inhabitants. The country was fertile, suitable for stock-raising, and rich in minerals, the latter being exploited in the year 1500 mainly by foreigners. The population was Catholic and divided into priests, nobles, and serfs. There was no middle class. The king was elective and very dependent on the Magnates, as the turbulent, independent nobles were called. The infantry and artillery were very weak and the cavalry, while excellently mounted, was poorly armed and badly disciplined. In 1526 the inferior political and military organization of the Hungarians led to their defeat by the Turks at the battle of Mohács. As a result of this battle the Kingdom of Hungary was long divided between the Turks and the Habsburgs.

THE OTTOMAN EMPIRE

The Ottoman Turks dominated the Christian nationalities of Southeastern Europe. About the middle of the thirteenth century this invading Moslem people had acquired a foothold in Asia Minor across the straits from Constantinople. During the next two centuries an extraordinary line of rulers had pushed their conquests in all directions. About the middle of the fourteenth century they had acquired a foothold in the Balkan Peninsula. In 1453 they had captured Constantinople, the capital of the Eastern Roman Empire. By the opening of the sixteenth century the Ottoman Empire included the Balkan Peninsula, the provinces around the eastern end of the Mediterranean Sea, and the northern coast of Africa as far west as Algiers.

In the Balkan Peninsula the Turks held a position similar to that of an invading army. They neither exterminated nor assimilated the conquered Greeks, Bulgars, Serbs, and Rumanians. They merely held the vanquished peoples in subjection and collected tribute from them. This policy kept alive the religious and national sentiment of the Balkan peoples which finally caused the dismemberment of the Turkish Empire.

At the beginning of the sixteenth century the Ottoman Empire was just entering upon a momentous career. For the next three centuries it ranked as a great power. Its dominions finally stretched from the borders of Persia to Morocco, and from Arabia to the Danube. Its rulers combined political despotism with the headship of the Moslem world. Its armies long menaced the very existence of Poland and the Habsburg State, and the fleets of the Turkish Empire and its Moslem allies, the corsairs of Northern Africa, constantly threatened the coasts of Naples, France, Spain, and the Papal States.

THE TEUTONIC KNIGHTS, POLAND, AND THE GRAND DUCHY OF MUSCOVY

In the regions now occupied by the new Baltic States, Poland and Russia, political control was very different in the year 1500 from that of to-day. Finland belonged to the Kingdom of Sweden; the Baltic coast from the Gulf of Finland to the Vistula was in the possession of the Teutonic Knights; the Kingdom of Poland and the Grand Duchy of Lithuania, united by the bond of a common ruler, occupied most of the region bounded by the Carpathian Mountains, the Dnieper River, and the Black and Baltic Seas; and the center of the great Russian plain was falling under the control of the rising Grand Duchy of Muscovy. The rest of the region was occupied by declining Russian principalities and by several powerful khanates, fragments of the once widespread Mongol Empire.

The Teutonic Knights was one of the semi-religious military orders, which had been founded during the period of the crusades. After the close of that movement they had established themselves on the shores of the Baltic Sea as a sort of vanguard of the advancing German civilization. In the year 1237 they had absorbed the Brethren of the Sword, a similar order, which had been established in Livonia in the year 1202 for the protection of the German merchants settled at Riga. For the next two centuries the combined orders waged a ceaseless struggle with the Prussians, the Lithuanians, the

THE OPENING OF THE SIXTEENTH CENTURY 43

Letts, and the Esthonians, and finally brought them under the control of the order. Thenceforth the knights, who were recruited from among the younger sons of the German nobility, lived in the region as a governing aristocracy and the conquered natives degenerated into a body of serfs. The political, economic, and cultural organization of the region continued to show the influence of its peculiar history until the Great War drove the German magistrates and landlords out of the country.

During the Middle Ages pressure from the Germans forced the Polish huntsmen, herdsmen, and tillers of the soil to form a Polish kingdom. The threat of conquest by the Teutonic Knights compelled the Lithuanians of the Niemen valley to form a state which an able line of rulers gradually extended over the region between the Carpathian Mountains, the Dnieper River, and the Black Sea, a region occupied by the Little and the White Russians. The union, in the year 1386, of the Grand Duchy of Lithuania with the Kingdom of Poland created a powerful state which was to dominate Northern Europe for more than two centuries.

From the thirteenth to the middle of the fifteenth centuries the Slavs east of the Dnieper had been ruled by petty princes, who paid tribute to the Mongols or Tartars living on the steppes north of the Black and Caspian Seas. The most important of these principalities was the Grand Duchy of Muscovy, a state which had grown up around the city of Moscow. John (Ivan) III, who was still ruling in the year 1500, threw off the rule of the Mongols in 1460, suppressed the princely appanages, which greatly weakened the State, and absorbed four rival principalities. The Grand Duchy of Muscovy later became known as Russia.

The Slavs of the great Russian plain were very inferior in civilization to the people of Western Europe. They had developed no industry or commerce of any importance. The economic foundation of the region was its large self-sufficing estates. The population, in consequence, consisted almost wholly of despotic landlords and heavily burdened free peasants. In customs and institutions this region was oriental in character. Geographically, it was a continuation of the continent of Asia. Greek missionaries from Constantinople had brought its religion and its civilization, and for two hundred years it had been subject to Asiatic Mongols. As a result of these influences Russia was destined to develop a civilization somewhat different from that of Western Europe.

THE OTHER STATES OF EUROPE

Thanks to their easily defensible position amid the Alps and to their indomitable spirit the Swiss continued to maintain their independence. They exercised considerable influence over the course of events in Europe by granting or withholding the privilege of recruiting mercenary troops in the Swiss cantons.

The three Scandinavian kingdoms lay outside the circle of the great political movements of the sixteenth century. Since 1397 the three states had been united by the Union of Kalmar, but the Swedes were on the point of regaining their independence. Denmark, the strongest and the most populous of the three kingdoms, included the southern part of Sweden, and by its conquest of Finland, Sweden had already taken the first step toward making the Baltic a Swedish lake.

This survey shows that, in the year 1500, Europe was just emerging from the ideas and institutions of the Middle Ages. The mass of the people lived on great estates in a condition of subjection to a small class of landlords. Commerce and industry were on a small scale, and cities, in consequence, were few in number and smaller in size than they are to-day. The economic organization led to the division of society into the privileged clergy and nobles, the unprivileged townsmen and peasants, and the middle class. In respect to religion the majority of the people in Europe were under the control of the Catholic Church. Intellectually they were just beginning to be emancipated from the bonds of Scholasticism through the efforts of the Humanists. Politically they were just commencing to substitute national states for the medieval Empire and the feudal kingdoms of the Middle Ages.

THE OPENING OF THE SIXTEENTH CENTURY 45

REFERENCES

RURAL LIFE AND ORGANIZATION IN ENGLAND
  W. J. Ashley, *English Economic History*, chapter I.
  E. P. Cheyney, *Industrial and Social History of England*, chapter II.
  F. A. Ogg, *Economic Development of Modern Europe*, chapter II.
  P. E. Prothero, *English Farming, Past and Present*, pp. 1–54.
  A. P. Usher, *The Industrial History of England*, chapter V.

VILLAGE LIFE IN ENGLAND SIX HUNDRED YEARS AGO
  A. Jessop, *The Coming of the Friars*, chapter II.

COUNTRY LIFE IN GERMANY AT THE CLOSE OF THE MIDDLE AGES
  E. B. Bax, *German Society at the Close of the Middle Ages*, chapter VII.

TOWN LIFE AND ORGANIZATION IN ENGLAND
  W. J. Ashley, *English Economic History*, chapters I–II.
  E. P. Cheyney, *Industrial and Social History of England*, chapter III.
  A. P. Usher, *The Industrial History of England*, chapters VI–VII.

TOWN LIFE AND ORGANIZATION ON THE CONTINENT
  C. Day, *A History of Commerce*, chapter VI.
  L. Thorndike, *The History of Medieval Europe*, chapters XVII–XIX.
  O. J. Thatcher and E. H. McNeal, *Europe in the Middle Ages*, chapter XXIV.

GERMAN TOWNS AT THE CLOSE OF THE MIDDLE AGES
  E. B. Bax, *German Society at the Close of the Middle Ages*, pp. 156–64, 203–18.

MEDIEVAL TRADE
  C. Day, *A History of Commerce*, chapters VII–IX.

THE FEUDAL ORGANIZATION OF MEDIEVAL SOCIETY
  C. Bemont and G. Monod, *Medieval Europe*, chapter XVI.
  E. Emerton, *Medieval Europe*, chapter XIV.
  J. H. Robinson, *History of Western Europe*, chapter IX.
  O. J. Thatcher and F. Schevill, *Europe in the Middle Ages*, chapter XI.
  O. J. Thatcher and E. H. McNeal, *Europe in the Middle Ages*, chapter VII.

THE MEDIEVAL CHURCH
  C. Bemont and G. Monod, *Medieval Europe*, chapter XXIX.
  E. Emerton, *Medieval Europe*, chapter XVI.
  J. H. Robinson, *History of Western Europe*, chapter XVI.

THE CULTURE OF THE MIDDLE AGES
  W. C. Abbott, *The Expansion of Europe*, vol. I, chapter I.
  J. H. Robinson, *History of Western Europe*, chapter XIX.
  F. Seebohm, *Era of the Protestant Reformation*, pp. 8–15.
  O. J. Thatcher and E. H. McNeal, *Europe in the Middle Ages*, chapter XXV.

THE ITALIAN RENAISSANCE
    W. C. Abbott, *The Expansion of Europe*, vol. I, chapter II.
    Cambridge Modern History, vol. I, chapter XVI.
    E. Emerton, *The Beginnings of Modern Europe*, chapter IX.
    J. H. Robinson, *History of Western Europe*, chapter XXII.
    L. Thorndike, *The History of Medieval Europe*, chapters XXXI–XXXII.
    E. R. Turner, *Europe, 1450–1789*, chapter IV.

THE NORTHERN RENAISSANCE
    Cambridge Modern History, vol. I, chapter XVII.
    E. Emerton, *The Beginnings of Modern Europe*, chapter X.

ERASMUS
    E. Emerton, *Desiderius Erasmus*.
    P. Smith, *Erasmus*.

SPAIN AT THE OPENING OF THE MODERN PERIOD
    E. P. Cheyney, *European Background of American History*, pp. 79–114.
    M. A. S. Hume, *Spain, 1479–1788*, chapter I.
    R. B. Merriman, *Rise of the Spanish Empire*, vol. II, chapter XV.

FRANCE AT THE OPENING OF THE MODERN PERIOD
    A. J. Grant, *Growth of the French Monarchy*, vol. I, chapter I.
    A. Tilley, *Modern France*, pp. 2–14.

GERMANY IN THE LATER MIDDLE AGES
    A. H. Johnson, *Europe in the Sixteenth Century*, pp. 106–28.
    L. Thorndike, *History of Medieval Europe*, chapter XXVIII.
    O. J. Thatcher and E. H. McNeal, *Europe in the Middle Ages*, chapter XXII.

EASTERN EUROPE IN THE LATER MIDDLE AGES
    Cambridge Modern History, vol. I, chapter III.
    F. Schevill, *History of the Balkan Peninsula*, chapters XII–XVIII.
    L. Thorndike, *History of Medieval Europe*, chapter XXIX.
    E. R. Turner, *Europe, 1450–1789*, chapter III.

MAPS
    Plan of a medieval manor. W. R. Shepherd, *Historical Atlas*, p. 104.
    Plan of a monastery. *Ibid.*, p. 101.
    Spain at the opening of the sixteenth century. *Ibid.*, pp. 82–83.
    France at the opening of the sixteenth century. *Ibid.*, p. 84.
    The hereditary possessions of the Habsburgs at the opening of the sixteenth century. *Ibid.*, pp. 86–87.
    The Burgundian Lands at the opening of the sixteenth century. *Ibid.*, pp. 84, 86–87.
    The Holy Roman Empire at the opening of the sixteenth century. *Ibid.*, pp. 86–87, 114–15.
    Italy at the opening of the modern period. *Ibid.*, p. 90.
    The Ottoman Empire at the opening of the modern period. *Ibid.*, p. 93.
    The Teutonic Knights. *Ibid.*, p. 88.
    The Swiss Confederation. *Ibid.*, p. 91.

CHAPTER II
BEGINNINGS OF OVERSEAS EXPANSION

DURING the Middle Ages most Europeans were acquainted with only a small part of the earth's surface. The world that they knew consisted of Europe and the parts of Asia and Africa that touched the Mediterranean Sea. A few Europeans had traveled in Southern and Eastern Asia, but China, India, and Japan still remained vague and almost legendary places. Since the fifteenth century men of European stock have explored the entire earth and have acquired control of the greater part of its surface. A large part of this work of discovery was done by the Spanish and the Portuguese in the latter part of the fifteenth and the first half of the sixteenth centuries.

In the early Middle Ages trade between Europe and the Far East almost entirely ceased, but after the time of the Crusades it steadily expanded. It consisted mainly in such luxuries as spices, drugs, sugar, precious stones, dyestuffs, alum, and textiles. The people of Europe used the pepper, cloves, cinnamon, nutmegs, mace, and ginger to season food and drink; the medieval apothecaries made use of the rhubarb, aloes, balsam, borax, gums, camphor, and other drugs in their prescriptions; the dyers employed the indigo, saffron and Brazil-wood in dyeing; and the prelates of the Church and the nobles wore the fine cottons and silks. The Italians had almost a monopoly in the distribution of these Eastern commodities to the countries of Western Europe. The political power of Genoa, Venice, and other Italian cities was based upon it. Sailing vessels and caravans carried these Eastern products from China, India, and the Spice Islands to the Eastern Mediterranean ports. From there the Italian merchants brought them to Italy where other merchants took them and distributed them to Western Europe. The inhabitants of Marseilles and Barcelona participated in this

MEDIAEVAL TRADE ROUTES

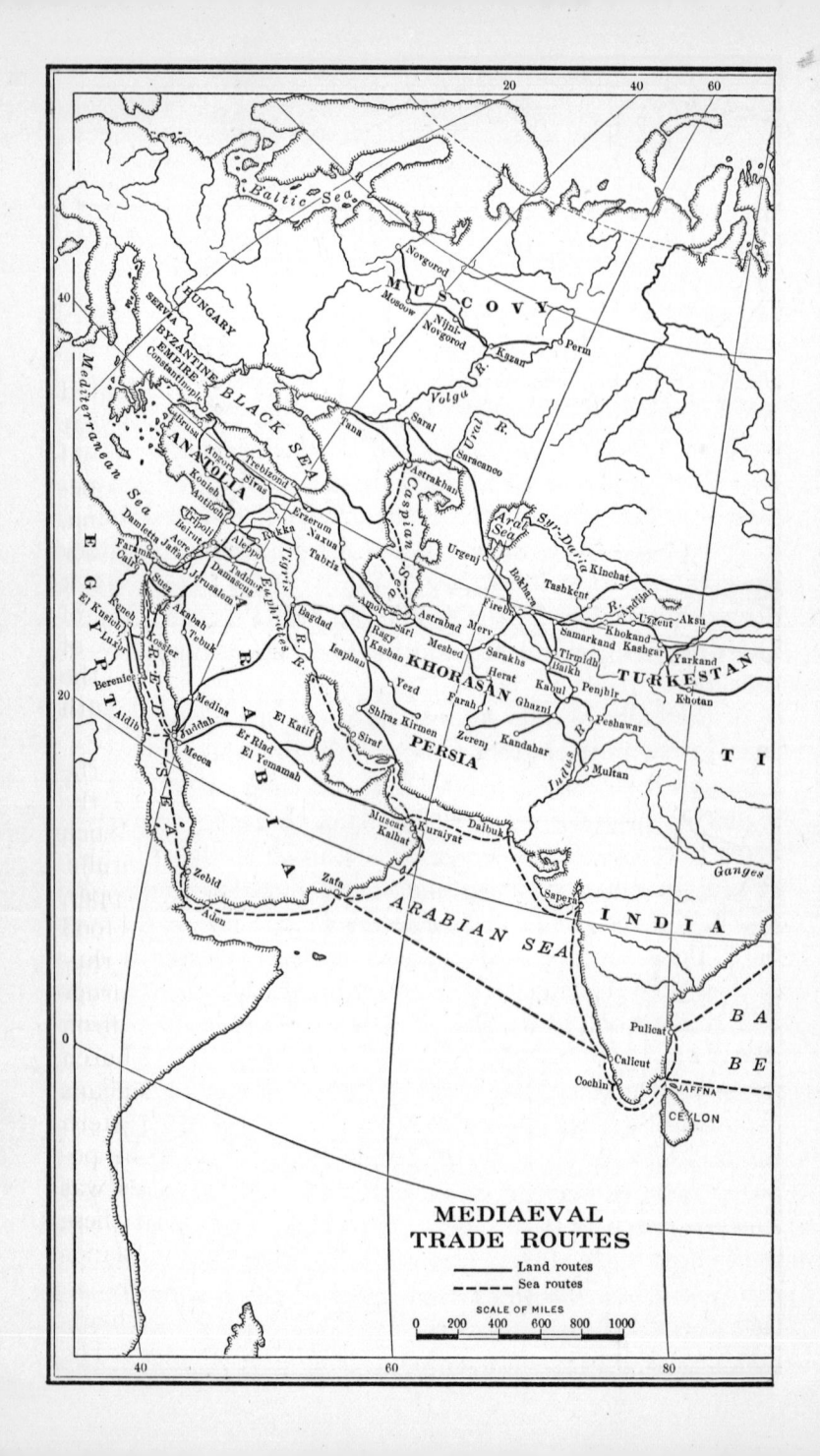

——— Land routes
- - - - Sea routes

SCALE OF MILES
0 200 400 600 800 1000

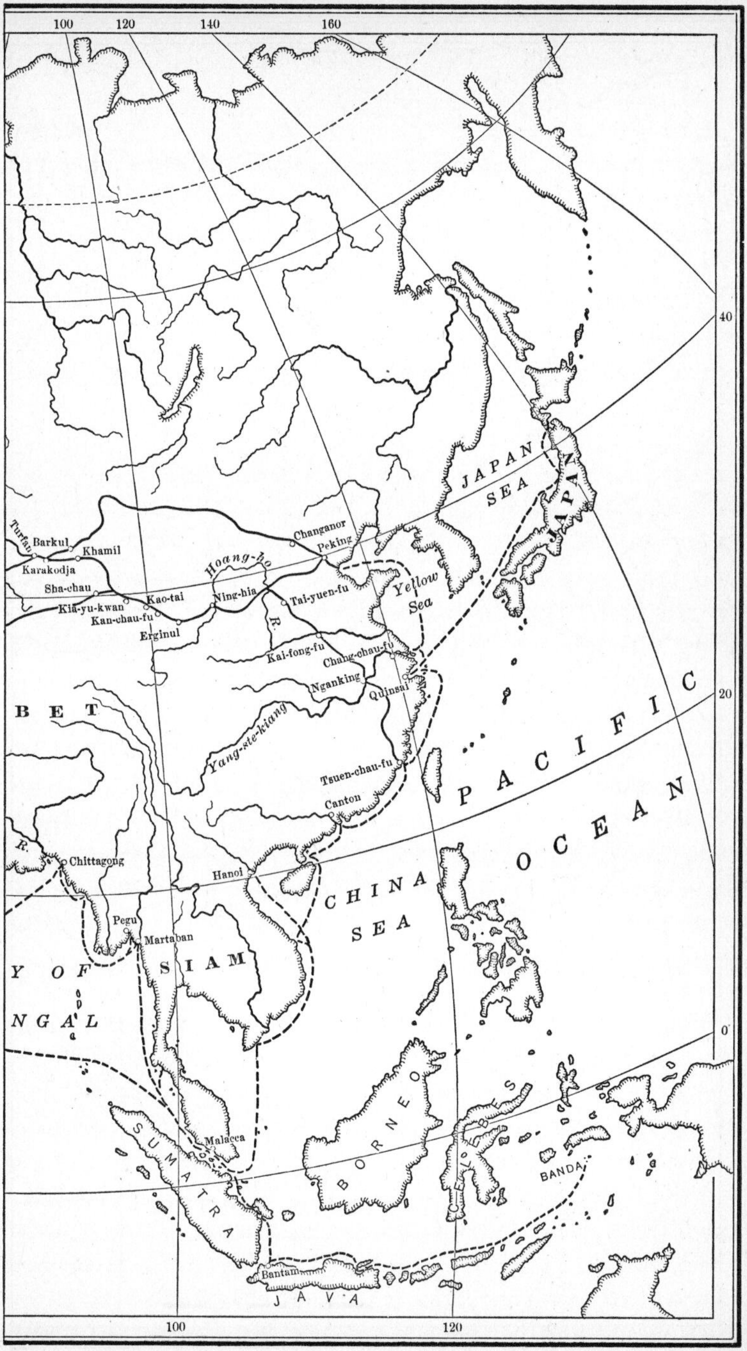

trade just enough to know about the profits of the Italians and to wish to break their monopoly.

The Portuguese were the pioneer explorers of the non-European world. The first leader in the work of Portuguese discovery was Prince Henry the Navigator (1394-1460), who devoted his life to the task of exploring the western coast of Africa. In 1419 he built a palace and observatory on Cape St. Vincent, a promontory of Southern Portugal. There he gathered around him a group of mathematicians and astronomers who studied geography and the art of navigation. Year after year his captains felt their way farther and farther down the African coast, and before his death, in 1460, they had reached the fertile, inhabited lands beyond the Senegal River. With this region the Portuguese soon began a considerable trade in slaves, gold and ivory.

A variety of motives inspired the Portuguese to carry on the work of exploring the African coast. With Prince Henry himself the desire for scientific information seems to have been the dominant motive, for he largely disregarded the opportunities for commerce, colonization, and the conversion of the negroes, and stuck to his self-appointed task of exploration. In the case of others the crusading, the religious, or the commercial motive predominated. As the Portuguese captains pushed farther and farther down the African coast, however, the idea of breaking the Italian monopoly in the exceedingly profitable trade in the products of the East by finding a new route to India probably took precedence over all other motives.

The Portuguese explorers had good reasons, therefore, for continuing their work of exploration after the death of Prince Henry. In 1471 they crossed the Equator for the first time; in 1482 they reached the mouth of the Congo River; and five years later Diaz rounded the cape now known as the Cape of Good Hope. Finally, in 1498, Vasco da Gama sailed around the Cape, felt his way up the eastern coast of Africa as far as the Equator, and then sailed boldly across the Indian Ocean in a northwesterly direction to Calicut in southwestern India. By courage and persistence the Portuguese had put them-

THE PRINCIPAL VOYAGES OF DISCOVERY
SPANISH
PORTUGUESE
First voyage of Columbus 1492-3
Second " " " 1493
Third " " " 1498
Fourth " " " 1502
Route of Hojeda, Cosa and Vespucci, 1499
Route of Pinzon, 1499
" " Pineda, 1519
" " Magellan and Elcano 1519-1522
Spanish trade routes
Route of Diaz, 1486-7
" " Vasco de Gama, 1497-8
" " Cabral, 1500
Portuguese trade routes
Route of John Cabot, 1497-8
First voyage of Cartier, 1534-5
Second " " " 1535-6
ABBREVIATIONS
J-Juana, (Cuba) E-Espanola, (Haiti)
LINE OF DEMARCATION, 1494
NORTH AMERICA
SOUTH AMERICA
EUROPE
ASIA
AFRICA
PACIFIC
OCEAN
ATLANTIC
OCEAN
INDIAN
OCEAN
PACIFIC
OCEAN.
ARCTIC CIRCLE
TROPIC OF CANCER
EQUATOR
TROPIC OF CAPRICORN
ANTARCTIC CIRCLE
ENGLAND
Bristol
St. Malo
FRANCE
PORTUGAL
SPAIN
Lisbon
Cadiz
NEWFOUNDLAND
VIRGINIA
Florida
SAN SALVADOR
DOM. OF New Spain
AZTECS
Vera Cruz (1519)
Acapulco
YUCATAN
HONDURAS
S. Domingo
DOMINICA
Route of Spanish fleets
TRINIDAD
Cartagena
NEW ANDALUSIA
QUITO
Spanish trade route
CANARY IS. 1341
C. VERDE IS. 1560
C. Verde 1445
C. Sierra Leone 1462
San Jorge da Minha 1482
FERNANDO PO 1484
CONGO
ANGOLA
Mombasa 1498
Mozambique 1498
Sofala 1500
Pernambuco
Bahia (1549)
Porto Seguro
BRAZIL
Rio Janeiro 1516
G. of St. Matias
G. of St. George
Port St. Julian
PATAGONIA
TIERRA DEL FUEGO
Muscat 1507
Diu
INDIA
Goa 1510
Cannanore 1512
CEYLON
Portuguese trade routes
CHINA
Macao 1557
SIAM
SUMATRA
JAVA
BORNEO
CELEBES
SPICE IS.
PHILIPPINES
NEW GUINEA
JAPAN
Spanish trade route

selves in a position to establish a monopoly over the trade in eastern products. As a result of the discovery of an all water route to the East, Portugal soon took the place of Venice as the chief distributor of eastern commodities, and the ocean soon superseded the Mediterranean as the center of the world's commercial activity.

Meanwhile Columbus, sailing under the auspices of Spain, had taken the first steps toward exploring the Western Hemisphere. He reached the West Indies in one bold voyage. In a sense, his achievement was just as much a culmination of the work of Prince Henry as the voyage of Vasco da Gama, for he obtained many of his ideas in Portugal. His distinctive merit lies in the fact that he actually put to the test the geographical ideas which many men cherished. The immediate results of his voyage were discouraging, for he found neither the mountains of gold, nor the Eastern products that he sought. His discoveries were interesting, but not immediately profitable.

The discoveries of Columbus brought up the question of the division of the newly discovered non-European lands between Spain and Portugal. The Spanish sovereigns hurriedly requested the Pope, who was still looked upon as a sort of arbiter of Europe, to confirm their right to their new discoveries. In 1493, consequently, the Pope decreed that all non-Christian lands lying one hundred leagues west of the Azores and Cape Verde Islands should belong to Spain, and that all lying to the east of the line should belong to Portugal. A year later this line, known as the Line of Demarcation, was moved to a point three hundred and seventy leagues west of the Cape Verde Islands. After Magellan circumnavigated the globe it was extended around the earth. This line later gave Portugal a claim to Brazil and Spain a claim to the Philippines.

Spain and Portugal promptly set themselves to the task of exploring and exploiting the areas assigned to them. Within a period of sixty years Spanish explorers traced the greater part of the coastlines of North and South America, explored the greater part of the interior of both continents, and made a beginning toward their settlement. Columbus himself discovered, during the course of three more voyages, the islands of Cuba, Haiti, Guadalupe, Porto Rico, Jamaica, and Trinidad, and touched the mainland of America near the mouth of the Orinoco River and on the coast of Central America. By 1525, as a result of the work of a score or more of Spanish explorers, the Atlantic coast from Nova Scotia to the Straits of Magellan, had been charted. In 1513 Balboa crossed the Isthmus of Panama and discovered the Pacific Ocean, and within a quarter of a century the Pacific coast from California to the Straits of Magellan, had been traced. Long before the task of mapping these coastlines was completed, however, the expedition of Magellan (1519-22) circumnavigated the earth, the greatest feat of navigation ever performed.

While Spanish navigators were tracing the coastlines of the Western Hemisphere, Spanish warriors explored and conquered the interior. In 1519 Cortez began the conquest of Mexico. In 1531 Pizarro conquered Peru. Shortly afterwards, other expeditions entered California, the Plata region, and Chile. From Mexico as a center Cortez sent out exploring parties in every direction. In 1540 Coronado with his companions traversed a large part of what is now Southwestern United States, finally reaching a point in Central Kansas. In 1539 De Soto led an expedition across the present states of Georgia, South Carolina, North Carolina, Alabama, Mississippi, and Arkansas, to a point in Oklahoma within nine days' march of the place reached about the same time by Coronado. About the middle of the century Orellana crossed the Andes and descended the Amazon to its mouth. By 1650, consequently, the Spaniards had a fairly accurate knowledge of the geography of South America and the southern half of North America.

Most of the Spanish conquerors were also colonizers. The newly discovered lands were sparsely populated and suitable for exploitation, and settlements and plantations were started in most of the new provinces. After the conquest of Mexico and Peru, the Spaniards worked the mines of precious metals in the two countries. Both in the mines and on the

BEGINNINGS OF OVERSEAS EXPANSION

plantations the settlers used the forced labor of the natives. By the middle of the sixteenth century, as a result of Spanish enterprise, settlements had been started at Buenos Ayres, Asunción, Santiago de Chile, Cuzco, Lima, Quito, Bogotá, Venezuela, Panama, and Mexico. In 1550 there were probably not more than 15,000 Spaniards in America, but twenty-four years later, a Spanish official estimated that there were 160,000 Spaniards in the New World. The new colonists were mainly men, who intermarried for the most part with the natives. A large part of the present population of Spanish America, for this reason, derives its blood in varying proportions from both the Spanish conquerors and the conquered natives.

While the Spanish conquerors were establishing the rule of Spain in America, the Portuguese were setting up a commercial monopoly in the East. The task of the Portuguese was very different from that of the Spaniards. The Spaniards were opposed by a relatively small and backward population, while the Portuguese had to establish themselves amid a teeming population and a highly developed civilization. The first task of the Portuguese was to overcome the opposition of the Arabs and Turks. This was accomplished by the decisive naval battle of Diu, won over an Egyptian fleet in the year 1509. This victory made the Indian Ocean practically a Portuguese sea for a hundred years. Under the rule of Albuquerque, probably the most famous administrator sent by Portugal to the East, great progress was made in acquiring strategic points and establishing Portuguese rule. In 1507 Socotra, commanding the entrance of the Red Sea, was seized and fortified. In 1510 the Portuguese captured Goa, the future capital of the Portuguese possessions in the East and one of the great markets of India. In the following year they took Malacca, the key to the spice trade. In 1515 Ormuz, the key to the Persian gulf, became a Portuguese protectorate. In six years, under the leadership of Albuquerque, Portugal had become supreme in the East. Subsequently the Portuguese opened up commercial relations directly with the Molucca or Spice Islands, China, and

Japan. The port of Macão, near Canton, is a present-day reminder of the magnificent commercial empire Portugal once had in the East.

The Portuguese also acquired a foothold in Brazil as the result of the discovery of Cabral, and the establishment of the line of demarcation by the Pope. While on his way to India in 1500, in command of the Portuguese fleet, Cabral sailed farther to the west than Vasco da Gama had done, and discovered a part of the Brazilian coast. The following year the Portuguese discovered that Brazil was a part of a continent. For many years, however, colonization progressed very slowly, because the East with its profitable spice trade offered to the enterprising greater immediate opportunities than Brazil.

During the sixteenth century the other nations of Europe played very little part in the discovery and exploitation of the non-European world. In 1497 John Cabot sailed from Bristol, England, and touched the mainland of North America, probably at some point near Cape Breton Island, and gave the English a basis for their later claims to North America. In 1524, Verrazano explored a considerable part of the Atlantic coastline of North America in the interest of France, and in the following decade Cartier led two expeditions to Canada which resulted in the exploration of the Saint Lawrence River as far as Montreal.

The discoveries and conquests made by Spain and Portugal in the sixteenth century were part of a movement known as the expansion of Europe. Toward the close of that century Spanish expansion overseas lost most of its momentum and the Portuguese movement actually lost ground, for after the union of Spain and Portugal under Philip II in 1580, Spain proved unequal to the task of defending both the Spanish monopoly in the West and the Portuguese monopoly in the East, and the place of Spain and Portugal, as the predominant commercial and colonial powers of Europe, was rapidly taken by the Dutch, who managed to maintain their supremacy during the greater part of the seventeenth century. The colonial and commercial predominance of the latter was finally destroyed as the result of the attacks of the English and French on the Dutch colonies and commerce during the latter half of the seventeenth century. The destruction of the power of the Dutch was the signal for a prolonged struggle for supremacy between England and France that finally resulted in the complete victory of the English in 1763. Ever since that date England has been the foremost colonial and commercial power of Europe. This expansion of Europe overseas has profoundly affected both the European and the non-European world. To a very large extent the modern world and its civilization was born of this movement.

As a result of it the world outside of Europe has been Europeanized to a large extent. Great numbers of Europeans have emigrated overseas and taken their civilization with them. The present populations, institutions, and customs of North and South America, South Africa, New Zealand, Australia, and Siberia are European in origin. Small European minorities have even imposed their political rule and to some extent their civilization over most of Africa and Asia, and Japan has only escaped the political control of Europe by adopting much of Western civilization.

In this work of Europeanizing the world, most of the peoples of Europe have played a part. The Portuguese race, language, institutions, and customs now predominate in Brazil; the Spanish race, language, institutions, and customs over practically all the rest of South America, Central America, Mexico, and most of the West Indies, and to less extent over the Philippine Islands and in the southwestern part of the United States. The Dutch still hold a large empire in the East Indies, and the Boers of South Africa and the descendants of the Dutch colonists in New York still show their Dutch origin. Indo-China and nearly half of Africa belong to the French Empire and Louisiana and French Canada still retain the language and institutions of France. The English are the masters of Canada, Newfoundland, Australia, New Zealand, South Africa, India, and a large number of islands and smaller territories. The Russian people have overrun all of Northern Asia. Every country of Europe has sent its emigrants to North and South America and the possessions of the British Empire.

The reaction of the non-European world, first on Spain and Portugal and later on the rest of Europe, has been as important as the Europeanizing of the world. It has revolutionized the commerce of Europe, created new financial institutions and situations, effected vast social and political changes, modified the religious concepts of Europe, and influenced profoundly the intellectual outlook of Europeans.

Two of the important effects of the discoveries of the Spanish and the Portuguese explorers have been the widening of the area of commerce and the changing of the routes of trade. The sailors of the Middle Ages clung to the waters of the Baltic, North, Mediterranean, and Black Seas and to the edge of the Atlantic Ocean. Even on these waters, the claims of different states to the control of a particular sea or coast frequently hampered commerce. The Hanseatic League, for example, controlled the Baltic Sea and Venice the Adriatic. The new discoveries made the whole world the field of commerce and the oceans the chief routes of trade. After the voyage of Vasco da Gama in 1598, the commodities of Asia came by the cheaper route around Africa, instead of by the older route across Asia, the Mediterranean, and the Alps. A single ship could carry more than several caravans and instead of being shifted many times the cargoes were loaded only once. Consequently commodities could be sent by the new route at about a third of the cost of the old. As a result of this change of routes, Spain and Portugal, and later The Netherlands, England, and France, rose in political and commercial importance while the city-states of Italy and the Free Imperial Cities of Germany sank into political and economic insignificance. Lisbon, London, and Amsterdam took the place of Venice, Augsburg, and Cologne.

The widening of the area of commerce and the discovery of cheaper routes increased both the volume and the variety of the wares of commerce. Europe knew already the products of Asia and Africa, but as long as commerce followed the old expensive routes of trade, only the rich could afford such costly luxuries as the gold, slaves, ebony, and ivory from Africa; the carpets, silk, and silver from Ormuz; the drugs, spices, and pearls of the Arabs; the pepper from Malabar; the opium and Indian cloths from India; the cloves and nutmegs from the Spice Islands; and the silk, lacquer, porcelain, and Chinaware from China. The route around Africa made possible larger cargoes and lower transportation charges. In consequence the Eastern products were sold at a great reduction over the old prices and the market for them greatly expanded. What had been luxuries within the reach of only the few became regular necessities for a considerable portion of the population. From the Western Hemisphere at the same time came gold and silver and new commodities like tobacco, cocoa, and sugar, that ultimately found their way into general use. By the end of the eighteenth century the trade in tea, coffee, and sugar alone constituted one fourth of the total imports of England.

The new commerce required a different organization from that which had met the needs of the Middle Ages. The wholesaler, the commission merchant, and the chartered company developed to meet the new situation. The last was the most important of the new agencies.

The chartered company was developed to provide more capital and more protection. The longer voyages and the larger cargoes required a greater outlay of capital; and the merchants had to be ready to ward off the attacks of hostile natives, pirates, and armed competitors. Spain and Portugal tried to meet the new situation by carefully regulating the trade with Asia, the East Indies, Africa, and America. The Spanish and Portuguese governments fitted out, officered, and managed the trading fleets. The merchants shipped their own goods on the government fleets, but the governments regulated and supported the merchants at every turn. In The Netherlands, France, and England commercial companies, chartered by the government, developed after the middle of the sixteenth century. These companies were of two kinds: the regulated company and the joint-stock company. The regulated company was a loose form of association in which the members shared in the privileges of the company but traded on their own capital for only such length of time as they wished. With such a form of organization little control could be exercised over the individual members and a continuous, active policy was practically impossible. These defects soon caused the regulated company to give way to the joint-stock company with its fixed capital and permanent board of directors, a form of organization which distributed the risk of loss and furnished the government a good means of regulating trade.

Another important result of the expansion of Europe was the discovery of gold and silver mines in Mexico and Peru. Prior to the discovery of America the stock of precious metals in Europe was comparatively small. A sheep or a pair of shoes could be bought for a few pence. The discovery of the mines in America increased the total stock of the precious metals and decreased the buying power of a given quantity. Prices rose two, three, and four hundred per cent, the amount varying from country to country. The increase in the stock of gold and silver in Europe also completed the process of putting Europe on a money basis. Barter gave way to a money economy.

The use of money as the regular basis of exchange led directly to the development of modern capitalism with its characteristic concepts, institutions, and situations. The willingness of the rising business class to pay for the use of other peoples' money caused society to conclude that the taking of interest was legitimate. The new opportunities for safe and profitable investment encouraged the saving of money and the accumulation of capital. Banking institutions arose for the handling of the new capital and exchanges for the sale of the new produce and the shares of the new commercial companies. The first modern center of finance was Antwerp. After the revolt of The Netherlands had caused the decline of Antwerp in the latter half of the sixteenth century, new financial centers developed at Amsterdam, London, Hamburg, Frankfort, and other cities. These business centers soon began to experience such periods of speculation as the South Sea and the Mississippi Bubbles.

A new economic theory, known as mercantilism, developed to meet the new economic situation. The statesmen of the rising national states became impressed with the importance of possessing adequate supplies of the precious metals. They attempted to acquire large stocks of gold and silver, to exalt foreign over domestic trade and manufactures over the production of raw materials, and to promote a dense population for the sake of national defense. They tried to attain these aims by high duties, bounties, the prohibition of imports and restrictions on the export of precious metals. The newly acquired colonies were treated as private estates to be worked for the benefit of the home country. Charles V first applied the new theory on a large scale, but his rivals quickly followed his example.

The new commodities and the increase in wealth gradually produced important social changes. General comfort, luxury, and ostentation increased. As gold and silver became plentiful, large quantities were used for purely decorative purposes. Cloth of gold and silver taffeta, silver plate, rings, watches, and neck chains came into general use. Gems came in great quantities from both Asia and America. Mexico and Peru furnished emeralds, turquoises, and opals, the West Indies pearls, and India diamonds. Calico, muslin, chintzes, ginghams, and many other new kinds of cloth became fashionable. From Asia, Africa, and America traders brought new foods such as potatoes, tomatoes, maize, sugar, molasses, peanuts, and, in more recent years, tropical fruits; new drinks such as tea, coffee, chocolate, cocoa, sassafras, lime juice, citron water, and rum; new social customs such as the use of tobacco and opium; and such things as chinaware, bric-a-brac, Indian screens, flowering plants, shrubs, and trees. These new products changed the diet, the dress, the social customs, and the surroundings of the people of Europe.

Still more important was the effect of the expansion of Europe on the organization of society and the position of the different social classes. Emigration to the New World furnished means of escape to the oppressed classes. To hold the lower classes in Europe the governing classes have been forced gradually to ameliorate social conditions. The introduction of a money economy modified the status of the peasants in many sections of Europe. The nobles in England and France became capitalists instead of feudal lords. They managed their estates in the way that would bring them the most money. In many cases they ceased to farm on their own account and became rent-collecting landlords. Consequently, they ceased to enforce their rights over their serfs and changed the old medieval payments in kind and service into definite money obligations. These changes led to the freeing of the serfs and the improvement of the status of many of the other peasants. The expansion of commerce and the development of capitalism, meanwhile, caused the growth of the middle class and its gradual rise in power.

The expansion of Europe also contributed to the rise of national monarchies. In the Middle Ages the kings had depended to a large extent on their feudal vassals for men to fill their armies and for officials to carry on the work of administration and justice. The economic developments that followed the expansion of Europe changed all that. The discovery of new mines of gold and silver and the great expansion of commerce so increased the royal revenues that the monarchs of Europe could hire troops and officials upon whom they could depend. The kings then deprived the nobles of their dangerous powers, leaving them only their privileges, and gave the important positions of the State to men of the middle class on whom they could rely. All power became centralized in the hands of the monarch. These forces were at work particularly in England under the Tudors (1485-1603), in Spain, after the division of the empire of Charles V in 1555, under the Habsburgs, and in France under the Bourbons.

The chief political effect of the expansion of Europe has been the rise of the middle class to political predominance. Its numbers grew with the development of commerce and banking; and its influence with the growth of capital. It could control even the policy of the absolutist kings through the power of its members to grant or withhold loans. At first the interests of the king and the middle class coincided and they entered into an alliance against the feudal nobles who stood for political and economic anarchy. The middle class supported the king in return for domestic order and favorable economic legislation. When the royal absolutism began to threaten its interests, however, the middle class opposed the monarch and established constitutional limitations on his authority. The English and French Revolutions were protests of the middle classes against the interference of the absolute monarchies.

The expansion overseas likewise affected the religious ideas of Europe. The first religious reaction of the new discoveries was the awakening of the missionary impulse. Close on the heels of the discoverers, conquerors, and merchants followed the heroic missionaries of the Church. Later came the Protestant missionaries. The contact of the various classes of Europeans with the different religions of Asia, Africa, and America, also had a number of unexpected results. In some cases the discovery of the diversity of religions led to a feeling of greater tolerance for divergent beliefs. In others the upsetting of old beliefs, that resulted from the new discoveries, gave rise to a skeptical or indifferent attitude toward the old form of religion. Later, the study of many different religions gave rise in our own day to the new science of comparative religions. Thus the expansion of Europe fostered the three modern tendencies of tolerance, skepticism, and the scientific study of religion.

Another effect of the expansion overseas was a stimulation of intellectual activity. The new herbs and drugs found in America and the Far East, the enlarged store of the old ones, and the contact of Europeans with Eastern physicians, changed the practice of medicine. Drugs in time took the place of blood-letting. The attention necessarily paid to meteorology, ocean currents, and trade winds advanced the science of navigation. The new discoveries gave Europe a knowledge of over half the world. This new information was organized by the makers of maps. Historians made great collections of accounts of the voyages of discovery, and the economists, philosophers, and writers found phenomena in the New World that stimulated and modified their thinking. The expansion of Europe thus affected the sciences of medicine, navigation, geography, history, and economics.

Finally, the expansion of Europe affected the mental attitude of Europeans. The work of discovery, settlement, and commercial exploitation called for and stimulated courage, enterprise, and initiative. The new achievements developed pride; the contact with inferior peoples aroused racial prejudice; and the new wealth fostered indolence, extravagance, and greed, as well as philanthropy.

Thus the expansion of Europe gradually modified all phases of European life. It widened the area of European commerce and changed the routes of trade. It slowly introduced new products into Europe and imported many old products in larger quantities. It made money the regular medium of exchange, developed new commercial institutions and new economic theories, and gave society a capitalistic organization. The economic changes in time caused an increase in general comfort, luxury, and ostentation, a readjustment in the position of the classes of society, and the rise first of the absolute monarchs and later of the middle class. Lastly the expansion of Europe gave rise to new religious conceptions, stimulated intellectual activity, and produced a change in the mental attitude of the Europeans. The expansion of Europe has been the chief factor in transforming Medieval into Modern Europe.

REFERENCES

MEDIEVAL TRADE ROUTES
  E. P. Cheyney, *European Background of American History*, chapter II.

ITALIAN CONTRIBUTIONS TO EXPLORATION
  E. P. Cheyney, *European Background of American History*, chapter III.

PIONEER WORK OF PORTUGAL
  W. C. Abbott, *The Expansion of Europe*, vol. I, chapter III.
  Cambridge Modern History, vol. I, pp. 7–20.
  E. P. Cheyney, *European Background of American History*, chapter IV.

BEGINNINGS OF OVERSEAS EXPANSION

M. B. Synge, *A Book of Discovery*, chapters XX-XXI, XXIV-XXV.
H. M. Stephens, *Portugal*, chapter VII.
C. Beazley, *Prince Henry the Navigator*.
Histoire Générale, vol. V, pp. 873-83.

The Discovery of America
J. S. Bassett, *A Short History of the United States*, chapter II.
H. E. Bolton and T. M. Marshall, *The Colonization of North America, 1492-1783*, chapters II-V.
E. G. Bourne, *Spain in America*, chapters II-XI.
R. B. Merriman, *Rise of the Spanish Empire*, vol. II, chapter XVII.
M. B. Synge, *A Book of Discovery*, chapters XXII-XXIII, XXVI-XXIX.
Histoire Générale, vol. V, pp. 914-27.

The Portuguese in the East
A. G. Keller, *Colonization*, chapter III.
H. C. Morris, *History of Colonization*, vol. I, pt. III, chapter I.
K. G. Jayne, *Vasco da Gama and his Successors, 1460-1580*.
H. M. Stephens, *Albuquerque and the Portuguese Settlements in India*.

The Portuguese in Brazil
A. G. Keller, *Colonization*, chapter IV.
H. C. Morris, *History of Colonization*, vol. I, pt. III, chapter II.
Histoire Générale, vol. V, pp. 883-900.

Spanish Colonization
H. E. Bolton and T. M. Marshall, *The Colonization of North America, 1492-1783*, chapters II-III.
E. G. Bourne, *Spain in America*, chapters XII-XX.
A. G. Keller, *Colonization*, chapters V-IX.
H. C. Morris, *A History of Colonization*, vol. I, pt. III, chapters III-VI.
W. R. Shepherd, *Latin America*, chapters I-VI.
Histoire Générale, vol. V, pp. 934-79.

Effects of the Expansion of Europe
W. Cunningham, *Western Civilization*, vol. II, bk. V, chapter II.
C. Day, *History of Commerce*, pp. 134-37.
J. E. Gillespie, *The Influence of Overseas Expansion on England to 1700*.

Maps
Medieval trade routes, W. R. Shepherd, *Historical Atlas*, pp. 98-99, 102-03.
Routes of the discoverers. *Ibid.*, pp. 107-10.

CHAPTER III

THE PROTESTANT REVOLT IN GERMANY AND INTERNATIONAL RIVALRIES

WHILE in the non-European world the explorers of Spain and Portugal were setting in motion many of the forces which were to transform the Europe of 1500 into the Europe of to-day, two important movements were at work in Europe — the Protestant Revolt and the struggle of France, Spain, and the Habsburgs for the control of Italy. The Protestant Revolt split Catholic Christendom into two warring camps and profoundly affected the political, social, and economic conditions in the Protestant portions of Europe. The international rivalries of the European Powers modified to some extent the political situation of Europe. The course of each movement decisively influenced the other.

THE LUTHERAN REVOLT

During the early Middle Ages the Church had become, in a sense, the framework of the whole social order. The vast organization developed to meet the many demands made upon the Church naturally cost a great deal of money. The Papacy in particular, with its large army of officials, was in constant need of revenue. Consequently, in an age in which the secular governments were developing new sources of income to take the place of the feudal method of personal relationships between governor and governed, the Church also did some experimenting with taxation.

In France and England, where strong national monarchies had developed, the secular governments held the Papal tax-gatherers in check. In Germany the weak central government was unable to prevent the Church from collecting large sums of money from the people. In Germany, consequently, the new financial policies of the Papacy brought violent protests from the secular princes, the rising middle class, and the spiritually minded in all classes, and subjected the whole structure of the Church to popular criticism.

Many of the ruling princes resented the privileges enjoyed by the Church and its clergy and coveted its wealth. These rulers objected to the appointive power exercised by the Pope, to his interference in the internal affairs of their states, to the jurisdiction wielded by the Church courts over the clergy and the laity, and to the exemption of the clergy and the property of the Church from taxation. They also wished to possess the actual lands, buildings, and movable wealth of the Church.

The knights — the lesser nobility — resented the changes which were destroying their power as individuals and as a class. They were growing poorer relatively and absolutely, at a time when luxury and display were increasing and prices were rising. Europe was getting on a money basis while the incomes of the knights continued to consist largely of the services of the peasants and payments in kind. At the same time, gunpowder, which had been introduced recently, was reducing the knights to political and military insignificance. The common man, armed with a gun, was becoming the equal of his lord. As a result the knights envied the wealth of the burghers and the power of the princes, hated the Church as the guarantor of the existing social order, and stood ready to join a revolt against the established conditions.

The leadership of the popular discontent was unexpectedly thrust into the hands of a humble German friar, Martin Luther. He was born of peasant stock at Eisleben in 1483, but spent most of his early life at Mansfeld, where his father was a miner. His first years were a time of poverty and severe discipline. His father, a man of strong character with a praiseworthy ambition for his son, planned to have Luther fit himself at the University of Erfurt for the practice of law, then the most lucrative profession in Germany. Little is known of Luther's life at the University. He seems to have taken mainly studies of the older type rather than those favored by the Humanists. As his enemies never attacked his early life, it was probably above reproach. He received his bachelor's degree in 1502, after a little more than a year's residence, and his master's degree three years later. He then took up the study of law, but within two months, for reasons that are not very well understood, he suddenly threw up the chance for a career as a lawyer and entered an Augustinian monastery.

Once in the monastery Luther began to wrestle with the problem of his soul's salvation. At first he tried the common monastic methods of fastings, prayers, and vigils, in the hope of winning salvation by his works, but they failed to give him the religious peace that he sought. He finally found that peace in the doctrine of justification by faith. This comforting belief came to him as a result of many serious talks with older members of his order and of much reading in the works of Augustine and the German mystics. For the rest of his life the phrase, 'The just shall live by faith,' remained fixed in his mind, and became the center of his teaching as a reformer. It served as the text of many lectures to the students of his university, and of many sermons to the townspeople of Wittenberg.

However, Luther did not spend all of his time in spiritual struggles. In 1508 he was called to the new university at Wittenberg, where for a year he taught the Ethics of Aristotle. Then for twenty-one months he was recalled to the monastery at Erfurt. During these months he made a visit to Rome, where he saw and heard much that strengthened him later in his opposition to the Church and the Papacy. Upon his return to Wittenberg in 1511, he took the degree of Doctor of Divinity, and entered upon his life-work of teaching and preaching. He began to lecture on the Psalms and the Epistles. His lectures were filled with many fanciful allegories and interpretations, but he impressed himself on his students as being a great teacher, and grew steadily in the esteem of his colleagues and townsmen. He began to preach with great success to the students and citizens, and in 1515 he was appointed provincial vicar of his order and thereby became superintendent of eleven monasteries.

Luther was engaged in his duties as preacher, professor,

and provincial vicar when he took the step which precipitated the religious revolution in Germany. On October 31, 1517, he posted ninety-five theses against indulgences on the door of the church at Wittenberg, and unwittingly touched the match to the waiting powder mine of Germany. To understand the significance of his acts it is necessary to know something of the history of indulgences.

From an early date the Church had imposed penances for sins. The act of penance, to be efficacious, had to be accompanied by contrition (or at least by "attrition"[1]) and confession, but from the first the Church had claimed the right to remit the penance it had enjoined, the remittance of the penalty of the Church being called an indulgence. From time to time the scope of the indulgences was enlarged, until at last the Church taught that souls retained in purgatory for venial sins could be aided by them. Little by little, also, the idea grew that a money equivalent might take the place of services or "good works," until finally, in 1517, Pope Leo X issued two bulls concerning the sale of indulgences in Germany that made extraordinary claims for the papal pardons and aroused the opposition of many patriotic Germans. One was issued for the purpose of raising money to repel the Turks, and the other to obtain money to aid in building Saint Peter's at Rome.

The two bulls were announced in Germany by permission of the Archbishop of Mainz. At the age of twenty-four this prelate had obtained the archbishopric of Mainz, the oldest, richest, and most influential bishopric of Germany, through the influence of his family and the payment to the Pope of 24,000 florins, an enormous sum for the time, for the pallium (the insignia of his office), and a like amount as annates (the first year's income from the position). He borrowed this large sum from the great Augsburg banking house, the Fuggers, and in order to recoup himself for his heavy outlay of money he struck a bargain with the Pope concerning the sale of indulgences in Germany. He agreed to permit their sale for a period of eight years in return for half of the proceeds,

[1] Grief arising from fear of punishment or from shame.

and then proceeded to exploit his "concession." He established a scale of prices, varying according to the financial ability of the individual, and promised complete remission of sins to every one who complied with the terms of the indulgence. He commissioned an unscrupulous Dominican monk named Tetzel to sell the indulgences and made every effort to impress people with their value. The Elector of Saxony refused Tetzel entrance into his electorate, but many of his subjects flocked across the border to purchase indulgences. As they were entirely out of harmony with the doctrine of justification by faith, the proceedings of Tetzel scandalized Luther. At first he innocently appealed to the Archbishop of Mainz to stop their sale. Only after the failure of this appeal did he take his epoch-making step of posting the theses on the church door at Wittenberg.

Luther's theses were merely ninety-five propositions for debate, such disputations being a usual part of the academic life of the time, but his propositions happened to strike a popular chord, since they contained many ideas found in the works of Wycliffe, Huss, and John Wessel, the latter a former professor in the University of Erfurt. They expressed clearly the vague thoughts of many men. In them, for example, Luther declared that the greater part of the people must need be deceived by the indiscriminate promise of release from penalties, and that those who believed in the certainty of their own salvation through letters of pardon would be eternally damned along with their teachers. For every Christian who feels true compunction has plenary remission of his sins already, and the buying of pardons should not in any way be compared to works of mercy. There was danger, Luther asserted, that people would ask why the Pope did not release souls from purgatory for the sake of charity instead of for money. As a result of asking such troublesome questions Luther quickly became a national hero, and his theses were soon on everybody's tongue, but no one was more astonished at the result of his action than Luther himself.

At the time he posted his propositions, Luther did not realize their implication, or the significance of the doctrines he had advocated for some years in his lectures and sermons. The Pope, too, looked upon the whole affair at first as a mere squabble of monks, but the friends of the Papacy quickly saw that an attack on indulgences was an attack on the Pope himself, and they began a vigorous assault on Luther. In defending himself against their counter-attacks during a famous debate held at Leipsic in 1519, Luther was finally driven into a position where he was forced to recognize that he was the leader of a revolt against the Church. In a discussion over the primacy of the Papacy, Dr. Eck, the Catholic opponent of Luther, forced him to admit that the heretic John Huss, the Bohemian reformer who had suffered martyrdom a century earlier, had taught good Christian doctrine and had been condemned unjustly. By this admission Luther asserted that the General Council of Constance had erred. This made him a rebel against the Church and a heretic. As the positions of Luther and the Church were really irreconcilable, the Pope finally excommunicated Luther in 1520.

At the time of his excommunication Luther was engaged in publishing three important pamphlets which practically constituted a declaration of independence from the Church. They were entitled the *Address to the Nobility of the German Nation*, the *Babylonian Captivity of the Church*, and the *Freedom of a Christian Man*. In the first Luther denied the extraordinary claims of the Pope and the clergy, advised the abolition of annates, pilgrimages, festivals, indulgences, monasteries, the Papal Court, masses for the dead, and all the practices of the Roman Curia designed to increase the Papal fees, and advocated that priests should be allowed to marry, that mendicancy be stopped, that the poor be cared for by the towns, that the number of the masses be greatly decreased, and that religious persecution be ended. The second pamphlet attacked the seven sacraments of the Church, advocated the reduction of the sacraments to baptism, communion, and penance, argued for the administration of both bread and wine to the laity at communion, and substituted for the Catholic doctrine of transubstantiation the peculiar doctrine of consubstantiation, according to which the body and blood of Christ were in the bread and wine as fire is in the hot iron. In the third pamphlet Luther declared that man was justified by faith and not by works. These stirring appeals to the German people rallied round the reformer for the time all the discontented elements in the nation.

At this point Charles V (1500–58) intervened in the controversy. He had just come into possession of the greatest empire Europe had seen since the days of Charlemagne. Through his mother he had received the Spanish and Italian lands of Ferdinand of Aragon and the Kingdom of Castile and its dependencies. Through his father he had inherited the hereditary possessions of the Habsburgs in the Danube Valley and the lands of Mary of Burgundy. He had just been crowned Emperor of the Holy Roman Empire at Aix-la-Chapelle after a tremendous contest with Francis I (1515–47) of France for the votes of the seven electors. More than any other man he seemed to hold the fate of Luther in his hands.

After some hesitation the Emperor summoned Luther to appear before the Diet at Worms. Under the protection of an imperial safe-conduct, Luther arrived at Worms on April 16, 1521, and on the following day he appeared before the Emperor and the assembled princes of Germany. They asked him to recant. For a time the black-robed friar seemed humbled by the brilliant gathering, but the next day he regained his courage and composure and defended himself in a respectful but bold speech. Before his Emperor and the greatest dignitaries of Germany, the humble friar declared, 'Unless I am convinced of error by the testimony of Scripture or plain reason ... I cannot and will not retract anything, for it is neither safe nor right to act against one's conscience.' After his departure from Worms, the Diet pronounced against him the ban of the Empire, but his words and actions won a great victory for his cause. Both the Papal bull and the ban of the Empire, directed against Luther, encountered the insuperable obstacle of public opinion.

Luther's dramatic appearance before the Diet of Worms was followed by his equally dramatic disappearance from public view. As he was returning from Worms to Wittenberg with several companions, armed horsemen seized him at a lonely point of the road and galloped away with him. His companions fled in terror and the German public for a time had no idea of his fate. The capture of Luther, however, was only a device of his prince, the Elector Frederick, to protect him. The Elector no longer felt able to defy the Pope and the Emperor openly, as he had been doing for three years, so he spirited Luther away to the castle at Wartburg, where he would be safe for a time. For the next ten months Luther lived and worked in this hiding-place. This proved to be a decisive period in the history of the revolt. Luther spent these months in writing and in planning for the future. He wrote an exposition of the Psalms, a treatise on monastic vows, and a tract on the misuse of the mass, but his most important work was beginning the translation of the New Testament into German.

This putting of the Bible into the speech of the people was an important event in the history of German literature. Luther's work holds the same place in German that the King James version does in English literature. Although he was not a great scholar, Luther had a genuine gift for writing and a feeling for the real spirit of the Bible. Though he took an earlier German translation as the foundation of his work, and made use of Erasmus's Greek edition of the New Testament, he really created literary German. He used his own Saxon dialect and enriched it with the best words from other German dialects. He was assisted by his learned young colleague, Melanchthon, and other Wittenberg friends, and the entire work was finally completed in 1534. The newly established printing presses of Germany soon made it possible for every middle-class family to possess a copy of Luther's translation.

At the end of ten months the course of events called Luther back to Wittenberg. During his absence men of radical views had begun to preach and to practice their ideas. The priests began to marry, the monks to leave the monasteries, and the clergy to administer both bread and wine to the laity. Mass was discontinued, and the images were being put out of the churches. Finally three men, calling themselves prophets, came from Zwickau. They denounced infant baptism, the Church, and learning, and preached that each person should seek direct revelation from God. Luther decided that his presence was needed at Wittenberg. For eight days after his arrival he preached the doctrine of moderation to the people, rebuking, exhorting, and persuading them. No changes, he told them, ought to have been made without the authority of their prince. But not even Luther could undo all that had been done in his absence, and in spite of his efforts the mass was slightly modified, communion was administered in both kinds to the laity, and the images continued to disappear from the churches. He could retard changes, but he could not entirely prevent them.

Until about the time of his return to Wittenberg from the seclusion of the Wartburg, Luther had the support and good will of a very large part of the German nation. Many of his supporters and sympathizers, though, were more interested in the amelioration of their own political, social, and economic situation than in the religious ideas of Luther. Dissensions and divisions inevitably appeared in the ranks of his followers. Luther alienated Erasmus and the Humanists by his violent methods, for Erasmus hated controversy and strife, while Luther actually enjoyed them. The great Humanist was a reformer; Luther, in comparison to Erasmus, was a revolutionist. The breach between the two leaders undoubtedly helps to explain the intellectual barrenness of the Lutheran movement in the next generation. Luther lost the support of the German knights, led by Ulrich von Hutten, by refusing to aid them in their struggle against the Church and the ruling princes and in their efforts to rescue their declining order and to build up a strong central government in Germany. Lastly, Luther killed the interest of the peasants in his movement by the attitude he took toward the Peasants' Revolt.

This revolt came in 1525. From time to time during the latter part of the Middle Ages the peasants of Southern Germany had risen in protest against their hard lot. Recent developments had made their condition seem even more intolerable. Prices had advanced; rents had increased; and the exactions of the lords constantly grew heavier. The German peasants, consequently, heard the doctrine of Luther gladly, since they thought he meant the reorganization of German society in accordance with their idea of the teachings of Jesus. They formulated their ideas into articles, and rose in revolt. According to modern conceptions the demands of the more conservative peasants were entirely reasonable. They asked that each community should have the right of appointing and deposing its own pastor, and of collecting the tithes to pay him; they demanded the abolition of serfdom, the obnoxious hunting rights, excessive services and burdens, and heriot,[1] and the removal of restrictions on the use of firewood and timber for repairs. But they made the serious mistake of resorting to violence to gain their ends. After a short period of hesitation, the nobles took up arms and put down the revolt with a savagery that far surpassed that of the peasants. Thousands of the peasants, as a result, lost their lives.

Luther played a futile and discreditable rôle in the revolt. Before the uprising he blamed the princes for the social conditions existing in Germany, but told the peasants that they had no right to attempt to correct the situation of which they justly complained. After the peasants ignored his advice and rose in revolt, he made a scathing attack against the 'robbing and murdering bands of peasants.' In a pamphlet he urged the lords to strike down the rebels like mad dogs. His policy was probably in part the result of his fear that the princes would withdraw their support from his movement and in part the expression of his natural conservatism. By his attitude toward their revolt, Luther permanently alienated the peasants from the Lutheran movement.

[1] By the right of heriot the lord seized the best beast or piece of movable property from his deceased tenant.

In spite of these divisions in the ranks of the reformers the Lutheran movement continued to spread. Both the monks and the parish clergy went over to the side of the new doctrines in great numbers. Some were moved by their consciences and others by self-interest. Many of the regular clergy welcomed an opportunity to escape from the monastic life and many of the secular clergy wished to have their marriages recognized and their children legitimized. In a great number of the parishes the priests became the first Lutheran pastors and conducted the new services in the old parish churches. The nuns adopted the new doctrines much more slowly. Far more important for the success of Luther than even the conversion of the clergy was the accession of many of the princes and the free imperial cities to the Lutheran movement. In 1525 Electoral Saxony, Hesse, and Prussia became officially Lutheran; and after the Diet of Speyer decreed in the following year that each prince of the Empire should decide the question of religion for himself, most of the states of Germany revolted from the Church. In Northern and Central Germany all the states except Brandenburg and ducal Saxony became Lutheran within a few years. In Southern Germany only Bavaria and the three archbishoprics of Mainz, Trier, and Cologne remained wholly Catholic. There was a tendency, though, for the cities of Southern Germany to be attracted by the Zwinglian [1] doctrines.

The accession of the princes and the cities to the Lutheran cause was not wholly the result of conscientious conviction. The members of the city councils and the rulers of secular states sometimes cared little and understood almost nothing about the doctrines of Luther, but they recognized very clearly the advantages which adherence to the new religious movement offered them. Both the princes and the councils of the free imperial cities increased their power and their revenues by adopting the Protestant cause. The Catholic hierarchy could no longer interfere with the internal affairs of the Protestant states; the secular courts no longer shared their jurisdiction with the Church courts; the Lutheran

[1] The doctrines of Zwingli are discussed in the next chapter.

clergy became submissive servants of the secular authorities; the clergy and the property of the Church no longer remained exempt from the control of the State; the lands and edifices of the monasteries and pious foundations fell into the hands of the cities and the secular rulers; and the ecclesiastical states came into the possession of princely administrators. To the cities the Protestant movement offered in addition the removal of the ecclesiastical restrictions on the taking of interest, the free play of commerce, and the capital which had so long been tied up in non-productive ecclesiastical institutions; to their citizens a position of greater honor in society. These powerful inducements were contributing causes to the success of the Protestant revolt in Germany.

The same causes that facilitated the spread of Luther's doctrines within Germany led to their adoption finally by the German states of Brandenburg (1539), ducal Saxony (1539), and the Palatinate (1545), and by a number of states outside of Germany. By the time of Luther's death in 1546 part of Southern Germany, all of the states of Northern and Central Germany, Sweden, Denmark, Norway, and the Baltic provinces, and many persons in Bohemia, Poland, Hungary, and Transylvania had declared for the Lutheran religion. In Sweden, Denmark, Norway, and the Baltic provinces, the rulers, who were hampered by the privileges of the nobles and the clergy and desired to increase the royal power and wealth, took the initiative. They usually permitted or actively aided the preaching of the new doctrines and then seized control of the Church and its property. In several of the states the rulers shared the property of the Church with the nobles. In Poland most of the burghers and many of the nobles became Lutherans; in Hungary and Transylvania the German settlers went over to the Lutheran Church almost in a body; and in Bohemia the followers of John Huss showed themselves friendly to the new religious movement. In the three Scandinavian kingdoms popular opposition to the Protestant policies of the rulers continued for a long time. In Bohemia, Poland, Hungary, and Transylvania the Protestant burghers and nobles encountered the hostility of Catholic sovereigns.

The immediate result of the revolt from the Church was invariably much religious confusion. As a usual thing, the reformers changed first the service, then the Church organization, and finally the doctrine. They thought the ceremony of the mass was discredited by the doctrine of justification by faith; they ceased to require confession and absolution; condemned fasts and asceticism, prayers to the saints, and pilgrimages; and no longer considered relics and shrines sacred. The monks and nuns deserted the monasteries and convents and the priests began to marry. Because of the emphasis they placed on the authority of Scripture, they gave the sermon the chief place of honor in the service, and German replaced Latin as the language of the Church. As a general policy Luther changed only such things in the service as he regarded contrary to Scripture.

The work of organizing the new Church usually progressed more slowly. Luther's first idea seems to have been to organize self-governing congregations such as the Baptists and the Congregationalists have in America to-day. The people generally showed themselves ill-prepared for such an ecclesiastical organization and the Peasants' Revolt completely discredited the democratic movement in the Church. Luther then left to the princes the task of organizing the new Church.

The first prince to act was Albert of Brandenburg, the Grand Master of the Teutonic Order. After the close of the Crusades the order had done a great work in extending the frontiers of Christendom and Teutonic civilization in the lands bordering the Baltic, but it had long outlived its usefulness. Although the knights of the order nominally still observed their monastic vows, their way of living had been long an open scandal. By 1525 they had lost control of West Prussia and seemed on the verge of losing East Prussia. Both their sovereign, the King of Poland, and their subjects were hostile to the order. The Grand Master's solution of his predicament was to turn the remaining lands of the order into an hereditary state, known thereafter as East Prussia, under his immediate rule and to become the vassal of the King of Poland. At the same time he assumed supreme ecclesiastical authority in East Prussia and with the aid of the two Prussian bishops introduced a Lutheran constitution and liturgy. In 1526 he married a Danish princess. Contemporaneously there occurred a wholesale spoliation of the property of the Church.

Other rulers quickly followed the example of Albert of Brandenburg. Strictly speaking they established as many different Lutheran churches as there were Lutheran states. Though the various churches differed from each other in details they resembled each other in general principles. In most of the states the sovereign appointed superintendents in place of the former bishops to watch over the lives and doctrines of the pastors, and consistories (commissions composed partly of ministers and partly of laymen), which had power over excommunication, civil punishment, suspension from office, and prohibition of labor, to take the place of the old court of the bishop. The churches did not appoint their pastors, exclude unworthy members, or exercise any self-government. Of course such an organization of the new Church greatly increased the power of the princes.

The Lutheran movement lacked the full statement of its doctrines that the Catholics and the Calvinists possessed. Luther was not an especially clear thinker and apparently never felt the need of such a complete statement of theology as Calvin gave his followers in the *Institutes of the Christian Religion*.[1] In 1529 Luther published his longer and shorter catechisms. In 1530 Melanchthon drew up for the Emperor and the Diet a statement of the Lutheran position, known as the Augsburg Confession, which still serves as the official statement of the Lutheran beliefs. The purpose of this celebrated document tended to make it somewhat misleading. It was written with the aim of presenting the Lutheran movement to the Emperor in as favorable a light as possible. Consequently, while it stated the Lutheran doctrines concerning justification by faith, good works, the eucharist, confession,

[1] The work of Calvin is explained later in the next chapter.

and the rôle of the sacraments clearly enough, it is silent on such important doctrines as the priesthood of all believers, predestination, indulgences, the power of the Papacy, the indelible character of the priesthood, purgatory, and the number of sacraments. The doctrine of justification by faith always remained the fundamental doctrine with Luther, but on other matters of belief he tended to become more conservative as he grew older.

The movement led by Luther was, therefore, a many-sided one. From one point of view it was a religious revolt of men no longer satisfied with the government, forms, and doctrines of the Church nevertheless, selfish and sordid motives contributed to its success. It was to the financial and political interest of the states to champion the reform movement. The ruling princes and the middle class triumphed with it. From other points of view the movement was a failure. Temporarily it diverted attention from the new intellectual movement, and accomplished little for religious liberty. It was not an immediate ethical force. A Protestant obscurantism succeeded the Catholic opposition to the advancement of knowledge so bitterly attacked by the Humanists. Unintentionally, nevertheless, it fostered the growth of the new intellectual spirit in accordance with which nothing is accepted on authority and everything is subject to inquiry.

The peaceful spread of the Lutheran movement was made possible by internal conditions in Germany and by the international political situation. As has already been shown,[1] the authority of the central government of the Empire was weak and most of the power was in the hands of the individual states. Consequently, the Protestant princes were in a position to protect the young Lutheran movement. Throughout the crucial years of the spread of Lutheranism, on the other hand, the attention of the Emperor was constantly distracted by the varied problems which arose out of the international situation.

[1] See chapter I.

INTERNATIONAL RIVALRIES

Immediately after the Diet of Worms pronounced the ban of the Empire against Luther, a war, which lasted ten years, broke out between the Emperor, Charles V, and his French rival, Francis I (1515-47). It really continued an old struggle for Italy. In 1494 Charles VIII (1483-98) of France had tried to conquer the Kingdom of Naples. His successor, Louis XII (1498-1515), had attempted to seize both Naples and Milan. The Italian possessions of Aragon had forced Spain to oppose the invasion of Italy by France. Twenty-one years of fighting and diplomatic maneuvering left Naples in the hands of Spain (1504) and Milan in the possession of France (1515).

The question appeared settled until the union of the territories of Ferdinand of Aragon, Isabella of Castile, Mary of Burgundy, and Maximilian, the Habsburg, put unprecedented resources in the hands of Charles V, and seemed to threaten the very existence of France by encircling it with a ring of hostile lands. On the south, Spain had seized Spanish Navarre in 1512 and menaced the safety of France through possession of the Province of Roussillon. On the northeast, Charles V held the Free County of Burgundy and claimed, on the ground of hereditary right, the adjoining Duchy of Burgundy. On the north, France held the portion of Flanders and the Somme Valley, which Louis XI had taken from Mary of Burgundy, the grandmother of Charles V. This situation led almost inevitably to a renewal of the conflict which had been raging between France and Spain.

The fighting began in 1521 and went on intermittently for eight years in Roussillon, in Navarre, in The Netherlands, and in Italy. The battle of Pavia (1525), in which Francis I and many of the notables of France fell into the hands of the Emperor, really decided the conflict, but the fighting dragged on four years longer. The cession of Milan to Spain was the most important provision of the Treaty of Cambrai, which finally concluded the war.

The conclusion of peace with France gave the Emperor no real respite from his political enemies. The Turks constantly threatened to attack the hereditary Habsburg lands lying in the Danube Valley. The French made strange alliances with the Hungarian nobles opposing the accession of Ferdinand, the brother of Charles V, in Hungary, the Lutheran princes in Germany, the Ottoman Turks, and the Moslem corsairs established in Tunis and Algiers. The Emperor made two expeditions to Africa and twice renewed the conflict with France. Engrossed as he was with these problems and activities, he had little chance to check the spread of the Lutheran movement.

Within the Empire the chief interest after 1530 was the effort of Philip of Hesse to organize the Protestants into a political and military party. He was the only Protestant prince with the least notion of the demands of statesmanship. As early as 1525 he took the first steps leading toward a Protestant alliance, and in the following year he concluded, at Torgau, a formal league with the Elector of Saxony, which was quickly joined by seven other states. The firm front presented by the new alliance was certainly partly responsible for the decree obtained by the Protestants at the Diet of Speyer in 1526, which practically left the religious question to the conscience of each prince. Philip of Hesse, however, planned to extend the alliance to include the Zwinglian cities of Southern Germany and the Protestant cantons of the Swiss Federation, but this statesmanlike plan was wrecked by Luther, who stubbornly insisted on a league of pure Lutherans. At the colloquy held between the two parties at Marburg, in 1527, Luther was so bigoted as to refuse to shake hands with Zwingli as a Christian brother, and only the preoccupation of the Emperor with other problems saved the Protestants from the natural consequences of Luther's folly.

For a time the situation looked ominous for the German Protestants. At the Diet of Speyer in 1529 the Emperor abolished the favorable decree of 1526 and left the Lutherans without any legal standing. His action caused the celebrated protest from which the Protestants derive their name. By 1532, however, the international situation had so changed that the Emperor agreed at the Diet of Nurem-

EMPIRE OF CHARLES V

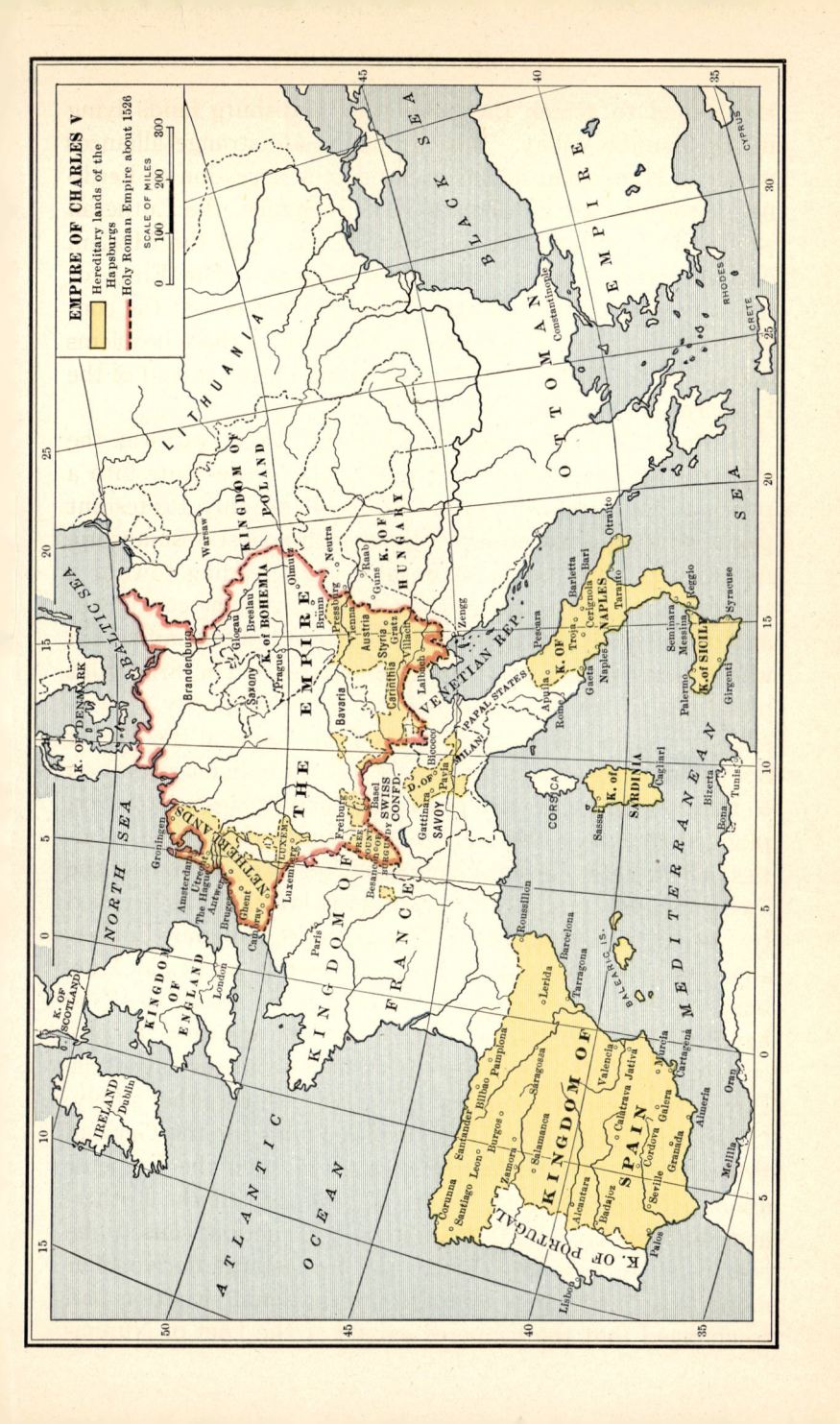

Hereditary lands of the Hapsburgs

Holy Roman Empire about 1526

berg, held in that year, that until the meeting of the general council none should molest or do violence to another, on account of his faith or for any other reason. This continued to be the situation of the Lutheran party until 1546.

In that year Charles V at last felt free to settle the Lutheran question. In 1544 he had signed a treaty of peace with Francis I and in the following year he had concluded a truce with the Turks. At the Diet held in Regensburg in 1546, therefore, he caused the request of the Protestant party for a renewal of the agreement of Nuremberg to be rejected. The Emperor then took the field against them with the avowed aim of punishing his disobedient and refractory subjects, but with the real purpose of restoring the Catholic religion. From his point of view religious unity was a necessary prerequisite for bringing about the political unification and centralization of Germany at which he was aiming. At first the situation looked favorable for the Protestants. They were slow in pushing their advantage, however, and their defeat finally was made certain by the desertion of Duke Maurice of Saxony from the Protestant party. At Mühlberg Charles V captured the Elector of Saxony himself, and a little later Philip of Hesse threw himself on the mercy of the Emperor. With the capture of its two foremost leaders, the Protestant cause seemed lost.

The triumph of Charles V at Mühlberg, though, was more apparent than real. He was nearly at the end of his resources and his troops soon began to desert him for lack of pay. He had really defeated only two of the Protestant princes; the Turks quickly renewed their attacks; in a short time Maurice of Saxony, whose desertion of the Protestant cause had made possible the victory of the Emperor, again changed sides; and Henry II (1547-59), the new French sovereign, allied himself with the Protestant princes of Germany in return for permission to occupy the important fortresses of Metz, Toul, Verdun, and Cambrai. This situation forced the Emperor to retire to The Netherlands, defeated and disheartened, and to leave his brother and regent, Ferdinand, to make what terms he could.

The defeat and flight of the Emperor brought the war to an end in Germany. The Treaty of Passau (1552), which ended the fighting, postponed the settlement of the religious and political affairs of Germany until the meeting of an Imperial Diet. The agreement finally drawn up by the Diet of Augsburg in 1555 allowed each secular prince to choose whether his state should be Catholic or Lutheran, permitted the Protestant sovereigns to retain the lands they had seized prior to 1552, and provided that an ecclesiastical prince should resign his office upon becoming a Protestant. Subjects who did not wish to conform to the religion of their state had to emigrate. The agreement failed to offer protection to the Calvinists or to enforce the restoration of Church property. After the conclusion of this Peace of Augsburg the Lutherans did little but consolidate their position.

In the same year Charles V began to abdicate his many thrones. Worn out by his numerous military campaigns, and prematurely aged by gluttony, he divided his dominions between his brother Ferdinand and his son Philip. To his brother he gave the hereditary Habsburg lands lying in the Danube Valley. To his son he left his Burgundian, Spanish, and Italian possessions. Thereafter the two branches of the family were known as the Austrian and the Spanish Habsburgs.

The Spanish Habsburgs continued the war with France and England until 1559. By the treaty of peace (Cateau-Cambresis, 1559), France gained Calais, the last English possession on the Continent, but continued merely to occupy Metz, Toul, and Verdun. It emerged from the long struggle slightly larger in area, but the second instead of the first Great Power of Europe. From this time forward it abandoned its efforts to conquer Italy and devoted its attention to obtaining its natural boundaries. The Spanish Habsburgs came out of the struggle dictators of Italy and the first Power of Europe. Thus the political results of these seemingly interminable wars were comparatively meager.

The incidental effects of the Italian wars were more important than their political consequences. The French kings, Charles VIII, Louis XII, and Francis I, and their French followers were amazed and delighted with what they found in Italy and returned to France filled with a desire to imitate the civilization they had seen. French architecture, painting, literature, and manners were influenced greatly by the contact of the French with the higher culture of Italy. In architecture the Italian influences tended to develop the Renaissance in place of the Gothic. This new style found its fullest expression in villas and palaces instead of in medieval cathedrals. Many Italian painters were drawn for a time to the French court. French writers began to imitate the eclogues, the tales, and the lyrics of Italian literature. The speech of French courtiers was so filled, for a time, with words of Italian origin that there was a real danger that many French terms would be supplanted by their Italian equivalents. Lastly, Italian modes and manners became for a while the standard for all who moved in the circles of the court.

THE ANABAPTIST REVOLT

Like many other responsible leaders of revolutionary movements, Luther found it impossible to satisfy and control all the forces of revolt. Zwingli, whose work in Switzerland will be described later, had the same experience. Both leaders were essentially conservative reformers and failed to hold their more radical followers. The various sects that rose in close connection with the reform movements of Luther and Zwingli are designated by the common name of Anabaptists. They sprang up more or less spontaneously in Germany, German Switzerland, and The Netherlands. One group gave Luther much trouble at Wittenberg in 1521. After their self-styled prophets were ejected from the cities of Saxony, the leaders of this group continued to trouble the countryside and to preach their revolutionary doctrines with growing vehemence, until the defeat of the peasants in 1525 led to the execution of most of the Anabaptist leaders and checked the movement for the time being. A second group arose at Zurich among the close followers of Zwingli. They were quiet, pious folk, led by saintly scholars, but their radical views concerning property, religion, and the taking of interest, and their refusal to bear arms, serve as civil officers, or take oaths, subjected them to savage persecution in both Switzerland and Southern Germany at the hands of Catholics, Lutherans, and Zwinglians alike. Hundreds were forced to recant, many died in prison, and after 1526 thousands were driven into Bohemia, Moravia, and Poland, and later into Hungary, Transylvania, and Southern Russia, where they almost completely disappeared in the eighteenth century. A third group owed its origin to the efforts of an extraordinary man named Melchior Hoffman, who carried on a wonderful propaganda in The Netherlands from 1530 to 1533, which almost destroyed the work of Luther and Zwingli in those regions. The excesses of a few of the leaders, who attempted to set up an Anabaptist state at Münster in 1532, caused the movement to collapse and made the name Anabaptist a term of reproach for the future. Fragments of the party were reorganized in 1536 into a body known as the Mennonites, still a quiet and respected religious sect in The Netherlands and the United States.

The Anabaptists were at the same time more revolutionary and more logical than Luther and Zwingli. Accepting the ideas of both these leaders concerning the authority of the Bible, they sought to build on the foundation of Scripture literally interpreted, a new church composed solely of baptized believers. This ideal involved social, political, and religious changes of a far more radical nature than Luther or Zwingli were willing or able to carry out. As there never was any organic unity between the different groups of Anabaptists, however, they differed considerably among themselves in spirit, aims, and points of doctrine.

Though the Anabaptists failed to found a permanent religious organization, their influence on religious history has been important. They weakened and hampered the work of the more conservative reformers like Luther and Zwingli without achieving their own aims. Nevertheless, they emphasized and kept alive many of the doctrines and practices which are now characteristic of the Baptists and other denominations with a congregational form of church government. They stood for the separation of Church and State, advocated religious freedom, opposed infant baptism, and emphasized the responsibility of the individual to God, freedom of the human will, the symbolical character of the Lord's Supper, congregational self-government, and simplicity of service. The connection between the Anabaptists and later bodies that held similar views, however, is not organic, but merely spiritual.

REFERENCES

Martin Luther
　J. Köstlin, *Life of Luther.*
　T. M. Lindsay, *Luther and the German Reformation.*
　A. C. McGiffert, *Martin Luther, the Man and His Work.*
　P. Smith, *The Life and Letters of Martin Luther.*
　Catholic Encyclopedia. Article: "Luther."

The German Revolt
　Cambridge Modern History, vol. II, chapters IV–VIII.
　G. P. Fisher, *History of the Reformation*, chapters IV–V.
　L. Haeusser, *The Period of the Reformation*, chapters I–IX, XIV–XVII.
　E. F. Henderson, *A Short History of Germany*, vol. I, chapters X–XV.
　A. H. Johnson, *Europe, 1494–1598*, chapters III–V.
　F. Seebohm, *Era of the Protestant Reformation*, pt. II, chapters III–V, pt. III, chapter I.
　F. Schevill, *A History of Europe*, chapter 5.
　P. Smith, *The Age of the Reformation*, chapter II.
　W. Walker, *The Reformation*, chapters III, V.
　T. M. Lindsay, *A History of the Reformation*, vol. I.
　J. S. Shapiro, *Social Reform and the Reformation.*
　H. C. Vedder, *The Reformation in Germany.*

Source Material on the German Revolt
　Translations and Reprints, no. II, vol. VI.
　J. H. Robinson, *Readings in European History*, vol. II, chapters XXV–XXVI.

The Revolt in Scandinavia
　R. N. Bain, *Scandinavia*, chapter V.
　Cambridge Modern History, vol. II, chapter XVII.
　G. P. Fisher, *History of the Reformation*, chapter VI.
　L. Haeusser, *The Period of the Reformation*, chapters XI–XII.
　F. Seebohm, *Era of the Protestant Reformation*, pt. III, chapter III.

The Struggle for Italy
　Cambridge Modern History, vol. I, chapter IV.

A. J. Grant, *Growth of the French Monarchy*, vol. I, chapter II.
A. H. Johnson, *Europe in the Sixteenth Century*, chapter I.
G. W. Kitchin, *A History of France*, vol. II, bk. II.
Histoire générale, vol. IV, chapter III.

CHARLES V
E. Armstrong, *The Emperor Charles V*.

THE ANABAPTISTS
T. M. Lindsay, *A History of the Reformation*, vol. II, bk. V, chapter II.
Article: "Anabaptists," in any of the encyclopedias.

MAPS
The Religious Situation in Europe about 1560. W. R. Shepherd, *Historical Atlas*, p. 116.

CHAPTER IV

THE PROTESTANT REVOLT IN OTHER LANDS

THE ZWINGLIAN AND CALVINIST REVOLTS

CONTEMPORARY with the German revolt against the Church was the Swiss revolt. The two movements differed in leadership, in the conditions under which they took place, and in results. The outstanding leaders of the Swiss revolt were Ulrich Zwingli and John Calvin. The first guided its earlier stages. The second carried the movement to its logical conclusion.

The extraordinary political situation in Switzerland strongly influenced the work of both these leaders. In the Middle Ages, the Swiss peasants had wrested their political freedom from the Habsburgs and had maintained it against the frequent aggressions of the surrounding princes. Each community or canton had a comparatively democratic form of local government, and the cantons were united into a loosely organized federal league. Some cantons were more democratic than others, and urban communities like Zurich and Berne had far more influence than the more sparsely settled and poorer cantons. The existence of various dependent common lands, furthermore, caused considerable trouble between the cantons. In spite of these weaknesses in organization, the Swiss held an important position in international affairs. The victories of the Swiss peasants over the Habsburgs and the Dukes of Burgundy had made the Swiss infantry the most highly prized mercenary troops in Europe, and the King of France, the Pope, and the Emperor eagerly sought the alliance of the Swiss cantons. The traffic in mercenaries, though, was undermining the primitive simplicity of the Swiss. The troops brought back the vices as well as the gold of France and Italy, and the influential men of the cantons accepted the bribes and pensions of foreign sovereigns. Nevertheless, the democratic political organization of the country led to a democratic organization of the Swiss Protestants, and the international importance of the cantons gave the Swiss reformers an opportunity to carry out their revolt against the Church unhampered by foreign interference.

To the Swiss cantons as to other parts of Western Europe came the Renaissance with its questioning of authority. The leader of the movement in Switzerland was Ulrich Zwingli. He was born in 1484 in Wildhaus, the highest village in the Toggenburg Valley. His family was the most prominent one in the village, for his father was its chief magistrate and his uncle was the parish priest. The traditions of his family marked him out for a clerical career. He studied at Basel, Berne, and Vienna, receiving his bachelor's degree from Basel in 1504 and his master's degree in 1506. In the latter year he began his career as a priest, serving first at Glarus, and later at Einsiedeln. In 1519 he was called to serve as people's priest at the great church at Zurich. Soon after he accepted this position he began his revolt against the Church.

The preparation of Zwingli for leadership against the Church was far different from that of Luther. The problem of his own salvation had never laid hold strongly on his imagination. He knew less than Luther about a deep personal religion and was primarily a Humanist. During the years of his residence at Glarus and Einsiedeln he had been engaged in the study of Greek and Hebrew. He studied the Bible as he would any other classic. His humanistic studies in time led him to the conviction that the Bible was authoritative and that indulgences and the hiring of the Swiss mercenaries were serious social abuses. His environment and training thus made democracy and the humanistic spirit the dominating influences in his life.

He made his first attacks on the Church, consequently, more in the spirit of his master Erasmus than in that of Luther. In 1519 he attacked the sale of indulgences at Zurich by Friar Sampson much as Luther opposed the activities of Tetzel at Wittenberg. The following year he began to preach against prayer to the saints, purgatory, monas-

THE PROTESTANT REVOLT

ticism, and tithes, and simplified somewhat the service of the Church. In 1522, under his influence, Zurich forbade all mercenary military service. Up to this point, however, Zwingli had not broken with the Church authorities. He continued to draw his papal pension until 1520 and the Pope chose to ignore the course of religious events at Zurich because of the political importance of the Swiss alliance. The early history of the Zwinglian revolt is thus in striking contrast to that of the Lutheran movement.

Zwingli was probably ready to go much further on the road toward reform and was only waiting for the magistrates of Zurich to take a forward step, when some of his impatient followers hurried him into open revolt against the Church. During the Lenten period in 1522 several of them publicly ate meat in the presence of Zwingli. A hot dispute quickly arose over the matter. The town council finally voted for the observance of the old rule for the sake of public peace, but in so doing it really substituted the authority of the town council for that of the bishop. After this revolutionary procedure the revolt progressed rapidly. In the same year ten priests joined Zwingli in a petition to the bishop, in which they prayed the latter to permit the marriage of priests. From this date on, the marriage of priests became ever more frequent. About the same time Zwingli published a full statement of his position. Toward the end of the following year the Great Council of Zurich caused a public debate to be held in the hope of settling the religious questions at issue. In order to regulate the discussion, Zwingli drew up sixty-seven theses or statements embodying his position. During the course of the debate Zwingli declared the whole body of Christians to be the Church, maintained the priesthood of every individual Christian and the authority of the Bible, proposed that the elected secular rulers should have the rightful authority over the Church, denied the power of the Pope, and the Catholic hierarchy, and opposed the mass, invocation of the saints, the doctrine of purgatory, fasting, clerical celibacy, and other characteristic doctrines of the Church. At the close of the arguments the burgomaster declared in the name of the council that Zwingli had not been convicted of heresy and ordered that he should continue to preach the gospel. In 1523, consequently, the city was committed to religious reform.

Religious innovations then followed quickly. Fees for baptism and burial were abolished. On Christmas Day, 1523, Zwingli announced the administration of communion in both kinds and the substitution of a sermon for the mass. Early in the following year indulgences and pilgrimages were abolished; celibacy of the clergy and the sacraments of penance and extreme unction were rejected; sacred pictures, statues, relics, and organs were destroyed; and the property of the Church was surrendered. As in Saxony the monks began to leave their monasteries. In 1524 the monks still remaining in the religious houses were united in one establishment where they were kept until they died. The income and property of the cathedral chapter at Zurich were devoted to education and the poor. In the spring of 1525 the mass was completely abolished and the memorial service of the Lord's Supper was substituted for it. By the end of 1525 the revolt against the old Church at Zurich was practically complete.

The results of the Zwinglian movement at Zurich differed considerably from those of the Lutheran movement in Germany. For the Pope and the Catholic hierarchy Zwingli substituted the elected authorities of Zurich instead of the princes. He retained, also, fewer of the elaborate ceremonies of the old faith than Luther, and used the plain interiors that have characterized the Protestant churches ever since. Zwingli was more revolutionary than Luther. Luther kept everything of the Catholic Church that in his judgment was not contrary to the Bible. Zwingli cut away everything from the government, doctrine, and services of the Church which, in his judgment, was not sanctioned by the Bible. The most fundamental difference between the two leaders was their interpretation of the Lord's Supper. To Zwingli it was merely a commemoration of Christ. To Luther, Christ was actually present in the bread and wine of the communion service.

These differences were sufficient not only to keep the followers of each leader apart, but to make them bitterly hostile to each other.

Meanwhile other preachers had been at work in German Switzerland. Most of them were followers or friends of Zwingli. In 1528, as a result of a public debate, Berne went over officially to the Protestant side. By 1529 revolts against the old faith had been carried through at Basel, Mühlhausen, Schaffhausen, Saint Gall, and other places in German Switzerland and at Augsburg, Ulm, Mainz, Frankfort, Strassburg, and other cities of Southern and Western Germany. The German cities were attracted to the Zwinglian movement by its democratic organization which gave control of religious affairs to the elected representatives of the people. In both Germany and Switzerland the teaching of Zwingli made the same strong appeal to the self-interest of the cities as the doctrines of Luther.

Upon the completion of the task of breaking away from the old Church at Zurich, Zwingli set to work on the problem of making the common lands of the Swiss Confederation safe for Protestantism and of opening up the Catholic cantons to the Protestant preachers. In his efforts to spread the new faith he resorted to political and military measures. The Protestant cantons organized a League of Christian Civic Rights and Zwingli urged a civil war to compel the acceptance of Protestantism by the Catholic cantons. The Catholic cantons, which were rural and keen enemies of innovation, in turn organized with Austria a league known as the Christian Union. War thus became almost inevitable. For two years the Canton of Berne prevented Zurich from forcing the issue, but in 1531 Zurich attempted to cut off supplies from the Catholic cantons and thus forced them to declare war. The forces of Zurich, ill-prepared for the struggle, were badly defeated, and at the battle of Kappel Zwingli himself was slain. The victors did not press their advantage, but at the time of the death of Zwingli his movement had reached its high point.

Although he left behind no powerful Church, as did Luther,

the influence of Zwingli on the Protestant movement was very important. He was the founder of a school of thought rather than of a Church. His political schemes miscarried, but his views on the Lord's Supper, public worship, and the organization of the Church, had a wide influence. Six of the thirteen Swiss cantons finally joined the Zwinglian movement. The work of Zwingli was soon taken up by John Calvin, who shortly afterwards assumed the leadership of the Protestant movement in Switzerland. Calvin undoubtedly learned much from Zwingli and concentrated and deepened the influences set in motion by his predecessor.

Calvin was a product of the reform movement in France. The French movement for reform like that of Zwingli had an entirely independent origin. The French felt almost as keenly as the Germans the need of changes in the Church and in the political and economic organization of the State. For a time the movement for Church reform went hand in hand with the agitation in favor of the new learning. The printers, the booksellers, the scholars, and many members of the clergy engaged in a propaganda for a reformation of the Church. Their agitation was the result of a closer acquaintance with the Bible. Hitherto even the educated had known the Bible mainly through the rites and ceremonies of the Church. The Gospels and the Epistles now revealed to them a new conception of religion. Christ stood forth as a living reality and the rites and ceremonies of the Church fell into a position of insignificance. The aim of the early French reformers was to restore the Church to what they considered its primitive simplicity.

The most important leader of the reform movement in France was Lefèvre d'Étaples, a celebrated professor of mathematics and physics, who at the age of fifty took up the study of theology. He influenced the French thought both through his writings, which began to appear in 1508, and his personal influence. In his writings he advocated the reading of the text of the Bible, disapproved of prayers in Latin, celibacy of the priesthood, and local superstitions, and affirmed the doctrines of the exclusive authority of Scripture and of salvation by faith instead of by works. In the years between 1523 and 1529 he gave his countrymen the Bible in their own language. At the same time he gathered around him men of his own and the younger generation, like Briçonnet, Cop, and Farel, who later left their mark on the reform movement in France and French Switzerland. Lefèvre d'Étaples, however, always considered himself a loyal member of the Church.

A promising result of the efforts of Lefèvre was the work of the reformers at Meaux. Briçonnet became Bishop of Meaux, and began to put the ideas of Lefèvre into actual practice. Under the protection of Margaret of Angoulême, the sister of Francis I, he summoned as preachers at Meaux picked young men who had been trained and inspired by the teaching and work of Lefèvre d'Étaples. This group emphasized the preaching of the newly discovered gospels and epistles, and neglected or actively opposed the ceremonies and pageantry of the old faith. Their work, however, encountered the same opposition as had that of Lefèvre.

The course of international affairs finally stopped the promising beginnings at Meaux and elsewhere. Upon the defeat of Francis I at Pavia in 1525, the regent, his mother, felt compelled to placate all the influential forces in the kingdom. These forces included the University of Paris, the Parlement of Paris, and the Paris mob, all of them fanatical opponents of Church reform. The price of their support was the suppression of the reform movement. Lefèvre, himself, who had been called to Meaux, was forced to flee to Strassburg for a time; the Bishop of Meaux rather weakly recanted the views and practices he had been advocating; and the group of earnest reformers which he had gathered around him fled in every direction. Some followed the example of their bishop. Like William Farel, others broke with the Church, became Protestants, and went into exile. The effort at pacific reform had failed, but scattered individuals and groups still cherished the new religious ideas.

John Calvin, the spiritual successor of Zwingli in Switzerland, was a product of the reform movement inaugurated in France by Lefèvre d'Étaples. Little is known of his childhood and youth. He was born in 1509 at Noyon in Picardy, where his father was a prominent citizen. Through his influence Calvin received, at the age of twelve, an ecclesiastical income that entailed no duties. There seems, however, to have been a strong anti-clerical feeling in the Calvin family that may have influenced the later career of John Calvin, for both his father and his brother died without being reconciled to the Church. In 1523 Calvin entered the University of Paris and in 1528, at the urging of his father, he began the study of law at Bourges and Orléans. After the death of his father in 1531 he seems to have given up the study of law and to have contemplated devoting his life to the classics.

The exact course of his intellectual and religious development at this time is unknown. Hitherto he had shown the qualities of a student. He was a hard worker, eager to be instructed, and possessed of a great capacity to assimilate knowledge. At some moment during these years he underwent what is usually described as his conversion. Henceforth to the end of his life his attention was devoted to theology. The turning-point of his career came in 1533, when his friend Nicholas Cop, who had been named rector of the University, delivered a discourse which was practically a manifesto of the party of Church reform. As a result of this discourse, both Calvin and Cop were forced to flee from France.

For two or three years thereafter Calvin moved around a great deal, but his main interest was centered in the preparation of that complete and systematic exposition of Christian doctrine known as the *Institutes of the Christian Religion*, which first appeared in 1536. This work is the acknowledged masterpiece of Protestant theology. It gave the Protestants for the first time a full, clear, and logical statement of their beliefs. The first Latin edition of the work appeared in 1536. A much fuller edition appeared in 1539. Two years later Calvin published a French translation. Many other editions appeared during the lifetime of Calvin and the work was translated into most of the European languages. In this celebrated treatise Calvin taught that God held a position of supreme importance in the universe. God was the creator of everything, and implanted a knowledge of himself in man. Through sin, however, man had fallen from his original state of purity and become in need of the further revelation of the Bible. Through the mysterious providence of God most men were destined to be lost and only a chosen few were foreordained to be saved. This doctrine, known as "predestination" and "election," was the distinctive feature of Calvin's theological ideas. Calvin's *Institutes* gave the Protestants a system of theology to oppose to the elaborate systems of the medieval Schoolmen.

As yet Calvin had no idea of becoming a great Protestant leader. His sole thought was to find a safe retreat in which he could devote himself to a life of study. While in search of such a place he chanced to stop for a brief time at Geneva, where William Farel, a student of Lefèvre d'Étaples and a former member of the reform group of Meaux, had been preaching the Protestant doctrines with great enthusiasm and success. Farel, realizing his lack of capacity for organizing the forces he had aroused, besought Calvin to remain at Geneva and help in the task of giving the city a new religious organization. After a dramatic interview Calvin reluctantly consented to stay, but the task of impressing himself on the life of the city still lay before him.

The situation of Geneva in 1536 was unusual. The city possessed great natural advantages. Situated at the point where the rushing Rhone leaves Lake Geneva, it commanded some of the important routes connecting Switzerland, France, and Italy. By 1534 the citizens of Geneva, with the aid of the Swiss cantons of Berne and Freiburg, had succeeded in freeing the city from the control of both the Duke of Savoy and his subservient tool, the Bishop of Geneva. The political revolt against the Bishop naturally led to a revolt against his religious power and beliefs. Influenced by the diplomatic pressure of Protestant Berne and the eloquence of William Farel, who had been working in the city since 1532, the citizens took an oath on May 21, 1536, to live according to the holy evangelical law and word of God. The preceding year the mob had forcibly installed Farel in the pulpit of the cathedral and broken the images in the churches. The destruction of the old religious organization had been completed and the task of building a new one to replace the old thus awaited Calvin. His task was greatly complicated, however, by the fact that the population of the city had acted as much from political as from religious motives.

At first Calvin held a very modest position in the city. His official title was only Professor of Sacred Letters in the church at Geneva. From the beginning, however, he exercised a profound influence over Farel.

The two colleagues immediately set to work at the task of making the Genevan church an institution for the worship of God, and the citizens of Geneva men fit to worship Him. In carrying out this task they prepared articles for the government of the church, a catechism, and a confession of faith. The catechism summarized the *Institutes* and the confession of faith came almost bodily from the catechism. The articles contained in an abbreviated form the ideas embodied later in the ordinances of 1541. As finally adopted they provided for the observance of the Lord's Supper, once a quarter; the exclusion of the unworthy from participation in the ceremony; and the establishment of a systematic discipline of personal conduct. This discipline was to be enforced by persons of good life and reputation chosen for the purpose. They were to admonish the delinquent fraternally at first; then to denounce him publicly to the assembly of the church. As a last resort the delinquent was to be excommunicated from the church and exiled by the city authorities. Many of the inhabitants of the city were opposed to the plans of Farel and Calvin. They had adopted Protestantism largely from political motives and they resented the close discipline which Calvin strove to impose on them. At the elections of 1538 they were victorious and soon afterwards they succeeded in driving Calvin into exile for three years at Strassburg.

This time of exile was an important period both in the life of Calvin and in the history of Protestantism. He broadened

THE PROTESTANT REVOLT

his acquaintanceship, widened his experience, and tried out for the first time a number of the features of church government with which his name is now regularly associated. During his stay at Strassburg he served as pastor of the band of French refugees who had come to the city. He introduced among them the strict discipline which he later set up in Geneva, adopted the forms of service that are still widely used in Calvinist churches, and began the singing of psalms and hymns as a regular part of the service. He modified somewhat the German service which he found in use at Strassburg and translated it into French. For the use of his congregation he also published a hymnal containing eighteen psalms and three compositions in French verse. Likewise the educational system established by Calvin at Geneva undoubtedly owes much to his three years' observation of the excellent educational facilities of Strassburg. The end of his period of exile from Geneva thus found Calvin better prepared to become a great Protestant leader.

Meanwhile affairs had gone none too well at Geneva. The faction hostile to Calvin and Farel mismanaged things and quickly discredited itself. Surrounded as it was by powerful foes, the little city was in a position of real danger. In their perplexity the citizens decided to recall Calvin, but only after much hesitation and the urgent solicitation of many of the Swiss pastors did he consent to return. His consent was conditioned, moreover, on the adoption of a program on which he had set his heart.

Calvin aimed to give Geneva an ecclesiastical constitution which should make the city a model Christian community. He embodied his ideas in the ordinances of 1541, which were an expansion of the articles of 1537 and which carefully regulated the life of the community. They provided for the selection and maintenance of a superior set of ministers and for what seems an excessive amount of preaching. The heart of the new system was the consistory, which was composed of the elders and ministers of the Church and met once a week. It had the power of examining, censuring, and excommunicating. It examined the citizens as to their religious knowledge, their criticism of the ministers, their absence from sermons, and their family quarrels. According to the records it punished the inhabitants of the city for having their fortunes told by gypsies, for dancing, for making a noise during a sermon, and for singing songs defamatory of Calvin.

The really novel feature of Calvin's system, however, was its rigid enforcement. Such legislation was common enough, but it was usually more or less a dead letter. Calvin, though, considered it the most essential feature of his reformatory plans. The ordinances of 1541 furthermore, made the church at Geneva far more independent of the city government than the policy of Zwingli had made the church at Zurich.

From this time on until his death Calvin was the leading citizen of Geneva. His advice was always sought and usually followed both in religious and in other matters, but his position was not assured until the last nine years of his life. At every election he was at the mercy of the electorate. Until the election of 1555 his life was a constant struggle and conflict. Many persons in the city bore very ill the dominance of Calvin and the French refugees and the close discipline exercised by the new consistory, and they opposed, criticized, and lampooned the reformer. During this trying period he showed both the strong and weak points in his character. He met all opposition with unflinching courage and firmness, but he considered himself the only true interpreter of Scripture and branded every attack on himself as an assault on God. The turning-point in the struggle was the execution in 1555 of the Spaniard Servetus for denying the Trinity. In their hatred of Calvin his opponents overreached themselves. They supported Servetus because he was an enemy of Calvin and thus put themselves in a position where they could be accused of abetting heresy. Calvin made use of his victory to admit to citizenship a sufficient number of the French refugees who sympathized with his views to make his own position henceforth unassailable. In modern eyes, however, the execution of Servetus is an ineffaceable blot on the record of the Genevan reformer.

In 1559 Calvin crowned his work at Geneva by the organization of the so-called Academy, which in time became known as the University of Geneva. In the mind of Calvin the school was an essential part of his church organization. After many delays the construction of the necessary buildings was begun early in 1558. The support of the school was largely obtained from gifts and legacies which Calvin solicited, and an adequate staff of instruction was provided by the chance disruption at just this time of a school at Lausanne. Theodore Beza, who continued the work of Calvin for forty years after the latter's death, was made rector of the new institution. The new academy was divided into a department of primary and secondary education and into a course of university grade, and not only furnished facilities for the adequate education of the children of the citizens, but also made Geneva the theological seminary of Reformed Protestantism. Students of theology soon came to Geneva in large numbers from France, England, Scotland, The Netherlands, Germany, and Switzerland, and most of the Protestant ministers of France received their training there.

Calvin continued his ceaseless activity until his death. Beza, his best friend and successor, reckoned that Calvin annually delivered nearly two hundred lectures on theology and preached close to three hundred sermons. Calvin also wrote voluminously. He revised his *Institutes of the Christian Religion* a number of times and wrote a large number of Biblical commentaries. He also maintained a remarkable correspondence, which he considered an important means of furthering the Protestant cause. He corresponded with most of the Protestant leaders in Germany, Switzerland, England, Scotland, Poland, and France. The French churches and pastors received his especial care. He selected and advised the pastors and they consulted him on all matters that concerned the welfare of French Protestantism. He exchanged letters also with many of the great of his day, numbering among his correspondents the sister of the King of France, the Kings of Navarre, Poland, and England, Admiral Coligny, Philip of Hesse, and the Elector of the Palatinate. His enemies called him the Protestant Pope. His frail body, however, finally broke under the tremendous strain and he died early in 1564. He died as he had lived, humble toward God, but confident that he was a chosen instrument in His service.

Through his correspondence and his personal contact with Protestant refugees at Geneva and in the Academy, Calvin exerted a tremendous influence outside of Geneva. This was particularly true in France, where informal assemblies of Protestants had existed at various points from the time of Lefèvre d'Étaples. The earliest converts were drawn from the artisan and middle classes. There, just as in Germany, thousands of down-trodden workmen had aligned themselves with the new movement. It furnished them the means of protest which they sought. Often the Protestant ideas started with the reading of pamphlets or from contact with wandering German workmen. Practically no nobles joined the revolt until after 1561. About 1555 a number of French churches were organized with pastors, elders, and deacons on the model of the church at Geneva. In spite of savage persecutions seventy-two churches were fully organized by 1559. In that year representatives of a few of the French churches secretly held a general synod at Paris.

In time Calvin also became the spiritual leader of those churches in Germany and in German Switzerland that had formerly looked to Zwingli for leadership. At first they looked on Calvin and his views with more or less suspicion, but in 1549 he obtained an agreement with the pastors of Zurich over the troublesome question of the interpretation of the Lord's Supper, that resulted in the general acceptance of his doctrines in a moderate form by all the Protestant churches of Switzerland. In Germany his doctrines but not his ideas with regard to discipline also made considerable progress. About 1560 the Elector of the Palatinate became a Calvinist. Shortly afterwards he caused the famous Heidelberg Catechism to be prepared and published. Before the close of the sixteenth century Nassau, Bremen, Anhalt, Baden, and Hesse had followed the example of the Palatinate, and in 1613 the important electorate of Brandenburg went over to the Calvinists. The German Calvinists, though, really occupied an intermediate position between Luther and Calvin.

Calvinism also made important gains in The Netherlands. From the beginning of Luther's agitation the inhabitants of The Netherlands favored the movement for Church reform. In May, 1521, Charles V issued an edict against heresy in his hereditary dominions, and two friars of Brussels became the first martyrs of the Lutheran revolt as a result of the enforcement of the decree. The execution of the decree depended mainly on the local authorities who were often friendly to the movement for reform. For a time, as we have seen, Anabaptist took the place of Lutheran influences in The Netherlands, but with the rise of Calvinism the people became adherents of the doctrines of Calvin. First under the influence of preachers from France the French-speaking provinces of the south became Calvinist. Later the northern provinces followed the example of the southern. In 1561 a Belgic Confession was adopted which became the doctrinal basis of the Dutch Reformed Church in The Netherlands. It followed the model of the one adopted by the French churches at Paris in 1559. The southern provinces, now included in the Kingdom of Belgium, in time returned to the Catholic Church, but the provinces now included in the Kingdom of The Netherlands have remained Calvinist for the most part since the days of their revolt against the Catholic Church and the rule of Spain.

The rise of Calvin's influence in Scotland is closely connected with the career of John Knox. After serving for some years as a priest of the old faith Knox became a Protestant pastor about 1546. The religious situation in Scotland and England drove him to Geneva where in 1555 he became pastor of the English exiles living in the city and a close associate of Calvin. After his return to Scotland, Knox became a leader in the Scotch revolt against the Church.

As elsewhere in Europe many factors contributed to the overthrow of the Church in Scotland. For many years there had been two factions in the country. One gradually became Catholic and pro-French in its sympathies; the other Protestant and pro-English. The Scottish sovereigns and political leaders, however, changed their party affiliations on the slightest pretext. Until about 1555 the reformers in Scotland outwardly conformed to the old Church, but in that year, upon the advice of Knox, they withdrew from the Church. Two years later the Protestant leaders subscribed to a covenant whereby they pledged themselves to "establish the most blessed word of God and his congregation." This action made civil war almost inevitable, and the struggle, which soon broke out, lasted from 1559 to 1560. The Protestant party was victorious, but it owed its victory largely to the money and troops furnished by England. The victorious Scottish party was influenced as much by the desire for the property of the Church and by patriotic resentment at the encroachment of the French as by zeal for the Protestant cause.

Knox played a more prominent rôle in organizing the new national church than in its establishment. Immediately after making peace, the Scotch Parliament passed acts abolishing the authority of the Pope and prohibiting the celebration of the mass and adopted a confession of faith that contained a summary of the main doctrines of Calvin. Knox also drew up a book of discipline, which aimed to introduce into Scotland the ideas adopted by Calvin at Geneva with reference to the organization of the church and the discipline of the private lives of the members of the community. Education was to be compulsory. Preachers, teachers, and the poor were to be supported by the property confiscated from the old Church. This last provision, however, ran counter to the interests of the nobles and remained a dead letter. The Church property left by the destructive mobs was seized by the grasping nobles. The lines which the new church was to follow were thus laid down as early as 1560, but the supremacy of Protestantism in Scotland was not absolutely assured until after the flight from the country of Mary, Queen of Scots, and the subsequent defeat of her party.

The influence of Knox was not confined to Scotland. It left its mark on northeastern Ireland and America. The Scottish colonists who migrated to the plantations of Ulster and the Scotch-Irish colonists who later went from there to the American colonies took both their religious ideas and their traits of character with them. Like Knox himself his fellow religionists were apt to be men of great force of character and almost fanatically honest, but hard, narrow, unreasonable, and intolerant. They believed themselves to be the elect of God and to have a divine mission. Everywhere they went they introduced the stern theology of Calvin and Knox, their democratic church organization, and their ideas of education and discipline. Some of the present troubles of Ireland and much that is finest in American life have their origin in the work of Calvin in Geneva and Knox in Scotland.

The influence of Calvin penetrated, likewise, into Poland, Hungary, and England. By the middle of the sixteenth century Calvinism had spread considerably among the nobles and educated classes of Poland, but it never took root among the lower classes and its influence later decreased as a result of religious dissensions and disputes. In Hungary Calvinism appealed especially to the Magyars and a Hungarian confession of faith was drawn up shortly after the middle of the century. At the present time something like one seventh of the Magyars are Calvinists. The Calvinist influence in England was exerted chiefly through the Puritans. Their rise will be explained in connection with the history of the Anglican revolt against the Church. The Puritans, however, came to America in considerable numbers under the Stuart Kings of England. Thus Calvinism reached America through the two important channels of the Scotch-Irish emigrants to the colonial frontier, and the Puritan colonists in New England and other colonies.

THE ANGLICAN REVOLT

In England the revolt against the Church took a different course from that followed by either the Lutheran or the Calvinist movements. In the fourteenth century Wycliffe had attacked the claims of the Papacy and the clergy, rejected the doctrine of transubstantiation, and advocated the confiscation of Church property. Under the name of Lollards his followers continued to criticize the Church throughout the fourteenth and fifteenth centuries. In the early years of the sixteenth century a distinguished group of Humanists, known as the Oxford Reformers, worked in England, and Lutheran, Zwinglian, and Anabaptist agitators visited the country, but there were no indications of a successful revolt against the established religion of the State until the King himself unexpectedly took the lead in attacking the Church. Eventually there might have been a popular revolt against the Church in England, but both the time and the form of the revolt which actually took place were dictated by the royal will. The general acquiescence of the English people in the royal policy was due to the great power wielded by the sovereign and to the failure of the Church to hold the popular respect and confidence.

The political power of Henry VIII (1509–47) was founded on his constitutional position and his personal popularity. His strong constitutional position had been bequeathed to him by his father Henry VII (1485–1509), and was the combined result of historical chance and the conscious policy of his father. At the close of the Middle Ages the War of the Roses had destroyed the power of the turbulent nobility and made the new middle class favorable to any government that seemed to promise peace and economic prosperity. Henry VII had taken advantage of this situation to establish a practical despotism while technically recognizing the constitutional position of Parliament. A policy of peace and economy made him largely independent of Parliament, and a long series of domestic measures and foreign treaties favoring the rising commercial and industrial classes made his dynasty popular with the middle class. The Tudor sovereigns were successful in retaining this strong position as long as their dynasty remained on the English throne.

The revolt of Henry VIII against the Church was based on very unworthy motives. While doubts concerning the validity of his marriage with the widow of his deceased brother and the desire for the male heir, so greatly needed on patriotic and dynastic grounds, may have had a considerable part in influencing the King's religious policy, his desire to marry Anne Boleyn, one of his Queen's ladies of honor, seems to have been the decisive factor in causing him to try to get rid of his first wife. The Church courts and the authority of the Pope, however, stood in the way of his plans, for the Church courts had jurisdiction over matrimonial cases and the Papal Court was the final court of appeal. All the precedents of the Church and the powerful influence of Charles V, nephew of Queen Catherine, stood in the way of the Pope returning a favorable answer to the suit of the English King. The appeal of Henry VIII thus put the Pope in a most trying position.

Confronted by this dilemma the Pope delayed his answer to the King as long as possible. On the other hand, the eager royal lover did all in his power to hasten a favorable answer to his suit. He first put pressure on the English clergy. Under threat of severe punishment for their technical disobedience to the laws of England the King forced the clergy to acknowledge him as supreme head of the English Church and to promise to hold no meetings and to pass no legislation without his sanction. Upon the royal initiative Parliament then adopted a series of measures which put the English clergy under the authority of the King and destroyed the income and authority of the Pope in England. Between 1529 and 1535 it cut off all money payments to the Pope from the English Church, forbade appeals to the Papal courts, put the nomination of bishops in the hands of the King, and made Henry VIII supreme head of the English Church. When these measures failed to force the Pope to favorable action, Parliament reënacted them and made them the permanent law of the land. This action cut the English Church off from all connection with the Pope, and gave the King more control of church revenues, appointments, legislation, and appeals than the Pope had ever enjoyed. The Church was completely subordinated to the State. Long before the quarrel of Henry and the Pope had reached its final stages, however, Henry had caused his own courts to grant him a separation from his wife Catherine and had married Anne Boleyn.

The desire of Henry VIII to get rid of Queen Catherine probably could not have led to this break with the Church if the revolt had not been in line with both the inclinations of the King and the spirit of the time. The King was an absolutist and every limitation on his authority aroused his opposition. The break with the Pope, furthermore, was a natural step in the development of the English national State. The whole tendency of English history for two centuries had been toward a diminution of the power of the Church and an increase in the power of the State. The divorce question merely precipitated a struggle toward which the two powers had been tending.

The English revolt against the Church could hardly stop with a change in its headship. Those in favor of reform attacked the doctrines, services, and institutions of the Church. The King himself favored the dissolution of the monasteries on account of the wealth they had accumulated, and caused Parliament to pass acts in 1536 and 1539 which dissolved the monastic communities and confiscated their property. Part of the property went into the royal treasury and part of it went to found or increase the fortunes of important private families of the kingdom. In many cases the reformers carried out the destruction of the monasteries with needless brutality and waste. They inflicted many hardships on the inmates of the dissolved institutions, and carelessly destroyed priceless objects of art.

In 1539 the English Government published a new English translation of the Scriptures, known as the Great Bible, and ordered a copy of it to be placed in each parish church of the kingdom. The language of the common people, also, came into greater use in the Church services. All parts of the Bible which were read in the services were put into English, and in 1544 a new litany was composed in the English language. However, during his lifetime Henry VIII successfully resisted all efforts to introduce innovations in doctrine.

The reign of Edward VI (1547–53), the son and successor of Henry VIII, saw the work of introducing Protestant reforms completed. The Protestant leaders prepared a new prayer book, which in a slightly modified form has been used ever since in the Church of England and in the Protestant Episcopal Church in America, removed the images and the crucifixes from the churches, permitted the glorious stained-glass windows to be broken, whitewashed or plastered over the religious pictures on the walls, and abolished fasting, pilgrimages, the use of holy water, and the imposition of penance. In addition they permitted the priests to marry, gave the prayer book a form acceptable to the Protestants, required everybody to use the new prayer book and to conform outwardly to the new religious innovations, summed up the new theological beliefs in forty-two articles, and completed the work of confiscating the property of the Church by dissolving the chantries, pious endowments which provided for the chanting of masses and the saying of prayers, usually in behalf of the soul of the founder. In making these changes the Government certainly went beyond the wishes of the great mass of the people.

In 1553, Mary Tudor (1553-58), the daughter of Henry VIII by his first wife, Catherine of Aragon, succeeded Edward VI on the English throne. Loyalty to her mother made the new ruler a Catholic in religion and the five years of her reign witnessed a Catholic reaction. She had the legislation of the reign of Edward VI repealed, then that of Henry VIII, and restored the Church as nearly as possible to the conditions which existed before the so-called Reformation Parliament began its work in 1529. She reintroduced the old Latin service, set up again the crucifixes, and caused the old customs to be resumed. She required the clergy who had married to put away their wives or to give up their places. Mary would gladly have restored to the Church the property confiscated in the reigns of her father and brother, but her advisers warned her that such a policy could not be carried out, for the new possessors were in no mood to relinquish their hold on it.

If Mary had been satisfied with these changes the Catholic reaction which marked her reign might have been permanent, but she thoroughly alienated her people by marrying Philip II of Spain and by persecuting many of her subjects on the ground of religion. Her policy of religious repression had the opposite effect from that which she intended. By burning several hundred English Protestants at the stake, she turned away the hearts of a large proportion of the English nation from herself and her religion. Many of the Protestant leaders went into exile on the continent of Europe, where they came into contact with Calvinism at Geneva and other Protestant centers. Upon the accession of Elizabeth, the daughter of Anne Boleyn and the half-sister of Mary Tudor, in 1558, these exiles returned and became the leaders of the so-called Puritan party. Disappointed in her hopes of winning the hearts of her subjects for herself and her religion, Mary Tudor died in 1558 of a broken heart. The crowning disappointment of her reign was the loss of Calais in 1558 to the French as a result of her alliance with Spain.

Elizabeth (1558–1603) on her accession to the throne found herself, in consequence, confronted by the problem of a suitable religious settlement. The circumstances of her birth, her own inclinations, and expediency dictated the adoption of a middle position between the conservative extreme of the Catholics and the radical extreme of the fanatical Protestants. In all matters of Church government, accordingly, Elizabeth went back to the system of Henry VIII and in most matters of doctrine and service to the position taken by the authorities in the reign of Edward VI. Two important laws were enacted which embodied this policy: the Act of Supremacy and the Act of Uniformity. The first abolished the authority of the Pope in England and made Elizabeth supreme governor of the English Church. The second measure did away with the mass, reintroduced the English prayer book issued in the reign of Edward VI, and ordered the ornaments and ceremonies used in the services to be the same as those used in the reign of her brother. All members of the clergy and officers of the Government, furthermore, were commanded to take an oath of obedience to the new legislation. A little later the Forty-Two Articles of the reign of Edward VI were slightly modified and reissued as the Thirty-Nine Articles. They have been ever since the official statement of doctrine for the Church of England and the Protestant Episcopal Church in America.

The religious settlement of Elizabeth made the Established English Church a very different institution from either the Catholic Church or the churches established by Luther and Calvin. It rejected the headship of the Pope, but retained the hierarchy of archbishops, bishops, and parish clergy. It adopted a service in which the old Catholic service was slightly modified and translated into English. It worded the doctrinal pronouncements of the English Church so as to permit wide differences of opinion among its members. This ambiguity in the official declarations made possible the rise of the High and Low Church parties within the present-day Church of England. The Established Church of England and the Protestant Episcopal Church of America are thus distinct from all other churches in government and service and tolerate a wide diversity of opinion.

The religious settlement of Elizabeth, however, did not satisfy all her subjects. On the one hand many of the nobles and gentry, particularly in the northern and the rural parts of England, remained loyal to the Catholic Church. On the other hand many persons wished Elizabeth to go much further on the road toward Protestantism. Led by the exiles, who had returned from Geneva and other Protestant centers on the Continent, they attacked everything which suggested the Catholic Church. They opposed the vestments worn by the clergy, the observance of saints' days, the sign of the cross in baptism, the use of organs, and many other forms and ceremonies, and denounced many of the popular amusements. They met secretly in so-called "conventicles" and held services which embodied their real religious beliefs. Because they wished to purify the services of the English Church they became known as Puritans. In time the Protestant extremists became divided into three groups: the Puritans, who wanted to purify the Church while staying in it; the Presbyterians, who were opposed to the government of the bishops and wished to introduce a form of church government similar to that used by Calvin at Geneva and Knox in Scotland; and the Separatists, who insisted on the right of each congregation to manage its own affairs. In spite of much repressive legislation the Government was never able to destroy either party of extremists. The present English Roman Catholics and most of the English non-conformist bodies of to-day are descended from these two groups of Elizabethan extremists.

RESULTS OF THE PROTESTANT REVOLT

The Protestant Revolt divided Western Christendom into two ecclesiastical parties, the Roman Catholics and the Protestants. The close of the revolt found the Roman Catholics still dominant in the states of Southern Europe, the Southern Netherlands, most of the territories of the Austrian Habsburgs, and much of Southern Germany, Poland, and Ireland. The Protestants dominated the remaining countries of Western Europe but they were divided into three principal churches. The three Scandinavian kingdoms, the provinces along the eastern shore of the Baltic, the majority of the states of Northern and Central Germany, and large numbers of the Czechs of Bohemia, the Germans of Transylvania, and the nobles and burghers of Poland were Lutheran. The more populous cantons of Switzerland, most of the free imperial cities of Southern Germany, the Palatinate and a few of the other German states, the northern provinces of The Netherlands, the Scottish Lowlands, a minority party in France, the Puritan party in England, and scattered groups in Bohemia, Poland, and Hungary were Calvinist. In England the Anglican Church was dominant.

In spite of their differences the Catholics and the three Protestant parties had much in common. Each of the four churches believed in the Trinity, the peculiar sacredness of the Bible, the fall of man, future rewards and punishments, and the necessity of salvation through Christ, and each taught the same code of ethics, but they were kept apart by differences in government, doctrine, and service.

In respect to Church government the four ecclesiastical

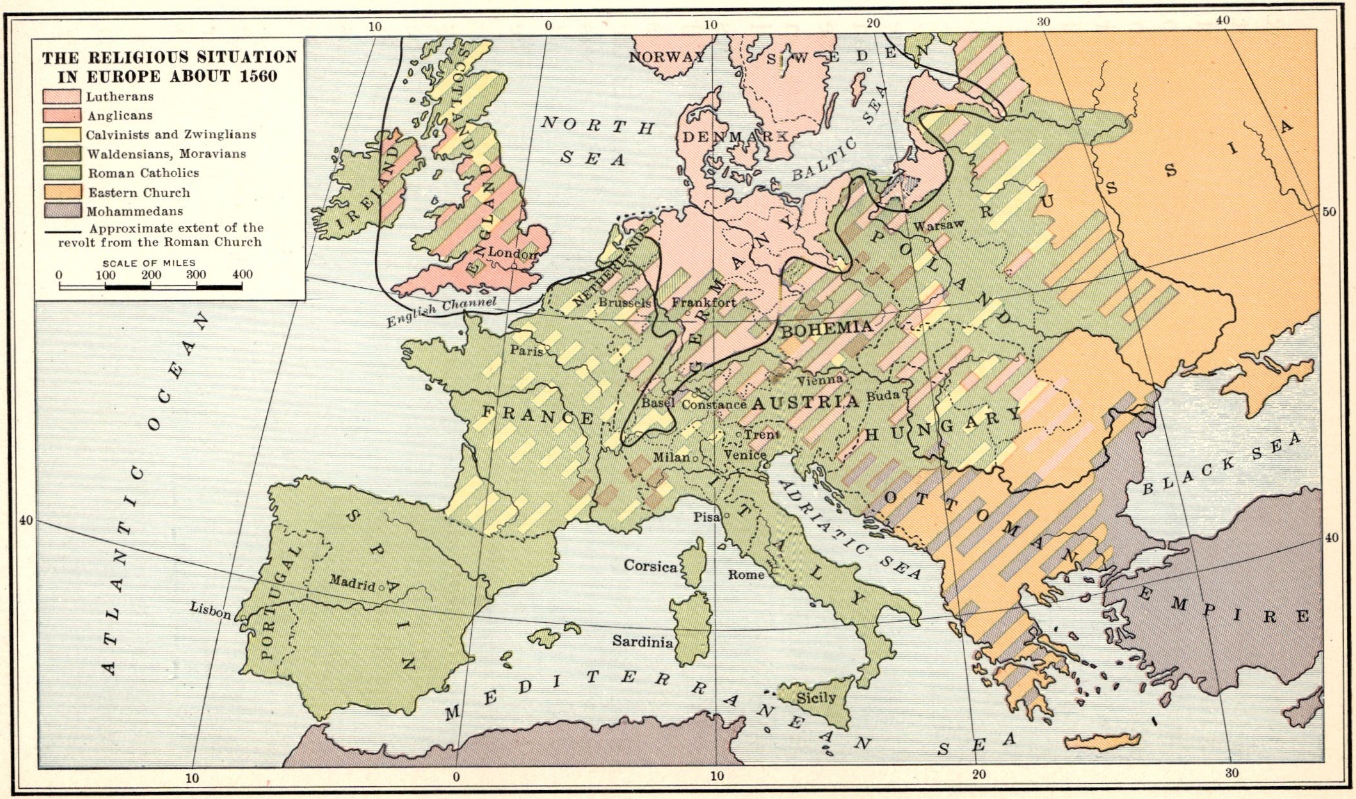
THE RELIGIOUS SITUATION IN EUROPE ABOUT 1560
Lutherans
Anglicans
Calvinists and Zwinglians
Waldensians, Moravians
Roman Catholics
Eastern Church
Mohammedans
Approximate extent of the revolt from the Roman Church
SCALE OF MILES
0 100 200 300 400
NORTH SEA
NORWAY
SWEDEN
DENMARK
BALTIC SEA
RUSSIA
SCOTLAND
IRELAND
ENGLAND
London
English Channel
NETHERLANDS
Brussels
Frankfort
GERMANY
POLAND
Warsaw
BOHEMIA
Vienna
Buda
AUSTRIA
HUNGARY
Paris
FRANCE
Basel
Constance
Trent
Milan
Venice
ITALY
Pisa
Rome
Corsica
Sardinia
Sicily
ADRIATIC SEA
OTTOMAN EMPIRE
BLACK SEA
SPAIN
PORTUGAL
Madrid
Lisbon
ATLANTIC OCEAN
MEDITERRANEAN SEA

parties divided over the question of the control of the Church. The Roman Catholics retained the Pope, the archbishops, and the bishops of the medieval Church. The English Church substituted the King for the Pope in the government of the Church, but retained the archbishops and bishops. The Lutherans, in most cases, put the secular government in place of that of the Pope and consistories and superintendents in place of the archbishops and bishops. The Calvinists adopted a more democratic form of Church government. With them assemblies, synods, and presbyteries, composed of elected representatives of the clergy and the laity, took the place of the medieval hierarchy. In a sense Protestantism was a protest against the cosmopolitanism of the medieval Church. In the Anglican and the Lutheran states it was the religious aspect of the developing political absolutism. Among the Calvinists and the Anabaptists it was the religious side of the rising democracy.

In regard to doctrine the four churches differed over the fundamental questions of the source of religious authority and the function of the clergy. The Roman Catholics held that the chief authority in matters of doctrine was the Bible as interpreted by the Church and that the intervention of the clergy was necessary for the salvation of the individual. The Protestants professed to believe in individual interpretation of the Scriptures and the priesthood of all believers. It was because they seemed to be based on the traditions of the Church rather than on the Scriptures that the Protestants rejected the claims of the Bishop of Rome, the jurisdiction of the Papal Government, and the doctrines of purgatory, indulgences, invocation of the saints, and veneration of relics.

The theory of the right of the individual to interpret the Scriptures gave rise to many differences among the three great groups of Protestants. Luther taught the doctrine of justification by faith; Calvin justification by election — that all those not predestined to be saved are to be lost; and the Thirty-Nine Articles of the Church of England left the whole matter in some doubt. The Protestants also differed in the number of sacraments they accepted and in the significance they attached to them. All three of the Protestant churches retained the sacraments of baptism and the Lord's Supper, but the Lutherans kept in addition the sacrament of confirmation and the Anglicans the sacraments of confirmation and ordination. For the Catholic doctrine of transubstantiation the Lutherans substituted the doctrine of consubstantiation. After 1561 the Calvinists looked upon all the sacraments as mere symbols. The Anglicans never reached any agreement on the question of their significance. In spite of their professed belief in the doctrine of the individual interpretation of the Bible all the Protestants except the Anabaptists tended to set up some official standard of doctrine in place of the Pope and the official pronouncements of the Church.

In respect to service the churches divided over the question of the retention of the language and the services of the medieval Church. The English Church translated the words of the service into English, but retained many of the Roman Catholic forms. The Calvinists adopted a simple service consisting of the reading of the Bible, the singing of hymns, extemporaneous prayers, and preaching. The various Lutheran churches tended to adopt a form of service midway between that of the Anglicans and that of the Calvinists.

The Protestant Revolt, however, was a political, social, and economic, as well as a religious, movement. In England, the three Scandinavian kingdoms, and the Protestant states of Germany the revolt enhanced the wealth and power of the secular heads of the states. The secular sovereigns ceased to share political authority with the Church and to be limited by its privileges. Instead they confiscated the wealth of the Church, taxed and judged their subjects without its interference, and appointed and controlled the clergy. In some cases the sovereigns shared with their nobles the property confiscated from the Church, but the rulers took great care to see that the nobility acquired no new political influence.

Another group benefited by the Protestant Revolt was the middle class. The bankers, merchants, and manufacturers profited by the removal of the restrictions on the taking of interest and the release of the land and capital which had been held immobile by the dead hand of the Church. In Germany the free imperial cities received the same political advantages as the princes. In the Calvinist states the democratic tendencies of Calvinism favored the development of the middle class, the element in society most capable at the time of profiting from the new liberty. The expansion of Europe, though, undoubtedly had more influence on the rise of the middle class than the Protestant Revolt.

The peasants, who constituted the great mass of the population, made no material gains from the Protestant Revolt. The absolutist princes had no mercy on the peasantry and the new lay proprietors proved harder taskmasters than the easy-going churchmen. The burdens of the peasants did not become appreciably lighter on the continent of Europe until the French Revolution set in motion the principle of individual liberty.

REFERENCES

HULDREICH ZWINGLI
  Cambridge Modern History, vol. II, chapter X.
  E. M. Hulme, *Renaissance and Reformation*, chapter XV.
  L. Haeusser, *The Period of the Reformation*, chapter X.
  T. M. Lindsay, *A History of the Reformation*, vol. II, bk. III, chapter II.
  P. Smith, *The Age of the Reformation*, pp. 146–60.
  Catholic Encyclopedia. Article: "Zwingli."
  P. Burckhardt, *H. Zwingli*.
  S. M. Jackson, *Huldreich Zwingli*.
  Histoire générale, vol. IV, chapter XI.

JOHN CALVIN
  Cambridge Modern History, vol. II, chapter XI.
  G. P. Fisher, *History of the Reformation*, chapter VII.
  L. Haeusser, *The Period of the Reformation*, chapter XVIII.
  T. M. Lindsay, *A History of the Reformation*, vol. II, bk. III, chapter III.
  F. Seebohm, *Era of the Protestant Reformation*, pt. III, chapter IV.
  P. Smith, *Age of the Reformation*, pp. 160–81.
  Catholic Encyclopedia. Article: "Calvin."
  H. Y. Reyburn, *John Calvin*.
  W. Walker, *John Calvin*.
  Histoire générale, vol. IV.

SOURCE MATERIAL ON JOHN CALVIN
  Translations and Reprints, vol. III, no. III, pp. 7–16.
  J. H. Robinson, *Readings in European History*, vol. II, pp. 122–34.

JOHN KNOX
    G. P. Fisher, *History of the Reformation*, chapter X.
    T. M. Lindsay, *A History of the Reformation*, vol. II, bk. III, chapter VI.
    P. Smith, *Age of the Reformation*, chapter VII.
    P. H. Brown, *John Knox, A Biography*.
    A. Lang, *John Knox and the Reformation*.

THE REVOLT IN FRANCE
    G. P. Fisher, *History of the Reformation*, chapter VIII.
    E. M. Hulme, *Renaissance and Reformation*, chapter XVI.
    T. M. Lindsay, *A History of the Reformation*, vol. II, bk. III, chapter IV.
    F. Seebohm, *Era of the Protestant Reformation*, pt. III, chapter II.
    P. Smith, *Age of the Reformation*, pp. 182–210.
    Histoire de France, vol. V, pt. II, pp. 183–249.

THE REVOLT IN THE NETHERLANDS
    Cambridge Modern History, vol. II, chapter IX.
    G. P. Fisher, *History of the Reformation*, chapter X.
    L. Haeusser, *The Period of the Reformation*, chapters XIII, XLI–XLII.
    T. M. Lindsay, *A History of the Reformation*, vol. II, bk. III, chapter V.

THE ENGLISH REVOLT
    Cambridge Modern History, vol. II, chapters XIII–XVI.
    T. M. Lindsay, *A History of the Reformation*, vol. II, bk. IV, chapters I–IV.
    P. Smith, *Age of the Reformation*, chapter VI.
    H. O. Wakeman, *An Introduction to the History of the Church of England*, chapters X–XIV.

RESULTS OF THE PROTESTANT REVOLT
    F. Seebohm, *Era of the Protestant Reformation*, pt. III, chapters VII–VIII.

MAPS
    The Religious Situation in Europe about 1560, W. R. Shepherd, *Historical Atlas*, p. 116.
    The Religious Situation in Europe about 1618, *Ibid.*, p. 120.

CHAPTER V

THE CATHOLIC REFORMATION AND THE ASCENDANCY OF SPAIN UNDER PHILIP II

DURING the latter half of the sixteenth century the Catholic Church took the offensive and checked the progress of Protestantism. The Church held a great council which defined anew the doctrines of the Church, reformed the crying abuses, and carried out many practical religious reforms, created new religious orders which battled successfully against Protestantism in Europe and won new empires for the Church in non-European lands, revived the inquisition, and inaugurated censorship of the press to combat the Protestant beliefs. Under the leadership of Philip II the crusading spirit of Catholic Europe was reawakened and directed against the rising tide of Protestantism in England, France, and The Netherlands. The Church was thus transformed from a passive victim into an aggressive opponent of the Protestant movement.

THE CATHOLIC REFORMATION

Loyal Catholics did not begin to realize their aspirations for Church reform until nearly the middle of the sixteenth century. The movement began with a revival of religious life combined with a strict adherence to the doctrines of the medieval schoolmen. With many it took the form of a restoration of the ideals of the old religious orders. Several of the monastic orders were brought back to their primitive austerity, and a reformed branch of the Franciscan friars, known as the Capuchins, was established, which played a very important part in bringing back to the Church the mass of the Italian people. The members of this order appealed to the populace and guided their religious thinking. The secular clergy, however, stood in need of reform even more than the monks and friars. In consequence an order, called the Theatines, was organized in 1524 for the purpose of remedying the inefficiency and corruption of the parish clergy. The members of the new order were ordinary secular priests bound together by the three monastic vows of poverty, chastity, and obedience. The new society found many imitators. Both the new and the old religious orders worked quietly and unostentatiously at the task of reforming the Church in Italy until they were reinforced by two powerful and militant agencies, the Inquisition and the Society of Jesus.

The medieval inquisition had been established for the purpose of searching out heretics and bringing them to repentance or of punishing them in proportion to their offenses, but by the fifteenth century the institution had little left to do. In 1477, however, the Catholic sovereigns of Spain requested its establishment in their dominions for the purpose of combating the pseudo-converts among the Jews and the Moslems, who were felt to be a menace to the State. The institution, accordingly, was set up in the older possessions of the Catholic sovereigns, and in the Spanish colonies, but in the newer provinces, like Naples and Milan, its introduction was successfully resisted. The rise of Protestantism gave the institution a new lease on life in Spain and called into being the Roman Inquisition which was introduced into Milan, Naples, and Venice, but was never established outside of the Italian peninsula.

The Inquisition has a bad reputation among Protestants. According to modern ideas its procedure was cruel and unfair and its punishments barbarous, but judged by the standards of the time, its procedure and punishments were no worse than those of the secular courts. The guilt of the accused was assumed and conviction rather than justice was sought. Every one was urged to inform on his neighbors. The prisoner was not confronted by the witnesses. Torture was frequently resorted to in order to obtain a confession of guilt. The inquisitors, who varied in number, were both judges and prosecutors. The defense, consequently, had an almost hopeless task. The punishments inflicted by the tribunal varied from mere reprimand to burning alive at the stake. The Inquisition supplemented and completed the work of the more pacific reformers. Through its work Protestantism was stamped out entirely in both Spain and Italy.

The second of the more militant agencies, employed to combat the spread of Protestantism, was the Society of Jesus, which was founded by a Spaniard, Ignatius Loyola. Its founder was converted from a careless sinful life while convalescing from a wound received in 1521 during the first war of Charles V and Francis I. The reading of some pious books during this time inspired Loyola with the wish to emulate the lives of the saints, and he took a vow of service to Jesus. Many years elapsed, however, before he was able to carry out his plans through the organization of the Jesuits. He spent long years at various points in Spain and at Paris in study and in the practice of asceticism. During this period of his life he worked out his famous Spiritual Exercises, the set of rules and counsels by which he later imposed his vision and his will on the men who became his followers. At Paris he followed the course in theology at the university only by surmounting the greatest obstacles.

At the University of Paris Loyola began to gather around him the band of followers that he finally organized into the Society of Jesus. In 1535 he and his first six recruits took vows of chastity and poverty and promised to devote their lives to the service of souls in the Holy Land. A renewal of the war with the Turks prevented them from going to Palestine, but they journeyed to Rome and put themselves at the service of the Pope instead. There the band encountered innumerable obstacles, but in 1540 a Papal bull, empowering the associates to organize their new order, was finally issued and Loyola was elected first head of the new society.

The founder and first general of the Society of Jesus was endowed with a will of iron, unconquerable perseverance, and an unshakable faith. His aim was the creation of a company of priests, organized on military lines and ready for any form of service. The society was extraordinary only in the thorough training given its members and in their unusual zeal, detachment, and self-sacrifice. The Jesuit had to be a man over thirty years of age, who had been undergoing for more than a dozen years a process of training under strict control. First came a novitiate of two years, during which the prospective member was subjected to all sorts of tests. Five or six years were then spent in study and as many more in teaching. Then followed a period of four years spent in the study of theology. Only after all these preliminary requirements had been met successfully was the member ordained to the priesthood. Lastly, after a second novitiate of a year, the candidate became a member of the society. A very small number of the picked men of the order took a fourth and special vow of obedience to the Pope and were known as the "Professed of Four Vows." "Making the spiritual exercises" of Loyola constituted an important part of the training of each Jesuit. The candidate first spent a considerable period of time in the contemplation of sin and of the life of Christ. Through this meditation and prayer he came to a realization that man's work is to do the will of God, and thus to throw himself wholeheartedly into the service of his order. The new order, furthermore, was organized much like an army and exacted more than military obedience from its members, who put their services wholly at the command of the society and its general.

These were the forces working toward the reformation of the Church when circumstances finally allowed the long deferred general council of the Church to meet. Such an assembly had long been advocated by those favoring reform of the Church, but many obstacles had prevented first the summoning and then the meeting of such a body. After the unhappy experiences of their predecessors with the general councils of the fifteenth century, the Popes wished to be sure that their authority would not be infringed upon by the council, and each political and religious faction desired a different place of meeting. Lastly the wars of Charles V and Francis I delayed for several years the actual calling together of the prelates of the Church. Trent, the imperial city nearest Italy, was at last selected as the place of meeting and the members of the Council were summoned to assemble there in March, 1545.

The first session of the Council of Trent was held in 1545 and the last one in 1563, but the body was not in continuous session for the whole eighteen years. Twice the Council was prorogued for considerable periods of time, the last intermission continuing for ten years. The assembly first took up the order of business and methods of procedure. The Council decided that the Papal representatives (known as legates) alone should have the right to preside over the sessions and to initiate legislation. All questions were to be discussed first in a special congregation or committee, and then in a general congregation of the bishops. Finally, at a formal session the adoption of the decrees of the Council was to be voted on without debate. It was also agreed that a question of doctrine and one of Church reform would be taken up and decided at each formal session of the Council. This was a defeat for Charles V, who wanted the question of reform taken up first, in the hope that timely religious reforms would restore the religious unity of his Empire. Voting, furthermore, was to be by head and not by nations. This assured the Pope and the Italians a steady majority in the assembly at all times. The Pope thus had nothing to fear from a council with such an organization.

There were in all twenty-five formal sessions of the Council. The results of its work are styled the canons and decrees of the Council of Trent. The doctrinal decrees deal exclusively with the doctrinal points emphasized by the Protestants. They declare both the traditions of the Church and the Bible to be the standard of authority for Christians, and the Vulgate edition of the Scriptures, the Latin edition of the Bible which had long been used in the Catholic Church, to be the authentic text of the Bible. This was in direct contradiction to the teaching of the Humanists, who alleged that they had discovered many errors in the Vulgate edition. The Council, furthermore, declared that salvation depended on both faith and works, and that the sacraments were indispensable, reaffirmed most of the medieval beliefs and practices, such as invocation of the saints, the use of images in the churches, purgatory, and indulgences, and adopted decrees condemning most of the abuses in the inner life of the Church that had been a subject of scandal. The work of the Council, therefore, greatly clarified the position of the Church with regard to doctrine and gave it a great impulse toward moral reform. The Church at last had a definite platform on which it could stand, and for which it could fight.

The Council left a number of matters of unfinished business in the hands of the Pope. In the year following the close of the Council, the *Tridentine Profession of Faith* appeared, which summed up in twelve articles the canons and decrees adopted by the Church at Trent. Two years later came the *Roman Catechism*, a long and comprehensive discussion of the doctrines of the Church drawn up for the instruction of the clergy. In 1568 a new breviary or devotional guide appeared, and in 1570 a new missal or liturgical standard. In 1582 the Pope published a revised edition of the canon law, and in the last decade of the sixteenth century a new edition of the Vulgate Bible. In 1564, also, the first index or list of books which good Catholics were prohibited from reading appeared at Rome.

The idea of censoring books arose with the art of printing. After the rise of the Lutheran heresy the universities began to publish lists of prohibited books. About the middle of the century the Pope ordered the Roman Inquisition to prepare a similar list of dangerous books. Finally the Council of Trent took up the matter and appointed a commission, which prepared the *Tridentine Index* of prohibited books, which appeared in 1564. Later in the century, the Pope entrusted a permanent commission or congregation of cardinals with the censorship of books. From time to time this body has published and revised lists of works forbidden to all Catholics. A separate *Index* was also established which pointed out all the passages which should be deleted or corrected in the works of science and literature. The efforts of the Church to censor the press seem to have been a failure as far as preventing scientific investigation or hindering the production of great literature, but it has undoubtedly had a tremendous influence on the thinking of the masses.

Having set its house in order by the measures just described, the Church began a vigorous offensive against the Protestants. During the last half of the sixteenth century the Church began to enforce the decrees of the Council of Trent concerning abuses in the inner life of the Church, won back much territory, and made many converts at the expense of the Protestants, and carried out vast missionary enterprises in Africa, the Far East, and America. The chief agencies of the Church in these achievements were the new religious orders, particularly the Society of Jesus.

Everywhere in Catholic Christendom the bishops set themselves to the task of reforming the clergy. They employed in this work the means especially recommended by the Council of Trent. They frequently visited the parishes, held regular meetings or synods of the clergy, and established seminaries in all the dioceses for the education of the clergy. By these measures they greatly improved the condition of the secular clergy.

Under the leadership of the Jesuits the Catholic attack on Protestantism made great progress. The first important gains at the expense of the Protestants were made in Bavaria. Following the letter of the Peace concluded at Augsburg in 1555, the Duke of Bavaria, in 1564, inaugurated the policy of excluding Protestants from his state, forced the University of Ingolstadt to accept the Tridentine Profession of Faith, and burned heretical books. Two Jesuits, Peter Canisius and a companion, served as professors at Ingolstadt for a time, and the education of the youth of the country was everywhere entrusted to the Society of Jesus. In adopting this policy the Bavarian ruler only imitated the policy followed by some of the Protestant princes.

The example of Bavaria was widely followed. The Margraviate of Baden, which the Duke of Bavaria was governing in the name of its young Margrave, was rewon for Catholicism shortly after the Duchy of Bavaria. Before the close of the century the Prince-Abbot of Fulda, the Archbishop of

Mainz, the Bishops of Würzburg and Paderborn, and the two Habsburg Archdukes ruling in Austria and in Carinthia, Carniola, and Styria had taken in their territories measures similar to those used in Bavaria. In each case the Jesuits powerfully seconded the efforts of the rulers. Everywhere they went the Jesuits led the reaction against the Protestants. As one of their most effective weapons, they established colleges in the large Catholic cities of Germany and in many points in Switzerland, The Netherlands, Bohemia, Hungary, and Poland, which became so famous that even many Protestant parents sent their children to them. Under the leadership of the Jesuits the Catholics regained considerable ground in Germany, Poland, and Hungary.

The Jesuits also made heroic efforts, in the reign of Queen Elizabeth, to win England for the Catholic cause. In 1580, thirteen priests, headed by Parsons and Campion, landed in England. Disguised as a gentleman, Campion traveled from place to place preaching to secret assemblies of Catholics. The English Government, however, which considered the acceptance of Roman Catholicism as disloyalty, captured and executed Campion and several of his companions on the charge of treason. Parliament then passed severe laws against the Jesuits and imposed heavy penalties for failure to conform outwardly to the Established Church of England. These measures had the effect of sharply dividing the Catholics in England from the Protestants. The Jesuits continued their activities, however, down into the Stuart period.

In the meantime the Jesuits and other religious orders had been carrying on a marvelous missionary campaign outside of Europe. Francis Xavier, the second recruit won by Loyola at Paris, was the first Jesuit missionary. Under the patronage of the Pope and the King of Portugal he went to India, where, beginning in 1542, he worked among both the Portuguese colonists and the natives of the country. Later he worked in the Malay Peninsula and in Japan. His labors resulted in the nominal conversion of hundreds of thousands of natives. Following his example, other missionaries went to China, India, Indo-China, Thibet, the Tartars north of the

THE CATHOLIC REFORMATION

Black Sea, and Abyssinia. Most of these early missionaries were men of marvelous character, but much of their work was superficial. Xavier learned only a few phrases of the native languages which he taught his hearers to repeat, and the missionaries spent hours in baptizing infants and the dying, in the belief that they were saving their souls for the Kingdom of Heaven. Two of the Jesuits laboring in India made such concessions to the spirit of caste that they brought on themselves the disapproval of other missionaries and of the Church. Many of the early converts, consequently, disappeared and much of the missionary work left no permanent trace.

The work of the missionaries in America was of a more enduring character. Everywhere the Franciscans, the Dominicans, and the Jesuits followed close in the footsteps of the Spanish conquerors, the Portuguese adventurers, and the French pioneers. Wherever they went they built churches and mission stations, and taught their religion by precept and example. At first the Spanish missionaries made little progress with the Indians on account of the cruelty of the conquerors, but after the abolition of Indian slavery, the Spanish missions began to prosper. With the help of the natives the missionary fathers built missions everywhere they went similar to those still to be seen in Texas, New Mexico, Arizona, and California. At first the wondering attention of the Indians was arrested by the vastness of the Christian edifices, the awe and mystery of the liturgy, and the self-sacrifice of the missionaries. Later, fragments of the Christian doctrine began to find lodgment in their hearts. The most remarkable achievement of the missionaries in America was the establishment of an independent Indian state in Paraguay. Colonies, known as "reductions," were formed among the Indians. There, separated from the Spaniards and guided by the fathers, the Indians lived lives that were increasingly civilized and Christianized. At the end of the seventeenth century, it is estimated that the Jesuit fathers had nearly 300,000 natives under their control in Paraguay. In Canada and the Mississippi Valley the French won the good will of the Indians from the start. The heroic achievements of Catholic fathers like Brébeuf, Jogues, and Marquette furnished Francis Parkman, the distinguished American historian, with materials for a veritable historical epic. The conquests made by these daring missionaries in the Far East and in America more than compensated the Church for the losses suffered at the hands of the Protestant reformers in Europe.

PHILIP II

The abdication by Charles V of his various crowns made his son, Philip II, ruler of the Emperor's Spanish, Italian, and Burgundian lands. In a dramatic scene at Brussels in 1555 Charles V handed over to his son the Free County of Burgundy and the seventeen provinces of The Netherlands. The latter had already been invested with the Duchy of Milan and the Kingdom of Naples, and in the following year he became ruler of Spain and its vast colonial possessions. As sovereign of the inexhaustible mines of Mexico and Peru, the great industrial and commercial centers of Italy and the Netherlands, and the magnificent infantry of Spain, Philip II was in a position to play a great rôle in the affairs of Europe.

Philip II was kingly in appearance and character. He had the manner and tastes, but not the appearance, of a Spaniard. He had large blue eyes and blond hair and beard. His steady gaze often unnerved those whom he was receiving. He invariably dressed with distinguished simplicity, in later life always in black. All with whom he came in intimate contact loved him. During his stay in England, after his marriage to Mary Tudor, he surprised all by his amiability. His letters show him sensible to the beauties of the world around him and interested in all that concerned his children and his servitors. The interior of his remarkable palace, the Escorial, still shows his extensive and profound knowledge of art. He had a very strongly marked strain of religious mysticism, an unlimited respect for the Church, and great zeal for its interests. He had a strong sense of duty and considered himself as merely the first servant of the State. In both life and death he was majestic and dignified.

THE CATHOLIC REFORMATION

The methods employed by Charles V and his son, as rulers, differed in many respects. The father was born at Ghent in The Netherlands, and had the international viewpoint. Philip II was born in Spain, and had the feelings and prejudices of his Spanish subjects. Charles V journeyed from country to country. Philip II seldom left the Spanish peninsula. Instead of wandering from city to city with a small retinue of officials, he made Madrid his permanent capital and created an elaborate bureaucracy. He passed a large part of his time in the Escorial, a palace built by his command on the slopes of the Guadarrama Mountains some distance northeast of Madrid to serve as a monastery, a royal residence, and a mausoleum for the sovereigns of Spain. From his own bare and modest apartment in this great edifice, Philip attempted to control every act of government. Early and late, throughout his life, he toiled at his self-appointed task, reading his orders and regulating everything. Matters were controlled from the Escorial, however, that should have been decided by subordinates, and Spanish officials lost weeks and months waiting for their slow and irresolute master to make his decisions. The very virtues of Philip were the cause of much of his ill-success.

The successor of Charles V applied his peculiar methods of government to two general tasks. In the Spanish peninsula he aimed at political and religious unity. In Europe he tried to be the champion of the Catholic Church. The first of these objects was achieved by the persecution and repression of Protestants and Moriscos, the annexation of Portugal, and the withdrawal of many of the privileges of the Kingdom of Aragon. The second led to the revolt of The Netherlands, war with England, and the Spanish intervention in the French Wars of Religion.

At the opening of the reign of Philip II several small groups of Protestants were discovered in Spain, Valladolid and Seville being their chief centers. This discovery aroused the Inquisition to new activity. It pitilessly punished and suppressed the Protestants. From that time on no one in the kingdom escaped the surveillance of the powerful institution.

Even men like the Archbishop of Toledo and Ignatius Loyola fell under its suspicion and were imprisoned by it. The King on one occasion sternly declared that he would bring wood to burn his own son, if his son were a heretic. In order to isolate his kingdom from heretical influences the King even recalled all of his subjects who were teaching and studying at foreign universities. By these measures Philip II saved Spain from Protestantism, but at the price of tremendous suffering on the part of the victims of the Inquisition, the intellectual stagnation of the country, and a popular odium from which Spain even yet has not wholly recovered.

This spirit of intolerance caused the revolt of the Moriscos, as the converts from the Moslem faith were called. They were as loyal, honorable, and industrious as any element in the Spanish state, but they refused to give up their racial and religious customs. Popular opinion was not yet ready to tolerate such religious differences. Stringent laws were passed, consequently, forbidding the use of Arabic, the wearing of the national costume, the taking of warm baths, and the employment of Arabic names by the Moriscos. The Inquisition was set up among them at Granada; their children were forced to attend Christian schools; and the whole race was subjected to a galling surveillance. The inevitable result of these measures was a rising of the Moriscos in 1568. Three years of barbarous warfare followed before the rebels were completely defeated. Many of them were killed; many were sold into slavery; and a minority were deported from Granada to other parts of Spain. Again the orthodoxy of Spain had been saved at a fearful price, for, by the ruin of the Moriscos, one of the foundations of Spanish prosperity was destroyed.

The annexation of Portugal, on the other hand, was one of the successes of Philip's long reign. It completed that political unification of the peninsula of which the sovereigns of Spain had long dreamed. The opportunity to seize Portugal came as a result of the dying out of all the legitimate, direct, male heirs to the Portuguese throne. Philip II seemed to have the best right of any of the claimants to the throne, but popular sentiment opposed the union of Spain and Portugal under his rule. Annexation was rightly felt to mean the incorporation of Portugal in the Spanish monarchy. The annexation, consequently, was carried out only by the use of military force, but after the defeat of the Portuguese national forces Philip was generally accepted by both the Cortes and the nation. Later events demonstrated, though, that Spain could neither hold Portugal nor defend its colonial empire, for within sixty years the Portuguese had regained their national freedom, and the Dutch had taken the place of the Portuguese in the Far East.

The last years of Philip's rule in Spain were disturbed by his contest with his former confidant and secretary, Antonio Perez. After having been only too useful a tool of the King, this unlucky official fell under the royal displeasure and fled to Aragon and its constitutional privileges for protection from the vengeance of Philip II. Perez finally escaped to France where he fabricated much of the propaganda against his former master which now passes for sober history, but Aragon was punished, by the loss of many of its political privileges, for the assistance extended to the King's former secretary through its laws and public opinion. This was an important step in the political unification of the peninsula and in the growth of the royal absolutism.

The foreign policy of Philip II was vitally connected with the history of The Netherlands, England, and France. The rôle played by Philip as the champion of orthodoxy in these three states can best be followed by tracing the history of each of these countries at this period.

THE REVOLT OF THE NETHERLANDS

The revolt of The Netherlands from the rule of Spain was the result of many causes. The grievances of the seventeen provinces, which had accumulated slowly during the reign of Charles V, caused an open revolt in the reign of his son. The nobles resented the giving of the highest offices of the state to foreigners. All classes opposed the presence of Spanish garrisons in the country. A proposed reorganization and reformation of the bishoprics also aroused much opposition, for the new regulations threatened to destroy many sinecures hitherto enjoyed by the nobles and gave the sovereign more votes in the Estates General and more authority over the clergy. The relentless persecution of the Protestants and the centralization of the government added to the popular feeling against Spain. Nevertheless, in spite of grave warnings concerning the danger of the policy he was pursuing, Philip II persisted until he drove the people of The Netherlands into open revolt.

The first organized resistance to the royal policy of repression came in 1566, when about two thousand prominent Catholic and Protestant nobles joined in a protest against the policy of Philip II. The merchants soon followed their example. The populace, however, carried matters to extremes. Calvinist mobs began to destroy the images, pictures, and other emblems of the Catholic religion. This violence did great damage to their cause. Many of the Catholic nobles refused to coöperate further with the movement, and Philip vowed to avenge God and his Church and sent the Duke of Alba to The Netherlands to carry out his policy. At the news of his appointment thousands emigrated to England and the Protestant regions of Germany, and even William, Prince of Orange, the future leader of the revolt, found it prudent to retire to his German estates for a time.

Immediately upon his arrival the Duke of Alba inaugurated a veritable reign of terror. Many nobles were seized and imprisoned, and two prominent members of the nobility were finally executed. A terrible Council of Troubles was created which the people justly named the "Council of Blood." Every one who had been connected with the political or religious opposition to Philip was denounced and hunted down by the dread tribunal. In one day five hundred persons were sentenced to death by it. A little later the Duke introduced a sales tax of five per cent on all exchanges of immovable property, and of ten per cent on all other sales. This meant ruin to the commerce and industry of the province. All classes protested at the policy of Alba. The butchers and bakers closed their shops; the merchants went on a strike rather than pay the tax; and even the Flemish bishops protested at the political and religious persecutions. The Duke and his royal master, however, remained deaf to every plea.

The early military efforts of William of Orange and his party were unsuccessful, but at sea the privateers authorized by the Prince did terrible damage. Finally in 1572 the "beggars," as the sailors manning the privateers were called, seized the port of Brill, in the Province of Zeeland. This was the signal for a general rising in five of the northern provinces of The Netherlands. From that time on the provinces of Holland and Zeeland, a region of islands and swampy coast one hundred miles long by thirty miles wide, were the base for all the military operations of the Prince of Orange.

In 1573, after he had done incalculable damage to The Netherlands and to the cause of Spain, the Duke of Alba was recalled. His successors — Requesens (1573–76) and Don Juan, the illegitimate half-brother of Philip (1576–78) — attempted to regain the revolted provinces by the introduction of more moderate policies, but their efforts came too late, and their negotiations failed. Their military operations, furthermore, were constantly hampered by the lack of money.

The chief interest of the period is the unsuccessful effort to organize all the seventeen provinces against Spain. In 1576 the deputies of the Catholic provinces met in Brussels simply as a measure of self-defense against the leaderless, unpaid, marauding Spanish troops, and opened up negotiations with the two Calvinist provinces of Holland and Zeeland. In the so-called "Pacification of Ghent" the two religious parties agreed upon the establishment of a general amnesty, the creation of an armed alliance for the expulsion of the Spaniards, the rehabilitation of those condemned by the "Council of Blood" and the restoration of their property, the recognition of the Prince of Orange as viceroy of the King, and the postponement of the settlement of the religious question until after the expulsion of the Spaniards. The mutual hatred of the Protestants and Catholics made a permanent union of the two religious parties impossible. The noble effort of the Estates General in 1578 to establish religious peace on the basis of religious toleration for all was ill received. The two religious parties were kept together, even for a time, only by their greater hatred of the Spaniard.

Conditions were favorable, therefore, for the policy of dividing the allies along religious lines, which was introduced in 1579 by the new representative of the King, Alexander Farnese, Duke of Parma. As a result of his skillful diplomacy the Catholics of Artois, Hainault, and the Catholic cities of Flanders soon separated themselves from the Estates General and formed the Union of Arras (1579). The new union provided for the maintenance of the provincial privileges of the members, the preservation of their Catholic faith as the sole religion, and the recognition of Philip as sovereign. The Protestants of Holland, Zeeland, Guelder, Utrecht, Groningen, and the Calvinist cities of Flanders and Brabant, thereupon formed a league known as the Union of Utrecht (1579). The military successes of the Duke of Parma then regained for Spain most of The Netherlands except Holland and Zeeland. Finally the Prince of Orange was assassinated at the instigation of Philip II (1584). The cause of the Dutch seemed lost, when the attention of the Duke of Parma was diverted to the war between Spain and England.

In their extremity the Dutch sought help from France and England, but they obtained no substantial assistance from either state. The final victory of the Dutch was due to their own efforts and to the leadership of John of Oldenbarnevelt and Maurice of Nassau, the latter being a son of the Prince of Orange. The former was the head and the latter the sword of the northern provinces. Within a few years the Dutch reconquered all the territory belonging to the seven northern provinces, firmly established the new republic of The United Netherlands, and made a substantial beginning toward the building up of a colonial empire, but the war dragged on until 1609, when it was terminated by a twelve years' truce, which practically recognized the independence of the United Provinces.

The truce left the seventeen provinces of The Netherlands divided into two distinct states. The ten southern provinces, devastated by marauding troops and decimated by war and emigration, were left under the control of Spain. They saved their Catholic orthodoxy at the price of their political liberty. The seven northern provinces, freed from the despotism of Spain and the intolerance of the Church, and enriched by the industry, the character, and the wealth of thousands of Calvinist immigrants driven out of the southern provinces, were ready to embark on a brilliant political and commercial career.

THE WAR BETWEEN ENGLAND AND SPAIN

Only the genuine desire of both the English Queen and the Spanish King to avoid war prevented the outbreak of hostilities between England and Spain immediately after the accession of Elizabeth to the throne of England in 1558. The English Queen and her advisers did not feel that their country was ready either politically or religiously for a war with the great Catholic power. Philip, on the other hand, hesitated to precipitate a war with England both on account of the strain it would impose on his overburdened finances and because of England's control of the sea route between Spain and The Netherlands. The struggle between Philip and Elizabeth, therefore, did not break out for nearly twenty years.

From the time of the accession of Elizabeth to the English throne, however, the probability of war steadily grew. Each sovereign gave aid and comfort to the enemies of the other as much as he dared. Elizabeth gave encouragement to the rival of Philip for the Portuguese throne, incited the people of The Netherlands to continue their revolt, and abetted the attacks of English seamen like Hawkins and Drake on the commerce and treasure ships of Spain. Philip, on his side, became increasingly involved in the Catholic plots against the throne of Elizabeth, which centered around Mary Stuart, the deposed Queen of Scotland.

War finally broke out between the two states in 1587 and lasted until the conclusion of peace in 1604. The most decisive and dramatic episode of the struggle was the defeat of the Spanish Armada in 1588. At great expense the Spanish sovereign gathered together and sent out from Spain a powerful expedition, which was to make a descent on England after taking on board the troops of the Duke of Parma stationed in The Netherlands. Although the preparations made by the Queen of England were inadequate and disgraceful, the great expedition failed, thanks to the incompetence of the Spanish admiral, the harassing attacks of the English seamen, and the destructiveness of a great storm encountered by the Armada. The chief results of the long war with England were the destruction of Spanish sea power and the further disruption of the finances of Spain.

THE WARS OF RELIGION IN FRANCE

The work of the Christian Humanists and the Calvinist ministers had divided the people of France into a Catholic and a Protestant party. Before 1559 only those moved by deep conviction joined the Protestant party. After that date large numbers of discontented nobles, who were actuated by political and personal motives, united with the party.

This transformation of the Calvinists into a political party is closely connected with the rise of the Guise family to power. One member of the family became leader of the military forces of the state; another became Cardinal of Lorraine and the real administrative head of the government; and their niece, Mary Stuart, Queen of Scotland and France, gained complete ascendancy over her weak young husband, Francis II (1559–60). The policies of the Guises soon created a great deal of opposition. They continued the policy of religious persecution followed by Henry II (1547–59) and carefully kept from power the closest relatives of the King, the Protestant King of Navarre, and his brother, the Count of Condé, who naturally felt that they had a better right to the offices of the state than the Guises. The King of Navarre and his brother became the leaders of those opposed to the rule of the Guises. These so-called "Malcontents" quickly saw the advantage of allying themselves to the powerful Protestant or Huguenot party and many of them turned over to Protestantism. Upon the death of Francis II, in 1560, his Queen returned to Scotland, and the Guise family lost control of the government. The chief result of their short period of power had been to divide France into two armed camps ready to plunge the country into civil war.

Upon the accession to the throne of the ten-year-old Charles IX (1560-74), the real power fell into the hands of his mother, Catherine de' Medici, who adopted the policy of playing off the Catholic and Protestant parties against each other for her personal advantage. One of her first acts was to stop religious persecutions and to authorize the holding of Protestant worship in certain places. Neither party understood or was satisfied with such a policy. Each party pillaged the property and murdered the adherents of the other party whenever a favorable occasion offered. Each really aimed at the extermination of the other.

The spirit animating the two parties is well illustrated by the famous Massacre of Saint Bartholomew (August 24, 1572). To frustrate the plans of Coligny, a trusted Protestant adviser of the King and his mother, the Catholic party persuaded Catherine de' Medici that Coligny was deceiving her. An unsuccessful attempt was then made to assassinate Coligny. To divert the anger of the young King from herself, his mother invented a story of a great Huguenot conspiracy, which brought the King over to the Catholic side. The Catholic leaders of Paris then arranged for the massacre of all the Huguenots who had gathered at Paris to witness the marriage of Henry, the Protestant King of Navarre, to the King's sister. The plot resulted in the death of hundreds of Huguenots at Paris and thousands in the provinces. To many of the Catholic leaders of Europe, however, the dreadful tragedy seemed merely a sign of the loyalty of France to the Church.

The civil war, which inevitably resulted from such a state of public opinion, broke out in 1562. The fighting went on almost continuously from that date until the termination of the war in 1595. The treaties of peace which were signed from time to time between the contending parties were really only temporary truces caused by fear of foreign intervention or the lack of funds to continue the struggle. The details of these wars are hardly important enough to be related in a work of this compass, but something ought to be said of the character of the fighting, the growth of the Protestants in organization, and the closing events of the struggle.

The armies of the time were small and composed mainly of mercenaries, especially German mercenaries. The fighting consisted of sieges, surprise attacks, and occasional pitched battles in the open field. Much of it was indecisive in nature. Throughout the war the country was terribly harassed by the undisciplined soldiers. The Catholics were aided by Philip II and by the Pope; the Protestants by Queen Elizabeth, the Prince of Orange, and the Protestant princes of Germany. The fortunes of England, France, The Netherlands, and Philip II were more or less interdependent. England, for example, was saved from invasion by the civil wars in France and the Dutch were preserved from Spanish rule by the diversion of the forces and resources of Philip to the Spanish Armada.

At each new peace the Protestants, though beaten in the actual fighting, were conceded, in the hope of obtaining peace for France, either the rights they already enjoyed or new privileges. In 1563 they were granted the right of Protestant worship in every bailiwick and in the houses of the nobles. In 1571 they were given freedom of worship in the entire kingdom, permission to fortify four cities as places of refuge and the right to hold any public office. After the treaty of peace of 1574 the Protestants organized a Protestant Union composed of cities which had practically usurped their autonomy. The representatives of the cities were to meet in local assemblies (representing the *généralités*) and representatives of the local bodies were to be united into a sort of Protestant Estates General. Thus there was gradually created within the state a federal republic of urban communities dominated by the Protestant nobles.

THE CATHOLIC REFORMATION

The formation of the Protestant Union was the signal for the organization of other federations. By 1585 the people of France were really divided into three leagues. In the south of France Henry of Navarre headed a Protestant league. In the North the Duke of Guise headed a Catholic league which was largely financed by Philip II of Spain. The people of Paris formed a third league that was both Catholic and democratic. By 1588 the two Catholic leagues had taken away from Henry III (1574–89) practically all his power. In revenge the King caused Henry, Duke of Guise, to be assassinated and allied himself with Henry of Navarre. The forces of the two kings seemed to be just on the point of taking Paris in 1589 when a fanatical Catholic assassinated Henry III. These two deeds of violence left Henry of Navarre, leader of the Protestants, the legal heir to the throne.

The next task of Henry of Navarre, henceforth known as Henry IV, was to conquer France and his capital in the face of the determined opposition of the Catholic League, the inhabitants of Paris, the Pope, and the money and soldiers of Philip II. He gained a number of important victories and once was only prevented from taking Paris by the forces of the Duke of Parma, but he was unable to bring the war to a decisive close. Four years of fighting convinced him that he must conciliate the religious prejudices of the majority of his subjects. In 1593, consequently, he renounced the Protestant faith and became a Catholic. After the King took this step the opposition rapidly disappeared. The leaders of the league were finally bought off one at a time. The war with Spain continued in The Netherlands and in the Free County of Burgundy, however, until Philip II, sick and about to die, caused the Treaty of Vervins to be negotiated in 1598. By the terms of this treaty everything was restored to the status established by the Treaty of Cateau-Cambrésis in 1559.

In victory, however, Henry did not forget his Protestant followers. In 1598 he issued in their behalf his famous Edict of Nantes. By this document the Protestants received certain religious, civil, military, and political rights. All persons possessing the right of high justice[1] or full military tenure were permitted to observe without restriction Protestant worship in their châteaux. Other gentlemen might worship according to the Protestant forms provided the number of persons present, other than members of the family, did not exceed thirty. The Protestants were permitted, furthermore, to have service in all villages and places of the kingdom where it had been established prior to 1597. The holding of Protestant services, however, was expressly forbidden at court and in the city of Paris. No distinction was to be made between Catholics and Protestants in respect to schools, hospitals, or public office. In addition, the Protestants were granted the right to hold general assemblies after the model of the Estates General and to have certain fortified places as cities of refuge. Their political privileges made the Protestants practically a state within a state, and put them in a position to hamper the work of the central government greatly during the ministry of Richelieu.

THE POSITION OF SPAIN AT THE CLOSE OF THE SIXTEENTH CENTURY

The sixteenth century ended with Spain defeated and half ruined. The Dutch had practically won their independence and had begun a brilliant commercial and colonial career at the expense of Spain. In England and France the plans of Philip II had failed completely. France was on the verge of assuming the place in international affairs which Spain had held in the sixteenth century.

The economic ruin of Spain was the result of the long wars of Charles V and his son and of the faulty economic policies of the Spanish Government. The wars of Philip II and his father involved tremendous expenditure. As Italy and Aragon contributed little or nothing to the treasury for thirty years, the burden of taxation fell with crushing weight on the people of Castile. Philip spent his revenue long before he

[1] The right of high justice gave a noble the right to inflict capital punishment in his court.

received it. The Spanish Government neither understood nor heeded the economic needs of the country. Agriculture was sacrificed in many places to the interests of the wandering sheep raisers (the *mesta*), who kept a vast area barren in order to have a highway for their sheep between the pastures of Northern and Southern Spain. A sales tax of ten per cent and a network of customs lines stifled commerce. The persecution of the Moriscos cost Spain a million, possibly, of its most industrious and skillful inhabitants. By attempting to monopolize the trade with the colonies, finally, the Government prevented the development of a normal colonial commerce. Consequently, the end of the century found Spain bankrupt and miserable.

In the first half of the sixteenth century Luther, Zwingli, Calvin, and their followers took the offensive against the medieval Church. In the second half of the century the forces of Catholic Europe took the aggressive against the enemies of the Church. Their weapons were the new religious orders, the Inquisition, the censorship of books, and the military forces of Philip II of Spain. Their attacks achieved a large measure of success. In Spain, Italy, the ten southern provinces of The Netherlands, and the hereditary lands of the Habsburgs ecclesiastical abuses were done away with and Protestantism was stamped out. In Germany and Poland much ground was regained. In France, England, and the seven northern provinces of The Netherlands, however, the Catholic forces were unable to suppress Protestantism.

REFERENCES

THE INQUISITION
  T. M. Lindsay, *A History of the Reformation*, vol. II, pp. 597–602.
  P. Smith, *Age of the Reformation*, pp. 411–17.
  Catholic Encyclopedia. Article: "Inquisition."
  H. C. Lea, *A History of the Inquisition of Spain*.
  E. Vacandard, *The Inquisition*.

THE JESUITS
  L. Haeusser, *The Period of the Reformation*, chapter XX.
  E. M. Hulme, *Renaissance and Reformation*, chapter XXI.
  T. M. Lindsay, *A History of the Reformation*, vol. II, bk. VI, chapter IV.
  P. Smith, *Age of the Reformation*, pp. 396–411.

Catholic Encyclopedia. Article: "Society of Jesus."
T. J. Campbell, *History of the Society of Jesus.*
S. H. Rose, *Loyola and the Jesuits.*
H. D. Sedgwick, *Ignatius Loyola.*

THE COUNCIL OF TRENT
E. M. Hulme, *Renaissance and Reformation,* chapter XXII.
T. M. Lindsay, *A History of the Reformation,* vol. II, bk. VI, chapter V.
P. Smith, *Age of the Reformation,* pp. 388–96.
Catholic Encyclopedia. Article: "Council of Trent."
J. Waterford, *The Canons and Decrees of the Council of Trent.*

THE INDEX
T. M. Lindsay, *A History of the Reformation,* vol. II, pp. 602–06.
P. Smith, *Age of the Reformation,* pp. 417–24.
J. Hastings, *Encyclopedia of Religion and Ethics.* Article: "Index."
Bettens, *The Roman Index of Forbidden Books.*
G. H. Putnam, *The Censorship of the Church of Rome and its Influence upon the Production and Distribution of Literature.*

THE REFORMATION IN SPAIN
T. M. Lindsay, *A History of the Reformation,* vol. II, bk. VI, chapter II.

THE REFORMATION IN ITALY
G. P. Fisher, *History of the Reformation,* pp. 385–97.
T. M. Lindsay, *A History of the Reformation,* vol. II, bk. VI, chapter III.

PHILIP II
Cambridge Modern History, vol. III, chapter XV.
C. E. Chapman, *History of Spain,* chapter XXIII.
M. A. S. Hume, *Spain, 1479–1788,* chapters II–V.
A. H. Johnson, *Europe in the Sixteenth Century,* chapter VII.
Histoire générale, vol. V, chapter II.

THE REVOLT OF THE NETHERLANDS
Cambridge Modern History, vol. III, chapters VI–VII, XIX.
L. Haeusser, *The Period of the Reformation,* chapters XXI–XXIV.
E. M. Hulme, *Renaissance and Reformation,* chapter XXV.
A. H. Johnson, *Europe in the Sixteenth Century,* chapter VIII.
J. E. Barker, *Rise and Decline of The Netherlands,* chapters V–VIII.
P. J. Blok, *History of the People of The Netherlands.*
Histoire générale, vol. V, chapter IV.
J. H. Robinson, *Readings in European History,* vol. II, pp. 171–79.

WILLIAM OF ORANGE
Ruth Putnam, *William the Silent.*
F. Harrison, *William the Silent.*

WARS OF RELIGION IN FRANCE
G. B. Adams, *Growth of the French Nation,* chapter XI.
Cambridge Modern History, vol. III, chapters I, XX.
A. J. Grant, *The French Monarchy, 1483–1789,* vol. I, chapters III–VI.
E. M. Hulme, *Renaissance and Reformation,* chapter XXVI.

L. Haeusser, *The Period of the Reformation*, chapters XXV–XXIX.
W. H. Hudson, *France*, bk. III, chapter X.
A. H. Johnson, *Europe in the Sixteenth Century*, chapter IX.
G. W. Kitchin, *History of France*, vol. II, bk. III, pt. II.
J. R. Moreton Macdonald, *A History of France*, vol. II, chapter XX.
A. Tilley, *Modern France*, pp. 21–31.
E. Armstrong, *The French Wars of Religion*.
J. W. Thompson, *The Wars of Religion in France*.
Histoire générale, vol. V, chapter III.

SOURCES ON THE WARS OF RELIGION IN FRANCE
Translations and Reprints, vol. II, no. III, pp. 16–32.
J. H. Robinson, *Readings in European History*, vol. II, pp. 179–85.

MAPS
Europe about 1560. W. R. Shepherd, *Historical Atlas*, pp. 118–19.

CHAPTER VI

DUTCH COLONIAL AND COMMERCIAL SUPREMACY, THE THIRTY YEARS' WAR, AND THE BEGINNING OF FRENCH ASCENDANCY

THE first six decades of the seventeenth century witnessed many important changes in Europe. The Dutch, freed from the restrictions of Spanish rule and prevented by Philip II from continuing the distribution of Portuguese colonial products from the port of Lisbon, entered after 1580 into direct competition with Spain and Portugal overseas and completely supplanted the Portuguese in the Malay Archipelago. During the same period the French monarchy, under the guidance of Henry IV, Richelieu, and Mazarin, became absolute at home and predominant in Europe, while Germany was being ruined by thirty years of civil war, and foreign intervention.

THE PERIOD OF DUTCH COLONIAL AND COMMERCIAL SUPREMACY

The geography of The Netherlands fitted its people to play an important commercial rôle. Their location at the mouths of the Rhine, the Meuse, and the Scheldt insured them easy access to the interior of Europe, and made the Low Countries the natural points of exchange between the Continent and England and between Northern and Southern Europe. The number and quality of their harbors also furnished the inhabitants unrivaled opportunities for fishing and trade.

Late in the Middle Ages the people of The Netherlands began to take advantage of this situation. The sailor folk of The Netherlands profited from a sudden migration of the herring from the Baltic to the North Sea. The Dutch became the chief distributors of the herring and invented a method for preserving them which gave the people of the northern Netherlands the markets of Europe. The growth of the fisheries led to the development of a merchant marine. Upon the discovery of the sea route to India the Dutch became the chief distributors of the Portuguese colonial products to the countries of Northern Europe. By the middle of the seventeenth century the Dutch carried the greater part of the trade of Western Europe.

In the closing years of the sixteenth century Philip II shut off the Dutch from this important distributing trade. In 1580 he annexed the Kingdom of Portugal to Spain and closed the port of Lisbon to his Dutch subjects who had been in open revolt against his authority since 1567. This action drove the Dutch to attempt to reach the East Indies for themselves. They made their first voyage in 1595, and by 1601 fifteen Dutch fleets, comprising in all sixty-five ships, had made the voyage to Asia.

The Dutch merchants, though, found that they were unable to protect themselves in those distant waters, and they competed with the natives, the Portuguese, and each other, in a manner which threatened to destroy the profits of the Eastern trade by raising prices in Asia and lowering them in Europe. As a remedy for this situation, the Dutch organized in 1602 an East India Company to perform the functions of government in the East, to carry on the struggles with Spain and Portugal, and to regulate trade. The Dutch merchants aimed to build a Dutch commercial monopoly in the Eastern hemisphere on the ruins of the former Portuguese monopoly. The Dutch authorities authorized the Company to perform in the East, between the Cape of Good Hope and the Straits of Magellan, practically all the functions of an independent government and encouraged all the citizens of the United Provinces to become shareholders in the Company.

The Company immediately set to work at the task of obtaining control of the areas in the Malay Archipelago which produced cloves and nutmegs. It attacked the fleets and trading posts of the Portuguese, and as early as 1603, it began settlements at Banda, one of the principal centers for nutmegs, and at Ternate, an important center for cloves. By 1611 it was established in Java. In 1641 the Company captured the strategic post of Malacca and in 1658 it obtained possession of the Island of Ceylon, a center for pepper and cinnamon. In 1652 the Dutch started a settlement at the Cape of Good Hope, an important port of call for water and provisions on the long voyage from Europe. While the Dutch were making conquests in the Malay Archipelago they were also opening up trading relations with China and Japan. These successes gave them the commercial supremacy they sought, and left the Portuguese but a few remnants of their former empire in the East.

The success of the Dutch East India Company led, in 1621, to the organization of the Dutch West India Company. It was founded as a war measure against Spain, with whom the Dutch had resumed the war at the expiration of the twelve years' truce signed in 1609, for the purposes of regulating and protecting the contraband trade they were carrying on with the American and African possessions of Spain and Portugal. For a long time the new Company derived its principal revenues from plundering the trading vessels and treasure ships of Spain, but it made some effort to found commercial colonies in both North and South America.

As early as 1609 the discoveries of Henry Hudson had called the attention of the Dutch to the territory around the Hudson River and from 1610 on the Dutch fur traders frequented the region. About 1623 the Dutch made a settlement on Manhattan Island which grew, in the course of the years, into the present city of New York. Throughout the period of Dutch rule, however, fur trading remained the main industry and agriculture prospered little. After 1629 the Dutch authorities made an effort to promote emigration to the colony by the establishment of the patroon system. To every person who brought over fifty families at his own expense, the Dutch Government granted a large tract of land with the title of patroon. This title conferred on the holder extensive civil and judicial authority and certain trading privileges. In 1664, as a result of the second Anglo-Dutch War, this rather weak colony fell into the hands of the English.

The Dutch attempts at colonization in South America met with a somewhat similar fate. In 1630 they succeeded in getting a foothold in the region of Pernambuco. Between 1636 and 1644 they widened their conquests until they included most of the northern coast of Brazil, but an insurrection against their rule broke out in 1645 which finally led, in 1654, to their complete expulsion. They continued to maintain themselves, though, in Dutch Guiana (Surinam) and on several islands along the coast which were situated advantageously for conducting a smuggling trade with South America.

During the first half of the seventeenth century the Dutch held as important a place in the commerce of Europe as in the trade overseas. In 1640 nearly one half of the ships passing into the Baltic were Dutch and thirty or forty Dutch ships went every year to Archangel, at that time the chief port of Russia. The Dutch almost monopolized, likewise, the trade between Spain and the North of Europe. Their commercial success was due in part to the preoccupation of England and France with other matters. The English were in the midst of the great struggle between the first two Stuart Kings and Parliament over the place of Parliament in the government. The French Government was centering its attention on establishing the absolutism of the King at home and the political supremacy of France in Europe.

In the latter half of the century the Dutch found it increasingly difficult to maintain their predominant position in the struggle for colonies and commerce, because they were forced to withstand simultaneous attacks on their supremacy by the French and the English. The English fought three Anglo-Dutch wars and adopted the Trade and Navigation Acts[1] in their efforts to overthrow the Dutch commercial monopoly. As a result of these attacks the Dutch were driven out of India in the East and lost their position as the chief carriers of English commerce in Europe. During the reign of Louis XIV, the French followed a policy similar to that of the English. The war of Louis XIV against the Dutch and the protective policy followed by Colbert were directed in part

[1] These acts are described in Chapter XIV.

against the commercial supremacy of the United Provinces. As a result of these simultaneous attacks of the English and the French the Dutch were losing their important position in commerce by the end of the seventeenth century and France and England were becoming the chief rivals in the struggle between the powers of Europe for colonial and commercial supremacy.

HENRY IV AND RICHELIEU

In 1598 the Treaty of Vervins and the Edict of Nantes finally gave France the peace it so sorely needed. The ending of civil and foreign war and the establishment of religious peace enabled its rulers to set to work at the task of restoring the country. For the next six decades France was fortunate in having successively as its rulers, a great king, Henry IV, and two able ministers, Richelieu and Mazarin. As a result of their work the monarchy became absolute in France and the French sovereigns became dominant in Europe.

Henry IV continued to rule France until he was assassinated in 1610. As leader of the Protestant party he had shown himself intrepid and clear-sighted in battle and tactful and conciliatory in dealing with opponents. As King of united France he showed himself to be gay and pleasure-loving in temperament, amiable and kindly toward his subjects, and firm and forceful as an administrator. His personality and his achievements in the work of restoring France have made him one of the popular figures in French history.

In 1598 France needed the services of a great king. Three and a half decades of civil war had left the state bankrupt and half ruined. As a result of the excesses of the soldiers, the executions and bloodshed, the emigration of Protestants, and the general misery, population had ceased to increase or had actually declined. In the country districts the farm animals had been killed off, the peasants were unable to plough the fields, the nobles had degenerated into leaders of pillaging bands of outlaws, and the peasants had become crafty, uncivil, and savage. Although better protected than the open country, many of the cities had suffered from pillage and exactions. The sea was infested with pirates and the land routes with marauding groups of disbanded mercenaries. Manufactures and commerce were at a standstill. The administrative machinery and the authority of the central government had been destroyed. The royal domains were mortgaged; the treasury, empty; and the State, bankrupt. Henry IV and his subordinates set themselves to the task of remedying these conditions.

As soon as he could, the King attacked the problem of repressing disorder. As early as 1597 the provincial governors and other administrative officers received orders to suppress the irregular bands which were harassing the open country and the thieves who were swarming in the streets of the cities. In the following year the Government prohibited the bearing of firearms. In the succeeding years the authorities caught and hanged many of the outlaws and vigorously pursued and destroyed the irregular bands.

The reforming of the finances of the kingdom was largely the work of the Duke of Sully. During the Wars of Religion he had attracted the attention of the King by his fidelity, courage, and administrative ability. His success in finding money for the King led to his appointment, in 1598, as sole superintendent of finance. Later he had many other administrative posts assigned to him. Sully's greatness as minister of finance lay in his success in administering the system he found in existence. He did nothing to remedy the fundamental injustice of the French financial system with its discrimination between classes and between regions. His principal achievements as superintendent of finance were the reduction of the public debt, the redemption of the royal domain, the creation of a surplus, and the lightening of the burdens of agriculture. He cut down the public debt a third, reduced the amount of the *taille* (a land tax on the peasants in some parts of France and a personal tax based on income in other parts of the country) and divided it more equitably, required the financial officials to observe the ordinary rules of bookkeeping in their accounts, and made the budget yield an average yearly surplus between 1600 and 1610 of one million livres. Under Sully, furthermore, the treasury ceased to be despoiled by royal mistresses, nobles, and courtiers. These measures furnished the King the means to make himself obeyed.

The reign of Henry IV is marked, too, by notable efforts to improve agriculture, industry and commerce. Something was done to relieve the peasants of their heavy burdens. The peasants, and, in consequence, agriculture were aided by the restoration of order and the reduction of the *taille*. The nobles were forbidden to hunt in the fields of growing grain or in the ripening vineyards. A serious effort was made also to introduce the culture of silk around Lyons and in the central part of France where it had never been established. In the neighborhood of Bordeaux a beginning was made in the draining of the swamps and low-lying lands. The introduction of new manufactures, such as silk, pottery, and glassware, was encouraged by the granting of funds and privileges to foreigners who settled in the country. Industry was favored much more, however, by the restoration of order. Commerce was encouraged by the building of roads, the repair of bridges, the digging of canals, and the conclusion of commercial treaties with foreign nations.

Simultaneously with the improvement in the administration and the restoration of the economic life of the country, there occurred a revival of the power of the central government and a development toward absolutism. The personality of the sovereign, the restoration of order, the improvement in the financial situation, and the revival of the economic life of the country, all contributed toward making such a development possible. The King removed the causes of discontent by his measures and at the same time won the hearts of his subjects by his personal qualities. He found little difficulty, consequently, in strengthening his position. As the reign progressed, the King deprived the governors of the provinces of many of their powers and destroyed the independence of many of the cities by taking from them the right to elect their own officials, by manipulating the municipal elections, and by taking away their civil and criminal jurisdiction. He also restricted the freedom of the French parlements[1] by similar measures. The tendency of these policies was to make France an instrument guided solely by the will of the sovereign.

In the reign of Henry IV two important steps were taken, also, in that steady march of the French boundaries toward the natural frontier of France which has been one of the striking movements of modern history. The accession of Henry IV opened the way for the incorporation of Navarre into the kingdom of France. A war with the Duke of Savoy caused the cession, in 1601, of the four small districts (Bresse, Bugey, Valromey, and Gex) which occupied the region just north of the Rhone River lying between the Saône and the Alps. Thus the boundaries of France reached the Pyrenees at another point on the south and the Alps at a new point on the east.

In 1610 Henry IV was assassinated. This left Louis XIII (1610–43), a boy of nine years, as nominal King of France and made necessary a regency. Through the efforts of some of the nobles and the action of the Parlement of Paris, Marie de' Medici, the mother of the new King, was appointed Regent. She showed little talent for government. During the seven years she was in power the country was a prey to disorder, corruption, and anarchy. Factions of nobles on several occasions openly rebelled against her government and in a vain effort to purchase the adherence of the great lords, she squandered the surplus so painfully amassed by Sully. The fall of the Queen from power as a result of a palace revolution brought a change in the powers behind the throne without changing essentially the conditions in the country. Not until the rise of Cardinal Richelieu to office in 1624 did France find a ruler capable of really governing the State and of continuing the policies inaugurated by Henry IV.

Richelieu rose to power in France by the means usually employed in the seventeenth century. At the early age of twenty-two the influence of his family obtained for him the

[1] Important courts of law in France.

comparatively poor bishopric of Luçon. After 1610 he paid assiduous court to Marie de' Medici and through her influence finally procured a cardinalate in the Church and the chief place in the Royal Council. Once he had the opportunity to display his ability his unusual talents kept him in office. His sovereign, Louis XIII, was not a great king, but he had the wisdom to recognize the greatness of his minister and the firmness to support Richelieu and his policies for eighteen years against the opposition of innumerable enemies.

The new minister was recognized, even in his own day, as an extraordinary individual. Though he was of no great stature and suffered from ill health all his life, he made a striking figure dressed in the red robes of a cardinal. He possessed an inflexible will, indomitable courage, quick decision, and a clear sharp eye for the present and immediate future. He put these qualities completely at the service of his country. His aim was to make his king absolute in France and the French monarchy predominant in Europe.

Richelieu immediately recognized that the Huguenots and the nobles were the principal obstacles to the absolutism of the King in France. The Huguenots put the interests of their religion and their faction above the interests of their country. The nobles often sacrificed the best interests of their country on the most frivolous pretexts. Consequently Richelieu set himself to the task of making both the Huguenots and the nobles obedient and docile subjects.

The conduct of the Huguenots in 1625 called the attention of the Cardinal to the danger arising from the political and military privileges granted to the French Protestants by the Edict of Nantes. While he was engaged in an important struggle in Italy the Protestant party rose in revolt and forced him to withdraw from the foreign war. Therefore, when two years later the Protestants of La Rochelle and the South of France made common cause with the English, who were at war with the French Government, the Cardinal determined to settle the Huguenot question once for all. He collected troops to the number of 25,000 for the siege of La Rochelle, encircled the city with troops, and closed the mouth of the harbor by an artificial dike built under immense difficulties for the purpose of preventing the English from bringing food and troops to the besieged. The siege lasted for months. Finally, after several efforts on the part of the English to relieve the city had failed and its population had been reduced by 16,000, as a result of hunger and pestilence, the city surrendered. During the next few months the remaining Protestant forces were defeated and disarmed. By these measures the power of the Huguenots was broken.

The Cardinal used his victory with extraordinary moderation. He destroyed only the political power of the Protestant party. He conceded to them all the religious and civil privileges granted by the Edict of Nantes and protected them against their enemies. Such discrimination as the Protestants suffered from, thenceforth, came from the local authorities and not from the central government. The Huguenots merely lost the power to interfere with the carrying out of the foreign policies of Richelieu.

The crushing of the nobles was a longer task. As early as 1626 the Cardinal attacked the custom of dueling and the practice of the nobles of maintaining private castles. Dueling was costing the lives of several thousand gentlemen every year and was the cause of much disorder. The fortified castles in the interior of the country formed natural centers of sedition and oppression. Although a few of the more notorious duelists were executed, the legislation against dueling had little effect until the custom died out as a result of changing fashions. The importance of the tearing down of the private castles in the interior of the country has been greatly overrated. Their destruction was chiefly significant as a sign of the new spirit actuating the Government. Gunpowder was already fast making the castles useless as a protection against the Government.

Far more important in destroying the spirit of faction among the nobles was the stern punishment of every act of insubordination. Every conspiracy was ruthlessly put down; every important conspirator was remorselessly punished. The inexorable Cardinal spared neither high nor low.

During his period of power Richelieu caused five dukes, four counts, a marshal of France, and many persons of inferior rank to perish on the scaffold, and drove the brother and the mother of the King into exile. This destructive work of the great minister bore fruit, however, in later reigns. After the time of Richelieu France experienced only one serious rising of the nobles, the movement known as the Fronde.

Richelieu was a politician and an administrator rather than a legislator. He was not an innovator, and left little mark on the institutions of France. The general effort of his rule, however, was to strengthen the royal power and to weaken every institution capable of offering opposition to the absolutism of the King. He completely muzzled public opinion and the nascent public press, never summoned the Estates General, and greatly restricted the power of the noble governors in the provinces by transferring their functions to officials recruited from the middle class who were more dependent on the Government. He relied a great deal on special commissioners to whom he delegated wide powers of administration. After his death these officials became established permanently in the different administrative districts of France (the *généralités*) and were known as "intendants." In time they became the most powerful representatives of the royal government. Richelieu also strictly limited the parlements to their judicial functions and rigorously repressed their tendency to obstruct the political action of the central government. In the provinces which retained some degree of local government, he largely destroyed the power of the Provincial Estates to thwart the will of the central government, and, by threatening to do away with their provincial privileges entirely, he limited the Provincial Estates to the function of dividing the burden of taxation among the local districts. He did absolutely nothing, on the other hand, to remedy the striking injustices of the French administrative system or to relieve the tremendous burdens of the peasants.

The greatest achievements of Richelieu were really in the realm of diplomacy. Although he did not live to witness the triumph of his policies, France, at the time of his death in 1642, was on the point of assuming the first place among the Powers of Europe, and both the Spanish and the Austrian Habsburgs were about to be humbled by the armies of France. The story of the humiliation of the Habsburgs, however, is a part of the history of the Thirty Years' War.

THE THIRTY YEARS' WAR

The Peace of Augsburg, which was signed by the Protestant and Catholic parties in 1555, merely gave Germany a temporary respite from civil war. It failed to allay the belligerent spirit of the religious factions and did little to remove the fundamental causes of strife. Surrounded by Catholics in the Southern Netherlands, the ecclesiastical states of the Rhine, Bavaria, and Austria, and afforded no legal protection by the Treaty of Augsburg, the Calvinists of Southern Germany were alarmed for their safety. The Catholics, reinvigorated by the Catholic reformation, were becoming aggressive, and were resenting more and more the continued seizure of Church property by the Protestants. The resulting tension led to innumerable incidents which inflamed public opinion, and to the organization of both the religious parties. In 1608 the Protestants of Southern Germany organized the Protestant Union, headed by the Elector of the Palatinate. In the following year the Catholics formed the League, led by Maximilian, Duke of Bavaria. Only the Lutheran princes of Northern Germany remained passive and indifferent. Divided, as it was, into two armed camps, Germany inevitably drifted toward civil war.

Events in Bohemia, where the religious situation had long had a disturbing influence on political conditions, finally precipitated a conflict in 1618. The Bohemian reformer, John Huss, had left behind him two groups of followers: a small group known as the "Bohemian Brethren," who separated entirely from the Church; and a larger group, called the "Calixtines," who had been regained by the Church only at the price of important concessions, which permitted the laity to partake of both the bread and the wine in communion. As a result of the similarity of the principles of Huss and Luther, Bohemia had proved fertile ground for the doctrines of Luther, most of the nobles becoming Lutherans. From the days of Luther on, there were constant disputes between the Habsburg rulers of Bohemia, who were Catholics, and their Protestant subjects. The rulers were alternately harsh and lenient. The nobles coerced the Catholic communicants among their peasant tenants on the one hand and, on the other, extorted for themselves a royal charter (1609), which granted religious toleration to persons living on the royal domains or on the ecclesiastical lands. This charter, however, was only the cause of endless episodes which embittered the relations of the religious factions. Two typical incidents, which were the immediate causes of the war, were the closing of one Protestant church and the demolition of another by order of the Archbishop of Prague.

The action of the Archbishop led to an assembly of Protestant nobles at Prague. After some discussion several hundred of the nobles rushed to the royal castle and hurled two detested regents of the Habsburgs, and a secretary, through the castle window to a moat a hundred feet below. As though by a miracle the royal representatives escaped with their lives, but this impulsive action of the incapable Protestant nobles plunged Germany into the civil struggle known as the Thirty Years' War.

The nobles and their leaders probably planned to throw off the rule of the Habsburgs and to reëstablish Bohemia as an independent state ruled by themselves under the nominal sovereignty of some puppet king, but they possessed neither the statesmanship nor the patriotism to carry through their program. They showed none of the spirit of the Dutch or the Swiss. Before precipitating the struggle they took no steps to secure the alliance of possible allies. After it began the Bohemian Diet actually dispersed without providing the money to pay for the maintenance of the troops which it had voted to raise. Its members seem to have thought about little except the fruits of victory.

The resources of the Emperor were so slender, however,

that at first it looked as if the Bohemian revolution might succeed. The Emperor had only an empty treasury, one Spanish general, and 1400 troops. During the first year of the revolt the rebels practically cleared Bohemia of the imperial forces and pressed up to the very gates of Vienna. At this point the arrival of Spanish and imperial troops stopped the victorious advance of the Protestant forces.

Both sides then turned to Germany for aid. In the vain hope that he might bring them the assistance of the Protestant Union organized in 1608, the Bohemians chose as king Frederick V, the Calvinist Elector of the Palatinate and son-in-law of James I of England. The Emperor obtained the help of the Lutheran Elector of Saxony and the Catholic League. The head of the League, Maximilian of Bavaria, stipulated, nevertheless, that the electorate of the Count Palatine of the Rhine should be transferred to himself, as a reward for his services, and that Upper Austria should be occupied by his troops as security for his expenses. The war thus broadened out from Bohemia to Germany.

In the ensuing campaign of 1620 the new allies of the Emperor made short work of the Bohemian revolt. Tilly, the general of the League, soon overran most of Bohemia, and the Elector of Saxony quickly subdued Silesia for the Emperor. The decisive battle of the campaign was fought at the White Mountain just outside of Prague. The Protestant forces proved to be no match for the veterans of the League. Frederick had brought his new subjects no substantial help and many of them were discontented with their new ruler because of his Calvinist tendencies. Everything was in disorder. In consequence the Bohemian troops quickly fled in panic and the Catholic forces took possession of the whole country.

The victory of White Mountain opened the way for the destruction of Bohemian independence and the suppression of the Protestant religion in Bohemia. The victorious Catholics, executed, imprisoned, or drove into exile the Bohemian nobility, and confiscated three fourths of their land. Catholic adventurers from Spain, Italy, and Germany, who became passive tools of the Habsburg despotism, then replaced the old nobility. The victors also transformed the Kingdom of Bohemia into a simple administrative district of the Habsburg state, abolished religious toleration, recalled the royal charter of 1609, banished the Protestant clergy, flooded the country with monks and Jesuits, and inflicted terrible persecutions on the Protestant laity to force their conversion to the Catholic faith. Only in Silesia and Lusatia, where the Lutheran Elector of Saxony had conceded rather liberal terms to the defeated Protestants in the name of the Emperor, did the Protestants manage to maintain their religion or any of their old rights. The Bohemians did not recover the political independence lost at the battle of the White Mountain until the crumbling of Austria-Hungary during the recent World War opened the way for the emergence of the new state of Czecho-Slovakia.

Upon the subjugation of Bohemia, the Upper and Lower Palatinate, the hereditary possessions of the defeated King of Bohemia, became the center of the military operations for two years. Little by little the forces of Spain and the League subjugated both territories. The Elector of the Palatinate was punished by the transfer of his electoral title and the Upper Palatinate to Maximilian of Bavaria. The Upper Palatinate was then subjected to treatment similar to that which Bohemia had received. Only in the Northern Netherlands, where the twelve years' truce of 1609 with Spain had expired, and in a few scattered districts in Germany were any troops still in arms against the Catholics.

Just when the war seemed on the point of ending for lack of fuel to feed the flames the struggle entered a new phase. Some of the Protestant princes in the region north and west of Brandenburg became alarmed for the safety of the Church lands which they had seized, and a little later (1625) Christian IV of Denmark entered the war for a similar reason. The Danish sovereign had obtained the bishopric of Verden and the eventual succession to the archbishopric of Bremen for one of his sons. In addition, James I of England, who was interested in the fate of his son-in-law, Frederick V, the exiled ruler of the Palatinate, held out the inducement of a substantial subsidy for the military intervention of Denmark in behalf of the Protestants of Germany. For a moment it seemed as if the advantage in resources and men was at last to swing to the side of the Protestants, but the failure of the promised English subsidies to arrive and the appearance of Wallenstein on the scene again swung the balance to the side of the Catholics.

Wallenstein was one of the most remarkable characters of modern times. He belonged to an impoverished branch of one of the great families of the Bohemian aristocracy. By 1625 his bravery had already won for him military rank; and a prudent marriage had brought him wealth and great estates. By extensive purchase of the confiscated estates he had become the greatest landholder in Bohemia. He now came forward with a proposal to raise an army of twenty thousand men for the Emperor and to maintain them without burden to the imperial treasury by a system of requisitions on the officials in the region where the troops were quartered. By the autumn of 1625 he was really at the head of fifty thousand men.

The subsequent campaign of 1626 was short and decisive. One Protestant army led by Christian IV marched up the Weser Valley against Tilly. Another led by Count Mansfeld pushed up the Elbe toward Wallenstein and made a long flanking march through Silesia and Hungary that ended in the dissolution of Mansfeld's army and the death of its leader. Meanwhile Tilly defeated the army of the Danish King at Lutter and drove it back toward Denmark. In 1629 Christian signed a treaty of peace at Lübeck at the price of surrendering Bremen and Verden. The defeat of the Danes left the Emperor supreme in Germany.

The Emperor threw away his opportunity, however, by issuing the Edict of Restitution (1629) and dismissing Wallenstein. By the first measure he deprived the Protestants at one stroke of two archbishoprics, twelve bishoprics, and about five hundred monastic properties, and restored to the Church all the property that had been seized by the Protestants.

This meant not alone the loss of much valuable property which the Protestants had had in their possession for three quarters of a century, but the reëstablishment of the Catholic religion in all the regained territories.

The Emperor dismissed Wallenstein as a result of the pressure of the League and of Maximilian of Bavaria. By 1629 Wallenstein was at the head of one hundred thousand men, scattered from the Baltic to Italy, and he refused to apply the Edict of Restitution in the territories under his control. The Catholic princes disliked his tolerance, objected to his requisitions, and mistrusted his designs. At the Diet of Regensburg in 1630, accordingly, they gave the Emperor the alternative of dismissing Wallenstein or of losing their support. Wallenstein was dismissed and the greater part of his army was disbanded just one month after Gustavus Adolphus and a Swedish army landed in Pomerania for the purpose of intervening in behalf of German Protestantism.

The interests of both his country and his religion led to the intervention of Gustavus Adolphus in the Thirty Years' War. History had almost inextricably entwined the causes of nationalism and Protestantism in Sweden. The dangers which threatened the Protestants of Northern Germany as a result of the Edict of Restitution and the predominance of Wallenstein, threatened Sweden as well, for after conquering Germany the Catholic Reformation would naturally spread to Sweden. At the same time the occupation of Northern Germany stood in the way of Swedish expansion. In the interest of Swedish security the Swedish sovereigns had been following a policy designed to turn the Baltic into a Swedish lake. During the preceding half-century all the lands on the eastern shore of the Baltic from Finland southward to Livonia had been conquered despite the opposition of Russia and Poland. The presence of imperial forces on the southern coast of the Baltic in Pomerania and Mecklenburg stood in the way of further Swedish expansion. The intervention of Gustavus Adolphus in the struggle in Germany was thus a mixture of religion and politics.

The new champion of German Protestantism brought to

DUTCH SUPREMACY AND FRENCH ASCENDANCY 157

the struggle qualities and resources such as Germany had not known before. In appearance Gustavus Adolphus was a typical Swede, and in action a veritable military hero. These qualities won for him the name of "Lion of the North." He brought to the struggle in Germany the military experience gained in twenty years of warfare with the Danes, the Russians, and the Poles, and a national army of seasoned veterans instead of the usual mercenary military force. Gustavus Adolphus and his army revolutionized the art of war. The Swedish commander mixed musketeers with his pikemen, abandoned the use of armor, lengthened the line of battle, made his battalions more mobile, increased the proportion of infantry, and enlarged the rôle of the artillery. Animated by patriotism, religious zeal, and enthusiasm for their great commander, the army of Gustavus Adolphus proved to be a powerful instrument of warfare.

At first the attitude of the Protestant princes of Germany greatly hindered the movements of the Swedish sovereign. His forces overran the provinces of Pomerania and Mecklenburg, but for a time the refusal of the Electors of Saxony and Brandenburg to abandon their neutrality blocked any further Swedish advance. Gustavus Adolphus brought the Elector of Brandenburg to reason by training his artillery on the city of Berlin, and the fall of Magdeburg, a great Protestant stronghold on the Elbe River, amid fearful scenes of pillage and conflagration, at last decided the wavering northern Protestants to risk something for their religion. About the same time an ultimatum of the Emperor to the Elector of Saxony had the unexpected effect of driving that ruler into alliance with the King of the Swedes.

While the German Protestants had been hesitating, substantial aid had come to the Swedes from France. Richelieu had long planned to raise the power of France by humbling the Habsburgs of Austria and Spain. Gustavus Adolphus now presented himself as a possible ally in carrying out this plan. After considerable negotiation, Richelieu and the Swedish King concluded a treaty of alliance (Treaty of Barwalde, 1631), in which Sweden agreed to maintain a force of thirty thousand foot soldiers and six thousand cavalry in return for a large French subsidy.

The conclusion of alliances with the German princes and with Richelieu paved the way for the remarkable campaign of Gustavus Adolphus which followed. The first decisive encounter of the new campaign took place at Breitenfeld (1631), near Leipsic. It resulted in a crushing defeat for the imperial troops commanded by Tilly, which demonstrated completely the superiority of the new Swedish tactics, and gave the Protestants possession of all Northern Germany. Gustavus Adolphus then turned his forces toward the Rhine. His march was little more than a military procession. His army overran the states in the valleys of the Main and the Middle Rhine, and then gained a victory at the Lech River which put Bavaria at the mercy of the Swedish forces and opened the way for an invasion of the hereditary territories of the Emperor.

In this crisis the Emperor recalled Wallenstein, who had been quietly waiting on his estates for some such turn of events. The latter stipulated terms which made him practically dictator of Germany. He demanded the recall of the Edict of Restitution and his own appointment to the sole command of the imperial troops. After months of preparation Wallenstein drove the Saxon allies of Gustavus Adolphus out of Bohemia and forced the Swedish commander to retrace his steps in order to prevent his line of communications from being severed. After much maneuvering for position the rival armies engaged in the decisive battle of Lützen (1632), a place not far from Breitenfeld. After hours of hand-to-hand struggle Wallenstein's army lost the battle, but the Protestants lost their incomparable leader. With the death of the Swedish King the war lost the last trace of moral or religious idealism.

Wallenstein did not long survive his great rival. His conduct subsequent to the battle of Lützen aroused the suspicions of the Emperor. Whether they were really justified is one of the enigmas of history, but the Emperor believed that Wallenstein was intriguing with the imperial enemies. Accordingly five of the great general's own officers were incited to assassinate him in the interest of the Emperor (February, 1634).

In spite of the passing of the old leaders the war dragged on in both Northern and Southern Germany. After two years of confused fighting a decisive battle occurred at Nördlingen (1634), which resulted in the flight or capture of an entire Protestant army and put the imperial and Spanish forces in control of all Southern Germany. Just as the battle of Breitenfeld had made Northern Germany Protestant, the battle of Nördlingen made Southern Germany Catholic. The diplomatic results of the victory were equally important. Saxony abandoned the side of the Swedes and signed with the Emperor the Peace of Prague (1635).

This treaty conceded to the Protestants permanent possession of all the Church property granted to them by the Peace of Augsburg in 1555 and undisputed possession for forty years of all Church property seized by them since 1552. The Elector of Saxony received for himself permanent possession of Lusatia, a province lying between Saxony and Silesia, and for his son the administration of the archbishopric of Magdeburg during his lifetime. The German princes with a few exceptions were invited to adhere to the treaty. As a result of this agreement only France and Sweden and three of the German princes were left to continue the war.

The defeat of Nördlingen and the defection of the German princes put Richelieu in a position where he had to act boldly if France were to draw the advantages he hoped for from the Thirty Years' War. The aim of his foreign policy was the territorial extension of France and the establishment of national security through the humbling of the Habsburgs. This had been his motive in subsidizing the Swedes since 1631, but subsidies were no longer enough. Direct intervention was necessary. In May, 1635, therefore, France declared war on Spain, which had intervened in the war on the Catholic side, with the province of Roussillon, the Free County of Burgundy, and the Spanish Netherlands as the immediate objects of the war.

At first the intervention of France had little effect on the struggle. Richelieu put into the field the enormous force, for that time, of one hundred and thirty-two thousand men, but neither the French troops nor their commanders were a match for the veterans of Spain. For several years they were outgeneraled and outfought in nearly every encounter. It was not until chance gave Richelieu control of the mercenary force of Bernard of Saxe-Weimar, a famous chieftain of the period, that the French began to win victories. In 1640 the French forces completed the conquest of Alsace. In the same year Catalonia and Portugal revolted from Spain. The revolt of the Catalans led to the conquest and occupation of Roussillon by the French; that of the Portuguese to the independence of Portugal. The Swedes in the meantime continued the struggle in Northern Germany where they inflicted many cruel losses on the imperial forces. Richelieu died in 1642, conscious that his policy was on the verge of complete success.

After the death of Richelieu his friend and protégé, Cardinal Mazarin, carried his policies to completion. France finally developed two commanders of the first rank. In 1643, at Rocroi, in the Spanish Netherlands, Condé and the French foot soldiers, using the tactics of Gustavus Adolphus, at last demonstrated their superiority over the hitherto invincible Spanish infantry and in the last three years of the war Turenne completely outmaneuvered his opponents, overran Bavaria, and desolated the country.

In 1648 the Peace of Westphalia at last put an end to the suffering of the German people. As the years went by the desire of the contestants for peace became stronger and stronger. With the passing of the earlier leaders from the scene, scarcely any serious German question remained to be solved. Both Protestants and Catholics were exhausted. Only the ambitions of France and Sweden stood in the way of peace. Although negotiations looking toward peace were begun as early as 1641, the diplomats did not actually open the sessions of the Congress of Westphalia until 1644. The representatives of France and of the Empire met at Münster; and those of the Empire and of Sweden at Osnabrück. The

EUROPE after the TREATY OF WESTPHALIA (1648)

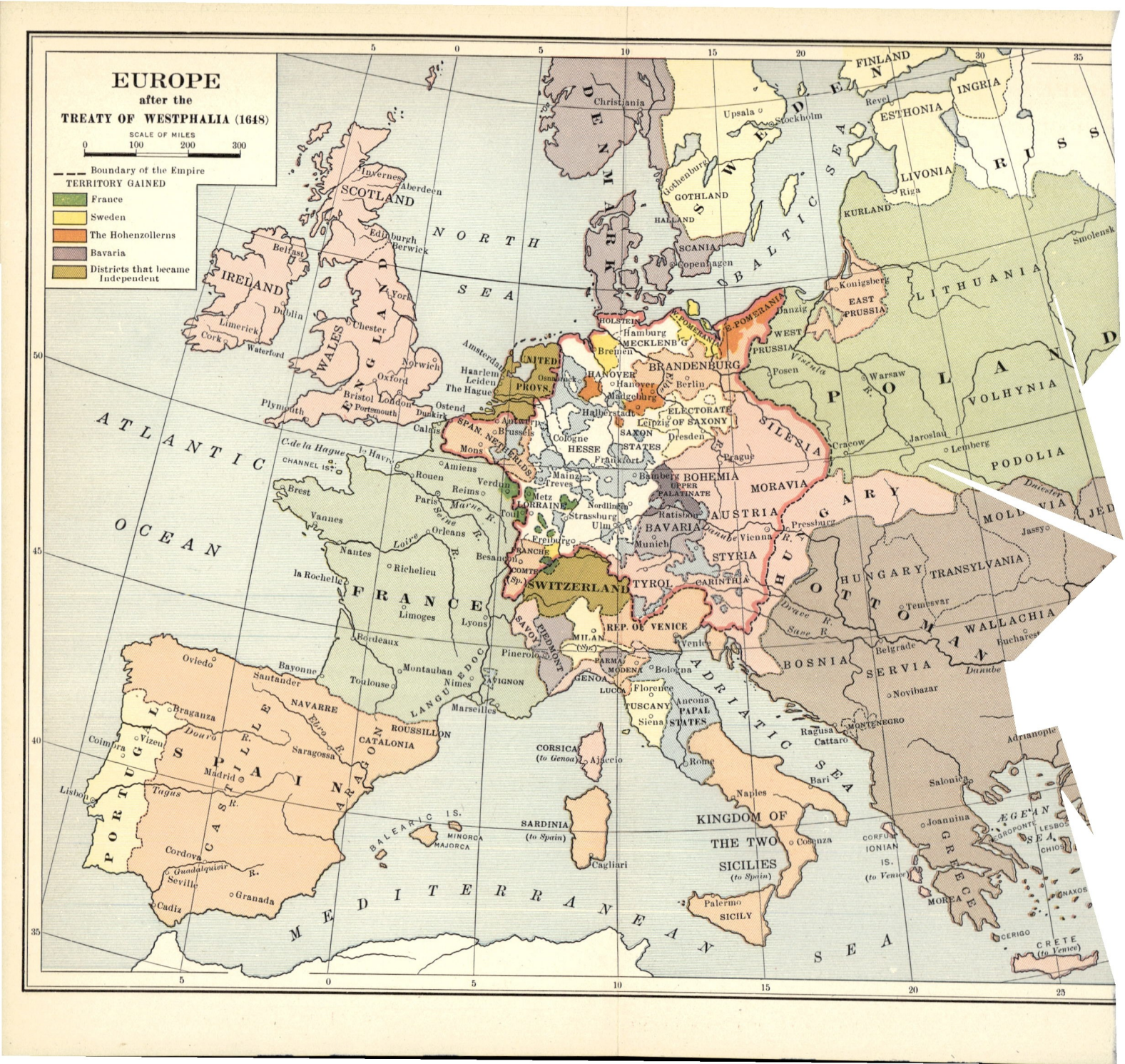

SCALE OF MILES
0 100 200 300

- - - Boundary of the Empire

TERRITORY GAINED
- France
- Sweden
- The Hohenzollerns
- Bavaria
- Districts that became Independent

whole series of treaties which resulted from their labors is referred to as the Treaty of Westphalia, from the general region in which the negotiations took place.

The agreements reached at Westphalia furnished the framework for international relations from 1648 to the outbreak of the French Revolution. By the terms of this treaty France gained legal possession and full sovereignty over the three bishoprics of Metz, Toul, and Verdun, which it had been occupying since 1552, and of the province of Alsace with the exception of the city of Strassburg. Sweden received Hither Pomerania, the bishopric of Verden, and the archbishopric of Bremen. These territories gave Sweden three votes in the German Diet, control of the mouths of the Oder, Elbe, and Weser Rivers, and a strangle-hold on German commerce. Brandenburg acquired Eastern Pomerania, the bishoprics of Halberstadt, Minden, and Camin, and the right of succession to the Saxon administrator of Magdeburg upon his death. Bavaria retained the Upper Palatinate and its hard-won electorate. An eighth electorate was created for the son of Frederick V of the Palatinate, who now entered into possession of the Rhine Palatinate. The independence of Switzerland and the United Provinces was recognized definitely. Each party was left in possession of the Church property it was occupying in 1624. Calvinism was put, at last, on an equal footing with Catholicism and Lutheranism, and the German princes were at liberty to choose the Calvinist religion for themselves and their subjects. The states of the Empire henceforth enjoyed the right of concluding treaties with each other and with foreign powers. The treaty of Westphalia was thus another step in that long process of weakening the Holy Roman Empire which began in the Middle Ages and which had been greatly accelerated by the revolt of Luther. The Diet, the Emperor, and the other machinery of the Imperial Government continued to exist, but they had practically ceased to function. The German princes henceforth coined money, organized armies, made war, and negotiated treaties almost unhampered by the nominal central government.

The end of the war found Germany in a terrible plight. For thirty years the armies of the warring Powers had marched over Germany, ravaging, robbing, and destroying everything which came in their way, until the armies themselves were reduced to poverty and misery by the general destruction. The armies of mercenaries with their plundering, their demands for quarters, and their requisitions were bad enough, but their enormous trains of camp followers were a veritable plague on the country. Often the camp followers were three or four times as numerous as the actual soldiers. In 1648, for example, the Imperial and Bavarian forces numbered forty thousand, the camp followers one hundred and forty thousand. Four Swedish companies included six hundred and ninety men, six hundred and fifty women, and nine hundred children. The women ranged from the proud and influential mistresses of the officers down to the worn-out hags, who hung on as beggars or servants among the common soldiers. The ordinary camp women lived under the little straw shelters with the soldiers, cooked their meals for them, washed their clothes, and cared for them when they were sick. On the march they looked after the children, the booty, and the utensils.

The coming of an army and its mob of camp followers meant ruin to any region. The countrysides, the villages, and even the cities had to furnish wood, straw, food, and fodder. Along the roads, toward a new camp, loaded wagons and herds of cattle began to move. The lumber and straw were used in building temporary shelters for the soldiers and the camp followers. During the first years of the war the villagers fled to places of refuge and tried to protect themselves. Upon the appearance of an army in a region the villages quickly vanished from the face of the earth. The camp followers wandered around plundering and stealing everything of value. Many villages were in ruins in the time of Gustavus Adolphus, and the destruction increased with great rapidity after his death. The population swiftly declined. The more well-to-do moved to the cities for protection. The land was worked little. Hunger and plague decimated the villages that remained and many peasants became outlaws.

The fate of the cities was only a little less severe. With the approach of a hostile army all commerce ceased. Often the city was ransomed at great expense. Leipsic, for example, was besieged five times; Magdeburg, six. If a city was captured the conquerors cut down the men in masses, dishonored the women, and destroyed everything on which they could lay their hands.

The loss of life and property was enormous. In the more fortunate provinces the population was reduced by half; elsewhere by three fourths or seven eighths. In Bohemia the population fell from three million to eight hundred thousand. The city of Augsburg had only sixteen thousand of its original eighty thousand left. In one district of Thuringia rather more fortunate than the rest, only 627 out of 1717 houses, 316 out of 1773 families, 244 out of 1402 oxen, and none of the 4616 sheep were left. Germany was a century in regaining what it lost in population and property as a result of the Thirty Years' War.

The spiritual, moral, intellectual, and social losses suffered by Germany as a result of the Thirty Years' War are equally important but more intangible. A whole generation had grown up in Germany without schools, without the ministrations of religion, and without the civilizing influence of gaining a livelihood by means of industry and sobriety. Gradually the churches had been plundered and destroyed. The clergy had been killed or driven off, so that religious life was practically at a standstill. The invading armies left their vices and their diseases. Drunkenness and immorality became prevalent. There was a senseless aping of foreign fashions and a contempt for honest toil. The upper classes had become harsh, narrow, and domineering; the lower classes, brutalized and cringing. The peasant no longer bore himself or was treated like a freeman. The life of all classes was coarser and ruder.

MAZARIN AND THE WAR WITH SPAIN

The treaties signed in Westphalia did not bring peace to all the warring countries. The war continued between France and Spain. The latter country, though, was in a desperate condition. Portugal had regained the independence of which Philip II had deprived it in 1580; Catalonia, with French assistance, was in full revolt; Roussillon and Cerdagne, the two Spanish provinces north of the Pyrenees, were in the possession of France; Flanders and the port of Dunkirk were in the hands of Condé; Naples was in open revolt; and as a result of a naval battle off the coast of Tuscany France was mistress of the Mediterranean. Only the outbreak of a civil war in France known as the Fronde saved Spain from the disastrous peace which the French arms were forcing upon it.

This movement is one of the most complicated episodes of French history. Louis XIII died within a few months after his great minister, Cardinal Richelieu, leaving an infant, Louis XIV (1643–1715), as his successor. For the greater part of two decades the King's mother, Anne of Austria, and Cardinal Mazarin were in control of the government. The court and the nobility hated the new minister because he continued the detested policies of Richelieu, and also because he was an Italian. The movement was partly an effort to remove Mazarin from office, partly an attempt of the Parlement of Paris to introduce various constitutional reforms suggested by English institutions, and partly an effort of the self-seeking nobles to obtain power and personal advancement. Not understanding the strength of the movement at first, the Cardinal and Anne of Austria dubbed it in contempt the "Fronde," the name of a children's game.

The revolt began in 1648 when the whole body of judges constituting the Parlement of Paris protested against the taxes being imposed by the Government and demanded the adoption of a program of reforms. The proposed program would have subjected the royal authority to the control of Parlement, reduced the important tax on the peasants known as the *taille*, abolished the officials known as intendants, and guaranteed personal liberty. A popular rising at Paris accompanied the demands of Parlement. Mazarin yielded for a moment to gain the time needed to gather military forces to suppress the revolt. The interest of Parlement, on the other hand, waned upon discovering the real intentions of their self-seeking, noble allies. Concessions were made on both sides and peace was restored.

This popular revolt led by the Parlement of Paris was soon followed by an aristocratic movement with which it had little in common. The second rising was the last effort of the nobles to maintain possession of the independence which was slipping away from them. It centered around the actions and ambitions of Condé, the great French general. He had the support of a large body of discontented nobles and of Spain, and, for a time, of the city of Paris. The two parties carried on a struggle of almost indescribable confusion. After a time the royal troops began to get the ascendancy, Paris made its peace with Mazarin, and Condé retired to Spain. The system of Richelieu was then restored completely.

Mazarin finally took up again the struggle against Spain but under far different conditions from those which existed in 1648 at the beginning of the Fronde. The resources of the state had been squandered, the military forces demoralized, and the authority of the royal government weakened. Spain, on the contrary, had regained the Spanish Netherlands and Catalonia. After three years more of fighting had failed to force either state to make peace, Mazarin concluded an alliance in 1657 with Cromwell, the Puritan master of England, by which the latter agreed to furnish Mazarin a fleet and six thousand of his veteran troops in return for the fortress of Dunkirk. With this assistance the French conquered and occupied most of the Spanish Netherlands as far as Brussels and gained important successes in Italy. These decisive victories paved the way (1659) for the treaty of the Pyrenees. By this agreement France gained Roussillon in the south and Artois and a number of cities and towns in the north, and its boundaries were extended to the Pyrenees and the Alps.

Mazarin survived his triumph only a few months and died

in 1661. Though he continued Richelieu's policies, Mazarin was the opposite of his great predecessor in many ways. He was soft and conciliatory in manner and graceful in address. He disarmed his opponents instead of conquering them. Management, not action, was his strong point. He was a master of dissimulation, extremely avaricious, and thoroughly Italian in his ideals and manners.

The first part of the seventeenth century was a period of transition. Europe was passing out of a period in which religion was the dominant interest into a period in which more secular affairs occupied the minds of European statesmen. During the first six decades of the century the Dutch became the leading colonial and commercial power, the French monarchy developed into an absolutism, France rose to first place among the states of Europe, and the Thirty Years' War nearly wrecked Germany. These movements led up to the Age of Louis XIV.

REFERENCES

DUTCH COLONIAL ACTIVITY
  W. C. Abbot, *Expansion of Europe*, vol. I, chapters XVII-XVIII, XX.
  Cambridge Modern History, vol. IV, chapter XXV.
  C. Day, *A History of Commerce*, chapter XX.
  A. G. Kellar, *Colonization*, chapters X-XI.
  H. C. Morris, *A History of Colonization*, vol. I, pt. III, chapters VII-VIII.
  J. E. T. Rogers, *Holland*, chapters XIX, XXII, XXVII.
  H. Robinson, *The Development of the British Empire*, chapter V.

HENRY IV
  Cambridge Modern History, vol. III, chapter XX.
  A. J. Grant, *The French Monarchy*, chapter VI.
  W. H. Hudson, *France*, bk. IV, chapter I.
  G. W. Kitchin, *History of France*, vol. II, pp. 399-487.
  J. R. Moreton Macdonald, *A History of France*, vol. II, chapter XXI.
  A. Tilley, *Modern France*, pp. 32-43.
  C. C. Jackson, *The First of the Bourbons*.
  P. F. Willert, *Henry of Navarre*.
  Histoire générale, vol. V, chapters VI-VII.

RICHELIEU
  Cambridge Modern History, vol. IV, chapter IV.
  A. J. Grant, *The French Monarchy, 1483-1789*, chapter VII-VIII
  W. H. Hudson, *France*, bk. IV, chapter III.
  G. W. Kitchin, *History of France*, vol. III, pp. 1-83.

J. R. Moreton Macdonald, *A History of France*, vol. II, chapter XXII.
H. O. Wakeman, *European History, 1598–1715*, pp. 132–53.
R. Lodge, *Richelieu*.
Histoire générale, vol. V, chapter VIII.

THE THIRTY YEARS' WAR
Cambridge Modern History, vol. IV, chapters I, III, V–VII.
E. F. Henderson, *Short History of Germany*, vol. I, chapter IX–XV.
L. Haeusser, *The Period of the Reformation*, chapters XXXII–XL.
H. O. Wakeman, *European History, 1598–1715*, chapters IV–VI.
S. R. Gardiner, *The Thirty Years' War*.
Histoire générale, vol. V, chapter XII.

SOURCES ON THE THIRTY YEARS' WAR
J. H. Robinson, *Readings in European History*, vol. II, chapter XXIX.

GUSTAVUS ADOLPHUS
R. N. Bain, *Scandinavia*, chapter VIII.
C. R. L. Fletcher, *Gustavus Adolphus*.

MAZARIN
Cambridge Modern History, vol. IV, chapter XXI.
A. J. Grant, *The French Monarchy*, chapter IX.
W. H. Hudson, *France*, bk. IV, chapter IV.
G. W. Kitchin, *History of France*, vol. III, pp. 84–142.
J. R. Moreton Macdonald, *A History of France*, vol. II, chapter XXIII.
H. O. Wakeman, *European History, 1598–1715*, pp. 153–64.
J. B. Perkins, *France under Mazarin*.
Histoire générale, vol. VI, chapter I.
Histoire de France, vol. VII, pt. I, pp. 1–117.

THE EDICT OF NANTES
Translations and Reprints, vol. III, no. III, pp. 30–32.
J. H. Robinson, *Readings in European History*, vol. II, pp. 183–85.

MAPS
Spread of Colonization, 1600–1700. W. R. Shepherd, *Historical Atlas*, p. 128.
Growth of France. *Ibid.*, p. 126.
Treaty Adjustments. *Ibid.*, p. 121.

CHAPTER VII

THE DEVELOPMENT OF PARLIAMENTARY GOVERNMENT IN ENGLAND

As she lay dying, Queen Elizabeth designated as her successor her kinsman, James VI of Scotland, the son of Mary, Queen of Scots. In English history he is known as James I (1603–25). His character and his ideas about "the divine right of kings" quickly set him in opposition to the spirit of political independence rising among his English subjects in the seventeenth century and to the closely connected growth of Puritanism. His contemporary, Henry IV of France, called him "the wisest fool in Christendom." He was highly educated, knew much about foreign countries, and was well versed in secular and religious history, and in matters that did not concern his own interests and feelings he was broadminded and good-natured. He lacked personal dignity, tact, and practical wisdom. He spoke indistinctly and with a decided Scotch accent, and shambled in his walk. He was so sure that he was right that he never made any effort to get the point of view of his subjects. He had none of the Tudor capacity "to know and conform to what the great mass of his subjects wanted." Worst of all he insisted on every possible occasion upon setting forth his lofty views concerning his own powers, authority, and responsibilities. He felt that he had been divinely selected for the task of ruling the state and resented the slightest opposition to his royal policies. These characteristics ill-fitted him to guide the destinies of the state at a time of political and religious change.

The religious settlement of Elizabeth did not satisfy many Protestants who wished for an independent, individual form of religion. This Puritan party had grown steadily during her reign in spite of the opposition it encountered at the hands of the Government. Its members wished for a simplification of the ceremonies of the Church, the abolition of bishops and archbishops, and the enforcement of sobriety in conduct. They entertained great hopes that a sovereign who had ruled over the Presbyterians of Scotland would make some concessions to the like-minded Puritans of England. Soon after the arrival of James in England, in consequence, the Puritan party prepared and presented to the King a great petition in which they merely requested a relaxation of some of the ceremonies of the Church to which they particularly objected. Their action resulted in the calling of a conference of representatives of the Puritans and the Anglicans[1] at Hampton Court near London.

The conference turned out badly for the Puritans. As soon as the King found out that they really aimed at the Presbyterian form of Church government, which he thoroughly disliked for the limitations it placed on the royal authority, he wrathfully broke up the conference and declared he would make the Puritans conform to the government and usages of the Established Church or drive them out of the country. Thereafter the Puritans suffered from a policy of repression that drove many thousands of them as colonists to America. The chief positive result of the conference was the appointment of a commission which prepared the King James version of the Bible.

In 1604, the same year in which the religious problem took an irrevocable turn, James involved himself in a serious political conflict with his subjects. Under the earlier Tudors the English had submitted without protest to the wide powers exercised by the monarchy because of the peace, security, and prosperity which the rule of the Tudors conferred. But already under Elizabeth Parliament had shown a decided tendency to demand a more independent position and a greater control over the policy of the Government. These tendencies ran absolutely counter to the character of James and to his theories about the divine right of kings. The result was a quarrel between King and Parliament, which lasted throughout the reign.

Immediately after his accession to the English throne,

[1] Representatives of the Established Church.

James unwisely precipitated the conflict. He showed a desire to dictate to his subjects whom they should elect as their representatives, informed the members of the newly elected Parliament that they enjoyed their privileges merely by royal favor, and then disputed, in two test cases, the right of Parliament to decide contested elections and the right of its members to be free from arrest during sessions. Both cases ended in victories for Parliament, which have had an important influence on constitutional law. At the close of its session Parliament asserted that the rights and liberties of the commons of England consisted chiefly in the right of its shires, cities, and boroughs to have free choice of their representatives, in the freedom of such representatives from arrest, and in their liberty to speak freely in Parliament.

A sharp conflict between James and his first Parliament also arose over finances. As a result of the rise in prices which followed the discovery of gold and silver in America, the royal revenues no longer provided for the legitimate needs of the Government. The King aggravated the situation by his extravagance. This forced him to make constant appeals to his reluctant Parliaments for funds and to resort to all sorts of devices to raise money. In particular the King sold monopolies in various lines of trade and revised the duties on commerce. At first the significance of the royal policy was not realized. For although a merchant named Bate did contest in 1606 the right of the King to levy a tax on commerce without the consent of Parliament, Parliament itself did not challenge the royal financial policy until 1610. The finances continued to make trouble throughout the entire reign of James I.

During the first sessions of Parliament, still other questions arose which caused trouble between the King and his people. James favored a more tolerant policy toward Catholics, persecuted the Puritans, concluded peace with Spain, and tried to unite England and Scotland into a country with a common set of institutions. Parliament opposed the King on all these questions. It favored severer laws against the Catholics, sympathized with the Puritans, opposed the establishment of peace with Spain, and set itself against the organic union of England and Scotland. While none of these questions were of major importance, each clash of opinion increased the friction between the King and Parliament.

The struggle begun in the first session of Parliament continued throughout the reign. James dispensed with Parliament for a period of ten years, permitted shameless proceedings among the courtiers at his court which alienated the better elements among his subjects, refused to intervene in the Thirty Years' War in behalf of the Protestant party, and exasperated the English nation by attempting to negotiate a marriage alliance for his son with Catholic Spain. Parliament attacked the monopolies which were frequently granted to unworthy courtiers, revived the constitutional process of impeachment, and insisted on its right to discuss foreign affairs. Behind each minor question really loomed the vital constitutional issue of whether the control of the Government rested in the King or in Parliament.

The reign of James witnessed considerable progress in the expansion of England into the British Empire. In 1601 a group of English merchants founded the English East India Company, which so long controlled English commerce with the East. In 1607 a group of English colonists settled at Jamestown in Virginia, and thirteen years later a band of Englishmen, who had fled to Holland to escape from persecution in England, established the Plymouth colony in New England. In 1610 English and Scotch settlers began the plantations of Northeastern Ireland that laid the foundations for the Scotch-Irish settlements of Ulster. The contemporaries of James hardly appreciated the significance of these three developments.

Charles I (1625-49) inherited his father's ideas and continued the quarrel of his father with Parliament. In 1625 Parliament refused to grant the money needed to carry on the war which had finally broken out with Spain in the preceding year. In the following session it attempted to impeach Buckingham, the royal favorite, because of his mismanagement of the Government. To save his friend, Charles dismissed Parliament without waiting for a grant of money of which he stood in desperate need. Thereupon the King found himself forced to resort to the quartering of troops on private citizens, to illegal means of raising money, to martial law, to arbitrary imprisonment, and to other illegal acts growing out of his financial situation. These royal measures led directly to the famous "Petition of Rights" of 1628, one of the fundamental documents of the English Constitution. In this document Charles I, who had been forced by his financial straits to summon Parliament again, declared illegal forced exactions, arbitrary imprisonment, martial law in time of peace, and billeting of soldiers. Finally in the following year the breach between King and Parliament became so wide that Charles dismissed Parliament, and for the succeeding eleven years endeavored to rule alone. This action directly joined the issue between King and Parliament.

The arbitrary government of the King, the High Church policy of Charles and his chief ecclesiastical adviser, Archbishop Laud, and the final revolt of Presbyterian Scotland against the royal efforts to force the forms and usages of the Church of England on the Established Church of Scotland marked this period of personal rule (1629–40). The King and his advisers resorted to all sorts of illegal financial expedients in their efforts to keep the royal treasury filled. In England Laud persecuted the Puritan ministers, imprisoned all who attacked the Established Church, restored order in the affairs of the churches, changed the ritual, and, as far as he could, enforced decency in conduct among the laity. In Scotland the King and the Archbishop attempted to increase the power of the newly appointed bishops, to make the Scottish clergy wear the surplice, and to force on the Scottish people a new prayer book. In England the Puritans and the upholders of the privileges of Parliament either suffered in silence or emigrated to America, where they settled in Massachusetts, Connecticut, and other colonies. In Scotland the people rose in armed revolt and refused to adopt the religious policy of the King and Laud. As he was without the troops or the funds needed to restore Scotland to order, or to prevent an invasion of England by the Scottish army, the King reluctantly summoned Parliament again.

The English Parliament, which met in 1640 in response to the royal summons, is known as the Long Parliament. It desired, above all, redress for its grievances. It released from prison all those who had suffered from the royal tyranny during the eleven years of personal rule, took vengeance on the Earl of Strafford and Archbishop Laud, two of the most unpopular advisers of the King, passed a measure which provided for the summoning of Parliament at least once in three years, deprived the King of the right to dissolve the Long Parliament, abolished several tyrannical courts and commissions, and declared illegal the arbitrary financial devices resorted to by the King during the period of personal rule. These measures put a fairly effective check on the power of the King.

Up to this point the members of Parliament had been almost a unit in their opposition to Charles I. Upon the appearance of new questions, however, the earlier harmony disappeared. The more conservative members of Parliament voted against a "Grand Remonstrance," which set forth with a great deal of boldness, but also with a great deal of exaggeration, all the crimes and wrongdoings of the King. The moderates in ecclesiastical matters opposed the efforts of the more radical members of Parliament to do away with the bishops, to adopt the Presbyterian system of Church government, to abolish the prayer book, and to make the whole English Church rigidly Puritan. These elements felt that Parliament itself was going too far. In the civil war which followed, therefore, they sided with the King.

The course of events in Ireland finally transformed the struggle between King and Parliament into civil war. The native Irish rose in rebellion against the English and Scottish settlers of Ulster and the whole English Government in Ireland. Story after story reached England of the slaughter and suffering of men, women, and children. The situation demanded prompt military action by the English authorities. Parliament, however, mistrusted the King and deprived him of effective control of the militia or "trained bands" as they were called. Charles thereupon raised the royal standard at Nottingham and summoned all loyal English to gather in its defense. This act completed the breach between King and Parliament, and precipitated civil war.

The opening of the armed struggle found England divided into two opposing parties. A majority of the members of the House of Lords, about one third of the members of the House of Commons, and most of the large landowners and the gentry sided with the King. The merchants and the yeomen supported Parliament. The royalists controlled the north and west of England; Parliament, the south and east. The King had more followers who had been raised to the profession of arms. Parliament had more money and the control of the navy and the seaports. To a large extent the struggle was a conflict between the rising, active-minded, middle class and the more conservative elements in English society.

The war lasted four years. At first the royalists followed the general plan of closing in on London from all sides and for a time the fighting went very generally in their favor. Later the Parliamentary authorities obtained the aid of an army from Scotland at the price of important religious concessions to the Scottish Presbyterians and learned to oppose the brave gentlemen of the royal army with the equally courageous and far more steadfast Puritans recruited by an English squire named Oliver Cromwell. These measures finally resulted in the defeat of the royal forces at Marston Moor (1644) near York and at Naseby (1645) in central England, and in the dispersion of the royalists, and the surrender of the King to the Scots.

Three years of confused negotiation followed the defeat and surrender of the King. The King, the Presbyterian majority in Parliament, the Parliamentary army, and the Scots worked at cross-purposes. The Presbyterians wished to get rid of the army. The army wanted a more tolerant policy than the Presbyterians favored, and felt a greater mistrust of the King. The Scots complained of the treatment which they had received at the hands of their English allies. The King negotiated with Parliament, with the army, and with the Scots, and played fairly with none of them. Alarmed at the turn of events, many of the more conservative opponents of Charles went over to his side. In 1648 risings in favor of the King even took place in southeastern England and in Wales and the Scots took up arms in his behalf, but the veterans of Cromwell quickly crushed the royalist opposition.

Embittered by the duplicity of the King and the renewal of the civil war, the leaders of the army returned from the war resolved to settle once for all with the ruler who had caused so much trouble and bloodshed. Taking the control of affairs into their own hands, they expelled their opponents from Parliament, set up a tribunal which tried and condemned the King to be executed, appointed a council of forty-one members to exercise executive power, abolished the office of King and the House of Lords, and declared England a Republic or Commonwealth. For the next eleven years the leaders of the army ruled without a king.

In foreign affairs the leaders of the Commonwealth attempted to break down the commercial and colonial position which the Dutch had enjoyed for half a century. In 1651 Parliament passed a "Navigation Ordinance" which provided that the goods of Asia, Africa, and America should henceforth be imported into England and the English colonies in ships owned and manned by Englishmen. Two years later England declared open war on the Dutch. These measures inaugurated a series of acts and wars that ended in the loss by the Dutch of their primacy on the sea.

In the main the Commonwealth failed in domestic affairs. The remnant of the Long Parliament proved itself corrupt. An assembly of selected "Godly men" — familiarly known as "Praise-God Barebones's Parliament," from the name of one of its members — which took the place of the Long Parliament for a time, showed itself impractical. The higher officers of the army then drew up a written constitution, known as the "Instrument of Government," which practically put the government of England into the hands of Cromwell as Protector.

Cromwell is one of the greatest characters in English history. He possessed a stalwart figure and a dignified and impressive demeanor. He liked music, art, and learning as well as hunting and the other vigorous exercises enjoyed by the ordinary English gentleman. He had an overwhelming sense of his own personal responsibility and of God's part in every event of his daily life. In political affairs he has been described as "slow and unimaginative, but clear-sighted and determined." In the religious controversies of his time he showed himself liberal and tolerant. His elevation to the Protectorate was not an accident. In the Long Parliament he had been "much hearkened unto." During the civil war he had organized the eastern counties into a stronghold of the Parliamentary Party, raised the remarkable regiment of cavalry known as "Cromwell's Ironsides," which decided the important battle of Marston Moor, and finally reorganized the whole army into the "New Model Army," which overwhelmed the royalists at Naseby. During the period of the Commonwealth he played a decisive rôle upon every critical occasion. When the Commonwealth proved a failure, his fellow officers of the army instinctively turned to him for leadership.

Cromwell justified his military associates' faith in him, particularly by his foreign policy. In 1654 he forced the Dutch tacitly to acknowledge the "Navigation Ordinance." During the next two years he captured from Spain a silver fleet [1] and the island of Jamaica. The great Mazarin courted his alliance and at his demand spared the persecuted Protestants of Savoy. England had not been so respected abroad since the days of Elizabeth.

In its domestic policy the Protectorate was practically a despotism. Cromwell found it impossible to work with his parliaments. He imposed taxes as heavy and as arbitrary as those levied by Charles I and established what was practically a military government. In consequence the hearts of the people turned back more and more toward the old ways and the old institutions.

---

[1] Once a year a Spanish fleet carried the gold and silver of the American mines to Spain.

The death of Cromwell in 1658 introduced a period of great confusion. His son Richard, who was neither a Puritan nor a soldier, succeeded him, but he soon found his position untenable and resigned his office. The officers of the army then invited the surviving members of the Long Parliament to come together again. Finally General Monk, commander of the English army occupying Scotland, came to London with his army and declared for a new, freely elected Parliament. This body immediately restored the monarchy and recalled Charles II, the son and heir of Charles I, to the throne.

Two factors contributed powerfully to bring about the restoration of the Stuarts. The English people had grown tired of political change and military rule. They desired a settled government by civil authorities. As their grievances against the Commonwealth and the Protectorate accumulated, their memory of the tyranny of the Stuarts grew dim. They stood ready to recall Charles II as soon as he assured them of their fundamental liberties. He gave that assurance in a message from Breda in Holland. In his declaration he offered a general pardon to all who had taken part in the recent Puritan Revolution except such as should be specially exempted from pardon by Parliament; agreed to leave undisturbed the owners of the estates which had been confiscated from the royalists, consented to the payment of arrears in wages due to the army; and promised to consent to any measure approved by Parliament that granted liberty of conscience. This voluntary acknowledgment of the power of Parliament led directly to the restoration of Charles to the English throne in 1660.

The restoration of the King left a good many questions to be settled. The hates engendered by the civil war, the Puritan army, the estates confiscated from the royalists, the vexatious financial problem, and the religious situation confronted the new Government. As far as it was possible the English nation returned to its old habits and customs, but it could not ignore entirely the new conditions produced by the long years of civil strife. In spite of the Declaration of Breda,

Parliament took revenge on a good many persons who had opposed the King in the civil war. Fourteen individuals were hanged, drawn, and quartered; nineteen were imprisoned for life; a like number were forced into exile; and great indignities were inflicted on the dead bodies of Cromwell and other Puritan leaders. Cromwell's veterans were paid their arrears in wages and the greater part of the regiments were disbanded. Estates which had actually been confiscated from the King and the Church were seized, but land which the royalists had been forced to sell was left in the hands of its new owners. Many of the vexatious dues inherited from feudal times were abolished, and the royal income was definitely settled for the lifetime of the King. These measures solved in a fairly satisfactory way the outstanding political problems.

The religious question proved more difficult. The Catholics and the Anglicans continued to exist during the disturbed years of the civil war and the Commonwealth and the Puritan party broke up into Presbyterians, Baptists, Quakers, Congregationalists, Unitarians, and queer sects like the Muggletonians. In 1644, as a result of the alliance formed with the Scottish Parliament, Parliament had abolished bishops and given the English Church a Presbyterian organization. This had vested the local government of the English Church largely in the hands of the ministers who were in charge of the various congregations. The more general matters of Church government were placed in the hands of district presbyteries, composed of ministers and elders, as well as in the hands of the General Assembly of the whole Church. In practice Cromwell had permitted Puritans of all shades of opinion to man the parish churches. Because of his interest in the Catholics the King favored a policy of toleration for all. Parliament discussed for a while a scheme for "comprehending" the Presbyterians in the Established Church, but the excessive demands of that church shipwrecked the whole scheme. The Anglicans desired simply a restoration of the old Established Church. An exceedingly complicated problem thus confronted the restoration authorities.

After a year of fruitless discussion and negotiation, Parliament adopted a policy of great severity toward all the new sects. An act of 1661 required all town officials to be loyal Anglicans and to take an oath declaring it unlawful to bear arms against the King. An act passed in the following year forced the clergy of the Established Church to assent to everything contained in the Prayer Book and caused thousands of English clergymen, the majority of them Presbyterians, to resign their ecclesiastical positions. The Conventicle Act of 1664 made it unlawful for those who refused to conform to the usages of the Church of England to assemble for worship as their consciences dictated. Finally in the next year the Five Mile Act made it illegal for ministers who had been dismissed from their posts to come within five miles of either a large town or any place where they had preached, unless they took an oath renouncing the law which made Presbyterianism the religion of the State and declared it unlawful to bear arms against the King. The Government applied these laws with great harshness. John Bunyan, the author of *Pilgrim's Progress*, spent twelve years in Bedford jail as a punishment for being a Baptist, and the Quakers suffered the cruel persecutions which led William Penn to found (1681) the colony of Pennsylvania as a refuge for them. All efforts to modify the religious policy of the English Government failed until the passage of the Toleration Act in 1689.

In domestic politics the reign of Charles II witnessed considerable constitutional progress. Neither King nor people forgot the lessons taught by the civil war. The King made no effort to impose arbitrary taxes on the nation, regularly dismissed his ministers as soon as they had lost the confidence of the majority in Parliament, and never pushed a contest with Parliament to the bitter end. In 1679 Parliament passed the Habeas Corpus Act, a measure which made it illegal to keep any one in prison for more than twenty-four hours without trial. These measures indicate clearly the growing power of Parliament during this period.

Another important development of the period was the

growth of permanent political parties. Some men became impressed with the importance of upholding the Government, the Church, and the whole established order. Others felt the need of protecting the individual from the tyranny of Church and State. Two political parties gradually developed which adopted these opposing points of view. They definitely crystallized into modern parties during the efforts of the party of individual liberty to exclude the brother of the King from the succession because he was a Catholic. The friends of the established order soon adopted the name of Tories; their opponents, the name of Whigs.

In foreign affairs Charles II allied himself with France and opposed the Dutch. In 1660 Parliament reënacted the Navigation Ordinance of 1651. Two years later it decreed that all the goods imported into English colonies must be bought in England. The efforts of the English Government to break down the advantageous commercial position of the Dutch brought on the second Anglo-Dutch War (1664–67). After an indecisive struggle the two Powers signed a treaty of peace, in which the Dutch surrendered their colony of the New Netherland (New York) to the English and the English gave up their claims to the Spice Islands. Five years later Charles II joined Louis XIV of France in a new attack on the Dutch. By this time, however, the English people were beginning to realize that the French were more dangerous rivals than the Dutch, and they forced their sovereign to withdraw from the struggle. From this time on the French King merely tried to keep the English neutral in the great struggles of the Continent. He secretly took Charles II into his pay in order that the need of money might not compel the English sovereign to summon a Parliament which, as the price of a money grant, might drive him into a war with France. The general policy followed by the English after 1651 cost the Dutch much of their commercial and political importance.

The reign of Charles II also saw some progress toward the settlement of America. In 1663 the King granted Carolina to eight of his associates. In the following year he granted to his brother, the Duke of York, the Dutch colony of New Netherland. In 1681 the King gave William Penn permission to found the colony of Pennsylvania as a refuge for the persecuted Quakers. By the end of his reign twelve of the original thirteen American colonies had been established.

Upon the death of Charles II, in 1685, his brother, James II (1685–88), succeeded to the English throne. The new sovereign had many of the faults of his father, Charles I. He was narrow-minded, intolerant, obstinate, determined to have his own way, and unable to understand the feelings of his subjects. Within three years his arbitrary government and his acts in behalf of the Catholic religion had alienated his subjects and brought on the Revolution of 1688.

One arbitrary measure after another followed the accession of James II. In his efforts to advance the interests of the Catholic religion the King dismissed the ministers and judges who opposed him, established a military camp not far from London, organized an Ecclesiastical Commission to discipline the clergy, which was practically the old, obnoxious Court of High Commission, appointed Catholics to offices in the army, the Church, and the universities, received a Papal legate in the country for the first time since the reign of Mary Tudor, authorized the opening of Catholic schools and the founding of monasteries, permitted the printing of Catholic books and pamphlets, and finally issued a Declaration of Indulgence, dispensing both Protestants and Catholics from conforming to the customs and usages of the Established Church. Even the Tories began to doubt the wisdom of keeping in office a sovereign who, in the interest of the Catholic religion, entirely disregarded the Constitution.

The issuing of the Declaration of Indulgence precipitated a crisis. The King ordered the clergy to read the declaration in the churches. The majority of the clergy refused to obey the royal order, and seven of the bishops, with the Archbishop of Canterbury at their head, petitioned the King to desist from his policy. Instead of listening to their advice, James II caused the bishops to be arrested and tried for libel. During the trial popular excitement rapidly increased and the news that the bishops had been acquitted by the jury roused public opinion to the highest pitch. The incident nerved the nation to resist the King.

The last straw for the nation in general was the birth of a male heir to the throne during the excitement over the trial of the bishops. So long as the nation could confidently look forward to the peaceful succession of Mary, the elder daughter of James II, and the wife of William of Orange, the Protestant Stadtholder of Holland, it tolerated James II in spite of his arbitrary government and his Catholic religion. The birth of an heir, however, opened up the prospect of an indefinite continuance of the detested policies of James II and convinced both Whigs and Tories that a revolution was necessary.

Accordingly, on the very day that the bishops were acquitted a group of prominent men, representing both political parties, invited William of Orange to come over immediately to England in order to preserve its liberties and to protect its Protestant religion. At the time this appeal reached him, William was thirty-eight years old. When only twenty years of age his country, because of the great name he bore, had chosen him Stadtholder of Holland and captain and admiral general of its military and naval forces, and called upon him to save the liberties of his country from Louis XIV. From that day until his death he led the forces of Europe in their great struggle against the ambitions of Louis XIV. Although he was not a brilliant general he brought to the task an indomitable will, singleness of purpose, and military and diplomatic talents of a superior quality. He cared for the invitation of the English leaders only because it offered him a splendid opportunity to bring England into the alliance against Louis XIV.

William, therefore, immediately made preparations for the invasion of England and finally landed with a few thousand Dutch troops at Tor Bay in Southwestern England. For a moment the English people hesitated. If William failed, his English supporters might lose both their lives and their property. Then the nation began to go over to him. The nobles and gentry commenced to declare for him and the very friends and courtiers of King James went over to him. Finally the King found himself deserted even by his daughter Anne and his favorite general, John Churchill, and realizing at last his unpopularity, and utterly discouraged, he fled to the Continent. His flight cleared the ground for the establishment of constitutional government in England.

For carrying out the work of setting up a new government, William summoned, upon his arrival in London, an irregular assembly known as the Convention Parliament. This body first declared the English throne vacant through the withdrawal of James II from the kingdom and offered the kingship to William and Mary as joint sovereigns. It next set forth its conception of the fundamental principles of the English Constitution in a document known as the Declaration of Rights, and thereby settled in favor of the nation the issues which had been in dispute between King and Parliament throughout the Stuart period. It declared illegal the alleged right to dispense with the laws, to levy taxes without the consent of Parliament, and to maintain a standing army dependent on the King, and asserted the right of petition, of choosing members of Parliament without royal interference, of freedom of speech, and of frequent meetings of Parliament to be inalienable rights of the English people. This document, in time, became a fundamental part of the English Constitution under the name of the Bill of Rights.

As a partial reward to the Protestant dissenters from the Established Church for their loyalty to the nation in its struggle with the King, Parliament passed in 1689 a Toleration Act. This measure allowed the dissenters, as they were called, to form independent religious congregations and to worship publicly according to their own forms. It did not put them on an equal footing with members of the Established Church. Until the nineteenth century dissenters suffered from the Test Act of 1673 (which excluded them from political office), from the Church rates (which forced them to contribute toward the support of the Established

Church), from the control of the Church over the registration of births, marriages, and deaths, and over cemeteries, and from the laws concerning education.

The full effect of the Revolution of 1688 was not realized immediately. The adoption of the Bill of Rights and the Toleration Acts and the establishment of the Protestant dynasty was gradually followed by a series of measures which insured the protection of the rights of Englishmen. From the Revolution onward Parliament authorized taxes for only a year at a time, a policy which tended to make certain the annual holding of Parliament. In 1695, by its failure to renew the licensing act, it removed many of the restrictions on the press. In the following year the King decided to choose his ministers entirely from the party in control of the House of Commons in order to insure harmony, and thus made an important precedent for cabinet government. In 1701 the Act of Settlement gave English judges tenure during good behavior and thus assured the independence of the courts. These measures, in a sense, completed the Revolution.

After 1715 the English Constitution was modified in two important ways. Queen Mary died in 1694 and King William III nine years later. William was succeeded by Anne, the younger sister of his wife. When Queen Anne died, in 1715, without surviving children, George I, King of Hanover, ascended the English throne because he was the nearest Protestant relative in the line of succession. As he could speak no English the new King left the Government largely in the hands of the cabinet, and made it necessary for one of its members to act as chairman or prime minister. Henceforth a cabinet led by a prime minister and composed of representatives of the political party dominant in Parliament really conducted the Government.

Parliamentary government in England was thus the result of a long development. Its forms arose during the Middle Ages. It gained its power and privileges as a result of the fierce struggles of the seventeenth century. It did not achieve its democratic basis until the nineteenth century.

REFERENCES

GENERAL ACCOUNTS

E. P. Cheyney, *A Short History of England*, chapters XIV–XVII.

A. L. Cross, *A Shorter History of England and Greater Britain*, chapters XXVII–XLI.

C. H. J. Hayes, *A Political and Social History of Modern Europe*, vol. I, chapter VIII.

A. B. Innes, *History of England and the British Empire*, vol. II, chapters X–XVI.

T. F. Tout, *An Advanced History of Great Britain*, pp. 420–569.

B. Terry, *A History of England*, part III, and bk. IV, chapters I–III.

G. M. Trevelyan, *England under the Stuarts*.

S. R. Gardiner, *The First Two Stuarts and the Puritan Revolution*.

O. Airy, *The English Restoration and Louis XIV*.

ENGLISH CONSTITUTIONAL DOCUMENTS

G. B. Adams and H. M. Stephens, *Select Documents of English Constitutional History*, pp. 326–490.

E. P. Cheyney, *Readings in English History*, chapters XIV–XVII.

H. Gee and W. J. Hardy, *Documents Illustrative of English Church History*, pp. 508–670.

J. H. Robinson, *Readings in European History*, vol. II, chapter XXX.

OLIVER CROMWELL

C. H. Firth, *Cromwell*.

S. R. Gardiner, *Cromwell*.

J. Morley, *Oliver Cromwell*.

T. Roosevelt, *Cromwell*.

CHAPTER VIII

ASCENDANCY OF FRANCE UNDER LOUIS XIV

To the first council of ministers held after the death of Mazarin, Louis XIV announced that henceforth he would be his own prime minister, and he forbade his subordinates to perform any important act of government without his foreknowledge and consent. No one supposed that the young, pleasure-loving monarch would stick long to his unexpected resolution, but for the remainder of his life he worked at public business for five hours a day, never allowing himself to be diverted by any amusement from the task of governing.

During the first half of his reign a remarkable group of ministers and generals aided him in his task. Colbert reorganized the finances, rebuilt the French marine, and stimulated the development of colonies and industries. Louvois gave the French army an organization superior to that of any other in Europe. Vauban, the greatest military engineer of the age, conducted the sieges of Louis XIV and fortified his border towns. Two remarkable generals, Turenne and Condé, led his armies. For a quarter of a century he shone in the glory reflected on him by this galaxy of great subordinates. When they died he filled their places with mediocre men who were unable to repeat the successes of their predecessors.

Colbert laid the foundation for the early successes of Louis XIV. Recommended to his sovereign by Mazarin, he had gradually risen in rank and power until he virtually became minister of marine, finances, agriculture, public works, commerce, and fine arts. His principal titles to glory are his achievements in the conduct of the finances, the commerce, and the marine of France.

As long as his sovereign would permit him to carry out his own ideas, Colbert put order in the finances, abolished abuses, and equalized to a slight extent the burden of taxation. To achieve these aims he established a special court to hunt out those guilty of corruption, which recovered enormous sums; he introduced a business-like system of accounting, suppressed many useless offices, reduced the rate of interest on the public debt, lowered and assessed more fairly the direct tax, known as the *taille*, which many had escaped paying, and augmented certain indirect taxes, which were borne by all. The adoption of these measures greatly reduced the cost of collecting the royal revenues and tripled the total income of the kingdom.

Colbert strengthened the existing organization of industry. He used the old craft gilds as agents for the enforcement of the innumerable regulations which he issued with a view to insuring the quality of French manufactures. As a result of his policy the gilds at Paris doubled in number, and until the French Revolution, the gild system continued to be a characteristic feature of French industry.

Colbert also attempted to establish many new industries. He gave financial assistance to manufacturers, enticed foreign artisans into the country, and started establishments for the manufacture of tapestries, plate glass, lace, and fine textiles. Many of the new industries, however, languished from the beginning, or declined after his death. The chief defect of his industrial policy was an over-regulation which frequently hampered French industry as much as it helped it.

In his commercial policy, as in his industrial policy, Colbert aimed to make France self-sufficient. With this end in view he undertook colonial projects and organized commercial companies, increased the export duties on raw materials and lowered the import duties on products needed in French manufactures; he raised the import duties on foreign manufactures considerably in 1664 and to a very high point in 1667. These measures tended to furnish the country an ample supply of colonial products, to provide French manufacturers with an abundance of cheap raw materials, and to protect them from competition.

Many other departments of French life felt the influence of Colbert. He encouraged the building of roads and canals.

He aided agriculture by reducing direct taxation, by forbidding the seizure of farm animals for debt, by encouraging better breeding of farm stock, and by draining swamps. He improved naval bases, provided a supply of timber for ships, and raised the number of naval vessels from thirty to two hundred and seventy-seven.

Louis XIV, however, dissipated the resources so carefully accumulated by Colbert. Both his own ambitions and the ideals of the age pushed the French King into a military career, which involved his country in four long, destructive wars. In the first three — the War of Devolution, the Dutch War, and the War of the League of Augsburg — he aimed to extend the limits of his kingdom to the natural boundaries of the Pyrenees, the Alps, the Rhine, and the ocean. In a fourth and greater struggle — the War of the Spanish Succession — he tried to seat a member of his family (the Bourbons) on the throne of Spain.

Louis XIV began the War of Devolution (1667–68) in the hope of obtaining the Spanish Netherlands and the Free County of Burgundy. After advancing the flimsy pretext that the provinces rightly belonged to his queen, as the firstborn of the late Spanish King by his first wife, he marched his troops into the disputed territories with little or no opposition from Spain. At this point, however, the formation of a triple alliance between the United Provinces, England, and Sweden for the protection of the threatened territories stopped the victorious advance of the French armies and forced Louis XIV to content himself with the acquisition of a few border fortresses in The Netherlands.

The French monarch already disliked the Dutch. He hated them for their republican form of government and for their policy of harboring French exiles and protecting the authors of books and pamphlets which were directed against himself. Their action in forming an alliance for the avowed purpose of thwarting his royal plans determined him to make war on the United Provinces.

Louis XIV made careful diplomatic and military preparations for his Dutch War (1672–78). First, he isolated the

EXTENSION OF THE FRENCH FRONTIERS, 1552-1766

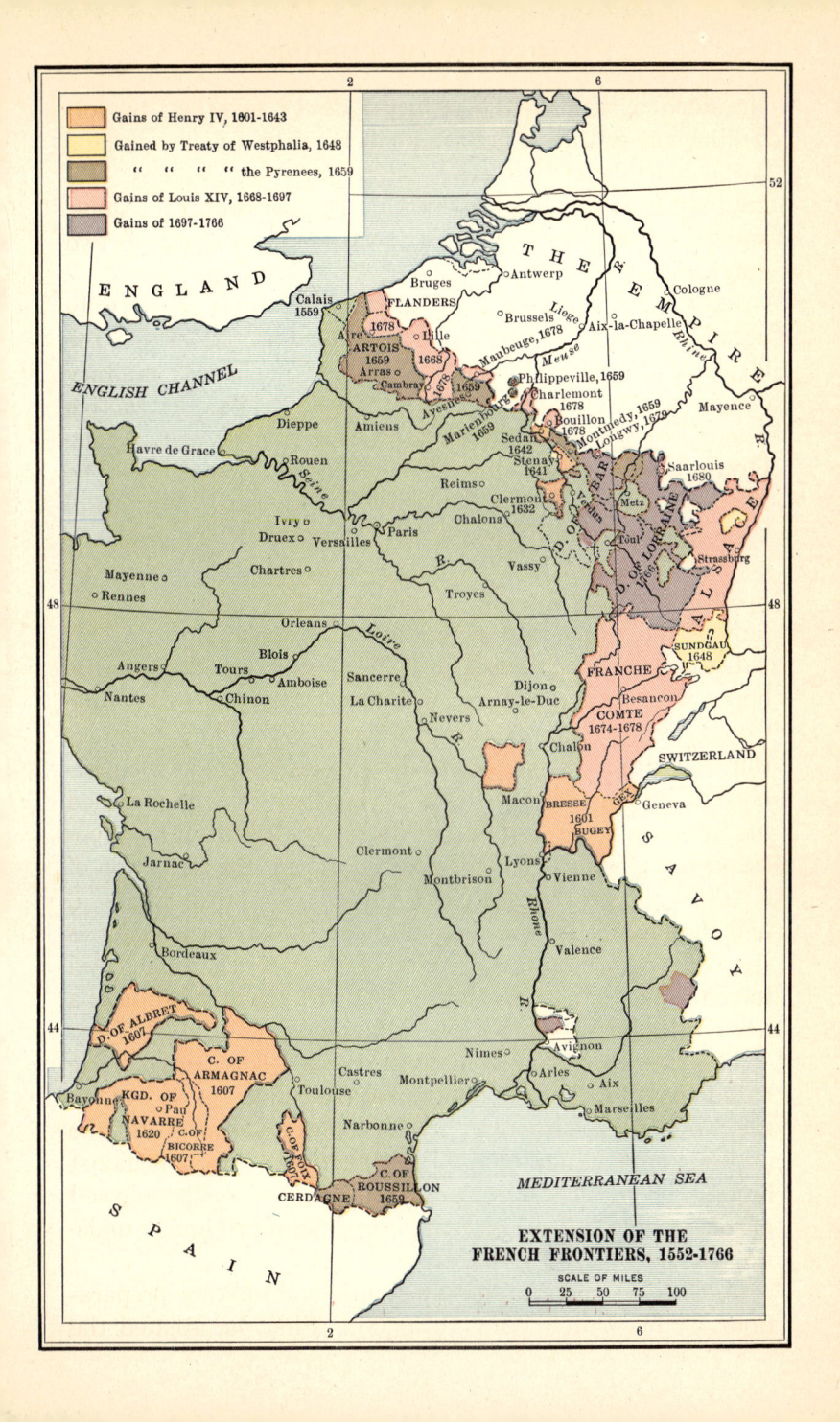

Legend:
- Gains of Henry IV, 1601-1643
- Gained by Treaty of Westphalia, 1648
- " " " the Pyrenees, 1659
- Gains of Louis XIV, 1668-1697
- Gains of 1697-1766

Dutch diplomatically by bribing the rulers of England, Sweden, and the various German states with money and promises of territory. Then Louvois, his great Minister of War, made careful provision for supplying the needs of the invading army. When all was ready the French marched into the United Provinces. The Dutch appeared doomed; they offered to pay Louis XIV a large indemnity and to cede to him several desirable territories. In the mistaken belief that they were at the end of their resources the French sovereign made still more humiliating and crushing demands. Contrary to his expectation his hard terms nerved the Dutch to a desperate resistance. Under the leadership of William of Orange (William III of England) they cut the dikes, compelled the forces of Louis XIV to leave the country, induced some of his allies to desert him, and organized a great European alliance against him. After four more years of indecisive fighting, the exhausted combatants concluded in 1678 a peace which preserved Dutch independence, modified in favor of the United Provinces the French tariff of 1667, and ceded to France, at the expense of poor and declining Spain, the Free County of Burgundy and another group of border towns belonging to the Spanish Netherlands.

For the next ten years Louis XIV remained nominally at peace with his neighbors. During this period he revoked the Edict of Nantes and inaugurated the policy of "Reunions." These are two of the most important episodes of the reign.

After their defeat at the hands of Richelieu, the Protestants had become a peaceful, industrious element in the nation. The great nobles had deserted the party after it ceased to offer them any political advantages, but many of the lesser nobles, a large section of the middle class, and numerous tillers of the soil remained loyal to the Protestant religion. Particularly numerous in the South of France and in the maritime provinces, they numbered about 1,200,000 persons and constituted about one twelfth of the population of France.

Many causes coöperated in deciding the French King to compel his Protestant subjects to change their religion. The

Protestants were destroying that unity in the State which all thoroughgoing absolutists desired. Louis XIV wished to prove his own orthodoxy. Madame de Maintenon, a pious lady, whom he had secretly married, favored a policy of repression. The French clergy had long clamored for either a stricter enforcement of the Edict of Nantes or its complete recall. The Revocation of the Edict of Nantes came in answer to these demands.

Persecution of the French Protestants had begun soon after Louis XIV became his own prime minister. As early as 1662 the French Government destroyed all the Protestant places of worship in the territory of Gex on the ground that Gex did not belong to France at the time that Henry IV issued the Edict of Nantes. In the following year it destroyed a hundred more places of worship because Protestant services had not been held in them prior to 1598. Each succeeding year the Government put greater pressure on the Protestants. It permitted their children to change their faith at the age of seven, gave Protestant officials a choice between apostasy and the loss of their positions, and closed many trades to Protestant artisans. In 1682 Bossuet and other zealous Catholics held missions throughout France for the purpose of converting the heretics. In 1684 the Government followed the policy of quartering rough dragoons in the houses of the Protestants of Southern France. Finally, in 1685, Louis XIV issued the Revocation of the Edict of Nantes. This decree revoked Henry IV's famous measure of religious toleration, abolished all Protestant worship, exiled the Protestant ministers, closed the Protestant schools, and forbade the Huguenots to emigrate from France. From this time on the laws declared France exclusively a Catholic country.

Events soon showed that the King had blundered. About ten thousand Protestant families had left France prior to the Revocation of the Edict of Nantes in order to escape the earlier repressive measures. After the appearance of that decree hundreds of thousands emigrated, in spite of the severe measures taken by the French Government to prevent a loss of population. Some managed to take most of their wealth with them, while others abandoned everything and threw themselves on the charity of foreign Protestants. Large groups of the proscribed established themselves in the United Provinces, England, and Germany, and smaller groups settled in Denmark, Russia, America, and the Dutch colony at the Cape of Good Hope. They enriched every country to which they went by their wealth, arts, and trade, and by their industry, probity, and piety.

Something like a hundred thousand Huguenots are thought to have settled in the United Provinces. The Dutch Calvinists welcomed their French brethren. They relieved the refugees for a number of years from paying taxes, allowed master artisans to exercise their crafts freely, advanced them money to establish manufactures, and supported the French ministers by state funds. The refugees made notable contributions to the wealth, industry, commerce, and culture of the United Provinces. They established manufactures of linen, woolens, silk, velvets, cloth, stockings, caps, and paper; and they brought so much specie into the country that between 1684 and 1687 the rate of interest at Amsterdam fell from three and one half to two per cent. Later a few of the Huguenot refugees from the United Provinces established themselves in the Dutch colony at the Cape of Good Hope.

Germany, too, offered places of safety to the Protestant refugees from France. Within a fortnight after the appearance of the Revocation of the Edict of Nantes, the Elector of Brandenburg issued a decree offering the Huguenots a place of refuge in his estates. The decree promised them that they should be met at Amsterdam, Hamburg, Cologne, and Frankfort by electoral agents, who would provide them with passports, money, and transportation, that certain places had been set aside for them, that homes would be furnished them, that they should be exempt from taxes for a period of ten years, that they should enjoy all the political and commercial privileges in the towns, and that their churches and ministers should be supported by the State. A number of other German princes offered similar inducements.

The response of the French Protestants to the invitations

of the German princes was large. Probably more than one hundred thousand of them settled in Germany, where they established themselves in considerable numbers in Brunswick, Hanover, Saxony, the Palatinate, Württemberg, Baden, and Brandenburg. More than twenty thousand settled in the estates of the Elector of Brandenburg. They made the same contributions to the life of the various states in Germany that they made in the United Provinces. Trade and manufactures really began in Brandenburg with the coming of the Huguenots. To the great delight of the Elector, the French immigrants also introduced the orchards and the market gardens to which they had been accustomed.

Although the English did not give the French refugees as warm a welcome as the Protestant princes of Germany and the Calvinists of the United Provinces gave them, something like a hundred thousand of them emigrated to England, Ireland, and the English colonies in America. Groups of them settled in most of the English colonies in America, but they put their mark most indelibly on South Carolina. England attracted in the main French artisans and manufacturers.

France thus lost a valuable element of its population, and much of its wealth, commerce, industry, and military skill. Although many of the emigrants reached England in a penniless state, it is estimated that they brought to the country on an average sixty pounds each. Lyons, which had employed eighteen thousand silk looms before the Revocation of the Edict of Nantes, had but four thousand at the end of the century. In 1727 Tours, which had had eight hundred mills, eighty thousand looms, and forty thousand people, had only seventy mills, twelve hundred looms, and about four thousand workers. In the twenty years following 1683 France lost 3,582,000 pounds sterling through the decrease of her exports to England and Holland alone. Vauban estimated that the naval forces of France lost in the neighborhood of nine thousand sailors and the military forces six hundred officers and twelve thousand soldiers. The total loss in population was probably four hundred thousand.

Simultaneously with his disastrous Huguenot policy,

Louis XIV pursued a policy of aggression against the Spanish Netherlands and the Empire that alarmed every state in Western Europe. The territories acquired by France since the Treaty of Westphalia had been ceded "with the rights and territories belonging to them." After the close of the Dutch War Louis XIV proceeded to interpret this vague phrase to suit himself. Under the pretext of determining his rights, he organized or designated courts composed of his own subjects to pass on his claims. The decrees of these prejudiced tribunals, enforced by the French armies, handed over to France ten border districts. They seized Strassburg, in Alsace, Casale, in Italy, and Luxemburg without even this flimsy pretext. These aggressions finally caused the alarmed states of Europe to organize the great alliance known as the League of Augsburg.

The organization of the league did not deter Louis XIV from further aggressions. A disputed election provided him with an excuse for occupying Cologne; and he invaded the Palatinate on the pretext that the succession rightfully belonged to his sister-in-law. These two invasions temporarily relieved the Dutch Netherlands from the fear of invasion and permitted William of Orange to slip over to England and drive James II from the English throne.

The general European war (1689–97) which followed these events was a dreary struggle. Neither side possessed a general of genius. The forces of France and of the alliance fought in The Netherlands, on the Rhine, in Italy, at sea, and in America (King William's War). At the end of the war Louis XIV surrendered most of the territories he had taken since the close of the Dutch War, agreed to allow the Dutch to garrison the Spanish Netherlands, and recognized William III as King of England.

The peace concluded at the end of the War of the League of Augsburg proved to be only a temporary one. Three years after its conclusion the pitiful, weak-minded Charles II of Spain died, leaving the Spanish throne to the younger grandson of Louis XIV. For a time it looked as if the Powers of Europe would acquiesce in the union of France and Spain in the hands of a single family (the Bourbons), but the indiscreet policy of Louis XIV in Spain quickly aroused the apprehension of the other states of Europe. He placed French garrisons in the Spanish Netherlands, constructed ships at Cadiz, and showed the English and Dutch that they could expect no favors in Spanish America. These measures aroused general opposition. The Emperor claimed the Spanish throne for one of his own grandsons. The English and the Dutch feared a strict enforcement of the commercial monopoly that was claimed by Spain in America. All the Powers feared that the union of France and Spain might upset the balance of power in Europe. Accordingly the Powers of Europe formed another great military alliance and began the struggle known as the War of the Spanish Succession.

The war lasted from 1702 to 1713. The fighting went on in The Netherlands, Bavaria, Spain, Italy, and America (Queen Anne's War). France lost practically all the important battles. The decisive battle of Blenheim (1704), in which Marlborough, the English commander on the Continent, marched his troops from The Netherlands to the Danube and formed a junction with the army of Prince Eugène, the celebrated Austrian commander, ended the war in Bavaria. Other successes drove the French out of Italy and The Netherlands and gave England possession of Gibraltar. The war seemed about to end in the complete humiliation of France when the flaring-up of national resistance in Spain, the response of France to the royal appeal, and the withdrawal of England from the war enabled Louis XIV to save something from the general wreck of his hopes.

The Treaties of Utrecht (1713), Rastadt, and Baden (1714), which concluded the War of the Spanish Succession, changed the map of Europe even more than those signed at Westphalia. Spain ceded Gibraltar and the island of Minorca to England, the island of Sicily to the Duke of Savoy, and the Spanish Netherlands (known as the Austrian Netherlands thereafter), Milan, Naples, and the island of Sardinia to Austria,[1] and granted England the right to sell negroes to the

---

[1] Austria later forced the Duke of Savoy to exchange Sicily for Sardinia and the title King of Sardinia.

Spanish colonies in America for thirty years and to send one merchant ship a year to the annual fair held at Porto Bello on the Isthmus of Panama. France ceded Acadia to England, acknowledged the English claims to Newfoundland and the Hudson Bay territory, and recognized the claims of Queen Anne and her Protestant heirs to the English throne. These treaties thus deprived Spain of its outlying possessions in Europe, wrested several important colonies from France, and strengthened England and the House of Savoy.

Next to the French King's love of war came his interest in building. During his reign he enlarged the palace of the Louvre, built the Hôtel des Invalides as a home for old soldiers, broadened many of the streets of Paris, and constructed the palaces of Versailles, the Grand Trianon, and Marly. The King made the grandiose palace of Versailles, with its great park, his official residence during the greater part of his reign.

Louis XIV built his costly and showy palaces for a serious purpose. He wished to dazzle his subjects with the splendor of his court and to gather his refractory nobles round himself for the purpose of breaking down their old policy of opposition to the central government. With this end in view he made himself the source of all honors, offices, gifts, pensions, and amusements. The new royal policy caused the sons of the factious nobles of Richelieu and Mazarin to abandon their roomy châteaux in order to live in small and uncomfortable quarters near Versailles. To be near the King came to be their greatest ambition.

Some knowledge of the extraordinary life led by the King and his courtiers is necessary for an understanding of the period. The daily life of the King became a public spectacle. The court accompanied him from morning to night. They watched him arise in the morning, assisted him to dress, served him at table, took a part in his amusements, and saw him to bed at night. An elaborate set of rules known as etiquette regulated the life of the court.

The court of Louis XIV cost the French nation a great deal of money. He maintained many sinecure positions for his nobles, paid the gambling debts of his favorites, gave expensive presents to his courtiers, and provided costly entertainments for the amusement of his whole retinue. The upkeep of the palace, the pay and food of the swarms of servants, and the necessary expenses of the court also took great sums of money. The burden of maintaining this costly institution fell almost wholly on the peasants and the middle class.

The French nation bore the drain of the wars, the building enterprises, and the court of Louis XIV with increasing difficulty. The strain of the Dutch War caused even Colbert to resort to many of the old bad financial devices. He created new offices, sold the royal domains, debased the currency, made the sale of tobacco a state monopoly, and imposed new taxes. As a last resort he tried to raise money by public loans. The treaty of peace brought little relief to the treasury, for the policy of "Reunions" necessitated the maintenance of a large army. The War of the League of Augsburg caused much suffering. The Government doubled the burdensome tax known as the *taille*, the peasants in many parts of the country had to subsist on boiled herbs, and bands of desperate, starving men roved the land robbing and killing all whom they encountered. At the end of the struggle, Vauban, the King's great engineer, estimated that one tenth of the population of France was reduced to beggary and that five tenths were too poor to assist the starving.

The War of the Spanish Succession caused still greater suffering. Taxes mounted to a point almost beyond human endurance. The country became impoverished, the Government could raise no further loans, and the State stood on the verge of bankruptcy. The terrible winter of 1709 added the horrors of famine and plague to the miseries of war. The cold killed the vines and the fruit trees. The soldiers lacked coats and shoes and food. Even the royal lackeys begged at the gates of the palace of Versailles. Upon his death in 1715 Louis XIV left behind him a country well-nigh ruined by his wars and his extravagance.

At the same time, that he was exhausting his kingdom, Louis XIV completed the task of making France an absolute monarchy, which Henry IV had begun and which Richelieu and Mazarin had continued. He suppressed practically every remaining vestige of local self-government. He ordered the parlements to register royal decrees without exercising the right of protest which they claimed. In the cities he named the candidates for municipal offices, confirmed elections, and placed officials under the control of the royal intendants. In the provinces he obtained docile provincial estates by inviting troublesome members to remain at home, by manipulating elections, and by bribing members. The police carefully censored the press, closely supervised the publication of new books, and hunted down the writers, printers, and distributors of pamphlets which attacked the Government. Intendants, drawn from the middle class and dependent on the monarchy for their position in the State, gradually replaced the noble governors in the work of administering the provinces. By the close of his reign Louis XIV could have truthfully said, "I am the State."

Its writers, its artists, and its savants, however, constituted the real glory of the reign. Through their panegyrics, histories, poems, statues, columns, triumphal arches, pictures, etchings, and tapestries they exalted the King in the eyes of his contemporaries. Colbert organized them into academies to which he assigned the task of establishing the standards for each department of knowledge or art.

The chief writers of the reign were Boileau, Molière, Racine, Bossuet, La Rochefoucauld, and La Bruyère. Boileau impressed on the reading public, by means of a series of satires and epistles which are no longer read, the high value of his great contemporaries. Molière founded modern French comedy by writing plays in which, for the amusement of Paris and the courtiers of Versailles, he hit off the affectations, absurdities, stupidities, and follies of humanity. Racine wrote swift but stately, flawless, poetic dramas, which contained nothing that detracted from the main crisis of the play. Fontaine became immortal through his simple but subtle fables; Bossuet, the orator, through his prose; La Rochefoucauld, through his epigrammatic maxims; and La

Bruyère as a moralist and an observer. These writers followed the classical ideal and drew their models and rules from antiquity. They were prejudiced against both the Middle Ages and nature.

For the King and Colbert alike the arts were only a sign of the royal wealth and power. Probably neither of them ever experienced the feeling of artistic pleasure in looking at a statue, a picture, or a monument. Le Brun directed most of the painting done under the royal patronage. His work is pompous, theatrical, and lacking in sincerity. His canvases reflect the mock-heroic spirit of the King. He tapestried the palace of Versailles with enormous battle pieces, in which Louis is always the victor.

In the interior the royal architects used papier-mâché and stucco freely in fanciful scrolls, wreaths, and shells, and they made large use of columns to adorn the exterior of the château. The palace of Versailles is the most characteristic, artistic monument of the reign.

The reign of Louis XIV was thus at the same time a very brilliant and a most disastrous period in the history of France. It enriched France with important additions of territory, with some of its most cherished monuments, with a brilliant court, and with the productions of writers, artists, and savants. It inflicted on the country political, economic, and social disasters which prepared the way for the French Revolution. The despotism and intolerance of the King, the bankruptcy of the State and the misery of the peasants, the privileges of the nobles and the frivolity of the courtiers made a revolution inevitable and necessary.

Long after the political, economic, and social forces set in motion by the policies of Louis XIV had undermined its political preëminence, France continued to dominate Europe in other ways. The court of Charles II of England aped the styles, the manners, and the amusements of Versailles. Every German princeling tried to build a palace like the château at Versailles and to imitate the life of the French court. The writers of Spain, Germany, and England, and to a slight extent Italy, imitated the great French writers.

French became the language of diplomacy and of polite society, French manners became the model of the aristocratic world, and French furniture and dress became the standard of good taste.

The age of Louis XIV was a sad period in German history. From the time of the Thirty Years' War onward invading armies had repeatedly devastated the Palatinate and some of the adjoining districts. During that struggle hostile armies ravaged the Palatinate eight times. During the Dutch War the French burned and plundered the region again; in 1680 they invaded the Palatinate in time of peace. Eight years later the French armies invaded the province still another time on the absurd pretext that it rightly belonged to the sister-in-law of Louis XIV, destroyed the beautiful castle of Heidelberg and the cities of Mannheim, Speyer, and Worms, kept the open country a desert in order that it might not serve as a granary for the enemies of France, and drove nearly half a million Palatines from their homes. These repeated invasions together with religious persecution, the tyranny of the princes and the nobles, and the failure of crops, set in motion a great tide of emigration from the Palatinate, Württemberg, Baden, and Switzerland to America. Since the greatest number came from the Palatinate their contemporaries called them all Palatines.

In 1708 the afflicted inhabitants of the region began an exodus from Germany that resembled in many respects the earlier flight of the Huguenots from France. Abandoning their homes without the permission of their own Government, they threw themselves on the generosity of the people of England. By October, 1709, thirteen thousand of the emigrants had reached London. The English authorities sent many of them on to America. One group settled in New York, another founded the town of New Bern, North Carolina, and great numbers of them established themselves on the frontier, where they shared with the Scotch-Irish the task of defending their fellow colonists. The policies of Louis XIV thus caused the emigration of both Huguenots and Germans to America.

REFERENCES

General Accounts

G. B. Adams, *Growth of the French Nation*, chapter XIII.
W. C. Abbott, *The Expansion of Europe*, vol. I, chapters XXV–XXIX.
A. J. Grant, *The French Monarchy, 1483–1789*, vol. II, chapters X–XV.
W. H. Hudson, *France*, bk. IV, chapters V–VII.
A. H. Johnson, *The Age of the Enlightened Despot, 1660–1789*, chapters I–III.
G. W. Kitchin, *A History of France*, vol. III, bk. V.
J. R. Moreton Macdonald, *A History of France*, vol. II, chapters XXIV–XXV.
J. H. Robinson and C. A. Beard, *The Development of Modern Europe*, vol. I, chapters I–III.
J. H. Sacret, *Bourbon and Vasa, 1610–1715*, chapters VIII–XII.
A. Tilley, *Modern France*, pp. 55–73.
H. O. Wakeman, *European History, 1598–1715*, chapters IX–XI, XIV–XV.
Histoire générale, vol. VI, chapters III–V.

Sources on the Period of Louis XIV

J. H. Robinson, *Readings in European History*, vol. II, chapter XXXI.
J. H. Robinson and C. A. Beard, *Readings in Modern European History*, vol. I, chapters I–III.

Colbert

A. J. Grant, *The French Monarchy*, vol. II, chapter X.
A. Tilley, *Modern France*, pp. 241–61.
H. O. Wakeman, *European History, 1598–1715*, chapter IX.
A. J. Sargent, *The Economic Policy of Colbert*.
S. L. Mims, *Colbert's West India Policy*.
Histoire générale, vol. VI, chapter V.

Louis XIV

A. Hassal, *Louis XIV*.

The Huguenots

A. J. Grant, *The French Monarchy, 1483–1789*, chapter XII.
H. M. Baird, *The Huguenots and the Revocation of the Edict of Nantes*.
Histoire générale, vol. VI, chapter VII.
Histoire de France, vol. VII, pt. II, pp. 39–80.

The "Palatines"

A. B. Faust, *The German Element in the United States*, vol. I, chapters III–VIII.

Maps

Military campaigns of the period of Louis XIV, W. R. Shepherd, *Historical Atlas*, pp. 125, 129.
Treaty adjustments, 1668–1713, *Ibid.*, pp. 125, 126, 133.

CHAPTER IX
THE RISE OF RUSSIA AND PRUSSIA

THE RISE OF RUSSIA

THE rise of Russia starts with the political consolidation of the greater part of the Eastern Slavs under the Grand Duchy of Muscovy and the revolt of this principality from the overlordship of the Tartars of the steppes. During the sixteenth and seventeenth centuries the Muscovite state steadily pushed back its boundaries at the expense of neighboring principalities; the central government developed into an autocracy; the peasants gradually sank into serfdom; and intercourse with Western Europe constantly increased. Finally, in the first quarter of the eighteenth century, Peter the Great anticipated the slow processes of evolution by revolutionizing many departments of the state.

Throughout this period certain fundamental factors vitally influenced the development of the Russian state. The unbroken plains and steppes, the lure of virgin soil, and the growth of the population invited continuous migration of the people and resulted in the expansion of the frontiers of Russia. The magnificent system of rivers offered Russian traders, hunters, soldiers, and settlers a convenient means of transportation and communication. The lack of outlets to the Black and Baltic Seas made wars with the Turks and the Swedes almost inevitable. The patriarchal organization of society, the adherence of the Russians to the Eastern Church, the self-sufficing nature of Russian agriculture, the social customs and modes of dress (which had been adopted as a result of the geographical connection of Russia with Asia), the commercial and cultural relations with Constantinople, and the long political subjection of the Russian people to the Mongols and the Tartars stood in the way of the opening of intercourse with Western Europe and the adoption of Western civilization by Russia.

The first ruler to make outstanding contributions to the development of the Russian state was John (Ivan) III (1462–1505). During his reign he consolidated the Muscovite state and freed it from the rule of the Tartars. He acquired, one at a time, the appanages which had been granted to his four brothers by his father, and incorporated them into the state. In 1578 he refused the demand of the Tartars for the customary tribute, and two years later he decisively defeated them. By these means he obtained the unity and freedom which were prerequisite for the development of the little Grand Duchy of Muscovy into a great state.

During the reigns of John III and his immediate successors the frontiers of the Grand Duchy were pushed out in all directions. The neighboring Slavic republics and principalities were recovered or conquered for the first time; the capture of the great commercial republic of Novgorod gave the developing Muscovite state an outlet to the White Sea. The boundaries of the Polish-Lithuanian kingdom were pushed far back toward the Dnieper and a region largely peopled by Little and White Russians was thereby included in the Russian state. In the reign of John (Ivan) IV (1533–84), who was known as "Ivan the Terrible," the grandson of John III, great progress was made in the conquest of the Tartar Khanates of Southeastern Russia and a beginning was made in the occupation of Siberia. In 1552 the Khanate of Kazan was conquered and four years later the Khanate of Astrakhan. In 1580 a band of adventurous Cossacks crossed the Ural Mountains into Siberia. By the end of the century the settlement of the Valley of the Obi had begun. By 1630 the Russians had reached the Sea of Okhotsk, an arm of the Pacific Ocean. Within a period of eighty years (1580–1660) the expanding Great Russians explored and conquered Siberia.

The story of the expansion of Russia is closely interwoven with the history of the Cossacks. The steady advance of free farmers over the steppes in quest of virgin soil gradually advanced the southeastern frontiers of both Russia and the Polish-Lithuanian kingdom. On the outskirts of this pacified territory a wild, free race of herdsmen and marauders, known as Cossacks, developed. Those in the valley of the Dnieper River at first acknowledged the nominal overlordship of the Polish-Lithuanian state. Later a determined effort on the part of the Polish Government to obtain actual control of its nominal subjects caused the Cossacks of the Dnieper River to transfer their allegiance from the declining Kingdom of Poland to the rising State of Russia. The Cossacks in the valleys of the Don and the Volga Rivers always recognized the nominal overlordship of Russia.

The conquest of Siberia provides a good illustration of the relation of the Cossacks to the whole movement of Russian expansion. In the second half of the sixteenth century the Stroganovs, an important industrial family of Russia, had established themselves on the Kama River at Perm, near the Ural Mountains. They engaged in salt-boiling, fur-trading, and the exploitation of the minerals of the region. From time to time the Mongols of the Obi Valley in Siberia crossed the Ural Mountains and attacked the fortified posts of the Stroganovs. To rid themselves of these attacks the latter induced Yermack, a Cossack chieftain who was out of favor with the Muscovite authorities because of his piratical attacks on the shipping of the Volga, to undertake an expedition into Western Siberia. Equipped with arms and supplies furnished by the Stroganovs, he crossed the Ural Mountains in 1580 with less than two thousand men and speedily drove the Mongols out of the valley of the Obi. He then regained the good will of John (Ivan) IV (1533–84) by presenting to him the newly conquered territory.

The mass of the Russian peasants did not feel the stimulating influence of this steady territorial expansion. While the upper classes were benefiting by the exploitation of the natural resources found in the newly acquired regions, the peasants were sinking from the position of free renters into a condition of actual bondage. This change in status was the result of a variety of forces. Toward the middle of the sixteenth century great numbers of peasants fell into debt to their landlords. At the same time the pressure of the land tax was increasing. Both movements gave rise to legislation and administrative practices which tended to tie the peasants to the land. The Government, in the interest of taxation, restricted the movement of the peasantry. The landlords, wishing to keep their labor force, held their debtor peasants, when it was possible, until they paid their debts. The landlords already exercised jurisdiction over minor offenses committed on their estates. Thus it came about that they held at the same time toward the peasants the positions of creditors, magistrates, public prosecutors, private litigants, and judges of their own causes. As a result of the action of these forces, the peasants either fled from such conditions to seek better opportunities on the frontier, or fell from the status of free peasants into serfdom.

This depression of the Russian peasantry had a number of important consequences. Only the upper classes derived benefit from the new influences that were penetrating into Russia. The peasants retained an archaic political, social, and economic status which was five or six centuries behind the development of Western Europe and did not share in either the political or the cultural advance of that part of the world. This situation gradually created a ruling class, consisting of nobles and bureaucrats, that was entirely out of sympathy with the mass of the population.

The new influences which slowly transformed the ideals and the manner of life of the ruling class in Russia came from Western Europe. Foreign merchants, soldiers, and adventurers penetrated into Russia, and Russians began to travel westward and make observations. John IV employed a body of German mercenaries and made an unsuccessful effort to bring German artisans into the country. In the last quarter of the sixteenth century Russia began to exchange embassies with other European states. At first the Tsar sent foreigners as his representatives abroad. Later the Russians became sufficiently adept in diplomacy and in foreign languages to undertake their own diplomatic missions. Another important factor in opening Russia to Western influences was the discovery of Russia in 1553 by the English.

This discovery came as a result of an attempt to find a northeast passage to Asia. In 1553 two English sea captains, Chancellor and Willoughby, found their way with three ships into the White Sea. Willoughby, with two of the ships suffered wreck, but Chancellor succeeded in landing at the spot where the city of Archangel now stands. The English knew so little about the political geography of the region into which they had penetrated that the letter of recommendation borne by Chancellor was merely addressed to any potentate or person of authority into whose hands it might come. The adventurers received, nevertheless, a hearty welcome from John IV, who saw in the expedition a means of obtaining the contact with the West which he so much desired. They received the right to trade freely in Russia, and in a short time Englishmen, Scotchmen, and other foreigners began to swarm into the country. As a result of the expedition an English commercial company, known as the Muscovy Company, was founded in the following year. The agents of this organization continued to develop the trade with Russia throughout the reign of Elizabeth, and even penetrated as far as the Caspian Sea and Persia.

The most outstanding ruler between John IV and Peter the Great was Boris Gudunov. John IV had created an autocracy of the Oriental type. One of his strong, energetic nobles, Boris Gudunov, rose first to the position of regent and, in 1598, to that of Tsar in the Russian state. During his period of power this ruler maintained the royal authority in the face of the opposition of the turbulent nobility, built towns and fortresses on the northeastern and southeastern borders of Russia to keep the Finns and Tartars in order, encouraged the colonization of Siberia, contributed to the transformation of the free peasants into serfs by forbidding them to transfer themselves from one landowner to another, and raised the head of the Russian Church to the rank of an independent patriarch. The new title tended to attract to the allegiance of the Tsars all communicants of the Eastern or Orthodox Church.

The years immediately following the death of Boris

Gudunov are known as the "Troublous Times." During this period domestic anarchy and foreign invasion threatened the state. Pretenders struggled for the throne, and the Poles and Tartars ravaged the state. The crisis ended in 1613 with the election of the Romanoffs to the throne.

The first great Tsar of the Romanoff dynasty was Peter the Great. In 1689 he took over the actual control of the Russian Government. He is the most remarkable character in Russian history. He found Russia a half medieval, half Oriental state. During his reign he completed the process of centralizing the Government, founded the Russian autocracy, and largely westernized his state. He raised and trained an army capable of competing with the troops of Western Europe, created a navy, built a new capital, reorganized the finances of the country, established the first Russian industries, made the Russian Church subordinate to the State, remodeled the political institutions, and carried out a foreign policy which gave Russia a temporary outlet on the Black Sea and a permanent port on the Baltic.

Peter the Great had a most extraordinary upbringing. He was only ten years old at the time of his father's death. The persons left in control of the Russian Government paid little attention to the education of the young Tsar. As a result he amused himself by wandering around the quarter of Moscow in which the foreign merchants and artisans lived. They taught him much that greatly influenced his later career. He learned to speak German and Dutch. A German physician taught him something of mathematics and of the art of fortification. A Dutch artisan repaired for him a boat with which he began to amuse himself. He learned a good deal about military tactics and strategy from drilling and maneuvering his attendants. Almost imperceptibly the amusements of the boy became the serious activities of the Russian Tsar. A seagoing vessel, built at Archangel, followed the little pleasure boat. The small company of attendants grew into the first regiments of the reorganized army.

The contact of the young Tsar with the life of the foreign quarter kindled in him the desire to see with his own eyes the wonderful civilization of the West. Protected by an incognito, he traveled in 1696 through Northern Germany, Holland, England, Italy, and Austria in the train of one of his own embassies. In every country he displayed an insatiable curiosity to see and to know. In Holland he worked a few days in the shipyards, talked with architects, dentists, and engineers, visited factories, etched a little, looked through a microscope, inspected laboratories, and examined scientific collections. He spent his time in other countries in much the same fashion.

Upon reaching Venice, Peter the Great learned that four of his regiments of old-fashioned troops had mutinied. Filled with a desire to transform Russia in accordance with Western models, and enraged with the reactionaries who had cut short his trip, he hurried back to Moscow. He first took terrible vengeance on the mutineers. He caused a thousand of them to be executed and the remainder to be knouted, mutilated, and exiled to Siberia. Next he attacked the flowing beards and long garments of the conservative Russians, which he regarded as symbols of their obstinate adherence to the traditional forms. He shaved off the beards of some of the reactionaries with his own hands, and stationed agents at the gates of the cities to cut down the long Oriental coats. By such violent measures he inaugurated a struggle to westernize his country which continued for the remainder of his reign.

One of the important reforms of Peter the Great was breaking down the Oriental seclusion of the women of the upper classes. Previous to this time they had lived in separate apartments, veiled their faces when appearing in public, and never mixed socially with men. The Tsar forced men and women to meet together in social gatherings called assemblies. His efforts did not meet with complete success. The women were timid and inclined to keep together in one corner of the room; the men were boorish and unused to the ways of mixed society. Both men and women were more likely to become intoxicated than to turn the neat phrases or make the courtly gestures for which the French salons were famous. In the end, however, the assemblies of Peter the Great did away with the barriers surrounding women and profoundly modified Russian life and character.

The Tsar also accomplished a great deal in respect to giving his people technical training. During his tour of Western Europe he induced hundreds of foreigners to settle in Russia and teach the Russians Western arts and trades. His ambassadors continued to act as regular agents for the attraction of persons of special skill or talent to Russia. By a decree of 1702 he guaranteed foreigners who settled in the country security, assistance, privileges, and religious freedom. He likewise sent many young Russians abroad to learn the art of war or the secrets of industry. It became a fad for the aristocratic youth of Russia to go to Western Europe to become familiar with the languages and the science of the West.

The skilled workmen who were brought into the country laid the foundation for Russian industry. At the opening of the reign of Peter the Great, Russia had no factories. At the close of his reign, it had two hundred and thirty-three public and private industrial establishments. The most successful of the new enterprises proved to be the iron mines which were opened in the Ural Mountains near Ekaterinburg. As a usual thing the State heavily subsidized the private owners. The difficulty in obtaining skilled workers to man the new factories proved the greatest obstacle to their progress. In consequence the factories resorted to the use of bonded serfs, and as a result practically became workhouses. The workers frequently lived in actual barracks, and were subject to the severest discipline. Such a labor force naturally produced goods poor in quality and high in price.

Another achievement of the Tsar was the establishment of a new capital at Saint Petersburg. Feeling that his old capital of Moscow was too remote from Western Europe and too conservative in its traditions, he chose a site on the banks of the Neva not far from the Gulf of Finland and there built one of the most beautiful cities of Europe on a low, swampy spot that seemed scarcely intended by nature for even a village. The city was both constructed and peopled by command of the Tsar. To drain the stagnant waters and fill the marshes required the labor of forty thousand peasants and soldiers. The departments of State did not move to the new city until late in the reign.

The Tsar himself probably considered his military and naval reforms as his greatest achievement. By the end of his reign he had an army of two hundred thousand men trained in Western tactics. Foreigners, to a large extent, furnished the officers for the new army, and landless vagabonds and runaway serfs provided the rank and file. The fleet, in the meantime, had grown from one small vessel to forty ships of the line and nearly eight hundred auxiliary ships.

In reforming the administrative machinery of the country the Tsar followed the Swedish models which he had observed in operation in the Baltic provinces. He established a senate of nine members to act as the supreme tribunal, to receive petitions and reports, to make appointments in the government services, to supervise finances, and to care for the recruiting and the equipping of troops, and he put boards or colleges of officials in charge of the government departments. For purposes of supervision he grouped the provinces into eight governments under the oversight of a governor and an elected council. Finally he gave Moscow and a number of the larger cities some measure of local government, in the hope of preventing corruption and the evasion of taxes. The senate and the administrative boards lacked initiative just as they did elsewhere in Europe, but the municipal reforms proved to be a decided success.

The Russian Church, naturally, did not escape the attention of the reforming autocrat. He created a docile Holy Synod to fulfill the functions of the Patriarch, seized the lands of bishops and archbishops, and forced the monasteries to support hospitals, schools, and invalid soldiers and to turn a large part of their revenues over to the imperial treasury. He granted religious toleration to foreigners, but held native Russians to a strict orthodoxy. His religious policy kept Russia orthodox and completely subordinated the Russian Church to the State.

While he was instituting these domestic reforms, Peter the

Great carried on a vigorous foreign policy with the aim of gaining an outlet to the Black and Baltic Seas and of bringing Russia into closer relations with Western Europe. His foreign policy involved him in wars with both Sweden, the master of the Baltic, and Turkey, the dominant Power on the Black Sea.

At the opening of the reign of Peter the Great, Sweden controlled the greater part of the Baltic coast. It had conquered Finland in the Middle Ages and in 1648, by the Treaty of Westphalia, it had acquired Western Pomerania, which controlled the mouth of the Oder River. After the lands of the Brethren of the Sword were secularized, in 1561, it had acquired Esthonia and later Livonia. A Russian outlet to the Baltic Sea, consequently, could be obtained only through the defeat of Sweden.

In 1699 conditions seemed favorable for a Russian attack on the Baltic provinces of Sweden. The new Swedish sovereign was an untried youth of seventeen; the nobility of the provinces of Livonia and Esthonia were disgruntled; and several of the political neighbors of Sweden were glad of an opportunity to attack her. The discontent of the nobles of the two provinces arose from the efforts of Charles XI of Sweden (1660–97) to regain lands from the nobles that a predecessor had given away with prodigal recklessness. Denmark, Brandenburg, Poland, and Russia all coveted territories in the hands of the Swedes. The leader of the discontented nobles, consequently, had no difficulty in organizing a great conspiracy against the young Swedish King.

The conspirators failed, however, to take into consideration the extraordinary military ability of Charles XII. Upon receipt of the news that the Danes had invaded Schleswig, that Augustus II of Poland and Saxony was attacking Riga, and that the Tsar of Russia was marching on Narva, the young King made a swift and unexpected attack on Denmark. At the end of six weeks the Danish sovereign surrendered all of his conquests and signed a treaty of peace. From Denmark Charles XII hastened across the Baltic to Narva, which Peter the Great was industriously besieging with an army of fifty thousand men. Without a moment's hesitation the young ruler of Sweden, with his little army of eight thousand men, attacked and defeated the motley forces of the Russian Tsar. The defeat of the Tsar left Charles XII free to settle with his remaining enemy, Augustus II, King of Poland and Elector of Saxony.

At this point in his campaign the Swedish King blundered. The campaign against the conspirators had thus far been admirably managed. He should have followed in Poland the same methods that he had employed in Denmark, but he was not content with forcing Augustus to make peace. Instead, he set himself to the task of completely crushing him. Taking advantage of the factional strife and political disorganization in Poland, he defeated the small military force which Augustus was able to assemble in the Polish-Lithuanian portion of his dominions, overran the country, and set up a puppet sovereign of his own. Then he followed his enemy into Saxony and forced him, in 1707, to sign a humiliating peace which left the King of Sweden for the moment the arbiter of Europe. He now had the choice of intervening in the War of the Spanish Succession or of returning to Northern Europe, where in his absence Peter the Great had overrun the Baltic provinces of Sweden.

He wisely decided to allow Western Europe to settle its own affairs and turned northward. At first he marched in the direction of Moscow with the idea of bringing the war to an end by the capture of that city. When the Russian defense stiffened, however, he recklessly cut himself off from all connection with Sweden and marched southeastward in order to join forces with the Turks and with Mazeppa, commander of a band of revolted Cossacks. The Swedish troops braved the swamps and forests of Southern Russia and the coldest winter of the century (1709) to find only a handful of Cossacks awaiting them. At Poltava on the extreme southern border of Russia they encountered the new army of the Tsar. In the battle which followed the Russians totally destroyed the Swedish army, and Charles XII escaped into Turkey with only a handful of followers. Although Sweden did not acknowledge its defeat until the Treaty of Nystad, signed in 1720, the battle of Poltava really decided the country's fate. Augustus II recovered his Polish throne, and Peter the Great acquired the Baltic provinces of Karelia, Ingria, Esthonia, and Livonia and the outlet to the Baltic Sea that he so much desired.

The struggle for an outlet to the Black Sea was of much less importance so long as the Ottoman Turks controlled the straits leading into the Mediterranean Sea. The Tsar temporarily acquired the port of Azov near the mouth of the Don River as a result of a campaign fought in 1694 and 1695. He lost it again, however, as a result of a war which Charles XII succeeded in stirring up in 1711 between his host, the Sultan of Turkey, and the Tsar of Russia. In an attempt to drive the Turks back from the Dniester to the Danube, the Tsar allowed his army to be hemmed in between the Pruth, some marshes and swamps, and the Turkish army. He was glad to save himself and his army from an ignominious defeat by handing back the port of Azov to the Turks.

The last campaign of Peter the Great was a punitive expedition against Persia. In 1722 he led an army of one hundred thousand men against the forces of the Shah of Persia and forced him to cede to Russia two ports and some other territory on the Caspian Sea. Peter the Great thus gave Russia control of the important trade-route between the Baltic and the Caspian Seas and prepared the way for the advances of his successors toward Central Asia.

Between the close of the Middle Ages and the death of Peter the Great in 1725 the little principalities of the great Russian plains were consolidated into a single state in which all authority was centralized in the hands of autocratic Tsars. These movements culminated in the reforms of Peter the Great. In spite, however, of the great Tsar's marvelous zeal and activities, his reforms left the habits and institutions of the mass of the Russian people almost untouched. He merely gave a Western façade to the Oriental edifice.

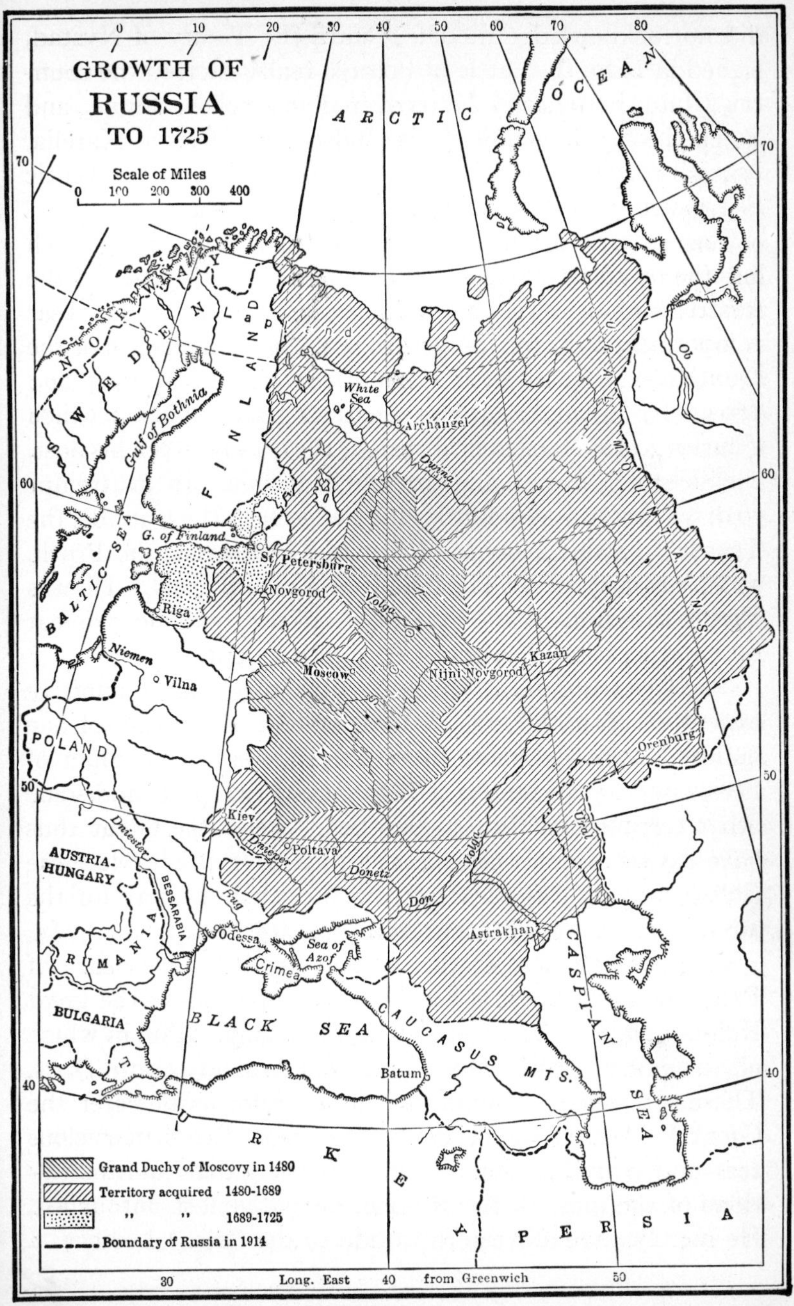
GROWTH OF
RUSSIA
TO 1725
Scale of Miles
0 100 200 300 400
ARCTIC OCEAN
NORWAY
SWEDEN
Lapland
FINLAND
Gulf of Bothnia
White Sea
Archangel
Dwina
URAL MOUNTAINS
Ob
G. of Finland
St. Petersburg
Novgorod
Riga
BALTIC SEA
Volga
Niemen
Vilna
Moscow
Nijni Novgorod
Kazan
POLAND
Orenburg
Kiev
Dniester
Dnieper
Poltava
Ural
AUSTRIA-HUNGARY
BESSARABIA
Bug
Donetz
Don
Volga
RUMANIA
Odessa
Sea of Azof
Crimea
Astrakhan
CASPIAN SEA
BULGARIA
BLACK SEA
CAUCASUS MTS.
Batum
TURKEY
PERSIA
Grand Duchy of Moscovy in 1480
Territory acquired 1480-1689
" " 1689-1725
Boundary of Russia in 1914
Long. East from Greenwich

RISE OF PRUSSIA

As a defense for their frontiers the medieval Emperors developed the political device of the mark or "march." The exposed border districts were put under counts of the march (markgrafen or marquises), who were armed with special powers and privileges and charged with the duty of defending the frontier. The East Mark grew into the State of Austria; the North Mark into the Electorate of Brandenburg.

For a long time the Mark of Brandenburg occupied a very inconspicuous position in the Empire. The early rulers spent the greater part of their time in conflicts with their own cities and nobles. In 1415 the Emperor granted the electorate to the Hohenzollern family, whose representative members until then had been counts in Southern Germany, ruling the territory around Nuremburg.[1] Until the seventeenth century there was little in the history of Brandenburg to suggest its later importance. The land was poor and out of the main current of trade.

Slowly and steadily, however, the Hohenzollerns set about extending their lands. In 1609 the Duke of Cleves died leaving no direct heirs. In accordance with a previous arrangement the Elector of Brandenburg began to occupy the Duke's various possessions, but he quickly found himself in competition with other claimants. After considerable negotiation the Elector temporarily took over in 1614 the administration of Cleves, Mark, and Ravensburg, three small territories situated in the Rhine Valley near the Dutch border. He never afterwards relaxed his hold on them.

In 1618 the Duchy of East Prussia came into the possession of the Electors of Brandenburg by inheritance. The duchy had formerly constituted a part of the possessions of the Teutonic Knights. Before the close of the Middle Ages the order had lost West Prussia to Poland as a result of the Treaty of Thorn (1466). Then in 1525 the last Grand Master of the order, Albert of Brandenburg, secularized East Prussia and the duchy became a Protestant principality

---

[1] The original Hohenzollern castle was in the south of Germany, by the upper Danube.

under the overlordship of the King of Poland. Upon the death of the Duke of East Prussia without heirs in 1618, the duchy was inherited by the electoral branch of the family of Hohenzollern.

Notwithstanding these two substantial territorial gains the Elector of Brandenburg played a dubious and unfortunate part during most of the Thirty Years' War. The reigning Elector was one of the weakest rulers of the Hohenzollern line; the Lutheran nobles were at odds with their Calvinist sovereign; and the chief minister of the state was probably an actual traitor to his country. The ruling Hohenzollern made hardly any effort to protect the electorate. The armies of every party marched through the state without molestation and quartered their troops on the unfortunate inhabitants. The fields were untilled, the towns were ruined, and the country was depopulated. The Mark of Brandenburg became such a desert that the court retreated to East Prussia for fear of running short of food. This was the situation in 1640 when Frederick William (1640–88), known in history as the Great Elector, came to the throne.

The first task of the new sovereign was to guide his state through the final stages of the Thirty Years' War. By skillful management and diplomacy he emerged from the peace negotiations with substantial territorial gains. By the terms of the Treaty of Westphalia, Brandenburg acquired Eastern Pomerania, Halberstadt and Minden, and the reversion of Magdeburg upon the death of its administrator. The acquisition of Cleves and East Prussia marked the ultimate limits of the state. The gains of the Treaty of Westphalia helped to bridge the gaps between Brandenburg and the recently acquired outlying territories of the Hohenzollerns.

The humiliating experiences of the Thirty Years' War had convinced the Great Elector of the need of a military force. At the close of the war he had a force of eight thousand men. Three years later he could muster an army of sixteen thousand men. By the opening of the Swedish-Polish War in 1655 the Elector had collected an army of twenty-six thousand men, an almost crushing burden for a state like Brandenburg. This was the beginning of the standing army in Prussia. From that date until the close of the Great War the rulers of Prussia considered the army the most vital institution in the Prussian state.

The Great Elector used the new standing army for the first time in freeing East Prussia from the suzerainty of the King of Poland. By changing sides in the most unscrupulous fashion in a war between Poland and Sweden he obtained from each of the warring Powers a recognition of the independence of East Prussia. In 1660 the Treaty of Oliva made the arrangement a part of the law of Europe.

The next task of the Elector was to make himself obeyed in his own dominions. The chief opposition came from the provincial estates. In the Mark of Brandenburg the opposition of the Diet was never very formidable, but in East Prussia and the former territories of the Duke of Cleves it assumed serious proportions. In Cleves, Mark, and Ravensburg, the authority of the Elector was finally recognized in 1666 after a sharp struggle. In East Prussia the task of the Elector was far more difficult. Both the nobles and the burghers were accustomed to a considerable amount of independence. The Great Elector was determined to be an absolute ruler as were other sovereigns in Western Europe. A prolonged struggle followed. The burghers of Königsberg were awed into submission by a mixture of intrigue and force, but the opposition of the nobles, who had the backing of the Kingdom of Poland, was not overcome until 1672. As a result of his struggles with the provincial diets the Elector became the real center and mainspring of his dominions.

Frederick William was as anxious to promote the prosperity of his provinces as to establish the authority of his dynasty. The awful scourge of the Thirty Years' War had left the naturally sterile soil of Brandenburg almost desolate. The population was less than half of what it had been before the war. The trade and industry of the country were practically extinct. The primary need of the land was human labor. The Elector began, consequently, a system of home coloniza-

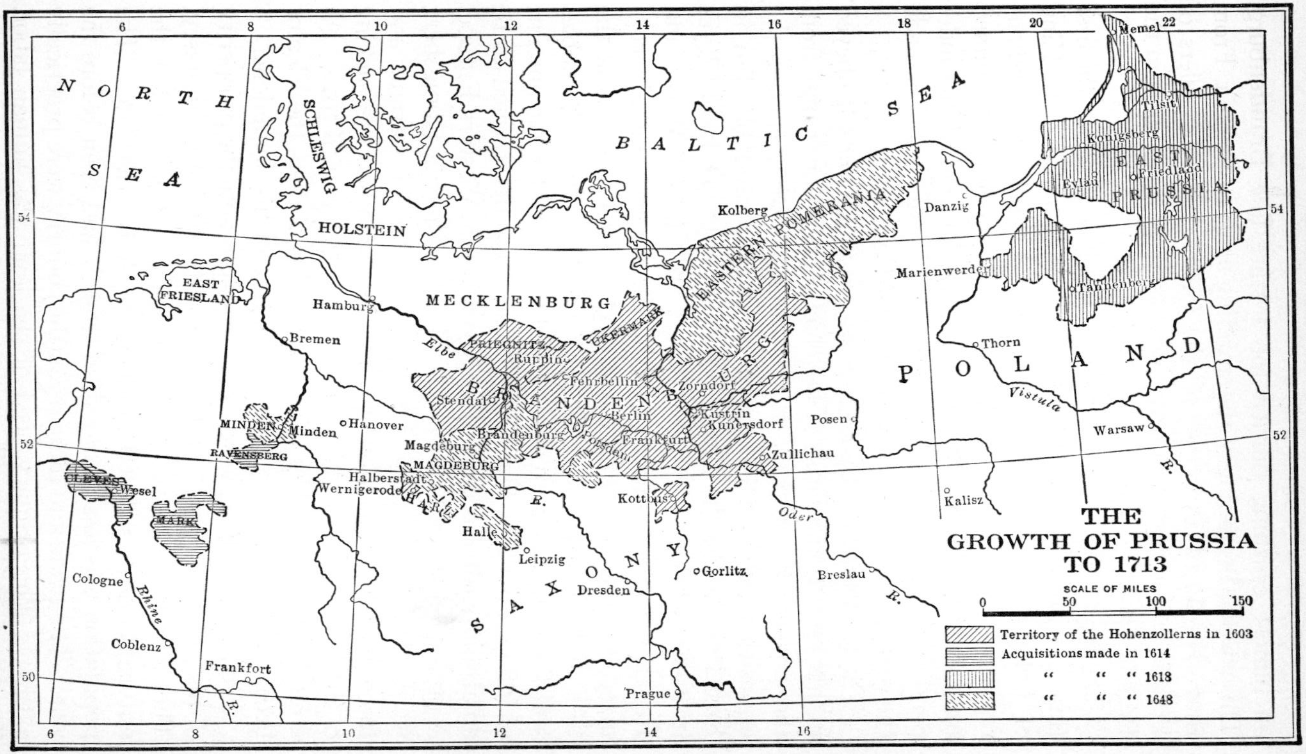
THE GROWTH OF PRUSSIA TO 1713
SCALE OF MILES
0
50
100
150
Territory of the Hohenzollerns in 1603
Acquisitions made in 1614
" " " 1618
" " " 1648
NORTH SEA
BALTIC SEA
SCHLESWIG
HOLSTEIN
MECKLENBURG
EAST FRIESLAND
EAST PRUSSIA
EASTERN POMERANIA
BRANDENBURG
POLAND
SAXONY
PRIEGNITZ
UCKERMARK
MAGDEBURG
MINDEN
RAVENSBERG
CLEVES
MARK
Memel
Tilsit
Konigsberg
Eylau
Friedland
Tannenberg
Marienwerder
Danzig
Kolberg
Thorn
Warsaw
Vistula
Posen
Kalisz
Zullichau
Kustrin
Kunersdorf
Zorndorf
Frankfurt
Berlin
Fehrbellin
Ruppin
Stendal
Brandenburg
Potsdam
Magdeburg
Halberstadt
Wernigerode
Halle
Leipzig
Dresden
Kottbus
Gorlitz
Breslau
Oder
Prague
Hamburg
Bremen
Hanover
Minden
Elbe
Wesel
Cologne
Coblenz
Rhine
Frankfort
R.
6
8
10
12
14
16
18
20
22
50
52
54

tion that is unparalleled in history. A century later six hundred thousand of the inhabitants of the state were immigrants or the descendants of immigrants. The new colonists came mainly from France and the United Provinces. While he was being educated in Holland the Elector had learned something of the aptitude of the Dutch for colonization. The Dutch immigrants taught the impoverished and disheartened inhabitants of Brandenburg how to drain their lands, to manage dairy farms, and to cultivate potato fields. The Huguenot immigrants also made incomparable contributions to the industrial, commercial, and intellectual life of the country. For the purpose of attracting such industrious and skillful immigrants to the depopulated country, the rulers of Brandenburg adopted the policy of religious toleration, for which the state became famous.

The later years of the Great Elector brought him little satisfaction. In the second war of Louis XIV, the Dutch War, the new army of Frederick William won a resounding victory at Fehrbellin, a point about fifty miles from Berlin, over the hitherto invincible Swedish allies of the French sovereign. The victory brought great prestige to the army of Brandenburg, but the diplomats of Louis XIV deprived the Elector of all of the expected territorial gains. A second marriage also caused him many domestic difficulties. Thus his career ended amid troubles of various sorts.

Frederick William was followed by his son, a ruler of very different mould. Frederick III (1688–1713) was vain, extravagant, and exceedingly fond of playing a part in pompous ceremonies. His grandson, Frederick the Great, said of him that he was great in small matters and little in great ones. His vanity led him to devote a large part of his time and thought to the task of winning the title of King for his House. The correspondence with Austria alone on this subject fills twenty-one folio volumes. The War of the Spanish Succession finally gave him an opportunity to satisfy his ambition. The Emperor needed the troops of the Elector of Brandenburg. In return for the assistance of eight thousand men of his splendid army, Frederick III received the coveted title of

King. At first he was merely known as Frederick I, King in Prussia, but in time the title was changed to King of Prussia. The name Prussia, likewise, was in time applied to all of the new King's dominions.

As a result of the work of the Great Elector and his son, Prussia rose from a position of insignificance to a place of importance among the states of Europe. The Great Elector won for his state the substance of power. His pompous son acquired its outward insignia. Their work made it possible for Frederick William I and Frederick the Great to raise Prussia, in the eighteenth century, to the rank of a great Power.

REFERENCES

GENERAL ACCOUNTS OF RUSSIAN HISTORY
  Cambridge Modern History, vol. V, chapters XVI-XVII.
  J. Mavor, *Economic History of Russia*, vol. I, chapters IV-VI.
  W. R. Morfil, *History of Russia*, chapter VII.
  R. Beazley, N. Forbes, and C. A. Birkett, *Russia from the Varangians to the Bolsheviks*, pp. 1-247.
  H. O. Wakeman, *European History, 1598-1715*, pp. 297-310.
  Histoire générale, vol. VI, chapter XIX.

PETER THE GREAT
  R. N. Bain, *The First Romanovs, 1613-1725*.
  O. Browning, *Peter the Great*.
  E. Schuyler, *Peter the Great*.
  K. Walewski, *Peter the Great*.

RUSSIAN EXPANSION
  F. A. Golder, *Russian Expansion on the Pacific, 1644-1850*.
  A. Rambaud, *The Expansion of Russia*.

SOURCES ON RUSSIAN HISTORY
  J. H. Robinson, *Readings in European History*, pp. 302-12.
  J. H. Robinson and C. A. Beard, *Readings in Modern European History*, pp. 57-63.

GENERAL ACCOUNTS OF PRUSSIAN HISTORY
  Cambridge Modern History, vol. V, chapters XX-XXI.
  E. F. Henderson, *Short History of Germany*, vol. II, chapter I.
  J. A. R. Marriott and C. G. Robertson, *The Evolution of Prussia*, chapters II-III.

GENERAL ACCOUNT OF THE HISTORY OF SWEDEN
  R. N. Bain, *Scandinavia*, chapters XI-XII.

MAPS
  The Growth of Russia, W. R. Shepherd, *Historical Atlas*, pp. 138-39.
  The Growth of Prussia, *Ibid.*, pp. 122-23, 130-31, 134-35.

CHAPTER X

THE STRUGGLE FOR COLONIAL AND COMMERCIAL SUPREMACY IN THE EIGHTEENTH CENTURY

THE struggle for colonial and commercial supremacy, begun by Spain and Portugal at the close of the fifteenth century as a result of the epoch-making voyages of Columbus and Vasco da Gama, continued unabated throughout the eighteenth century. The Dutch and Portuguese played a comparatively little part in the conflict, but the French, English, and Spanish waged a long series of wars between 1689 and 1815 for predominance overseas.

In 1689 these five competitors differed greatly in respect to their military power and their colonial possessions. The Portuguese retained only Brazil and a few unimportant posts in Africa and Asia and had practically dropped out of the colonial struggle. The Dutch still possessed islands of commercial importance in the West Indies, a valuable point of call at the Cape of Good Hope for ships using the route around Africa to India, and important possessions in the East Indies. Spain held the Philippines, Central America, Mexico, Florida, all of South America except Brazil, and most of the larger islands of the West Indies. The French colonial empire included Acadia and Canada, many of the smaller islands in the West Indies, two posts on the west coast of Africa, and two important trading posts on the east coast of India. In addition the French had already explored the Mississippi Valley and were reaching out to possess Newfoundland and the Hudson Bay region. The English had acquired a strip along the Atlantic Coast from Maine to Florida, a number of islands in the West Indies, and trading posts in Gambia and on the Gold Coast in Africa and at Bombay, Madras, and Calcutta in India. Consequently, the French and the English confronted each other in India, Africa, the West Indies, the Mississippi Valley, and Canada;

THE COLONIAL SITUATION ABOUT 1689
British possessions
Dutch possessions
French "
Portuguese "
Spanish possessions
NORTH AMERICA
Hudson Bay
NEW FRANCE
LOUISIANA
NEWFOUNDLAND
TEXAS
NEW SPAIN
Florida
Bahama Is.
Bermudas
St. Domingue
Hispaniola
Porto Rico
Cuba
Guadeloupe
Martinique
Granada
Barbados
Caracas
New Granada
Cayenne
PERU
SOUTH AMERICA
BRAZIL
CHILE
FALKLAND IS.
C. Horn
PACIFIC OCEAN
ATLANTIC OCEAN
AZORES IS.
MADEIRA IS.
CANARY IS.
C. VERDE IS.
Goree
Cape Coast Castle
ST. HELENA
St. Paul
ANGOLA
Sofala
Cape Colony
C. of Good Hope
AFRICA
BRITISH ISLES
England
DUTCH REP.
FRANCE
SPAIN
PORTUGAL
Gibraltar
EUROPE
RUSSIA
SIBERIA
ASIA
INDIA
BENGAL
Calcutta
Aracan
Bombay
Goa
Madras
Pondicherry
CEYLON
SUMATRA
Ft. York
JAVA
BORNEO
CELEBES
MOLUCCAS
NEW GUINEA
PHILIPPINES
Macao
REUNION
INDIAN OCEAN
PACIFIC OCEAN
ARCTIC CIRCLE
TROPIC OF CANCER
EQUATOR
TROPIC OF CAPRICORN
ANTARCTIC CIRCLE

the English and the Spanish in the Caribbean; the French and the Spanish in the West Indies and the Mississippi Valley.

Each region produced one or more commodities of commercial value. In India the Powers competed for the trade in textiles, precious stones, drugs, tea, coffee, cotton, and other luxuries of Eastern origin; in Africa, for gold, ivory, wax, and negro slaves; in the West Indies for various colonial products, but especially for sugar; in the Mississippi Valley for furs; and in Canada for fish and furs. The desire to monopolize the trade in these products gave the states of Europe a powerful incentive to expand their colonial dominions. As a result each general war in Europe after 1689 had a phase in which colonial and commercial questions were the chief issues.

The first of these general European wars was the War of the League of Augsburg (1689–97), known in America as King William's War. In Europe the conflict was in the main a struggle against France for the maintenance of the balance of power; in England the free development of parliamentary government and the Protestant régime were at stake; while in America colonial and commercial questions were the issue. The continental struggle has already been discussed in connection with the period of Louis XIV.

The English issues were particularly affected by the fighting at sea and the campaign in Ireland. A naval battle at Beachy Head in 1690 gave the French command of the sea until their defeat two years later at La Hogue; and a dangerous rising of the Catholics of Ireland in behalf of James II menaced the throne of William III and the principles he represented, until it was suppressed in 1690 at the battle of the Boyne. The victories of La Hogue and the Boyne assured England freedom of action in developing constitutional government and the protection of her Protestant régime.

In America neither the French nor the English colonies were in a position to wage a decisive conflict. The French Government had restricted colonial emigration to orthodox Catholics. As a result Acadia had a population of about 3000 and Canada of 12,000. In contrast the English colonies had a population of 200,000, composed largely of persons discontented with the religious, social, and economic conditions in the Old World. The English colonies were too disunited, however, to throw their united strength into the struggle with France. The French contented themselves, therefore, with French and Indian raids on weak and isolated settlements on the English frontier, which excited the horror of the English without accomplishing the slightest military result. The English planned expeditions by land against Montreal and Acadia and another by sea against Quebec, but their sole success was the capture and pillage of Port Royal in Acadia.

The military and economic situation in Europe brought the war to an end in 1697. The treaty of peace recognized the claims of William III to the English throne, but ignored completely the success of the English colonists at Port Royal. So the fighting in America really settled none of the questions at issue. The real results of the war for the colonists were the destruction of frontier settlements, the impoverishment of the colonial governments, and the birth of a spirit of self-reliance that was later to have important consequences.

The War of the Spanish Succession quickly followed the War of the League of Augsburg and involved the French and English colonists in the conflict known as Queen Anne's War. The English fought the Spanish and French in many different regions. The French and English fought over Newfoundland, Acadia, Canada, and the Hudson Bay Region. On the Florida frontier the English colonists of the Carolinas fought the Spanish settlers of Florida and the French colonists of Louisiana. In the Caribbean area the English contested possession of the West Indies with the forces of France and Spain. The outstanding success of the war was the capture of Acadia by the English, who rechristened their new province Nova Scotia.

The Treaty of Utrecht, signed in 1713, brought the war to a close. A number of its provisions affected the territorial and commercial situation in America. Spain granted England the right to sell to the Spanish colonies each year negro slaves to the number of 4800 and permission to send once a year one ship of 500 tons burden to trade at Porto Bello on the Isthmus of Panama. France ceded to England all its claims to Acadia, Newfoundland, and the Hudson Bay region. England consequently gained, by the treaty, important commercial rights in the Spanish colonies, a menacing position in respect to the French colony in Canada, the valuable fisheries of Newfoundland, and the fur trade of the Hudson Bay region.

The conclusion of peace at Utrecht caused no abatement of the colonial and commercial rivalries of England, France, and Spain. The English colonists continued their steady expansion toward the interior; English merchants and shipowners hastened to exploit the opportunities for trade and smuggling in Spanish waters; French explorers, traders, and missionaries spread with great rapidity over the Mississippi Valley; and the Spanish made important advances on the northern and northwestern frontiers of Mexico. It is necessary to know something of French aggression, Spanish expansion, and English intrusion to understand the history of the years between the Treaty of Utrecht and the outbreak of the War of Jenkins's Ear (1739).

Even before the opening of the War of the League of Augsburg the French had begun to establish themselves in the Mississippi Valley. Father Marquette, Joliet, La Salle, Tonty, and other explorers disclosed the general nature of the region. Adventurers and traders in search of furs completed the work of the more famous explorers, and consecrated fathers of the Catholic Church began the work of converting the Indians to Christianity. In 1699 the French began the settlement of Louisiana. Within twenty years the colony had a population of five thousand. Before war broke out again, in 1744, the Illinois country had become a source of grain supply for the French posts on the Great Lakes, New Orleans, Mobile, and even Europe; the lead mines of Missouri were being exploited on a large scale; and the Rocky Mountains had been reached by explorers and traders, who made their way up every important river valley of the Western Plains. Only the hostility of the Iroquois Indians shut the French out of the Upper Ohio Valley. To protect their settlements, missions, and trade, the French built forts at Louisburg on Cape Breton Island to guard the mouth of the Saint Lawrence from naval attacks and to threaten Acadia, at Crown Point on Lake Champlain to bar the only practicable route from New York to the Saint Lawrence, at strategic points on the Great Lakes like the sites of Forts Frontenac and Niagara, and along the Wabash and Mississippi Rivers. To the enemies of France, however, the fortification of these posts appeared as a threat and an aggression.

The Spanish kept pace with the French by extending their frontiers into Texas, Arizona, and California. They acted with the avowed purpose of forestalling the French in these regions. The Spanish missions, which in time dotted the Spanish frontier from the Pacific Ocean to the Gulf of Mexico, greatly assisted the soldiers and adventurers of Spain in the task of pushing forward the Spanish frontiers. The Spanish fathers constructed, for example, six such establishments at San Antonio, Texas, and over thirty within the limits of the present State of California. These devoted missionaries erected churches and mission settlements with the aid of the Indians and gathered the natives into communities, where they were gradually taught the rudiments of civilization and the Christian religion. Only the kinship of the French and Spanish royal families and the overshadowing rivalry of France and England prevented Spain and France from becoming involved in wars over border questions.

Meanwhile the old ill-feeling between England and Spain over commercial questions was becoming stronger. The English sea captains resented their exclusion from the trade with the Spanish colonies and engaged in smuggling operations at every opportunity. The efforts of the Spanish coast guards to prevent the illicit trade frequently led to the seizure of English ships, the mistreatment of their crews, and exaggerated tales of Spanish cruelty. A protest presented to Parliament in 1738 told of fifty-two such cases. The natural result of this growing irritation was the War of Jenkins's Ear, which began in 1739. This conflict received its peculiar name from an extravagant tale of alleged maltreatment related by a certain Captain Jenkins, who came to London and displayed an ear which he claimed the Spaniards had cut off seven years earlier. Though of doubtful authenticity the story greatly inflamed English public opinion and gave its name to the struggle which followed.

The war was in the main a maritime struggle. One English fleet plundered a Spanish fort on the coast of Peru, captured a Spanish galleon on its way to Manila, seized Spanish colonies and ships in the Indies, and returned to Portsmouth, after a voyage of four years, with holds full of gold and silver. Another fleet captured Porto Bello on the Isthmus of Panama. But all told the English experienced more failures than successes. On the mainland the Spanish colonists of Florida did considerable fighting with the settlers of the newly established English colony of Georgia. In 1744 the war with Spain became merged in a new commercial and colonial struggle with France.

The new war is known as the War of the Austrian Succession (1740-48) in Europe [1] and as King George's War (1744-48) in America. Fighting went on in Europe, America, and India. The events in America hardly merit a detailed discussion. On land the English captured the fortress of Louisburg at the mouth of the Saint Lawrence River, and the French made an unsuccessful attack on their old province of Nova Scotia and renewed their raids on the frontier settlements of New England. At sea the English practically destroyed the French navy. The fighting in America really settled none of the issues in dispute.

The situation in India differed vastly from that in America. The country contained a large, dense, and heterogeneous population, which was nominally under the rule of a line of sovereigns known as the Mogul Emperors, whose power had largely fallen into the hands of subordinate officials and native princes. Both England and France had entrusted their interests in the peninsula to chartered companies, which enjoyed exclusive trading privileges. The English East

[1] The European phase of the struggle is discussed in Chapter XI.

India Company had small, fortified trading posts at Bombay, an island just off the western coast of India, at Madras on the southeastern coast, and at Fort William (later known as Calcutta) in the delta of the Ganges; the French Company, at Chandernagore near Calcutta, at Pondicherry and Karikal near Madras, and at Mahé on the southwestern coast. Both companies cared solely for profits. During the earlier European conflicts they had maintained a strict neutrality. The policy of Dupleix, the remarkable French governor in India, finally forced the two companies to abandon this policy.

After a brilliant record in subordinate positions this celebrated colonial administrator took charge of the French posts in the Indian peninsula in 1741. Immediately after taking office he began a series of reforms. He attacked abuses, reduced expenses, stimulated commerce, disciplined his European troops, fortified Pondicherry, and organized a native military force known as Sepoys. Upon the outbreak of the conflict with England he quickly displayed his unusual talents. His forces captured the English post at Madras in 1746, defeated decisively two native armies in the Carnatic (the province surrounding Pondicherry), and thwarted the efforts of the English to capture Pondicherry. As the treaty of peace handed back Madras to the English in exchange for Louisburg, the fighting in India was no more decisive than that in America.

The Treaty of Aix-la-Chapelle, signed in 1748, was little more than an armistice. The rivalry of France and England continued with unabated keenness. In India Dupleix carried on the struggle indirectly by intervening in the affairs of native states in the interest of the French. In America the French interfered in Acadia, occupied the Upper Ohio Valley, and stirred up the Indians on the frontiers of the Carolinas and Georgia. These activities of the French, particularly their occupation of the Upper Ohio Valley, quickly brought on a struggle known as the French and Indian War (1754–63) in America, which was merged two years later into the European struggle known as the Seven Years' War (1756–63).

INDIA
IN THE TIME OF
CLIVE AND DUPLEIX

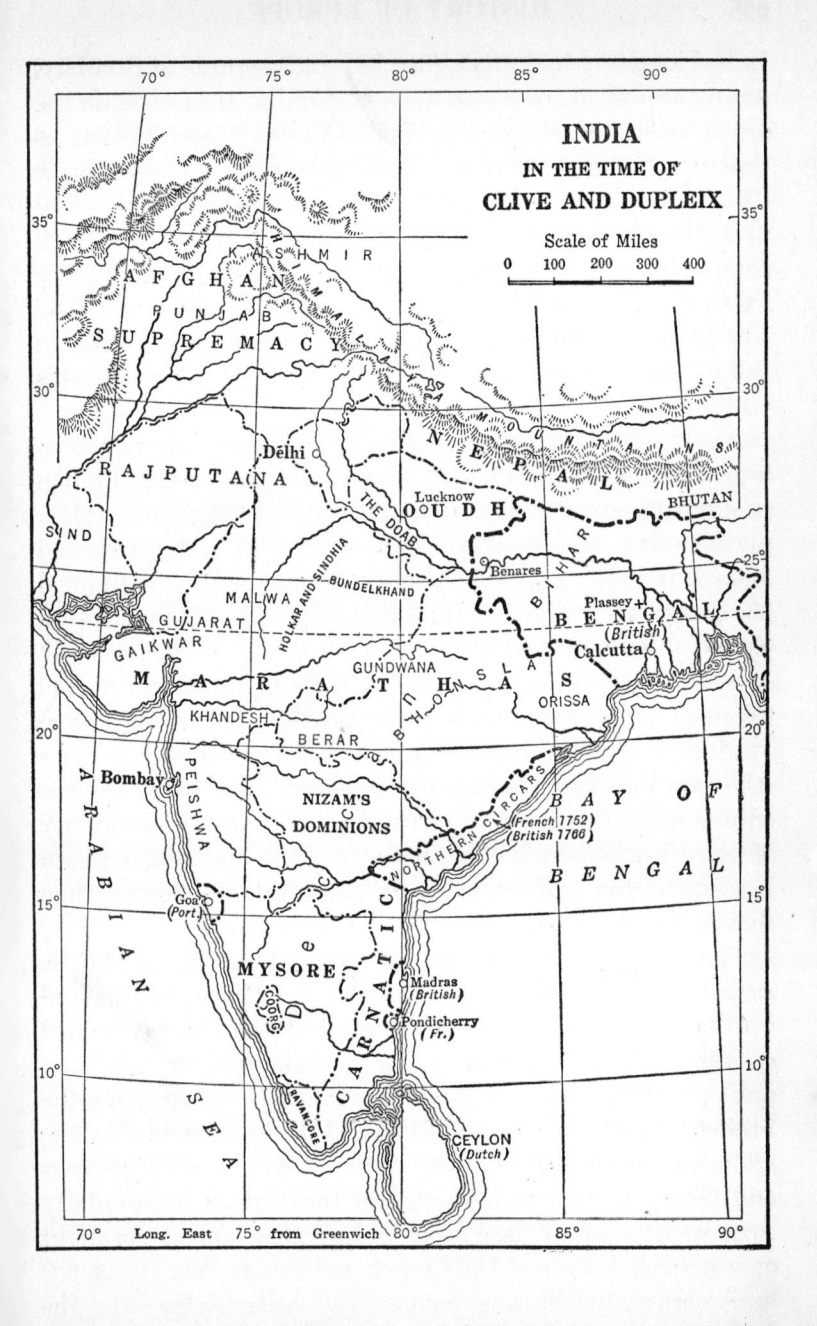

The conflict never really stopped in India. In spite of the Treaty of Aix-la-Chapelle, Dupleix placed on the thrones of Arcot in the Carnatic, and of Hyderabad in the Deccan (a native state situated immediately west of the Carnatic in the interior of the peninsula), princes favorable to France, and forced the Mahratta princes of West Central India to acknowledge the suzerainty of the French. In carrying out the policy of Dupleix the French troops rivaled the exploits of the Spanish conquerors in America. French forces, consisting of a few dozen Europeans and a few hundred Sepoys, defeated native armies numbering tens of thousands. As a result of these victories several of the French posts were ceded outright to France; the ruler of the Carnatic became a mere puppet in the hands of the French; and a military force, composed of French and native troops and commanded by the ablest lieutenant of Dupleix, was stationed at the capital of the ruler of Hyderabad. By 1751, Dupleix was virtually dictator of Southern India.

The great administrator did not maintain his advantageous position long. The French Government and the French East India Company failed to support his ambitious schemes, and in 1750 the English began to abandon their policy of nonintervention. Neither the French East India Company nor the French Government understood the situation in India, the astounding achievements of Dupleix, or the significance of his plans. They saw merely that his policies yielded no immediate revenue. In the hope of propitiating the English and increasing the dividends of the French East India Company, the French Government recalled Dupleix in 1754 and thereby lost an empire.

While the French were sacrificing Dupleix in the interest of peace in India, they were making the outbreak of war in America almost certain by their policy on the upper waters of the Ohio. To forestall the English traders and land speculators, who were making their way into the region, the French began to build a series of forts along a line running north and south through the Allegheny Valley. In 1753 they built fortified posts on the present site of the city of Erie and on

COLONIAL AND COMMERCIAL SUPREMACY

French Creek. In the following year they constructed Fort Duquesne at the point where the Allegheny and Monongahela Rivers join to form the Ohio. A struggle for its possession immediately followed, which finally broadened out into the great Seven Years' War.

After being defeated in the first skirmishes in the Ohio Valley by the French, the English drew up in 1755 a general plan of campaign with the object of driving the French out of both the Ohio Valley and Canada. They planned to drive the French away from Fort Duquesne and the posts guarding Lake Ontario, to force a passage into Canada by way of Lake Champlain and the Richelieu River, and to open the way for the ascent of the Saint Lawrence by the capture of Louisburg. The capture of these French strongholds would prepare the way for a converging attack on Quebec and Montreal.

For two years the efforts of the English forces in America met with little success. The campaign of 1755 ended in the complete failure of the English expeditions against Fort Niagara and Crown Point and in the disastrous expedition of Braddock against Fort Duquesne. In the following year the French captured Fort Oswego on Lake Ontario and built Fort Ticonderoga on Lake Champlain. These French successes threatened to cut the English colonies in two and laid the frontiers of Pennsylvania and Virginia open to disastrous Indian raids.

In 1758 the tide at last turned in favor of the English. The English victories are inseparably associated with the name of William Pitt, the first English statesman to point out clearly the tremendous importance of the colonial struggle. Under his leadership the war in the colonies became a national struggle. He put capable officers like Wolfe and Forbes in command in America, and sent fleets, troops, supplies, and money to the colonies. England had at last found a minister with an imperial imagination.

Upon the rise of Pitt to power the English took up in a new spirit the old general plan of campaign. An army of 7000 men under General Forbes forced its way across the mountains and through the forests of Pennsylvania, and took possession of Fort Duquesne, which was rechristened Fort Pitt in honor of the great minister. A force of 12,000 men, aided by a great fleet, captured the fortress of Louisburg and opened the way for Wolfe's expedition against Quebec in the following year. The capture of Fort Frontenac at the northeastern end of Lake Ontario and of Oswego on its southern shore tended to cut off the French settlements in Canada from the French posts in the Mississippi Valley and along the Great Lakes. Then English naval victories in the East, off the port of Havre, and in the Mediterranean drove the French from the sea. These victories prepared the way for the final English attack against the French possessions in America.

In 1759 the English were ready to attack Canada. Nine thousand men under the command of General Wolfe and a great fleet moved against Quebec. After weeks of fruitless effort, the English discovered an unguarded path that led to the plateau on which the upper city was built. There on the Plains of Abraham occurred the decisive battle of the war in America. At the moment of victory for the English (September 13th), both the French and the English commanding officers fell mortally wounded. Four days later the British troops entered the city. The following year three English armies, converging from Quebec, Lake Champlain, and Lake Ontario, forced the surrender of Montreal. The capture of the remaining French posts on the Great Lakes and in the Upper Mississippi Valley left Louisiana as the sole French possession in America.

The victory of the English in America was almost inevitable. The French colonies were vastly inferior to the English in population and resources. Daring leadership and the negligence and disunion of the English colonies gave the French arms success in the early years of rivalry, but the 1,200,000 English colonists were certain to triumph in the end over the 60,000 French colonists in Canada and the few thousand French settlers in Louisiana. The situation in Europe was equally favorable to the English cause. France was a continental power with European interests. The

COLONIAL AND COMMERCIAL SUPREMACY

French Government could never give its undivided attention to colonial problems. England lay detached from Europe by the English Channel and the North Sea and, therefore, was in better position to concentrate its resources on the colonial issue. Finally the English superiority on the sea cut off the French colonies from the aid of the mother country and thus assured the ultimate collapse of the French power overseas.

The insular position of England and her control of the sea influenced the war in India as well as in America. The sacrifice of Dupleix did not prevent a continuance of the struggle of the French and English East India Companies for supremacy. The conflict was renewed in two distinct regions of the peninsula; in Bengal, a populous province in the Ganges Valley, and in the Carnatic.

The war in Bengal arose out of a dispute between the English and the Nawab or native ruler of that province. The young, ignorant, self-indulgent, and headstrong prince attacked and captured Calcutta because the English authorities there had incurred his displeasure by protecting one of his relatives and by fortifying the post. One hundred and forty-six of the captured garrison were thrust for the night into the small, poorly ventilated, underground military cell of the fortress, known as the "Black Hole," where one hundred and twenty-three of them died in the stifling atmosphere. The incident led to immediate action on the part of the British authorities. A military force composed of 900 English troops and 1500 Sepoys and commanded by Clive was dispatched to Bengal from Madras. It quickly recaptured Calcutta, conquered the French post of Chandernagore, and forced the Nawab to conclude a defensive and offensive alliance with the English. In spite of this alliance the situation remained so unsatisfactory that the English plotted the overthrow of their nominal ally. Their plans finally resulted in the overwhelming victory of Plassey (1757), where 1000 English troops and 2000 Sepoys under the command of Clive defeated and destroyed a native army of 50,000 commanded by the Nawab. The English then installed a candidate of their own as ruler in Bengal. The price of his elevation to the throne was the payment of heavy indemnities to the Company and private individuals for their losses at Calcutta and the gift of enormous gratuities to Clive and other officials of the Company. One of the first results of the new position of the English in the province was the reduction of the Dutch establishment in Bengal to the status of a mere trading post. A stupid act of inhumanity was the immediate cause of the establishment of English rule in India.

The English conquest of Bengal was followed by that of the Carnatic. Lally, the successor of Dupleix in India, quarreled with all of his subordinates and allowed the diplomatic structure so skillfully reared by Dupleix to go to pieces. The recall of Bussy, the French commander in the Deccan, angered the Nizam (a native ruler of Hyderabad) and caused him to transfer his allegiance to the English. The English command of the sea made the situation of the French desperate even in the Carnatic. In 1761, the English won the decisive battle of Wandewash and one by one reduced the French posts in the Carnatic. The fall of Pondicherry in 1761 marked the end of French dominion in India.

By what seems in retrospect an incredible act of folly, Spain allowed herself to be drawn into the colonial struggle too late to save France but in time to share her disasters. Spain entered the war for a variety of reasons. Family ties and formal alliances bound the French and Spanish royal houses together. Questions of trade continued to cause difficulty between the Spanish and the English; England barred Spanish fishermen from the waters of Newfoundland; and English dyewood cutters had established themselves in Central America on territory claimed by Spain. The Spanish lost Havana and Manila, and their intervention in the conflict did nothing to stop the progress of the English arms.

The military and naval situation in Europe and the desire of the English Government for peace finally led to the conclusion of the Treaty of Paris in 1763. By the terms of this agreement, France recovered its trading posts in India, but the opportunity to create a great empire by the methods of Dupleix had passed into the hands of the English. On the continent of North America, France ceded to England Canada and all her possessions east of the Mississippi River with the exception of the city of New Orleans and two small islands in the Gulf of Saint Lawrence useful for drying fish. In the West Indies the French retained only Guadeloupe, Martinique, and Saint Lucia; and in Africa only Gorée. England restored Havana and Manila to Spain, receiving in exchange the province of Florida, a territory of indefinite extent stretching northward toward Goorgia and westward to the Mississippi River. To compensate Spain for its loss of Florida, and to retain the Spanish alliance, France gave the Spanish Government, by a secret agreement, the city of New Orleans and all the French possessions west of the Mississippi River. The Seven Years' War deprived France of her colonies, her marine, and her political and military prestige, revealed Spain as a weak and incapable military Power, and made England the predominant colonial and commercial Power of Europe.

The wars of the eighteenth century thus greatly modified the standing of the colonial Powers. In 1689 the Portuguese had lost most of their former overseas possessions and the Dutch and the Spanish seemed satisfied to be left in undisturbed possession of the great empires they had occupied. The French and the English were just on the eve of their great colonial careers. During the eighteenth century the Spanish, though repeatedly defeated, succeeded in extending their rule over much of the territory now included in Southwestern United States; the French won and lost great empires in India and North America; and the English established their preëminence among their competitors for dominion overseas. The English victories of the eighteenth century contributed greatly toward the creation of the present British Empire.

REFERENCES

The Rivalry of France and England in America
 J. S. Bassett, *A Short History of the United States*, chapter VI.
 H. E. Bolton and T. M. Marshall, *The Colonization of North America, 1492–1783*, chapters XIV–XX.
 H. Robinson, *The Development of the British Empire*, chapter VI.
 J. H. Robinson and C. A. Beard, *Development of Modern Europe*, vol. I, chapter VII.
 W. H. Woodward, *A Short History of the Expansion of the British Empire*, pp. 64–69, 85–176, 182–96.

Sources on the Rivalry of France and England in America
 J. H. Robinson and C. A. Beard, *Readings in European History*, vol. I, chapter VII.

Development of Spanish Colonial Power in the Seventeenth and Eighteenth Centuries
 H. E. Bolton and T. M. Marshall, *The Colonization of North America*, chapters XIII–XVI.

The Rivalry of France and England in India
 Cambridge Modern History, vol. VI, chapter XV.
 H. Robinson, *The Development of the British Empire*, chapter VI.
 J. H. Robinson and C. A. Beard, *The Development of Modern Europe*, vol. I, chapter VI.
 W. H. Woodward, *A Short History of the Expansion of the British Empire*, pp. 69–85, 176–81, 198–208.
 Lyall, *The Rise of British Dominion in India*.
 Histoire générale, vol. VII, chapter VI.

Sources on the Rivalry of France and England in India
 J. H. Robinson and C. A. Beard, *Readings in Modern European History*, vol. I, chapter VI.

Maps
 The struggle for colonial dominion, 1700–63, W. R. Shepherd, *Historical Atlas*, p. 136.

CHAPTER XI

AUSTRIA AND PRUSSIA IN THE EIGHTEENTH CENTURY

THE Holy Roman Empire was even weaker at the opening of the eighteenth century than in the year 1500. The authority of the Emperor and the Diet had been steadily transferred to the states composing the Empire. Among these states the rising Kingdom of Prussia and the loosely organized state of Austria, composed of the hereditary lands of the Habsburg Emperors, had the deciding voice. The petty and middle-sized states wielded comparatively little influence.

AUSTRIA IN 1740

The Habsburgs created the modern state of Austria. During the latter part of the Middle Ages they had gradually acquired control of Austria proper and the adjoining provinces of Styria, Carinthia, Carniola, and Tyrol. Just at the opening of the modern period Ferdinand, the brother of Charles V, had laid the foundation for the modern state of Austria-Hungary by joining in a personal union the kingdoms of Bohemia and Hungary to the hereditary Habsburg possessions. Then in 1555 the Austrian lands had been separated from the remaining territories of Charles V in Western Europe and started on a separate career.

Thereafter, the realm, which centered at Vienna, participated in most of the movements which affected Western Europe. For a time the Protestant revolt threatened its religious unity. The Catholic Reformation, however, regained Austria and Styria for the Church, and the Thirty Years' War stamped out Protestantism in Bohemia. From the time of this war onward the policy of humbling the Habsburgs, inaugurated by Richelieu and continued by his successors, menaced the life of the Austrian state. As a result of this policy the Austrian Habsburgs lost Alsace to France by the Treaty of Westphalia (1648), but gained Naples, Sicily,[1]

[1] In 1720 Savoy exchanged Sicily for Sardinia and the title King of Sardinia.

and the Spanish Netherlands by the Treaty of Utrecht (1713). These acquisitions increased the complexity of the problems confronting the Habsburgs.

In the meantime on their eastern boundary the Austrian Habsburgs had been engaged in a severe struggle with the Turks for possession of the Danube Valley. In 1526 the disastrous battle of Mohács had put the Turks in possession of the greater part of Hungary, and in 1683 only the timely intervention of the Poles had saved Vienna, the Austrian capital, from capture. In the closing years of the seventeenth century, however, the Habsburgs had finally succeeded in clearing Eastern Hungary, Croatia, and Transylvania of Turkish invaders.

In the eighteenth century the question of the succession became the chief problem of the Habsburg monarchy. Charles VI, who came into possession of the various Austrian provinces in 1711, had no male heir. He devoted his reign to the task of insuring the peaceful succession of his daughter, Maria Theresa, to the Habsburg possessions. First he wrested the assent of his various dominions to the fundamental law, known as the Pragmatic Sanction, which set forth the rights of his daughter. Then he spent the rest of his life in negotiating, bargaining, and fighting with the Powers of Europe in an effort to obtain their support. In consequence, by the time of his death in 1740, every important state of Europe had recognized by treaty the claims of his daughter.

Therefore the War of the Austrian Succession, which broke out in 1740, found the Austrian state ill-prepared to sustain a prolonged attack. The new ruler was a woman with no experience in ruling. Her peaceful accession to her wide-flung empire depended largely on the paper promises of jealous, land-hungry neighbors: for her father had disregarded the blunt advice of Prince Eugène that a good army and a well-filled treasury would be the best guarantee of her rights.

PRUSSIA 1713–40

In contrast with his Austrian contemporary Frederick

William I of Prussia believed thoroughly in the advice of Prince Eugène. Upon his accession in 1713 he found his widely scattered territories unprovided with natural boundaries, devastated by plague, bankrupted by his display-loving predecessor, and surrounded by aggressive neighbors. He left it twenty-seven years later with a superbly drilled army, a well-filled treasury, and a highly centralized government.

This ruler combined many sterling qualities with strange eccentricities that aroused the mirth of his contemporaries. He treated his own family harshly. His ready cane fell on the backs of his servants, his soldiers, and his subjects. He had a mania for tall soldiers. He discussed public affairs in a rude assembly, composed of his intimates, which he called his "Tobacco Parliament." His economies bordered on avarice. These qualities the facile, malicious pen of his own daughter have distorted into a caricature of the real Frederick William I. His virtues deserve more attention than they have received. He had an almost boundless energy. His moral rectitude "transformed the whole tone of his surroundings." He had a great capacity for attention to detail. In a real sense he made himself the first servant of the State.

Before his pompous, theatrical father had been dead an hour, Frederick William struck the keynote of his reign in a dramatic way. Calling for the household accounts he drew a line through the whole list of court lackeys and pages. The same fate overtook the court poet, the twenty-five trumpeters, and many other individuals who had ornamented the court of his father. He likewise sold the fine jewels, the beautiful furniture, and the costly equipage collected by his father. He reduced his own court to about the limits deemed suitable for the establishment of a wealthy private gentleman. He spent the money saved by these economies on the army.

Frederick William I made this institution his first care. He increased it from 38,000 to 80,000. As a result of this increase Prussia, the twelfth state of Europe in respect to population, ranked fourth from the point of view of its military establishment.

The King maintained such a military force only by resorting to extraordinary measures. At first he relied on voluntary enlistments and impressment to keep up its numbers, even permitting recruiting officers to surprise congregations during Sunday service and carry off the largest and strongest young men for the army. In 1733 he adopted the cantonal system of recruiting. He divided the country into cantons containing about five thousand families, each canton being expected to supply the recruits for one regiment. In practice the nobles furnished the officers for the army, the peasantry the rank and file, and the middle class escaped military service entirely.

The maintenance of such a large army put a tremendous strain on the Prussian state. For its support the Government depended mainly on the income derived from the royal domains and from taxation. The King found his domains heavily mortgaged, and one third to one half of the tenants carried off by plague. He leased the royal estates on more advantageous terms and settled the waste lands with colonists. By this policy he more than doubled the income derived from the royal estates.

In colonizing his waste lands with immigrants Frederick William I followed in the footsteps of the Great Elector. He advertised through the Dutch press and other agencies for settlers, and offered them inducements similiar to those earlier extended to the Huguenots. He attracted some 30,000 colonists to the country by these methods. About one half of them came from Salzburg, where the Protestants were being persecuted by a newly elected archbishop. Their story has been immortalized by Goethe in his *Hermann und Dorothea*. The remainder came mainly from the Swiss cantons and from the south and west of Germany. They settled for the most part in East Prussia, where they made notable contributions to the civilization of the province.

In opening his state to the victims of economic misfortune and religious persecution, the thrifty Prussian King did a good stroke of business. He sold the colonists horses, oxen, and cows at a substantial profit, settled them on the inferior lands of the domain, and made a good return on his investment. He repeopled in this way fifty-nine royal domains, three hundred and thirty villages, and six cities.

The King was not so successful in increasing the revenue derived from taxation. By rigidly enforcing the existing tax laws, reorganizing the administration, improving the economic condition of the kingdom, and substituting a money tax for the old feudal obligations of the nobles, the King only increased the yield from taxation by a third. The abolition of feudal tenures, however, had considerable political and social significance.

In his efforts to improve the economic condition of the country the King was a thoroughgoing mercantilist of the school of Colbert. He facilitated the export of Prussian manufactures, discouraged imports, and stimulated domestic manufactures. His legislation concerning the woolen industry well illustrates both the royal policy and its results. He forbade the export of raw wool, prohibited the importation of woolen manufactures, extended assistance of all sorts to domestic manufacturers, and induced skilled foreign artisans to settle in the kingdom. As a result of the royal policy the Prussian woolen industry employed by the end of the reign five thousand men, supplied the demands of the army and the country, and produced a large surplus for export to Russia and other countries. Similar schemes for the encouragement of tobacco warehouses and silk and linen factories proved less successful.

Frederick William also transformed the finances of the kingdom. In 1713 he found his subjects too poor to advance money to their government and foreign countries unwilling to make loans to his state. The Prussian armies had been kept in the field by foreign subsidies during the War of the Spanish Succession. By careful economy, skillful management of the royal domains, the fostering of industry, and more effective management of taxation he nearly doubled the royal revenues and created a large royal treasure.

Much of the improvement in the finances of the state was due to the reorganization of the administrative machinery.

The Great Elector had transformed the semi-feudal into an absolutist state. Frederick William I gave it unity and system. A general directory divided into five departments was established at Berlin in 1722 under the presidency of the King. Subordinate to this central body were chambers of war and domains in the provinces. At the base of the administrative hierarchy were royal commissioners who supervised rural districts or groups of towns. Drastic punishment was provided for peculation and laxness. The officials were to be trained men, and were not to be appointed to positions in their own provinces. Both the strength and the weakness of the system lay in the fact that everything depended on the sovereign.

In ecclesiastical matters Frederick William adopted in the main the policy of the Great Elector. He treated the Jews severely, and suppressed the dissenting Protestant sects; but he tolerated the Catholics, with the exception of the Jesuits. He made unsuccessful efforts to abate theological strife and to unite the Lutherans and the Calvinists. In comparison with his contemporaries he followed a tolerant policy.

For culture and education beyond the rudiments of learning, the coarse, blunt King had nothing but contempt. He reduced the yearly allowance made to the Academy of Arts from a thousand to three hundred thalers, and charged the society rent for the rooms that it occupied. He cut off the pension of Leibnitz, the great philosopher and mathematician, and upon his death appointed a court fool in his place as president of the Academy of Sciences. He neglected the royal library and diverted its funds to other uses. The universities suffered from the kidnaping of students by the recruiting officers, lack of funds, and the contempt and abuse heaped on their faculties. As a result of the royal policy the Prussian state produced nothing in the realm of letters, science, or the arts during the reign.

In spite of the militarization of the state the reign of Frederick William was comparatively peaceful. The single important event of the period, in respect to foreign affairs, was the acquisition of Stettin, the port of Berlin. The King first obtained from Peter the Great the right to occupy Swedish Pomerania during the Northern War; then he purchased the district from Sweden by the Treaty of Stockholm (1720).

Much that has been most characteristic of the Prussian state thus dates from the reign of this harsh, arbitrary, peculiar sovereign. He continued the policies of colonization and toleration bequeathed to him by his predecessors. He was one of the founders of the bureaucracy, the army, and the domineering officer class of Prussia. His ideals rose no higher than the level of the barracks, but he made possible the rise of Prussia under the guidance of his famous son to the position of a great European Power.

THE WARS OF FREDERICK THE GREAT

The death of Frederick William I in 1740 made his son, Frederick II, master of the army, the treasury, and the absolutist state his father had done so much to create. His richly endowed nature had already been gnarled and twisted by his tragic quarrel with his father. Frederick had shown a detestation for military life, vigorous amusements, and the coarse companions of his father, and a decided inclination for music, literature, gay clothes, and flighty companions of both sexes. Frederick William, alarmed for the permanence of his life-work, had tried to force his more delicately organized son into the same coarse, rough mould that had produced his own blunt, rugged, God-fearing nature. His policy had estranged Frederick II and driven him to make an unsuccessful attempt at flight from the kingdom. As a punishment the father had forced his son to witness the execution of one of his companions, and to learn by the most intense application the details of governing a country and commanding troops. The stern discipline of the father laid the foundation for much of the later success of Frederick II, but at the price of a bitterness of spirit that colored his whole outlook on life.

Shortly after his accession to the Prussian throne, Frederick II cynically marched his troops into the undefended Austrian province of Silesia without the formality of a declaration of war, occupied the greater part of the province, and thus started the War of the Austrian Succession (1740-48). The conflict was waged both in Europe and overseas. On the Continent the European states fought for possession of Silesia and over the balance of power; in America and India (1744-48) for colonies and commerce. The chief events of the overseas struggle and of the War of Jenkins's Ear which merged with it have already been narrated.[1]

The Prussian occupation of Silesia and the decisive victory of Frederick II over the Austrian forces sent to drive him out of the province disclosed to the other states of Europe the military weakness of Austria. Disregarding their solemn promises to the father of Maria Theresa, Spain, Bavaria, and Saxony prepared to push their claims to the Austrian succession, and France, urged by a war party to complete the humbling of the Habsburgs, finally entered the conflict. Thereupon they formed an alliance with Prussia for the dismemberment of the inheritance of Maria Theresa (1741). Only England, which confined its assistance mainly to advice and subsidies, appeared to remember its promise to stand by the "Pragmatic Sanction."

In Europe the struggle went on in three general areas. In Italy the forces of Austria and Sardinia fought those of France, Spain, and Naples for control of the peninsula. In Central Europe Austria carried on an unequal struggle with Prussia, Saxony, Bavaria, and France. In the Austrian Netherlands the French forces opposed English, Dutch, and Austrian troops. In Italy four years of warfare left the political situation practically unchanged. In Central Europe the Austrian efforts against Frederick II failed and, with the assistance of a large French army, the Elector of Bavaria overran Upper Austria and Bohemia and obtained the imperial crown. Fortune then veered to the side of Maria Theresa. Her forces cleared Upper Austria and Bohemia of invaders, occupied Bavaria, and forced the new Elector of Bavaria to redeem his territories at the price of surrendering his father's imperial claims. In the Austrian Netherlands

[1] In Chapter X.

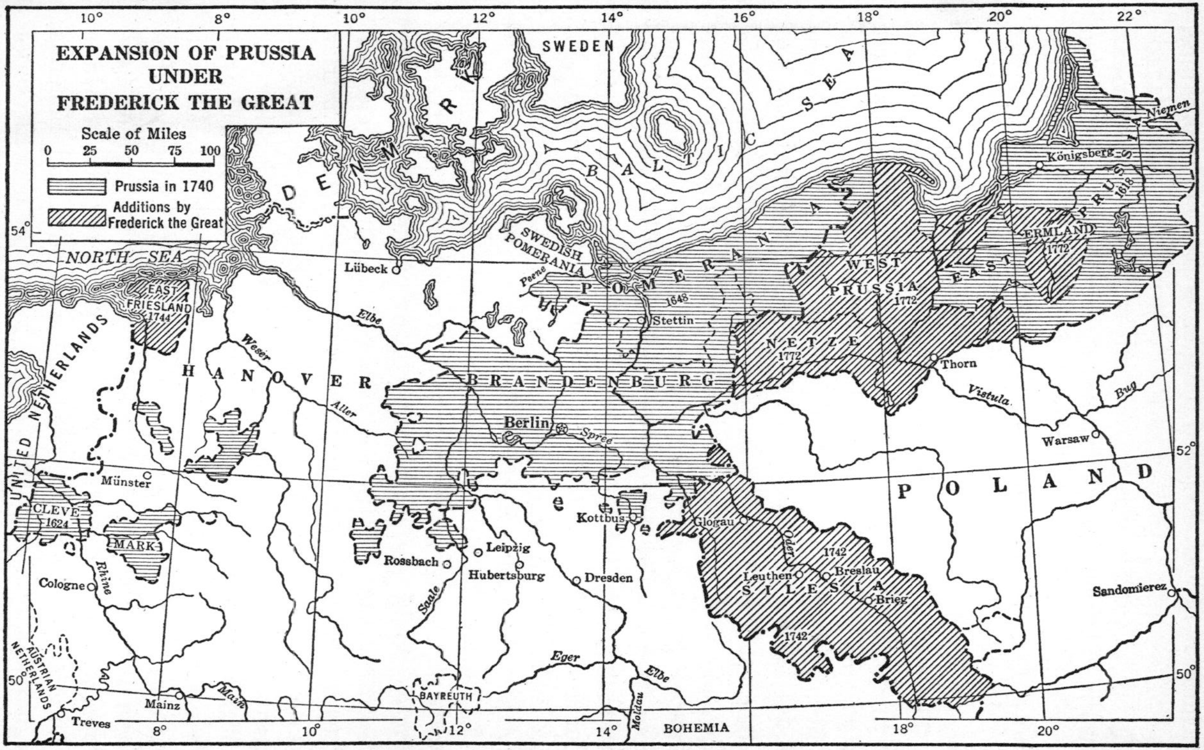
EXPANSION OF PRUSSIA
UNDER
FREDERICK THE GREAT
Scale of Miles
0 25 50 75 100
Prussia in 1740
Additions by Frederick the Great
SWEDEN
DENMARK
BALTIC SEA
NORTH SEA
EAST FRIESLAND 1744
UNITED NETHERLANDS
HANOVER
SWEDISH POMERANIA
POMERANIA
1648
Stettin
Lübeck
BRANDENBURG
Berlin
Spree
Elbe
Weser
Aller
Peene
WEST PRUSSIA
1772
NETZE
1772
EAST PRUSSIA
1618
ERMLAND
1772
Königsberg
Niemen
Thorn
Vistula
Bug
Warsaw
POLAND
Sandomierez
SILESIA
1742
Glogau
Oder
Breslau
Leuthen
Brieg
Kottbus
Leipzig
Rossbach
Hubertsburg
Dresden
Saale
Eger
Moldau
BOHEMIA
BAYREUTH
Münster
CLEVE
1624
MARK
Rhine
Cologne
Mainz
Main
Treves
AUSTRIAN NETHERLANDS
54°
52°
50°
8°
10°
12°
14°
16°
18°
20°
22°

the French forces overran a large part of the province. The French success in the Austrian Netherlands and the Prussian seizure of Silesia were the two outstanding military achievements of the European struggle.

The King of Prussia conducted the struggle with characteristic duplicity. After sending to Maria Theresa at the time of her accession to the Austrian throne a formal recognition of her position and the offer of military assistance in case of need, the Prussian monarch invaded the Austrian province of Silesia without declaring war, representing to the inhabitants that he was acting in the interest of Maria Theresa and with her approval. Then twice during the war (1742 and 1745) he deserted his allies and made a separate peace with Austria, cynically remarking after the negotiation of the second treaty of peace, "Happy are they who, having secured their own safety, can look tranquilly on the embarrassment and anxiety of others." He left his allies to make the best terms they could.

The eight years of indecisive fighting made little change in the map of Europe. By the treaty of peace signed at Aix-la-Chapelle in 1748, Frederick II kept Silesia, and added to his territories an area of great industrial and agricultural value, covering 15,500 square miles, and containing a million and a quarter of inhabitants. Sardinia extended the eastern boundary of Piedmont to the Ticino.

The treaty of peace signed in 1748 could be little more than a truce. The war had crushed none of the combatants and the peace settlement had satisfied none of the Powers. Neither France nor England had gained anything. Prussia was uneasy about the safety of its newly acquired province; and Austria was not reconciled to its loss. The general situation made a reopening of hostilities almost a certainty.

Maria Theresa especially prepared for a renewal of the war. The success of Prussia in the War of the Austrian Succession had convinced her and her advisers of the necessity of transforming the Habsburg state according to the Prussian pattern. Accordingly, they set about to improve the machinery of government, to increase the resources of the state, and to strengthen the army.

The great political need was centralization of authority. The central government deprived the nobles and the provinces of much of their power and required the provincial estates to vote a fixed sum for ten years instead of making annual contributions of money and men. This gave the central government control both of the army and of a fixed revenue. Simultaneously the machinery of government was simplified and modernized. Each branch of the central administration was put under a separate department and a council of state was created to coördinate and control the various branches of the government.

At the same time drastic educational, religious, industrial, and commercial reforms were introduced. The reformers started a system of primary education, established or improved technical schools of various sorts, brought the universities under the control of the State, and built hospitals and asylums. In the ecclesiastical sphere they regulated carefully the monasteries and their property, decreased the number of holidays in the interest of industry, and for political reasons subjected to royal control the communication of the Pope with the Austrian clergy. Manufactures of cloth, porcelain, silk, and other articles were established, and roads and canals vastly improved. As a result of these measures Austria entered the Seven Years' War strengthened and reorganized.

The building-up of a strong army was of even more importance for the carrying-out of the plans of Maria Theresa and her ministers. A system of conscription, following the general lines of that used in Prussia, was introduced in all the Habsburg dominions except Hungary, Tyrol, The Netherlands, and the Duchy of Milan; the size of the army was increased; incompetent officers were removed; military schools were created; and many of the Prussian methods were adopted. As a result of these reforms Maria Theresa was able on the outbreak of the Seven Years' War to put an admirable military force into the field.

While the Austrian administrators were busy reorganizing the Habsburg state, the Austrian diplomats were engaged in laying the foundations of a great coalition against Frederick II of Prussia. The formation of such an alliance necessitated a realignment of the Powers that has aptly been described as the "Diplomatic Revolution." Only the principal steps in the long and complicated negotiations can be given. Austria began the revolution by making diplomatic advances to France, its chief enemy since the days of Richelieu, because by this time Austria and England did not have enough interests in common to maintain the alliance formed between them in 1689 on the eve of the War of the League of Augsburg. England, on the other hand, was more interested in the fate of the Hanoverian possessions of the King of England than in the fate of Silesia. For this reason England concluded a treaty with Frederick II that provided for the protection of Hanover and the maintenance of German neutrality in case of war between France and England. By this treaty Frederick hoped to ward off the danger of being asked by his French ally to attack England through an attack on Hanover in case of an Anglo-French war, a move which would give Russia and Austria an opportunity to attack his own possessions. France, however, looked upon this Anglo-Prussian agreement as a defection on the part of Prussia from the French alliance and at once signed a defensive treaty with Austria. These agreements of Prussia and England and of France and Austria completely reversed the European system of alliances.

Austria next united the states hostile to Prussia into a defensive alliance. Russia, which had been an ally of Austria almost continuously since 1726, readily agreed in 1756 to furnish 80,000 men for an attack on Prussia. Austria was to regain Silesia, and Russia was to have East Prussia. The Elector of Saxony was gained for the league against Prussia by the prospect of having his elective kingship in Poland changed into an hereditary office. Sweden was won by the promise of Prussian Pomerania. Finally, after an unheralded attack of Prussia on Saxony to prevent the resources of

AUSTRIA AND PRUSSIA

that state being placed at the disposal of the coalition, that Frederick well knew was being formed against him, France signed a treaty by which she agreed to furnish 105,000 men and an annual subsidy to the new alliance being constructed by Austria. This agreement completed the great coalition against Frederick II.

The war, started on the Continent by the attack of the Prussian King on Saxony, is known as the Seven Years' War. Like the earlier War of the Austrian Succession, it was carried on in America, in India, on the sea, and on the Continent. The overseas struggle of England with France (and for a short time with Spain) over colonies and commerce has already been described. As France and, to a much less extent, England (on account of Hanover) were interested in both the continental and the overseas struggles, there was a tendency for the outbreak of fighting in one place to bring about a renewal of hostilities in the other.

The continental struggle was carried on in two different areas and was divided into three distinct periods. In Western Germany two armies, one composed exclusively of French troops and the other of French and imperial forces, operated from the Rhine and the Main Rivers as bases. In Eastern and Central Germany Frederick faced Austria, Russia, and Sweden.

The first period of conflict included the campaigns of 1756 and 1757. The sudden invasion of Saxony by the Prussians, which has already been described, was followed by the overrunning of much of Bohemia and the investment of Prague, its capital city. Fortune then turned against the King of Prussia. An Austrian army sent to relieve Prague defeated Frederick himself and forced him to evacuate Bohemia. The defeat and capitulation of the Hanoverian forces in Western Germany followed this disaster; the Swedes entered Eastern Pomerania; and the Russians took Memel and Tilsit in East Prussia, and won the victory of Jaegersdorf over the Prussians. Just as all seemed lost for Prussia, Frederick II extricated himself from his perilous position by two crushing victories: one at Rossbach in Saxony over the army of the

French, and one at Leuthen in Silesia over the Austrians. The first period ended with Saxony and Silesia in possession of Prussia and with the Russians and Swedes in retreat.

The second period of the war closely resembled the first, except that Frederick II was almost wholly on the defensive. In 1758 Prussian forces drove the French armies back to the Rhine and the Main, while the Russians in East Prussia and the Austrians in Silesia defeated Frederick himself. In the following year the Russians overran the Prussian dominions as far as the Oder and the Austrians gave the Prussians the worst defeat of the war at Kunersdorf in Silesia. Only the diversion of the Russians to Silesia and their subsequent withdrawal to East Prussia saved Prussia from defeat. The campaign of the succeeding year was very much a repetition of that of 1759. The Russians greatly harassed the eastern provinces of Prussia, while the Prussians defeated the Austrians in both Silesia and Saxony. The second period of the war thus ended with Prussia cleared of enemies and Saxony still in the hands of Frederick.

In the third period of the conflict Prussia was saved as a result of changes in Russian policy. The Prussian armies did manage to throw the French armies back across the Rhine and Main Rivers in 1761 after various engagements, but they failed to protect East Prussia and Pomerania from the Russians. Just as the forces of Frederick were reaching complete exhaustion, however, the Tsarina Elizabeth, the implacable enemy of Frederick, died, and Peter III, a great admirer of the Prussian King, came to the Russian throne. One of his first acts was to order his troops to fight thereafter on the side of Prussia. As a result of a palace revolution, Peter III was assassinated too soon to play an important part on the Prussian side, but his successor, Catherine II, aided Frederick by adopting a policy of neutrality. The withdrawal of Russia left Frederick in possession of Silesia and his enemies too weak to wrest the province from him.

The war weariness of the remaining combatants led to the negotiation of peace at Hubertusburg. By the treaty signed there early in 1763, Frederick retained Silesia and promised

Joseph, the son and heir of Maria Theresa, his vote in the coming imperial election. The Elector of Saxony recovered his German dominions. The Seven Years' War thus left England mistress of the seas, France deprived of her colonies, her marine, and her political and military prestige, and Prussia actually the chief state in Germany, and firmly established as a great Power.

FREDERICK THE GREAT AS AN ENLIGHTENED DESPOT

Frederick II was one of the first sovereigns of Europe to show an interest in the intellectual movement led by Voltaire, Montesquieu, and other French writers and thinkers of the eighteenth century.[1] He corresponded with Voltaire, induced a number of the French literary men to settle in Berlin, surrounded himself with wits and writers of French origin, professed to believe the doctrines of the French philosophers, and made some show of applying their principles in the government of his state. He was the most prominent of the eighteenth-century group of rulers known as the "enlightened despots."

The Prussian King had two opportunities to apply the ideas of the French philosophers to the problems of his government. The first came in the decade that intervened between the withdrawal of Frederick from the War of the Austrian Succession and the opening of the Seven Years' War; the second after the conclusion of peace in 1763. As a result of the ravages of the Seven Years' War in Prussia much of the work of the first period had to be done over again. In both periods Frederick followed the same general principles and used the same administrative methods. Consequently the whole work of Frederick II as an enlightened despot may well be studied in one place.

The close of the Seven Years' War found the Prussian state terribly devastated and its population actually decimated. Silesia had been the scene of five military campaigns and had lost 50,000 of its inhabitants. The Prussian provinces east of the Oder, which had been repeatedly overrun

[1] This movement is discussed in Chapter XII.

by the Russians, had lost proportionately five times as many people. Frederick himself estimated that one ninth of his subjects had disappeared during the war. Berlin had been raided three times; the army cut to pieces; the treasury practically exhausted; and the coinage debased. Ruin, misery, and waste prevailed where seven years earlier there had been prosperity and progress.

Immediately after the conclusion of peace Frederick set himself resolutely to the task of reconstructing his state. He gave rations to the needy out of the military magazines, remitted taxes for six months in Silesia and for two years in Pomerania and the eastern part of Brandenburg (known as the New Mark), donated timber and money for the rebuilding of the houses and farms destroyed by fire, and distributed seed, oxen, horses, sheep, pigs, and cows to the peasants free of charge. As a result of these measures Prussia quickly recovered from the effects of the war and the royal Government soon began to reap a reward for its efforts at reconstruction in the form of rents, taxes, and increased population.

These temporary measures were supplemented by more permanent policies. Throughout his reign Frederick carried on the policy of attracting immigrants to Prussia, begun by the Great Elector and continued by Frederick William I. He established immigration agencies at Hamburg and Frankfort, and offered immigrants traveling expenses, building material, money, and exemption from customs duties, taxes, and military service. Every weaver immigrating into the state received a free loom; peasant farmers, seed and cattle; and manufacturers, assistance in starting new industries. The new colonists came from every part of Germany. All told three hundred thousand immigrants are estimated to have settled in Prussia. By the close of the reign one sixth of the royal subjects were either immigrants or the children of immigrants.

Many of the colonists were established on lands that had been reclaimed at the direction of the King. Frederick strove to make every acre of his dominions productive. If he observed in his tours of inspection through his provinces a waste place capable of improvement he reported it to the proper provincial chamber of war and domains as a site for a certain number of villages of a given size. The methods of Frederick are well illustrated by his work in reclaiming the great swamps along the Oder below the city of Frankfort. The work of drainage was begun in 1747, soldiers being placed at the disposal of the officials in immediate charge of the work. Five hundred thousand thalers were expended on the undertaking. Two hundred and fifty villages were established by immigrants from the Rhineland, Mecklenburg, Sweden, Saxony, Bohemia, Poland, and Austria. By the use of such methods over fifteen thousand square miles of territory were reclaimed during the reign.

Frederick adopted without question the mercantilist theories of his contemporaries. Industries were artificially developed and prohibitions of imports and exports followed each other in rapid succession after 1763. In the interest of domestic manufactures the export of Silesian wool to Austria was stopped. After the discovery of rich strata of iron ore in Upper Silesia, in 1768, the importation of Swedish iron and of pig iron and raw steel from Austria was forbidden. Frederick aimed to develop within his boundaries all the industries necessary to a great state.

In an effort to carry out this policy, establishments for the spinning and weaving of linen, wool, cotton, and silk, the refining of sugar, and the manufacture of porcelain and glassware were actually started. In every industry employers and employed alike were assisted with free gifts, pecuniary advances, indemnifications, and premiums. Public warehouses for wool, silk, and cotton were established, and the whole traffic in raw materials was supervised and controlled by the State. Two million thalers were spent on developing the silk and velvet manufactures alone and the industry grew steadily. The Prussian porcelain industry was a by-product of the Seven Years' War. During the occupation of Saxony by the Prussians the secret of the famous Dresden ware was extorted from the employees of the Elector of Saxony. No effort was spared to make the most of the discovery. The manufactory at Berlin was bought; the purchase of rival products from abroad was prohibited; porcelain was substituted for gold and silver plate on the royal table; and Jews who wished to marry were compelled to purchase a service of porcelain. Although at Frederick's accession Prussia made only a few manufactured articles, toward the end of his reign one of his ministers could boast that the kingdom produced every conceivable manufacture.

The influence of the French philosophers is most clearly to be seen in the judicial and legal reforms of Frederick. He abandoned the use of torture to obtain evidence in trials. With the aid of Cocceji, a jurist, the King abolished superfluous courts, reduced the number of judges, and quickened procedure. A great code of civil law was projected, but the work was not completed until the succeeding reign. Up to this time Prussian law had been a mixture of Roman law, Church law, and old Germanic customs.

In spite of his boasted enlightenment the King was essentially a conservative. He continued in the main the administrative, financial, military, social, and religious policies handed on to him by his father. He made no material change in the administrative machinery, but he established a department for the supervision of trade, manufacture, post, and immigration in 1740, and one for military affairs in 1746. He continued to collect the old taxes, and imposed a number of new ones. He steadily increased the army in numbers and equipment. He continued the traditional policy of the Hohenzollerns in respect to toleration. He made no fundamental change in the inner organization of the state. For the sake of maintaining an officer class and an ample supply of recruits, he preserved the privileges of the nobles and the serfdom of the peasants. The shock of the disasters of the Napoleonic period was needed to make the leaders of Prussia ready for a thoroughgoing reform of the Prussian state.

The last twenty-three years of the reign of Frederick II were thus mainly taken up with the activities of peace. Foreign affairs played a much less important part than in the years prior to 1763. The foreign event of most permanent interest in these years was the acquisition of West Prussia by the Prussian state as a result of the partition of Polish territory between Russia, Prussia, and Austria in 1772. By acquiring this Polish province the Prussian state materially shortened its boundary line. As the partitions of Poland are primarily facts of Polish history, they will be fully discussed in the chapter on "Slavic Europe and the Ottoman Empire in the Eighteenth Century."

As a result of the various activities of Frederick II in behalf of his state, Prussia was much stronger at the time of his death in 1786 than at his accession in 1740. The number of inhabitants in the state had grown as a result of the annexation of Silesia and West Prussia, the policy of colonization, and the natural increase of the population from 2,200,000 to over 4,000,000. The army had been doubled, the fortresses rebuilt, magazines established, and equipment provided for an army of 200,000 men. The finances showed each year a comfortable surplus of revenues over expenses and the treasure stored away for use in time of war amounted to more than the revenues of the state for two years. Many marshes had been drained, woods planted, and wastes cultivated. The number of cattle and horses had doubled. Under the leadership of Frederick II Prussia achieved as much as its antiquated, medieval organization would permit.

Thus the rise of Prussia from a small state of the Empire to a position of equality with the great Powers of Europe was accomplished in less than a century and a half under the leadership of four members of the House of Hohenzollern. In developing their state they followed with fidelity certain clearly marked principles. Territorial expansion of the state, development of the army, the establishment of a centralized absolutism, encouragement of immigration, and tolerance in religion are policies which characterized each of the four reigns. No state in Europe is as much the product of the policies of its rulers as Prussia.

JOSEPH II AS AN ENLIGHTENED DESPOT

A far more faithful disciple of the French philosophers than Frederick II of Prussia was Joseph II, the son and successor of Maria Theresa. Although he was associated with his mother in the government for fifteen years as co-regent, he never felt free to follow his own inclinations until her death in 1780. Once freed from her control he undertook to inaugurate in his various dominions most of the measures that appeared reasonable and necessary to the reformers of the eighteenth century.

One of the first reform decrees of Joseph II was his patent of toleration. In all places where they had sufficient numbers to defray the cost of worship, he permitted Protestants and Greek Catholics to build places of worship on condition that their religious edifices should have neither bells nor steeples and should bear no resemblance to churches. Protestants and Greek Catholics could become members of trades and corporations and receive academic degrees. By special dispensation of the Emperor they also might be permitted to hold public office.

Several of the reforming decrees dealt with the monasteries. They were prohibited from recognizing the authority of foreign superiors. The contemplative orders were suppressed, and the congregations occupied with the care of the sick and teaching were forbidden to admit new members for a period of ten years. Their property was to be used in pensioning the monks and in sustaining schools and humanitarian institutions. As a result of these confiscatory measures some seven hundred out of more than two thousand monasteries were suppressed, the number of monks in the state was reduced more than half, and revenues amounting to more than thirty-five million gulden were accumulated.

Great efforts also were made to subordinate the Church to the State. The archbishops, bishops, and other religious authorities were forbidden to receive bulls or letters from the Pope or communications of any sort from foreign ecclesiastical authorities without the approval of the Emperor. Appeals to the court of Rome were prohibited. Marriage was made a civil matter and divorce was instituted in defiance of the teachings of the Church. The bishops were required to take an oath of allegiance to the Emperor and were compelled to submit their instructions and pastoral letters to the temporal authorities for approval. State seminaries were established to give a modern education to candidates for the priesthood. The object of the Emperor in all this legislation was to be master in his own dominions.

Each of the "enlightened despots" did something to improve the legal and judicial institutions of his state. In Austria Joseph II completed the work commenced by his mother. He abolished torture and the old inquisitorial procedure, made the punishments inflicted by the penal code more humane, considerably reduced the cost of justice, and created a hierarchy of courts, with tribunals of first instance, appeals, and final revision. No distinction was made between classes of society. Thus the Austrian judicial and penal code owed much to the reforms of Joseph II.

The sympathies of the Emperor were also aroused by the condition of the peasants. He found them serfs, unable to leave the estates on which they lived or to marry without their lord's consent and subject to a thousand forms of servitude. He freed them from serfdom, compelled the lords to sell to the peasants the land they cultivated for themselves, and gave them the right to change their domiciles and to marry as they pleased.

The political aim of the Emperor was to weld his German, Slav, Belgian, Hungarian, and Italian subjects into a united, compact people. German was made the official language of the state. The rights and powers of the provinces and the cities were greatly curtailed. The functions formerly performed by them were handed over to a centralized administration. The whole state was divided into uniform administrative districts with identical political organs.

The introduction of so many reforms in so short a time soon aroused serious resistance in the Austrian Netherlands and in Hungary. The general uneasiness created by the religious and social legislation of Joseph II was followed by open revolt after the publication of political reforms designed to supersede provincial institutions of long standing. The result of these revolts was the defeat of most of the reform measures of the Emperor. Just before he died Joseph II himself restored to the Hungarians their old constitution, and immediately after his death his brother and successor, Leopold II, followed the same policy in Belgium. Although he died bitterly disappointed at the failure of most of his reforms, a survey of the reign of Joseph II is of value because it clearly portrays the aims and hopes of the reformers of the eighteenth century.

German history between 1713 and 1789 is divided into three rather distinct periods. In the first Charles VI of Austria was attempting to insure the succession of his daughter, Maria Theresa, to the Austrian throne, while his rival, Frederick William I of Prussia, was centralizing political authority in his state, strengthening his army, and building up his treasury. In the second, Prussia and Austria were engaged in a great struggle which resulted in the transfer of the Austrian province of Silesia to Frederick the Great and demonstrated the right of Prussia to be considered as a Power of the first rank. In the third, Frederick the Great and Joseph II tried to apply in their dominions some of the doctrines of the French philosophers, and thereby won for themselves an important place among the group of rulers known as the "enlightened despots."

REFERENCES

AUSTRIA UNDER CHARLES VI
Cambridge Modern History, vol. VI, pp. 201–05.
S. Whitman, *Austria*, chapter XVI.

PRUSSIA UNDER FREDERICK WILLIAM I
E. F. Henderson, *A Short History of Germany*, vol. II, chapter III.

THE WARS OF FREDERICK THE GREAT
Cambridge Modern History, vol. VI, chapters VIII–IX.
A. Hassall, *European History, 1715–89*, chapters VI–IX.
E. F. Henderson, *A Short History of Germany*, vol. II, chapter IV.
J. A. R. Marriott and C. G. Robertson, *The Evolution of Prussia*, pp. 113–38.
G. M. Priest, *Germany since 1740*, chapter II.

J. H. Robinson and C. A. Beard, *The Development of Modern Europe*, vol. II, chapter V.
F. Longmans, *Frederick the Great*.
R. A. Hall, *Frederick the Great and his Wars*.
Histoire générale, vol. VII, chapters IV–V.

FREDERICK THE GREAT AS AN ENLIGHTENED DESPOT
Cambridge Modern History, vol. VI, chapter XX.
E. F. Henderson, *A Short History of Germany*, vol. II, chapter V.
G. M. Priest, *Germany since 1740*, chapter III.
W. F. Reddaway, *Frederick the Great*, chapter X.
T. Campbell, *Frederick the Great*, chapters XV–XVIII, XXXI–XXXVII.

FREDERICK THE GREAT
W. F. Reddaway, *Frederick the Great*.

SOURCES ON THE PERIOD OF FREDERICK THE GREAT
J. H. Robinson and C. A. Beard, *Readings in Modern European History*, chapter V.

MARIA THERESA
J. F. Bright, *Maria Theresa*.

JOSEPH II
Cambridge Modern History, vol. VI, chapter XVIII.
A. Hassall, *European History, 1715–89*, chapter XIII.
S. Whitman, *Austria*, chapter XIX.
J. F. Bright, *Joseph II*.

CHAPTER XII

SLAVIC EUROPE AND THE OTTOMAN EMPIRE IN THE EIGHTEENTH CENTURY

THE IMMEDIATE SUCCESSORS OF PETER THE GREAT

DURING the period between the death of Peter the Great (1725) and the accession of Catherine II (1763), Russia made comparatively little progress along the lines marked out by the great Tsar. As there was no law regulating the succession to the throne, the period was a time of political intrigue, palace revolutions, and frequent changes of rulers and ministers. Catherine II was the first ruler to take up again the policies of Peter the Great.

The outstanding movements of this period were the intervention of Russia in the Seven Years' War, a reaction toward religious intolerance, and the substitution of French for German cultural influences. Because of the change in its foreign policy, Russia had to be considered henceforth as a Power to be reckoned with by the states of Western Europe. Upon the adoption of a more reactionary policy in religion, the Government drove the Jews into Poland, closed the Protestant churches, and destroyed most of the mosques of the Tartars situated north of the Black Sea. As a result of the change in cultural ideals, French tutors and governesses became common in the houses of the Russian nobles, and Russian students and travelers became so numerous in Paris that a Russian chapel was erected in the French capital for their use. Russia thus emerged from the period during which the reforms of Peter the Great were in abeyance with its upper classes more French in culture, with its government more intolerant in religion, and with its prestige enhanced as a result of the victories of the Russian troops in the Seven Years' War.

In 1762 a new palace revolution elevated Catherine II to the Russian throne. She proved to be the greatest ruler, with the single exception of Peter the Great, in the long line of Russian sovereigns. The most important phases of her reign were her enlightened despotism and her intervention in the affairs of Poland and Turkey. Her foreign policy led to the partition of Poland and the dismemberment of Turkey.

CATHERINE II AS AN ENLIGHTENED DESPOT

No ruler of the eighteenth century enjoyed a greater reputation for enlightenment than Catherine II. In the main her reputation was the result of her careful cultivation of relations with the French philosophers. She understood thoroughly the importance of winning the approbation of Europe for herself and her country. With this end in view she maintained an active correspondence with Voltaire for over fifteen years, induced Diderot to make Saint Petersburg his home for a time, offered d'Alembert the post of tutor to her son, Paul, and expressed the greatest admiration for the work of Buffon. Flattered by these royal attentions, the French philosophers represented Catherine II to Europe as one of the most enlightened of contemporary sovereigns.

Her actual achievements did not correspond to her great reputation. Her reforms were limited to a slight increase in religious toleration, the further secularization of the property of the Russian Church, the colonization of the sparsely settled steppes of the Don and the Volga, and the establishment of a few institutions for secondary education and public assistance. She did practically nothing to alleviate the hard lot of the Russian serfs, to lessen the inefficiency of the Russian Government, or to Europeanize the great mass of the Russian people.

Catherine II opened her reign with a decree that seemed to promise much for the future of Russia. For the purpose of drawing up a new code of laws for the Russian people, she summoned to Moscow an assembly which represented every element in the population of Russia. For the guidance of this body the Tsarina drew up a set of instructions that owed much to the maxims of Montesquieu and Beccaria. The assembly, however, accomplished little. Its members had little practical experience with deliberative bodies, and

Catherine II and her advisers were not ready for radical reforms. A few of the recommendations of the assembly were finally embodied in decrees, but the most important result of calling the body together was the enlightenment of the Tsarina as to the condition and needs of her empire. Some fifteen hundred statements of grievances, which threw a flood of light on the situation of her state, were brought to Moscow by members of the assembly.

In respect to the serfs the results of the reign of Catherine II were equally disappointing. Instead of freeing the serfs or alleviating their lot she actually enlarged the area of serfdom by extending the right of bondage to Little Russia and gave away to her favorites estates populated with about 800,000 souls. The masters continued to control the marriages of their serfs, to assign them tasks, and to inflict terrible punishments upon them. Early in her reign she forbade the selling of serfs and the dispersion of their families, but a decree forbidding serfs to complain of their masters made these prohibitions practically ineffective. In spite of an apparent desire to improve the condition of the Russian peasantry, the net result of the reign of Catherine II was to tighten the bonds of serfdom and to extend its area.

A similar fate overtook the Tsarina's dreams of creating a great national system of education, consisting of primary, secondary, and higher schools. She established only a few secondary institutions. During this period, however, the upper classes increased their acquaintance with French culture. Frenchmen became more numerous in Russia, their language became more widely used, and their arts and literature more appreciated. In 1783 a Russian Academy was founded in imitation of the famous French Academy. This absorption of French culture was confined entirely to the upper classes of Russia, and tended to deepen the chasm already separating the aristocracy from the peasant masses.

The Tsarina did something for the promotion of public health by founding a college of medicine, by opening a number of hospitals, and by popularizing the custom of inoculation for smallpox. By having herself inoculated in 1768 by an English physician, she put in vogue the practice, and thus did a great deal toward eliminating an important cause of depopulation in Russia.

In matters of religion Catherine II shared the views of the French philosophers. During the course of her reign she secularized the lands of the Russian Church and introduced a greater degree of religious toleration. A decree of 1764 secularized the Church lands of Great Russia and Siberia. The Government then greatly reduced in number and amount the heavy and complicated payments of the peasants on these lands, and entirely abolished forced labor. As a result of the more tolerant policy adopted by the Tsarina in religion, the Moslems reopened their mosques in Southern Russia, and the Jesuits reëntered the empire.

POLAND ON THE EVE OF THE FIRST PARTITION

At the opening of the modern period of history, Poland was the largest state in Europe and the dominant Power in the North. Before the close of the eighteenth century it had ceased to exist. This startling political transformation was the logical result of certain fundamental weaknesses in the Polish state.

Poland did not have a homogeneous population. Five discordant peoples inhabited the state. Poles and Germans lived in West Prussia; Lithuanians and Russians in Lithuania; Poles in Poland proper; and a large Jewish element in the cities. The large Russian element in the population was the result of the eastward expansion of the Polish-Lithuanian state; the German, of immigration and the conquest of West Prussia by the Teutonic Knights; and the Jewish, of the emigration of Jews from Russia and Western Europe to escape religious persecution. These diverse racial elements had never been welded into a single nation.

The differences in race were accentuated by differences in religion. The Russians were adherents of either the Eastern Church or the Uniate branch of the Roman Catholic Church.[1]

---

[1] The Uniates acknowledge the supremacy of the Pope, but retain the liturgy of the Eastern Church and permit the marriage of priests.

In either case they were looked down upon by the Roman Catholics as an inferior class of Christians. The Germans were Lutherans, and the Poles and many of the Lithuanians were Roman Catholics. The adherents of the Eastern and the Lutheran churches were alike known as "Dissidents."

For a time during the Protestant Revolt the Lutherans and the Calvinists had made great progress in converting the inhabitants of the Polish-Lithuanian state to Protestantism. Most of the Germans became Lutherans, and many of the nobles and their dependents Calvinists. Several hundred of the Catholic churches were turned into Protestant places of worship, and Protestant ministers were substituted for the Catholic priests. During the Catholic Reformation which followed, the Roman Catholic Church regained much of the ground it had lost. The Protestants became restricted to a few of the cities, and adherents of the Eastern Church were forced to join the Uniate branch of the Roman Catholic Church or undergo many forms of religious persecution. As a result of the policy followed by the dominant religious party of the state, the Russian Dissidents looked to Russia for defense and the Protestants to Prussia.

Another serious defect in the organization of the state was the special position held by the nobles. Nearly a million and a half persons out of a population of twelve to thirteen millions were nobles. In theory every noble was the equal of every other. In reality they varied in wealth and influence from the sixteen or seventeen powerful magnates who maintained courts of almost barbaric splendor and private armies numbering thousands of retainers down to the mass of poverty-stricken nobles who owned a bit of land and eked out a living as soldiers or domestics in the employ of the more fortunate members of the nobility. The nobles had reduced the other classes to a nullity. The Polish peasants were the most miserable class in Europe. They knew nothing but poverty, hard work, and cruel treatment. The burgher class had been nearly destroyed by unwise legislation and the results of foreign invasions. The policy of the nobles deprived the peasants and the burghers of all participation in the affairs of the state.

The nobles had been equally keen to seize all authority in the state. After the extinction of the strong Jagiello line of sovereigns in 1572, the kingship became elective in Poland in practice as well as in theory. Thenceforth, at each election of a sovereign the monarchy was despoiled of essential prerogatives by pre-election bargains. As a result of this custom the King was at the mercy of the nobles and the Diet by the end of the eighteenth century.

The nobles, however, showed no fitness to use the power they had seized. Out of the theory of the equality of the nobles they had developed two customs exceedingly detrimental to the state: the *liberum veto* and the practice of "exploding" the Diets. As a result of the first practice one member of the nobility after 1652 could block any measure before the Diet. By means of the second a single noble could not only thwart the will of the majority of a Diet in respect to one measure, but he could nullify their whole previous work. Between 1652 and 1704 forty-eight out of fifty-five Diets were "exploded"; and in the reign of Augustus II every Diet was broken up in this way. These two customs opened the way for bribery and corruption. At least one noble could always be purchased by an interested foreign Power. Beginning with Richelieu the French and Habsburg rulers vied with each other in influencing Polish affairs through an unscrupulous use of secret service funds. Louis XIV is said to have spent 50,000,000 livres in this way and the Habsburgs spent nearly as much. After 1669, the foreign Powers, with no interest in the welfare of Poland, became the controlling factors in Polish politics.

As early as the seventeenth century the weaknesses of the Polish state began to cost Poland its border provinces, its prosperity, and its independence. As a result of the efforts of Sweden to make the Baltic a Swedish lake, Poland lost in 1660 the province of Livonia, a territory gained in 1561 by the secularization of the lands of the Brethren of the Sword. In the same Treaty of Oliva, Poland recognized the complete independence of East Prussia. By a skillful balancing of Sweden against Poland the Elector of Brandenburg had managed to obtain a recognition of the independence of East Prussia from both states. During the Great Northern War (1700–20), in which the sovereigns of Denmark, Poland, and Russia attempted to despoil the youthful Charles XII of his possessions, Swedes, Saxons, and Russians marched over and plundered Poland as if it had no political existence. Again in the War of the Polish Succession (1733–38), Poland was at the mercy of the troops of the foreign Powers struggling to control it. In spite of these repeated warnings the nobles with incredible blindness refused to reform their Constitution or to make reasonable preparation for the defense of their country. Although the Polish state had no natural boundaries except the Carpathian Mountains on the southwest, Poland had for its defense only one fortress, empty arsenals, and an army of 8000 to 10,000 men, while much smaller states had forces ten to twenty times as large. Long before its actual partition at the hands of Russia, Prussia, and Austria Poland was plainly marked for political extinction.

THE PARTITION OF POLAND AND THE DISMEMBERMENT OF TURKEY

The neighbors of Poland wished to continue this state of anarchy indefinitely. With this end in view, Frederick II of Prussia and Catherine II of Russia signed a treaty in 1764 which provided for their joint support of Prince Stanislaus Poniatowski, a favorite of the Tsarina, for the vacant kingship of Poland, the protection of the Polish Dissidents, and the maintenance of the anarchical constitution of the Polish-Lithuanian state. By a liberal use of money and Russian troops, Catherine II then forced the election of her favorite as king, brought Poland under her complete control, prevented the reform of the Polish Constitution, and forced the Polish Diet to enfranchise the Dissidents. The action of the Tsarina in favor of the adherents of the Eastern Church led in 1768 to the organization of a great Catholic confederation

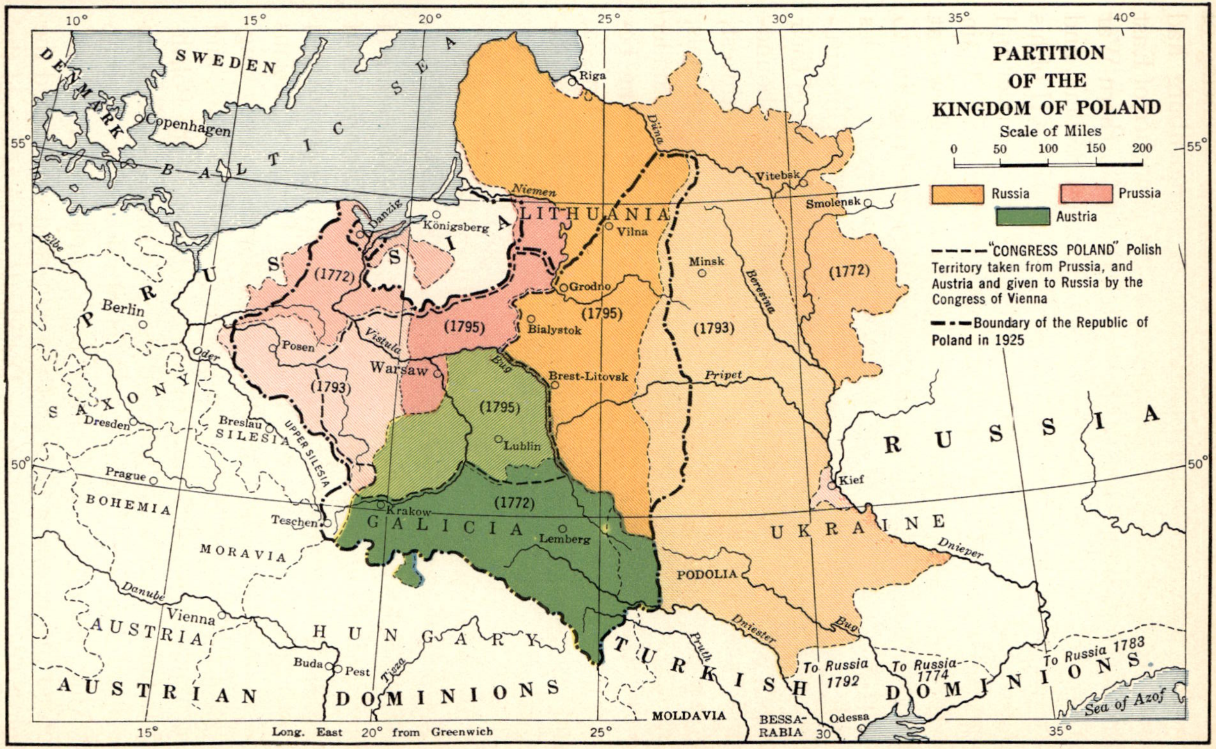

PARTITION OF THE KINGDOM OF POLAND
Scale of Miles
0 50 100 150 200
Russia
Prussia
Austria
"CONGRESS POLAND" Polish Territory taken from Prussia, and Austria and given to Russia by the Congress of Vienna
Boundary of the Republic of Poland in 1925
SWEDEN
DENMARK
Copenhagen
BALTIC SEA
PRUSSIA
LITHUANIA
Riga
Düna
Niemen
Vitebsk
Smolensk
Danzig
Königsberg
Vilna
Minsk
Beresina
Grodno
Bialystok
Berlin
Posen
Vistula
Warsaw
Oder
Bug
Brest-Litovsk
Pripet
SAXONY
Dresden
Breslau
SILESIA
UPPER SILESIA
Lublin
RUSSIA
Prague
BOHEMIA
Kief
Krakow
Teschen
GALICIA
Lemberg
UKRAINE
Dnieper
MORAVIA
PODOLIA
Danube
Vienna
AUSTRIA
HUNGARY
Dniester
Bug
Pruth
Tisza
Buda
Pest
AUSTRIAN DOMINIONS
TURKISH DOMINIONS
To Russia 1792
To Russia 1774
To Russia 1783
Sea of Azof
MOLDAVIA
BESSARABIA
Odessa
Long. East 20° from Greenwich

in Poland and to an insurrection in defense of the Roman Catholic religion.

At this point the Polish question became intertwined with the Turkish question. In attempting to crush the opposition of the Roman Catholic party to the intervention of Russia, the troops of Catherine II, in pursuit of fugitive Polish confederates, had attacked and burned Balta, a town belonging to the Tartar allies of Turkey; Russian agents had been stirring up the Christian population of the Balkan Peninsula against their Turkish masters; and the French allies of the Roman Catholic party in Poland had been striving for some time to bring about the intervention of the Turks in behalf of Poland. In 1768 these various causes finally induced Turkey to intervene in behalf of Poland.

The intervention of Turkey quickly confronted Europe with an exceedingly serious diplomatic situation. The Turks were unsuccessful in their struggle with Russia. The Russian troops defeated them in a number of engagements, occupied the provinces of Moldavia and Wallachia (the two provinces which later united to form Rumania), and seized a number of Turkish strongholds north of the Black Sea while the Russian fleet defeated the Turkish fleet in the Ægean Sea. The occupation of Moldavia and Wallachia brought the Russians to the Danube. An advance of Russia across the Lower Danube would involve both Austria and Prussia in the war. Austria was vitally concerned in the question of the control of this important outlet for its products, and the entrance of Austria into the war would force Prussia to come to the assistance of its Russian ally.

As a solution of the problem Prussia and Austria proposed the partition of Poland. By such an arrangement Russia would forego its Turkish conquests in return for Polish territory, and the balance of power would be maintained by assigning to Austria and Prussia shares of Polish territory. A series of complicated treaties, which embodied this compromise, were then negotiated in 1772 between the three Powers. As a result of these agreements the Polish state lost one fourth of its territory and one third of its inhabitants; Russia annexed the region east of the Dnieper and the Düna Rivers; Austria acquired Galicia and other territories immediately to the north of the Carpathian Mountains; and Prussia took West Prussia, the territory lying between the Prussian provinces of Brandenburg and Pomerania and the Prussian province of East Prussia. Austria gained the largest area, population, and revenue, but added another element to its already heterogeneous population and gave up the easily defensible boundary of the Carpathians for a frontier without natural defenses. Prussia, on the other hand, linked up its central group of territories with the province of East Prussia and considerably shortened its boundary line.

The partition of Poland temporarily saved Turkey from serious dismemberment. By the treaty of peace finally signed by Russia and Turkey, in 1774, at the little Bulgarian village of Kutchuk-Kainardji, Russia recovered Azov and a number of points along the northern shore of the Black Sea; Turkey renounced its sovereignty over the Tartars of the Crimea and adjoining regions; Russian merchantmen obtained the right to trade freely in the Black and Mediterranean Seas and to pass through the Straits of the Bosphorus and the Dardanelles; Turkey recovered the provinces of Moldavia and Wallachia on condition that they were to be better governed; and Russia gained the right to act as protector of certain Christian churches in Constantinople. Turkey thus lost only its suzerainty over the Moslem Tartars living north of the Black Sea.

This treaty, nevertheless, had a number of important results. From being the protector of a few of the Christian churches of Constantinople, Catherine II quickly transformed herself into the "protector" of all the Christian subjects of the Turkish Sultan, and within a decade she completely subjugated the Tartars north of the Black Sea. The Tsarina thus carried to completion Peter the Great's policy of gaining an outlet for Russia on the Black Sea. By a mixture of persuasion and menace, meanwhile, Austria cajoled Turkey into ceding the province of Bukowina on the ground that the threat of Austrian intervention had saved to Turkey the provinces of Moldavia and Wallachia.

The shock of the first partition of Poland brought a large part of the Polish nation to a realization of the need for radical measures of reform. The renewal of warfare between Russia and Turkey in 1788 gave Poland an opportunity to formulate and institute, undisturbed by Russia, the legislation required to reorganize and strengthen the Polish state. A law of 1791 gave the cities of Poland autonomy in government, admitted the middle class to offices in the Church and the army and conceded to them the right to purchase the land of the nobles, and permitted the nobles to engage in commerce and industry. The constitution adopted in the same year granted Protestants and adherents of the Eastern Church freedom of worship, abolished the *liberum veto*, and invested the King with real executive powers. Serfdom was condemned but not suppressed.

These patriotic measures of the Poles came too late to save their state from destruction. The conclusion of a treaty of peace with Turkey in 1792, by which Russia advanced its boundaries from the Bug to the Dniester River, gave Russia a free hand in Poland.

Immediately upon the conclusion of peace, Catherine II demanded the restoration of the old constitution of Poland and quickly overcame the resistance of the Polish troops. Then in 1793, while Austria was involved in the wars of the French Revolution, Russia and Prussia proceeded to partition Poland a second time. Prussia acquired by this partition about a million and a half more Poles and the important cities of Danzig, Thorn, and Posen, while three million more Russians and Lithuanians fell to the share of Russia. A rising of the Polish patriots in behalf of their liberties led two years later (1795) to a third and final partition of the unfortunate state, in which Russia, Prussia, and Austria all received shares of Polish territory. As a result of the three partitions Russia acquired all of the former Grand Duchy of Lithuania and Little Russia; Prussia obtained the lower valley of the Vistula, including Warsaw; and Austria received Galicia and the upper valley of the Vistula.

The loss of its independence as a result of the three partitions of Poland by no means destroyed the Polish nation. From the time of the final partition of Poland in 1795 to the end of the World War of 1914-18, the desire for national freedom lived on in the hearts of the Polish subjects of Russia, Prussia, and Austria. In each of the three states the Poles proved to be a serious and continuous problem. In the Napoleonic period and in the revolutions of 1831 and 1863 the Poles gave convincing evidence of the vitality of their national feeling. Finally, at the end of the World War their fidelity was rewarded by the reëstablishment of Poland as an independent state of Europe.

THE SOUTHERN SLAVS AND THE OTTOMAN TURKS

The history of the Southern Slavs is a long and complicated story. About 500 A.D. bands of Slavic origin began to harass the Danube frontier of the Eastern Empire, and to force their way southward into the Balkan Peninsula. By 700 A.D. these invaders had absorbed or expelled most of the natives of the peninsula. The original inhabitants held their ground in some measure in only three regions. In Albania the ancient Illyrian stock survived, along the coasts of Greece and Asia Minor and in the islands of the Ægean, the Greeks, and in the fastnesses of the Eastern Carpathian Mountains, possibly the Roman provincials.

As a result of time and chance the new and the old inhabitants of Southwestern Europe became organized into ill-defined national groups and rude political divisions, differing in location, dialect, customs, and in some cases in religion. Some of the Slavs and the natives united to form the Rumanian nation and established themselves on both slopes of the Eastern Carpathians in the Kingdom of Transylvania and the principalities of Moldavia and Wallachia, but the native strain predominates in that strange "Latin" people. Other Slavs coalesced with the remnants of the ancient Greek stock to form the modern Greek nation. The survivors of the old Illyrians became the ancestors of the modern Albanians. The remainder of the Southern Slavs fell apart into four groups: the Slovenes, the Croats, the Serbs, and the Bulgars. The Slovenes and the Croats, located between the Drave River and the Adriatic Sea, became in time Roman Catholics and subjects of the Habsburgs. The rest of the Southern Slavs and their Christian neighbors became adherents of the Eastern Orthodox Church and subjects of the Ottoman Turks. The Bulgars, however, descended from a small tribe of Asiatic invaders of that name who entered the Balkan Peninsula in the latter part of the seventh century, brought some of the Slavs into subjection, while adopting their language and culture.

After building up a considerable state in Northwestern Asia Minor, the Ottoman Turks crossed the Dardanelles in 1354 and created a great empire in Southeastern Europe at the expense of the Southern Slavs and their neighbors. About 1361 the Turkish invaders captured the city of Adrianople, made it their capital, and transformed it into a fit center for an elaborate Oriental court. In 1389 they crushed the Christian forces of the Balkan Peninsula on the plain of Kossova. This victory carried the boundary of the Turkish Empire northward to the Danube River. In 1453 the Turks crowned their work by the capture of Constantinople, the last independent remnant of the once proud Eastern Empire. By the end of the fifteenth century only the Serbs of Ragusa and Montenegro retained any semblance of their former independence.

After its conquest by Mohammed II, Constantinople took the place of Adrianople as the capital of the Turkish Empire. The Sultan whitewashed the marvelous mosaics of the Church of Saint Sophia, transformed the famous church into a mosque, built an immense palace, covered the new capital with fine edifices, and laid the foundation for the present cosmopolitan character of the city by permitting, and in many cases even compelling, Christians and Moslems of every description to come in and repeople his capital.

The Sultan treated the conquered Christians with a mixture of leniency and cunning. He promised the Greeks toleration and protection, assigned to them a quarter of their own in the city, restored to them many of their churches and monasteries, and put them under the immediate rule of a patriarch of their own nationality, who enjoyed special protection and privileges and a wide jurisdiction over his co-religionists. The Sultan shrewdly selected a patriarch, however, who abhorred the Roman Catholics, thereby insuring the maintenance of the schism existing between the Christians of the East and the West.

In the sixteenth century the Turkish Empire continued to expand. Under Selim I (1512-20) the Turks extended their rule far toward the borders of Persia, well into Mesopotamia, and over Egypt, and gained the overlordship of Arabia. These successes gave the Turkish sultans possession of the standard of the Prophet, the guardianship of the holy places of Mecca and Medina, and the headship of the orthodox Moslems of the world (the Caliphate). During the reign of Solyman the Magnificent (1520-66) the Turks captured the strategic points of Belgrade and Rhodes, formed an alliance on more than terms of equality with Francis I of France, crushed the Hungarians on the field of Mohács, retained the greater part of Hungary in their own possession, and forced Ferdinand, the brother of Charles V, to pay a heavy tribute. In the meantime the allies of the great Sultan, the corsairs of the Barbary States, terrorized the coasts of Italy and Spain. At the time of its greatest extent the Turkish Empire reached from Mesopotamia to Algeria and from Arabia to the region north of the Black Sea.

In Europe the Turks never constituted more than a military aristocracy. The all-powerful Sultan parceled out the conquered lands to his retainers as fiefs. In return for their lands his Moslem vassals gave the Sultan military service and furnished armed contingents. They lived by exploiting the Christian and Moslem peasants living on their great estates.

The Turks did not treat the different conquered nationalities alike. The Rumanians of Moldavia and Wallachia retained their own institutions intact on condition of paying a moderate tribute and furnishing a contingent to the Ottoman armies. The Greeks with superior intelligence soon made themselves indispensable to their Turkish conquerors and received many favors at their hands. The Greeks carried on the commerce of the Empire, paid a large share of its revenues, and rose to the higher positions in the administration and the Church. The Serbian and Bulgarian peasants, on the other hand, lay entirely at the mercy of the landed proprietors, the Turkish administrative officials, and the Greek rulers of the Eastern Church.

The Turkish Government discriminated in three ways against practically all the Christians of the Empire. It forbade them to bear arms, compelled them to pay heavier taxes than the Moslems, and, until the custom was given up in 1676, forced them to pay a cruel tribute of children. Once in five years shrewd appraisers of human flesh visited the Christian villages and seized the most likely looking boys and sent them to Constantinople to be trained for the Sultan's service. After receiving a careful training these boys entered the administrative service of the Sultan or enrolled in the Janissaries, the most famous military organization of the Empire.

In time the Turkish administrative system became oppressive to both the Moslems and the Christians. After the middle of the sixteenth century the Turkish Government sold many of its important offices in the army, the administration, and the judiciary to the highest bidder. In turn the higher officials reimbursed themselves by selling the lower offices within their gift. In the final analysis the common people paid the cost of the system in corruption and extortion. The administrative system, combined with the shift in trade routes, led to the neglect and desertion of farmsteads, depopulation and decreased production, and a general decline in prosperity. The Eastern Church suffered from the same evil. The Greeks, who were the most prosperous of the Christian subjects of the Sultan, also bought the lucrative posts in the Church. As a result of this system of purchasing offices the general body of the clergy was mainly Greek. To recoup themselves the Greek priests burdened their parishes with all kinds of dues and tithes.

After the great conquests of Solyman the Magnificent the Turks experienced a century of stagnation followed by a long period marked by their gradual decline and retreat. The Sultans ceased to lead their armies in person. Eunuchs and harem women began to wield a preponderant influence over the policies of the Government. The Janissaries became at the same time less formidable as a military power and an increasing source of danger to the state. The Austrians, the Poles, and the Venetians proved themselves foes of sterner stuff than the Greeks and the Southern Slavs. The Turks failed to keep pace with the Powers of Western Europe in the art of war. Probably only the dissensions of Christendom saved the Ottoman Turks from defeat long before their repulse in 1683 in front of the walls of Vienna at the hands of John Sobieski, King of Poland.

After this defeat the brunt of the task of driving the Turks out of Europe fell to the lot of Austria and Russia. Between 1684 and the end of the eighteenth century the two Powers repeatedly attacked the Turkish Empire in the hope of destroying and dismembering it. By the treaty signed at Carlowitz in 1699, Austria gained all of Hungary, including the Kingdom of Transylvania and Croatia-Slavonia. As a result of treaties signed with the Ottoman Empire in 1774 and 1792, Russia acquired the region between the Bug and the Dniester Rivers.

The efforts of Austria and Russia to dismember the Turkish Empire aroused the hopes of the oppressed subjects of the Sultan. The failure of the two states to carry out their proposed plans greatly disappointed the Christian subjects of the Turks. Nevertheless, their efforts had some important results. The slumbering spirit of nationality, stirred into action by the wars against the Ottoman Empire, became a powerful force among the Serbs, the Greeks, the Rumanians, and the Bulgarians which finally shattered the power of the Ottoman Turks in Europe.

REFERENCES

THE IMMEDIATE SUCCESSORS OF PETER THE GREAT
J. Mavor, *Economic History of Russia*, vol. I, bk. I, chapter VII.
W. R. Morfil, *History of Russia*, chapter VIII.
R. Beazley, N. Forbes, and C. A. Birkett, *Russia from the Varangians to the Bolsheviks*, bk. II, chapter VI.

CATHERINE II
A. Hassall, *European History, 1715–89*, chapter XIII.
J. Mavor, *Economic History of Russia*, vol. I, bk. II, chapter VI.
W. R. Morfil, *History of Russia*, chapter IX.
R. Beazley, N. Forbes, and C. A. Birkett, *Russia from the Varangians to the Bolsheviks*, bk. II, chapter VII.
J. B. Bury, *Catherine II*.
E. A. B. Hodgetts, *The Life of Catherine the Great of Russia*.
Histoire générale, vol. VII, chapter IX.

POLAND ON THE EVE OF THE PARTITIONS
J. S. Orvis, *A Brief History of Poland*, chapters III–IV.

THE PARTITIONS OF POLAND
W. R. Morfil, *Poland*, chapter XI.
J. S. Orvis, *A Brief History of Poland*, chapter V.

THE SOUTHERN SLAVS AND THEIR NEIGHBORS
F. Schevill, *The History of the Balkan Peninsula*, chapter XIX.

MAPS
The Growth of Russia in Europe, W. R. Shepherd, *Historical Atlas*, pp. 138–39.

CHAPTER XIII

THE INTELLECTUAL REVOLT AGAINST AUTHORITY

In the year 1500 the minds of the greater part of even the intellectual class were in bondage to a mass of more or less erroneous scientific, philosophical, religious, and political ideas, which had received the sanction of the schools and of the political and ecclesiastical officials. The intellectual history of the next three centuries is the story of the struggle of scientists and thinkers against the dominance of these conceptions, a struggle often waged in the face of the stubborn prejudice of the mass of the people and the determined opposition of the constituted authorities.

The medieval thinkers had worked out a world scheme based on data given by the senses and supported by the physics of Aristotle, the astronomy of Ptolemy, and passages in the Bible. According to the medieval theory the world was the center of the universe. Around the earth revolved in circular or in epicyclic orbits the moon, the planets, the sun, and the stars, all held in place and controlled in their motions by transparent crystalline spheres. Enclosing the whole was the immovable empyrean. Comets were the harbingers of direful events. Both the earth and the heavens were supposed to have been created instantaneously. All the sciences were yet in a very elementary stage. Astronomy had not advanced beyond astrology. Chemistry was fettered by its connection with alchemy. Little was known about the character of the earth's crust. Fossils were considered models used by the Creator during creation, relics of the deluge, or tests of faith. Theological misconceptions prevented the development of a rational science of anthropology. Devils were supposed to swarm like bacilli and to be the cause of storms, insanity, deafness, dumbness, epilepsy, epidemics, pestilence, and sin. Magic took the place of physics and chemistry. Giving up belief in witchcraft was considered equivalent to giving up belief in the Bible.

Various Renaissance thinkers contributed toward shaking the medieval, homocentric conception of the universe, but the real founder of the modern view was Nicolaus Copernicus (1473–1543). He was born of a well-to-do-family at Thorn in Poland. He probably sprang from a German family that had long been resident in Poland. After studying the humanities, mathematics, and astronomy in the flourishing university of Cracow, he became, through the influence of his uncle, the Bishop of Ermeland, a prebendary, or canon, in the Cathedral of Frauenburg, where he lived more like a nobleman than a monk. He spent the first ten years in his new position in studying astronomy, medicine, and the humanities at the universities of Bologna, Rome, and Padua. After his return from Italy he lived for a time with the Bishop of Ermeland in the capacity of both physician and courtier. Upon the death of his uncle he took up his residence at Frauenburg. His last years were troubled by the attitude of the new bishop toward the development of the humanistic spirit.

Copernicus seems to have begun to busy himself with his new conception of the universe shortly after the opening of the sixteenth century. Starting from certain suggestions of the Greek philosopher Pythagoras, Copernicus advanced the revolutionary hypothesis that the earth is merely a planet such as Mars or Venus and that the earth and the other planets revolve around the sun in circular orbits. The acceptance of this idea had staggering consequences. People had to believe that the supposedly solid earth, with its trees and houses, its cities and countries, its mountains and seas, was at the same time spinning like a top on its own axis and rushing in its annual course around the sun at the rate of nineteen miles every second. The earth ceased to be the all-important center of the universe; the sun, the moon, and the planets lost the position of subsidiary lights set in the heavens for the benefit of man; and the universe broadened out illimitably.

Fortunately for the peace of Copernicus, few knew about his ideas until after his death. He formulated his hypothesis and gathered his supporting evidence slowly, and set forth his ideas only in lectures to his own students. Consequently, even scholars knew very little about his doctrines, and the intellectual, political, and ecclesiastical authorities left him undisturbed. He did not permit his manuscript to be published until he was an old man at the point of death.

The Protestant theologians attacked the new hypothesis earlier than the Catholic. Luther called Copernicus a fool who wished to reverse the entire science of astronomy. Luther's chief lieutenant, Melanchthon, deduced nine proofs of the proposition that "the earth can be nowhere if not in the center of the universe." Calvin thought to clinch the argument against the theory of Copernicus by quoting from the first verse of the Ninety-Third Psalm, "the world also is stablished, that it cannot be moved." The Catholic theologians did not begin to denounce the new hypothesis until seventy years later, when it began to be asserted as a fact. An unauthorized preface to the work of Copernicus, which represented the new theory as merely an hypothesis not intended to be taken seriously, disarmed their opposition at first. The Ptolemaic astronomy,[1] however, continued to be taught even in the universities for over a hundred years.

The great need of the new astronomy was adequate and accurate data. The supplying of this was the great achievement of Tycho Brahe (1546–1601), a Danish astronomer sprung from a noble family. While observing a conjunction of Jupiter and Saturn in 1563, he discovered that even the old astronomical tables of Ptolemy were highly inaccurate.[2] He devoted his life to improving them. For twenty-one years he worked as a pensioner of the King of Denmark, at an extraordinary observatory constructed for his use on an island in the narrow channel which separates Denmark from Sweden. After the death of his protector he became a protégé of the Emperor Rudolph II, but he died soon after taking up his work at Prague. His chief services to astronomy were the construction of improved astronomical instruments and his

---

[1] The system attacked by Copernicus.
[2] Ptolemy was considered by the Middle Ages as the chief authority on astronomy.

INTELLECTUAL REVOLT AGAINST AUTHORITY

accurate observations. He was the greatest astronomical observer before the invention of the telescope.

The scientific heir of Tycho Brahe was Kepler (1571–1630). Born in Württemberg of poor parents, he struggled throughout his whole life against poverty, ill health, and adverse conditions. At first he intended to become a Protestant minister, but his acceptance of the Copernican theory of the universe disqualified him, in the eyes of the theologians, for such a career. He then turned for a short time to the teaching of mathematics, but soon became an assistant of Tycho Brahe at Prague. After the death of Tycho Brahe, Kepler became imperial mathematician in his place and devoted himself to the study of the records left by his former chief. His study of these records led to the discovery of his three celebrated laws of planetary motion, which introduced order and simplicity into what otherwise would have been a chaos of detailed observations and paved the way for the greater generalization of Newton.

Another notable contributor to the advance of science was Galileo (1584–1642), a contemporary of Kepler. After receiving a good education at the expense of his father, he became in 1589 a lecturer in mathematics at the university of his native city, Pisa. During the three years he held this position he made two interesting discoveries. While praying in the cathedral one day he conceived the idea of the pendulum as a measurer of time from observing the action of a lamp left swinging by a verger. Some time later he discovered that Aristotle was mistaken in thinking that bodies fell at rates of speed depending on their weight. A five-pound weight really did not fall through the air five times as fast as a one-pound weight. One morning, before the assembled university, Galileo proved his own views about falling bodies by dropping simultaneously a one-hundred-pound shot and a one-pound shot from the top of the famous leaning tower of Pisa. The two bodies hit the ground at the foot of the tower at exactly the same time. The dramatic demonstration aroused a storm of opposition. The adherents of medieval philosophy refused to accept the evidence of observed facts when it contradicted the principles of their master Aristotle, and Galileo found it prudent to leave Pisa.

Through the influence of friends Galileo then obtained from the Venetian Senate the chair of mathematics in the University of Padua. For the next eighteen years he occupied this post with increasing renown. At first he cautiously concealed his real views concerning the universe and taught the old Ptolemaic system of astronomy. The course of events, however, finally enabled him to take a bolder stand. Having heard a rumor of a toy, rigged up by a Dutch apprentice from a couple of spectacle lenses, which greatly enlarged near-by objects, Galileo invented a small telescope and began scanning the heavens with his rude instrument. The new invention proved to be a tremendous weapon against the Ptolemaic system. Galileo showed that the moon, instead of being a smooth and perfect sphere of different nature from the earth, possessed hills and valleys and other features resembling the earth. He found, likewise, that the planet Jupiter had satellites, thus disclosing a miniature solar system and confirming a prediction made by Copernicus many years before, and that Venus had phases as did the moon. The last discovery turned against the opponents of the Copernican theory their own weapons; for they had pointed out the lack of such phases in respect to Venus and Mercury as a proof of the falsity of the new hypothesis concerning the universe. Finally Galileo discovered spots on the sun. This discovery proved the rotation of the sun and the erroneousness of the old assumption that the sun was incorruptible. These discoveries led Galileo to come forward as an avowed and strenuous advocate of the Copernican system.

The battle waged against the new theory by its opponents was a long and hotly contested one. The adherents of the old system refused to believe their own eyes. They either declared the newly discovered satellites of Jupiter to be an illusion created by the Devil or they took the still safer course of refusing to look through the new telescope at all. They feared for the credit of the Scriptures, the letter of which they supposed to be the supreme authority in matters of science as in all others. According to their interpretation of the Bible the account of Joshua staying the sun in its course and the statement that the earth was immovable made the theories of Copernicus and Galileo unscriptural and consequently heretical.

This fear for the credit of the Bible brought Galileo into conflict with the Inquisition. He was first interrogated by this tribunal in December, 1615. As a result of this first interview the hypothesis of Copernicus was declared heretical and scientifically false, and Galileo renounced his belief in the theory, and promised to teach it no more. This was the occasion for putting the works of Copernicus on the *Index*. Contrary to his promise, however, Galileo continued to advocate the Copernican theory. This led in 1633 to his trial by the Inquisition, his condemnation by that body as "vehemently suspected of heresy," and his incarceration at the pleasure of the dreaded tribunal. Galileo rested under this sentence until his death nine years later. The Church, however, cannot be held accountable for much of the unhappiness of Galileo's declining years. He was confined either at his own home or in the homes of his friends, and he even drew a pension from the Pope during his last years. The Church was in no way responsible for his blindness or for the death of members of his family.

He spent the years of his imprisonment in investigating the field of mechanics. His work along this line was actually of greater importance than his more spectacular contributions to astronomy. His investigations proved that falling bodies descend toward the earth with uniformly accelerated motion. He showed that the path of a projectile is a parabola. He demonstrated that the floating of solid bodies in a liquid depends on their specific gravity relative to the liquid rather than on their form as previously believed. He ascertained most of the known facts about the transverse strains and the strength of beams. He thought out the application of the pendulum to clocks, and invented the first thermometer. By his clear grasp of the idea of force as a mechanical agent he extended to the external world the conception of the invariability of the relation between cause and effect, and did more by these investigations to establish the Copernican system as an accepted fact than by his discoveries with the telescope.

The new astronomy founded by Copernicus, and built up by Tycho Brahe, Kepler, and Galileo, was completely formulated and mathematically interpreted by Sir Isaac Newton (1642-1727). He was the son of a small English freehold farmer. His distaste for agriculture caused him to be sent to the University of Cambridge, where he quickly distinguished himself in mathematics. By the time he was twenty-four, Newton had laid the foundations for each of his great contributions to science: the invention of calculus, the law of gravitation, spectrum analysis, and the formulation of the three laws of motion. In 1669 he became professor of mathematics at Cambridge, a post which he held for thirty years. Thenceforth he spent most of his days in thought and study, free from the ordinary cares and interruptions of life. But for the intervention of friends, however, much of the result of his thinking would have been buried with him, for the idea of publishing his discoveries seems never to have occurred to him. His later years were marked by no great discoveries. For a time he served as a member of Parliament. After the Revolution of 1688 he filled the post of Master of the Mint. For the last twenty-four years of his life he acted as president of the Royal Society.

The most important of Newton's discoveries was the law of gravitation. Galileo had stated the laws of falling bodies. Kepler had shown how the solar system moved. Newton pointed out the force which caused the heavenly bodies to move through the heavens in accordance with immutable laws, by deducing the idea that the same force of gravitation that makes a free body fall to the earth causes the motion of the moon around the earth and the motion of the earth and the other planets around the sun.[1]

---

[1] Every particle of matter in the universe attracts every other particle with a force which acts in a line joining them, and whose intensity varies as the product of the masses and inversely as the squares of their distance apart.

These advances in astronomy were closely linked with the development of mathematics. By the end of the sixteenth century Arabic figures had for the most part taken the place of Roman characters in arithmetic. Decimal fractions, better methods of division and multiplication, and the signs for plus, minus, and equality were introduced, and geometry was revived and further developed. Early in the seventeenth century logarithms were worked out as an aid in computations; analytical geometry was developed by the famous French philosopher, Descartes; and calculus was discovered by both Leibnitz and Newton. By the eighteenth century the processes and symbols of modern algebra had been pretty well established.

While the astronomers had been exploring the universe, other scientists had been making progress in discovering the laws of the human body. Vesalius (1514–64), a Belgian educated at Paris, was the first person in modern times to dissect the human body and to publish drawings of his dissections. By the thoroughness, the boldness, and the brilliance of his work he broke the bondage of medical men to the authority of the ancients, of Galen in particular, in the field of anatomy. He is said to have laid the foundation of modern biological science. An Italian contemporary of Vesalius, Eustachia, found the tube connecting the throat and the middle ear, now named for him. The name of Fallopio, another contemporary, is similarly associated with the human oviducts. His disciple, Fabricius (1537–1619), discovered the valves in the veins. Fabricius in turn was the teacher of the Englishman, William Harvey (1578–1657), who did for the study of function what Vesalius had done for the study of structure. Although Harvey is remembered chiefly as the discoverer of the circulation of the blood, he made many other notable contributions to science, and his methods mark him as one of the great pioneers in the revival of the method of experiment for the improvement of knowledge. In the latter part of the seventeenth century the utilization of the microscope opened virtually a new world for biologists in the study of the minute anatomy of man, of the lower animals and of plants. The Italian anatomist, Malpighi (1628–94), discovered the corpuscles of the blood and the Dutchman Leeuenhoek (1632–1723) brought to light the existence of protozoa.

Some interesting and fruitful discoveries were also made in the seventeenth century in the fields of chemistry and physics. In Italy Torricelli (1608–47), a disciple of Galileo, discovered the existence of atmospheric pressure, determined the weight of the atmosphere, and invented the barometer. His investigations were carried forward by Pascal (1623–62), a Frenchman, who investigated the pressure of the atmosphere at different altitudes. Toward the end of the century, Huygens (1629–95), a Dutch physicist, applied pendulums to clocks and spiral springs to watches, developed the wave theory of light, and published important treatises on light and weight. During the first half of the seventeenth century Jan van Helmont (1577–1644) made a special study of gases and coined the term "gas." During the latter half of the century an Englishman, Robert Boyle (1627–91), made notable contributions to the study of the atmosphere, gases, and other substances, and formulated the famous law that the volume of a gas varies inversely with the pressure exerted on it.

In the latter half of the seventeenth century scientific investigation began to be organized and subsidized. The Governments of Europe began to take an interest in promoting general scientific progress and no longer left the advancement of science entirely to individual initiative. In England the Royal Society was established in 1662, and fourteen years later (1674) the famous observatory at Greenwich was completed. In France, Colbert made the French Academy of Sciences an official institution in 1666, and in the following year he established the observatory at Paris. In the last year of the seventeenth century the Prussian Royal Academy of Sciences was founded at Berlin. These societies stimulated the advancement of science by their discussions and by the publication of proceedings and learned journals. In 1769 the English, French, Danish, and Russian

INTELLECTUAL REVOLT AGAINST AUTHORITY

Governments coöperated by sending out scientific expeditions to widely separated points on the earth's surface for the purpose of determining more exactly the distance of the earth from the sun.

The eighteenth century witnessed great progress in the field of chemistry. Boerhave (1668–1738), a Dutch physician and botanist, subjected organic substances to chemical processes and founded organic chemistry. In 1750 a Scotch physician, Dr. Joseph Black, revolutionized contemporary conceptions of heat and chemical decomposition by his experiments with limestone. In the latter half of the century three British scientists made important discoveries: Cavendish discovered hydrogen (1766), Rutherford, nitrogen (1772), and Priestley, oxygen (1774). In 1784 Cavendish produced water by a synthesis of hydrogen and oxygen. Chemical discovery in the eighteenth century culminated with the French chemist Lavoissier (1743–94). He invented much of the nomenclature of modern chemistry and by his constant use of the balance in chemical analysis he founded quantitative chemistry.

During the eighteenth century important advances were also made in the field of physics. While experimenting with the heating of water, Dr. Black discovered latent heat. Notable discoveries were also made in electricity. The existence of positive and negative electricity was ascertained; the differences in the conductivity of various substances was discovered; and the identity of the electrical spark and the bolt of lightning was shown by Benjamin Franklin's famous kite experiment.

A beginning was made, also, toward the development of a number of other sciences. In 1740 Lazzaro Moro put forward the revolutionary hypothesis that the rocks must have been in process of formation when the fossils now found in them were included in them and that the crust of the earth must consist of superimposed strata. Buffon (1707–85), the French naturalist, made important contributions to zoölogy in his vast *Natural History*. At the same time the Swedish naturalist Linnæus (1707–78) founded the science of botany.

These notable scientific discoveries were made possible by a great change in the mental habits of seekers after truth. Medieval man, as has been shown, never resorted to observation and experiment. He sought rather for the pertinent texts in the Bible, in the writings of Aristotle, and in other authoritative works and used them as infallible premises from which to deduce truth. The great advances in science since 1500 have been made possible by adopting new methods in the search for truth. The results gained by careful observations and by experiments made with instruments of precision have supplanted the results obtained by ingenuously interpreting old texts.

The advance of science had a number of important practical results. The discoveries in physics and chemistry led up to the Industrial Revolution. For example, the investigations of Black concerning latent heat were utilized by Watt in developing the steam engine, and the discoveries of the chemists, Scheele and Berthollet, were applied to the bleaching of cottons. The physicians were slow in applying the discoveries concerning the cure of the sick, but in time the new facts produced a revolution in the practice of medicine. The greatest effect of the progress of science was its influence on the intellectual outlook of an increasingly large number of people. Intelligent men began to lose their awe and credulity concerning their environment. In the place of spirits, demons, and supernatural forces, they found natural and immutable laws.

While the scientists were overthrowing the scientific ideas of the Middle Ages, the philosophers were undermining its philosophical conceptions. During the Middle Ages the scholastic philosophers had given a theological explanation of the universe. The Humanists, who revived the various philosophical systems of antiquity, were the first to challenge the views of the medieval philosophers. They were soon followed by thinkers who evoked entirely new interpretations of the universe.

One of the first martyrs of the new scientific ideas was Giordano Bruno (1548–1600). At the age of sixteen he entered a monastery, but found himself unable to conform to its discipline. In consequence, he soon fled from the monastery and passed the rest of his life in wandering from place to place. He spent more or less time in Italy, Geneva, France, England, and Germany, and lectured at many universities on astronomy and the philosophy of Aristotle. As time went on he formulated the ideas of Copernicus more clearly in his own mind and taught them to his students with increasing boldness. At the invitation of a Venetian nobleman he finally returned to Italy. Soon after his return he fell into the clutches of the Inquisition. The Roman inquisitors made out a list of eight gross heresies found in his writings. At the head of the list stood his denial of the Catholic doctrine of the Eucharist. Probably his idea that there were an infinite number of worlds counted against him. Faced with the charges of the Inquisition, Bruno refused to recant and defiantly answered his accusers, "Ye who pass judgment over me feel, maybe, greater fear than I upon whom it is passed." He met death by burning with the most steadfast courage, a martyr to the cause of free inquiry into truth.

Another early thinker to revolt against the scholastic philosophers was Francis Bacon (1561-1626). To him the Aristotelian philosophy of the universities seemed productive mainly of vain contentions and disputations. His great achievement as a philosopher is his clear statement of the faults of medieval thinking. He advocated the employment of careful observation and induction in the search for truth and the establishment of a sort of laboratory for the promotion of science. As a result of a brief statement in one of his works in which he assigns sensations as the source of all knowledge, Bacon is regarded as the forerunner of John Locke and the founder of the empirical school of philosophy. He was neither the great constructive philosopher nor the lonely scientific pioneer that he has often been credited with being. He merely stands high among the men of his time who were striving toward a new intellectual activity.

The real founder of modern philosophy is Descartes (1596-1650). His chief importance in the history of thought is his declaration of intellectual independence against the bondage of medieval philosophy. He asserted the worth of his own mental processes. He sought to evolve the truths concerning the universe by deducing by the same rigid methods employed in mathematical science the conclusions that of necessity flow from a few simple, certainly known intuitions. He tried to substitute a mechanical explanation for the old theological explanations of the universe. Using this method, Descartes, Spinoza, Leibnitz, and other modern philosophers of the same school worked out complicated theories regarding God, the universe, man, and their relations to one another. To understand them is the work of a lifetime. Each thinker of this so-called rationalist school of philosophers, however, sought to make a new synthesis which would embody the vast store of new scientific facts.

The second great school of modern philosophy is the empirical school. Its founder was John Locke (1632–1704). He gave his philosophical ideas to the world in his *Essay concerning Human Understanding*. Locke felt that preceding thinkers had extended their inquiries into matters beyond the reach of the human understanding. He confined himself mainly to the problem of how we know. He came to the conclusion that our ideas originate either with our five senses or with reflection.

Contemporary with the growth of science and partly arising from the advance in scientific knowledge there developed a skeptical attitude toward religion. Men began to doubt the teachings of both the Protestant and the Catholic theologians. They refused to believe that God constantly interfered with the immutable laws that the men of science had discovered in the universe. They rejected the miracles related in the Bible and in the lives of the saints. They denied that God on certain special occasions had revealed himself to the Jews alone. They refused to believe in the doctrine of the fall of man preached by the theologians. On the contrary, they believed man capable of indefinitely improving his own conditions and that of his fellows by freeing himself from the errors and superstitions of the past.

The ideas of these thinkers were given clear statement in the works of the English Deists. They agreed only in casting off the trammels of authoritative religious teaching in favor of a free and purely rationalistic speculation. As nearly as their doctrine can be summarized, the Deists taught that the first cause of the world is a personal God, who is apart from the nature which he created and unconcerned as to the details of its working. They rejected the miraculous element in the Bible. They denied the doctrine of the Trinity, the mediatorial character of Christ, the idea of the atonement, and the doctrine that either the Jews or the Christians were the "chosen people." They raised their voices on every occasion against ecclesiastical authority.

Long before the opening of the eighteenth century both the course of events and the trend of political thought in England were tending to undermine political absolutism. In opposition to the theory that kings rule by divine right and that subjects have no recourse against them, the Parliamentary party, in the struggle with the Stuarts which preceded the Puritan Revolution of the middle of the seventeenth century, emphasized three principles: that the king was subject to law, that law had its source in the people instead of in the monarch, and that the people consisted of individuals with personal rights rather than of privileged groups or associations. In the "Petition of Right" of 1628 the Parliamentary party wrung from Charles I a recognition of four specific privileges. During the period of personal rule (1629–40), and after the assembling of the Long Parliament, life, liberty, and property were repeatedly claimed as fundamental liberties. Finally the Parliamentary party even caused the execution of the King. The general effect of the Puritan Revolution on contemporary thought and political theory is best illustrated by a survey of the theories of Milton and Harrington.

John Milton (1608–74) is a notable character in the history of both English literature and political theory. He received a good education and traveled considerably in Europe. Prior to the Puritan Revolution he wrote a number of his most famous shorter poems. In 1644 a quarrel with the Stationers'

Company, the body in control of censorship, led to the writing of his *Areopagitica*, a spirited vindication of the liberty of the press, and brought him into great prominence. In the conflict between the King and the army at the close of the Puritan Revolution, Milton sided with the army. In 1649 he became Latin Secretary of the Council of State, a post which he retained, in spite of being overtaken by blindness, until the restoration of Charles II. For a time after the return of that sovereign to England, Milton was in considerable personal danger, but the Act of Indemnity put an end to his troubles. He spent the greater part of his later years in the composition of his *Paradise Lost* and *Paradise Regained*.

Two of the most fundamental concepts of Milton's political thinking concern the questions of sovereignty and liberty. In his philosophy ultimate power rests in the people. Kings and magistrates thus are merely the agents of the people and possess no power save what is delegated to them. Individual liberty, likewise, is the birthright of men and of nations. In the name of liberty, Milton demanded religious toleration, freedom of the press, the abolition of efforts to enforce a rigid and austere code in diet, dress, and amusements, and a republican form of government. The literary ability of Milton coupled with his great prestige gave his political philosophy a wide hearing.

The work of James Harrington (1611–77), a contemporary of Milton, formed a complement to the work of the latter. The substance of his philosophy is embodied in his *Commonwealth of Oceana*. The work contains a scheme for a constitution providing an oligarchical republic for Great Britain, to be instituted by Cromwell. The government was to be in the hands of the owners of property. His advocacy of the secret ballot and other devices for insuring the absolute freedom of the voter from constraint upon his choice, foreshadows political developments of the nineteenth century. Milton was concerned mainly with the subject of individual freedom; Harrington with the scope and operation of government.

The next great shock to the fortress of political authority came from the Revolution of 1688. During the reign of

INTELLECTUAL REVOLT AGAINST AUTHORITY

Charles II every effort to liberalize existing English ecclesiastical and political institutions met with obstinate resistance. By his religious policy favoring Catholics, however, James II alienated from the side of the monarchy many of its natural supporters and precipitated the Revolution of 1688. For the second time in half a century the English people exercised successfully the right of popular revolt against their constituted sovereigns. A liberalizing of the English Constitution followed the Revolution. Thenceforth religious toleration, popular sovereignty exercised through Parliament, and the rights of Englishmen, formed fundamental principles of the Constitution.

The Revolution of 1688 quickly found a defender and expounder in the aforementioned philosopher, John Locke (1632–1704). After completing a course at Oxford he served for fifteen years as confidential secretary of the Earl of Shaftesbury. Through Shaftesbury he obtained office in the English Government. Upon the fall of his patron he lost his political position and even retired for a time to the United Netherlands. After the Revolution of 1688 he again came into office. His most famous political works are his *Letters on Toleration* and *Treatises on Government*.

In explaining the origin of political authority, Locke started with the conception of a state of nature in which men have no political superior, but enjoy such natural rights as life, liberty, and property. The right to property arises as a result of putting labor into a particular object. The inconveniences of the state of nature made it burdensome. Therefore civil society arose to take the place of natural society. This was created by each individual contracting with every other individual. The society thus formed then entered into a compact with its ruler for the establishment of a civil government which should assume the obligation of protecting life, liberty, and property. Society thus became vested with the functions of determining offenses against the law of nature and of punishing violations of that law. According to the philosophy of Locke, life, liberty, and property were to be made secure by separating the executive, the legislative, and the federative functions of the government. By the federative power of the government Locke meant that power which was concerned with the conduct of international relations. He did not separate the executive and the judiciary. He considered the legislature as the supreme power in the government. This legislative power was, nevertheless, only a trust to be employed in the interest of society. Failure on the part of the government to fulfill its trust justified popular revolution. The tendency of the political doctrines of Locke was to promote the idea that institutions are made for man, not man for institutions.

In the eighteenth century a remarkable group of Frenchmen known as the "Philosophers" or the "Encyclopedists" became leaders in the revolt against authority. While they made some contributions to European philosophy, their main function was to popularize the dominant currents of thought. They united in their writings the scientific ideas of the men of science, the philosophic tendencies of the time, the skeptical doctrines of the Deists, and the political theories of the writers on politics. They exercised a tremendous influence on the group of eighteenth-century rulers known as the "enlightened despots" and on the thinking of the upper and the middle classes in France and the rest of Europe.

The oldest member of the group known as the French philosophers was Montesquieu (1689-1755). By hereditary right he became president of the Parlement of Bordeaux. In 1721 he published his *Persian Letters*, in which he ridiculed the religious, political, social, and literary life of his countrymen. He put his comments into the mouths of two Persians supposed to be traveling in Europe. Although the book was published anonymously, Montesquieu was known to be the author and he quickly acquired a great reputation. This satire nearly cost him his election to membership in the French Academy in 1728. Since his fortune enabled him to gratify his taste for study and travel, he resigned in 1726 his office in the Parlement of Bordeaux and spent some years traveling in the principal foreign countries of Europe. A sojourn of two years in England gave him an opportunity to meet influential people of that country and to observe English political conditions. He spent his remaining years mainly in the preparation of his history of the Roman people and his *Spirit of Laws*.

The great reputation of Montesquieu is based largely on his *Spirit of Laws*. As a result of his studies and travels, Montesquieu learned that laws varied from nation to nation. He concluded that this resulted from the application of reason to the particular circumstances of a given society. Montesquieu classifies governments into democracies, aristocracies, monarchies, and despotisms. He finds democracies moved by love of country and of equality; aristocracies, by moderation; monarchies, by a high sense of the rights and privileges pertaining to each preëminent class or individual; despotisms, by fear. Education and legislation in each state must correspond to the principle which moves the government. Montesquieu's discussions of liberty and slavery are especially famous. Like Locke he attached great importance to the separation of the powers of government. He, however, classified those powers as executive, legislative, and judicial. He regarded this separation of powers as indispensable for the existence of liberty in a state. Montesquieu thought that he found this situation only in England. The laws concerning accusations of crime must also be framed on sound principles. In this part of his work Montesquieu made a notable contribution to the discussion of criminal law and procedure. Against slavery he shows himself a radical and uncompromising foe. He believed that climate and environment had an important effect on legislation. He held that liberty flourished better in cooler climates. He found Protestantism better suited to republics; Catholicism, to monarchies; and the Moslem religion, to despotisms. Laws should conform, too, to the peculiar spirit of a nation.

The *Spirit of Laws* had a great influence. It was one of the first works in modern times to discuss in an enlightened manner the question of civil liberty. In his discussion of crime and punishment, Montesquieu was a forerunner of

Beccaria. While the *Spirit of Laws* did not advocate the complete reform of the French monarchy along the lines of the English Constitution, it showed clearly Montesquieu's profound admiration for English institutions and held up for comparison the liberty of the English and the tryanny of the French monarchy. The French philosophers, the moderates of the French Revolution, and all those whose enthusiasm for reform was wisely tempered by moderation greatly admired the work. No book save the treatises of Locke on government was better known to the leaders of public opinion in America during the period of the War for Independence and of the making of the Constitution.

The most prominent of the French philosophers was Voltaire (1694–1778). Upon the completion of his formal education he was introduced into the best society of the last years of the reign of Louis XIV. In this environment he soon became known as a somewhat dissipated young man endowed with a brilliant and sarcastic wit. His first definite achievement was as a writer of plays for the French stage. In 1726 a quarrel with a member of the powerful family of Rohan led to the exile of Voltaire to England for a period of twenty-six months. There he associated on terms of intimacy with Lord Bolingbroke, Swift, Pope, Gay, and other famous contemporary Englishmen, studied the writings of Bacon, Newton, and Locke, and acquainted himself with the social and intellectual life of the country.

A new period in the life of Voltaire began with his association with Madame du Chatelet, a woman of high intellectual gifts and scientific attainments. By the strange moral code then accepted in French high society he was permitted to live in the closest intimacy with her without even causing a break between her and her husband. He spent these years mainly at her château. They were years of prodigious intellectual activity. Voltaire wrote many plays, worked at a history of the reign of Louis XIV, gave the French public a popular account of the ideas of Newton, and produced an almost endless stream of tales, novels, satires, and poems. In 1746 he received the coveted honor of membership in the

INTELLECTUAL REVOLT AGAINST AUTHORITY 293

French Academy. The death of Madame du Chatelet in 1749 closed this period in his life.

He then took up his residence for two years with Frederick the Great at Berlin. Although each was flattered at first by the attentions of the other, the despotic temper of the Prussian King and the sharp tongue of the French man of letters quickly embroiled the two friends in a bitter quarrel which led Voltaire to return to France. Frederick the Great even went so far as to have Voltaire arrested as he was leaving Germany.

Some years after his departure from Berlin, Voltaire bought the estates of Ferney and Tournay near the Swiss border. He spent the last twenty years of his life at the Château of Ferney. There he felt fairly secure from attack, and he assumed, accordingly, a very aggressive attitude toward all the abuses that he wished to destroy. He sent forth hundreds of short writings, issued under all sorts of names and printed in many places, which found their way to the public in spite of the opposition of the French authorities. The main theme of Voltaire during this period of his life is the fight against religious intolerance and fanaticism. He stands always for the sovereignty of reason.

There was another side to the personality of Voltaire. The little village of Ferney remembers him as its benefactor. On the monument raised to his memory in the village, Voltaire is credited with the construction of a church, a school, a hospital, a reservoir, a fountain, and more than one hundred houses, with lending money without interest to the neighboring communes, with draining the marshes, and with sustaining the people of Ferney during the famine of 1771. In fact every man who suffered from intolerance found in Voltaire an eloquent and a powerful defender.

For forty years Voltaire was the leader of the philosophic group in France. He should be looked upon as a man of action who used literature as a weapon in behalf of his own creed. According to the creed of Voltaire man knows only by his own reason. What the senses do not tell us we cannot know. "All men who pretend to supernatural revelation are swindlers, and those who believe them are dupes." Freedom of opinion and of expression should be allowed at least to all educated men. Men should be granted personal liberty. The burdens of taxation should be equalized. Serfdom should be abolished. The feudal dues should be suppressed. Probably the works which best embody this point of view are his *Letters on the English*, which appeared shortly after his return from England, and his *Handy Philosophic Dictionary*. In the former Voltaire touched on such subjects as religious toleration in England, the guarantees enjoyed by British subjects, liberty of speech, freedom of the press, the political life manifested in the English Parliament, and the scientific and philosophical contributions of Locke and Newton. The letters compelled Frenchmen to think about the conditions under which they lived and to question the political and social systems of France. The *Handy Philosophic Dictionary* was a series of short, biting essays directed for the most part against the Church. In them Voltaire is often superficial, but he is always clever.

A writer of a very different character from Voltaire was Jean Jacques Rousseau (1712–78). For the facts of his early life his biographers are forced to depend on the highly improbable account given by himself in his *Confessions*. For the first ten years of his life he seems to have been brought up in a very haphazard way at Geneva by a dissipated, violent-tempered, foolish father. At the age of sixteen he ran away from Geneva and started an extraordinary series of wanderings and adventures. In 1741 Rousseau arrived at Paris. For several years he resorted to various means of earning a livelihood. During this period he served for a time as a private secretary, wrote for the stage, copied music, and mingled with the artists, writers, and thinkers of Paris. He also formed an irregular connection with an illiterate woman of the servant class by whom he had five children, all of whom were sent to a foundling home soon after birth.

Rousseau grew more and more displeased, however, with a social order in which he knew he could not occupy a position in keeping with his mental superiority. His developing views are shown by two essays written in competition for prizes offered by the Academy of Dijon. In 1750 he won the prize with an essay which maintained that civilization had not made morals purer. Rousseau's paradoxical assertion of the superiority of the savage state took the artificial society of the time by storm. Four years later he wrote an essay on inequality in which he advanced the claims of all men to an equal share in the government and in the enjoyment of nature's blessings. Henceforth Rousseau was a confirmed democrat.

His three most famous works, *Julie, ou La Nouvelle Héloïse*, the *Social Contract*, and *Emile*, appeared about ten years after Rousseau had begun to attract attention. In the first he expressed his feelings about nature and love; the second explained his ideas about government; and the third unfolds his ideas about education. The influence of the three works has been tremendous.

The later years of Rousseau were a time of trouble. His works involved him with the Governments of Europe; his temperament embroiled him constantly with those who admired his genius and tried to befriend him. He has been described as sensitive, emotional, self-conscious, and impatient of control. Both neglect and too much attention made him indignant. "He never developed beyond the stature of a spoiled child." These qualities made him incapable of friendship and social intercourse with rational people. In his later years he was actually half insane.

After the appearance of his three most important books, Rousseau was much on the move. The Parlement of Paris condemned his *Emile* and ordered the arrest of its author. Warned by friends of his danger, Rousseau fled from France. Both Bern and Geneva, however, ordered his withdrawal and condemned his works. From this time on until his death he moved from place to place, a prey to the idea that his friends were persecuting him.

In the *Social Contract* are to be found the principal contributions of Rousseau to political thought. In this work he tried to reconcile liberty with authority. In solving the problem he assumed, like most writers of the seventeenth and eighteenth centuries, the existence of a pre-social condition of mankind, antecedent to the establishment of government, in which every individual was free to do as he liked. In his earlier essays Rousseau regarded this state as the ideal one for mankind. By the time he wrote the *Social Contract*, however, he had come to the conclusion that the social state was preferable. He considered that the development of society was inevitable because of the inherent sinfulness of men. Man escaped from the natural state by means of a social contract through which each individual put himself and all his power under the supreme direction of the general will. As a result of the social contract, sovereignty, regardless of the form of government, resides in the society thus formed. In fact, Rousseau was not greatly concerned about the form of government, which he thought of as the result of a legislative act. Law should express the general will; and the government should act merely as the agent of the sovereign people. Although it did not solve the problem of reconciling authority and liberty, the *Social Contract* of Rousseau exercised a tremendous influence on the thinking of the more democratic elements in the population prior to and during the French Revolution. He furnished the catchwords of French democracy and promoted the idea of the national state. His writings gave an importance to the common interest and the general will which they had never before possessed. The followers of Rousseau, who were more definite and more radical than their master, wielded an even greater influence.

Rousseau's work entitled *Julie, ou La Nouvelle Héloïse*, caused a veritable revolution in the manners of French society. Modern readers find this novel, which is written in the form of letters, too sicklied over with Rousseau's own sentimentality, but it created a great sensation among his contemporaries. By its description of the simple living and the pleasures of country life it made simplicity and nature the fads of high French society.

The *Emile* of Rousseau was also a novel. It is the story of the education of a boy. In theory it holds to the maxim

"Trust to Nature." In practice the education of the boy is guided by a tutor who interferes openly or secretly in every part of his pupil's life. The function of the tutor, according to Rousseau, is to arouse in his pupil an interest in learning. The work emphasized many points that needed to be stressed, particularly the duty of giving children liberty to develop and of stimulating them to learn by arousing their interest.

The first French writer to devise a practical method for giving expression to the general will emphasized by Rousseau was Sieyès. He held that the way to make a constitution was to convene an extraordinary constitutional assembly. His proposals were first actually put into practice during the French Revolution.

Of much more importance than the work of Sieyès in influencing the course of events in Europe was the effect of events in America. In the American Revolution, which was in reality an application of the liberal ideas developed in England, many Frenchmen imagined they saw the application of the ideas of their own philosophers. In the written constitutions adopted by the American states, furthermore, Frenchmen found a precedent which suggested the written constitutions of the period of the French Revolution.

Montesquieu, Voltaire, Rousseau, and their numerous followers devoted their attention particularly to the intellectual problems of society. Another group of French thinkers centered their attention on its material problems. The theme of their discussions was the functions, relations, and prosperity of the farming, manufacturing, and commercial classes in the state. Like all their contemporaries they assumed the validity of the ideas of the age about a state of nature, natural law, and the social contract. Their reasoning led them to the conclusion that governments should be allowed to interfere only so far as was absolutely necessary for securing to each member of society the natural rights of man. Labor, manufacturing, and commerce should therefore be free and unfettered. In consequence they opposed the monopoly of the gilds and the hampering of commerce. Their most specific demands were the abolition of internal duties on grain and the introduction of a single tax on the land. The latter demand was based on the fallacy that agriculture alone contributed toward increasing the wealth of the nation. They are known as the Physiocrats.

Although his philosophy was broader than that of the Physiocratic group, Turgot, who was the first reforming minister of Louis XVI, supported the system of the Physiocrats in both his writings and his official policy. The general tendency of the teachings of the school was to challenge the policy of universal regulation that was advocated by the mercantilists and made the regular practice in France by Colbert.

Across the English Channel Adam Smith, a professor in the University of Glasgow, discussed some of the same problems. He began to speculate upon the laws by which a nation might increase its wealth. He came to the conclusion that the governments should abolish the greater part of the existing monopolies, restrictions on trade, customs duties, and burdens on industry. The good of all would best be promoted by each person's being left free to follow his own personal interests. His conclusions were embodied in his famous work, *The Wealth of Nations*, which appeared in 1776. Much of the misery of the lower classes in the nineteenth century arose from a too literal application of the economic principles of Adam Smith.

The classic protest against the method used in the eighteenth century, in the trial and punishment of accused persons, was made by an Italian nobleman, Beccaria (1735–93). Accepting the current political theories of his age he argued in favor of a clear, compact, and explicit code of criminal law, and for the abolition of torture and the death penalty. His ideas were published in his famous *Crimes and Punishments*.

The ideas of the French philosophers were best summarized and set forth in the great coöperative work known as the *Encyclopedia*. At first the French publishers planned to translate the English encyclopedia of Chambers. After Diderot (1713–84), an important member of the French philosophic group, became editor, he persuaded them to un-

INTELLECTUAL REVOLT AGAINST AUTHORITY

dertake a far more original and comprehensive work. The prospectus published in 1750 called for a work of eight folio volumes and at least six hundred plates. The first volume appeared in 1751 and the last in 1765. The completed work actually included seventeen volumes of text and eleven volumes of plates. Diderot had the assistance of Voltaire and many less famous members of the group known as the French philosophers. In consequence, the *Encyclopedia* was at the same time a work of reference and a vehicle for the propagation of the doctrines of the editors and contributors. The obstacles encountered by the publishers and editors furnish an excellent illustration of the political and intellectual situation in France. In 1752 a decree of the royal council suppressed the first two volumes as injurious to religion and to the king's authority. Through the connivance of the official in charge of the censorship of books, the manuscripts and plates for the *Encyclopedia* found a safe hiding-place in the house of the director of censorship himself. After the appearance of the seventh volume the Parlement of Paris again stopped the sale and publication of the work. The mistress of the King and high officials of the Government, however, secretly supported the enterprise, and Diderot continued his task on condition that the remaining volumes should appear at one time. Much of the success of the philosophers was due to the approval of the very classes against whom their attacks were being made.

The three centuries lying between the opening of the modern period and the French Revolution thus witnessed a general attack on authority. The men of science overthrew the scientific conceptions of the Middle Ages by substituting the ideal of natural law for the supernatural explanations of the theologians. The philosophers revolted against the ideas of Aristotle. The skeptics doubted the doctrines of the Church. English political leaders and thinkers undermined the royal absolutism. Finally, in the eighteenth century a remarkable group of French writers combined these currents of thought in their writings and made them part of the thought of the enlightened classes in that century.

REFERENCES

THE OVERTHROW OF THE MEDIEVAL CONCEPTION OF THE UNIVERSE
O. Lodge, *Pioneers of Science*, chapters I–IX.
W. T. Sedgwick and H. W. Tyler, *A Short History of Science*, chapter X.

THE PROGRESS OF SCIENCE
W. T. Sedgwick and II. W. Tyler, *A Short History of Science*, chapters X–XV.

THE WARFARE OF SCIENCE AND THEOLOGY
A. D. White, *History of the Warfare of Science with Theology in Christendom*.

THE DEISTS
Article: Deists — any encyclopedia.

FRANCIS BACON
C. C. J. Webb, *A History of Philosophy*, pp. 135–43.

DESCARTES
C. C. J. Webb, *A History of Philosophy*, chapter VII.

THE PHILOSOPHY OF JOHN LOCKE
C. C. J. Webb, *A History of Philosophy*, chapter VIII.

THE POLITICAL THEORIES OF MILTON
W. A. Dunning, *Political Theories*, vol. II, pp. 241–48.

THE POLITICAL THEORIES OF HARRINGTON
W. A. Dunning, *Political Theories*, vol. II, pp. 248–54.

THE POLITICAL THEORIES OF JOHN LOCKE
W. A. Dunning, *Political Theories*, vol. II, chapter X.

MONTESQUIEU
W. A. Dunning, *Political Theories*, vol. II, chapter XII.
E. J. Lowell, *The Eve of the French Revolution*, chapter X.

VOLTAIRE
E. J. Lowell, *The Eve of the French Revolution*, chapter V.
J. Morley, *Voltaire*.

ROUSSEAU
W. A. Dunning, *Political Theories*, vol. III, chapter I.
E. J. Lowell, *The Eve of the French Revolution*, chapters XVIII–XIX.
J. Morley, *Rousseau*.

THE ENCYCLOPEDIA
E. J. Lowell, *The Eve of the French Revolution*, chapter XVI.
J. Morley, *Diderot*.

CHAPTER XIV

THE BRITISH EMPIRE IN THE LATTER HALF OF THE EIGHTEENTH CENTURY

BETWEEN 1500 and 1763 England grew from a small state into a great empire. In the next fifty years the Empire witnessed many important changes. In England proper the introduction of machinery and steam power transformed English industry; the enclosure of the open fields and the adoption of scientific methods of farming revolutionized English agriculture; the preaching of Wesley stirred the consciences of Englishmen; and the agitation of the reformers threatened to democratize the political constitution of England. In America the Empire lost its most important colonies. In India and Australasia it gained important new territories.

ENGLAND IN 1750

The transformation of industry, the revolutionizing of agriculture, and the stirring of the political and religious consciences of Englishmen profoundly changed the structure of English society. A survey of the chief features of English society about 1750 will furnish a fixed point from which to measure the progress and significance of these important economic, religious, and political movements.

About the year 1750 England had a population of about 6,500,000 inhabitants. By far the larger part of this population lived in rural communities in the southeastern half of the country. Comparatively few of the people lived in cities or in the northern and western districts of England.

In rural England many features of medieval times still survived. Villages with open fields, interspersed strips, and common pastures existed in all parts of the country. Most English farmers left a third of their arable land idle each year, wasted a good deal of land in balks and unused strips, and employed in farming antiquated tools and methods.

A few enterprising men like Jethro Trull, Lord Townshend, Robert Bakewell, and others furnished exceptions to this general situation. As a usual thing they first acquired complete control of their lands by enclosing them. They obtained an act of Parliament authorizing the enclosure of all or of a part of the land included in a parish, surveyed the land to be enclosed, and finally assigned to each person affected by the enclosure a compact plot of ground that was equivalent in value to what he had surrendered — that is, interspersed strips and the common rights in the open fields, meadows, pasture land, and woodland. Each landholder then enclosed, improved, and managed his own plot or plots of ground as he chose. The introduction of better methods of farming usually followed the enclosure of the land. The larger farmers, at least, carefully drained and fertilized their land, planted wheat and turnips by drilling them, instead of by sowing them broadcast, used better seed, kept down the weeds by careful cultivation, scientifically rotated the crops, and paid judicious attention to the segregation and breeding of stock. The general adoption of these principles later produced the Agricultural Revolution.

This transformation of English agriculture had not proceeded far enough in 1750 to disturb seriously the old organization of English society. The gentry and the titled members of the aristocracy still stood at the top of the social hierarchy. They lived in great houses, employed many servants, held large estates, and exercised, as justices of the peace, wide powers of local government over their tenants and neighbors. Since the sixteenth century their numbers had been augmented by the addition of successful merchants who had bought estates to bolster up their social position. Below the landlord class ranked the freeholders, copyholders, and leaseholders. With the aid of agricultural laborers they did the greater part of the actual farming of the land. They differed greatly among themselves in respect to the size and value of their holdings, the terms on which they held their land, and in social position. Many of the freeholders (frequently referred to as yeomen) carried on some by-industry, such as weaving, in addition to their agriculture. For several decades there had been a noticeable decline in the number of the yeomen. Next in the social scale came the cottagers, farm servants, and squatters. The pittances which they received from the landlords and farmers as wages constituted the greater part of their incomes.

Although England produced in 1750 most of the goods required by its own population, it was not in the modern sense of the word a manufacturing country. The most important and the most ancient of its manufactures was the woolen industry. The manufacture of woolens for domestic use was carried on in all parts of the country. The weaver and his family, assisted at most by a laborer or two, carried on the processes of carding, spinning, weaving, and dyeing. Since they lived in the rural districts, the regulations of the gilds did not hamper them. Often the weaver combined some agriculture with his weaving. In this case he held a few acres, raised some vegetables, grew the oats for his porridge, and kept a pig, a cow, a horse, and some poultry. This method of manufacture is known as the domestic system.

In 1750 the weaver was ceasing to be his own master. In many districts the capitalists already owned the looms and the raw material, paid the weaver for working the yarn up into cloth, and disposed of the finished product. The intervention of the capitalist in the domestic system was an important step toward the establishment of the factory system. The next and final step was to bring the machinery and workers together under one roof.

None of the other English industries approached the woolen industry in importance. The once flourishing iron industry had greatly declined as a result of the destruction of the forests through the manufacture of the charcoal that was necessary for smelting the iron. Some glassware, linen, silk goods, and rude pottery were manufactured, and quantities of liquor were brewed or distilled. All of these industries were carried on by the domestic system of manufacture.

In the middle of the eighteenth century English commerce was still small in bulk, but as a result of the growth of the

British Empire it was rapidly expanding. Both exports and imports had doubled since the beginning of the century. The condition of the roads made the pack horse still the usual means for transporting commodities from one part of the country to another. The wares of commerce were regularly distributed through fairs, special markets like the market for cloth at Leeds, traveling merchants, and peddlers. Retail shops existed only in the cities.

As a result of the struggle for parliamentary government in the seventeenth century, the powers formerly exercised by the King had definitely passed into the hands of Parliament. This body represented mainly the landlords and the merchants. The membership of its upper house consisted of hereditary peers, the two archbishops, and most of the bishops. The peers controlled a large proportion of the seats of the lower house through the manipulation of the restricted electorate by the use of bribery and influence. The English aristocracy controlled local government also. In their capacity as justices of the peace they had gradually supplanted the manor courts, the parish vestries, and other organs of local government. On one occasion the Duke of Buckingham tried and convicted a man in the ducal kitchen, upon the evidences of his own keepers, for hunting on his ducal estates. Such episodes force one to the conclusion that only the upper classes fully enjoyed the boasted rights of Englishmen.

THE INDUSTRIAL REVOLUTION

The Industrial Revolution profoundly modified many features of the society just described. This movement came as a result of the interaction of a number of forces. The religious persecutions and the devastating wars of the continent of Europe had driven to the shores of England many craftsmen who brought into the country the slowly accumulated skill and ingenuity of the Continent. Particularly in the North of England, where town life developed after the gilds and the medieval town restrictions had gone out of vogue, these foreign artisans found greater freedom and opportunity for plying their trades. The work of the scientists and thinkers had freed the minds of an increasing number of people from the grip of the supernatural and led to the development of a rationalism which culminated in an unusual curiosity, a search for the natural causes of phenomena, and a widespread use of scientific methods of investigation. These conditions inevitably quickened the inventive faculties and led to the invention of machinery.

A second factor in producing the Industrial Revolution was the unusual opportunity for the profitable use of mechanical inventions. The expansion of commerce created new markets for English goods and increased the wealth of England. The new markets and the new wealth, in turn, increased the demand for English goods. The new demands for English products created a demand for a larger output, and the growth of English capital made possible the rise of the new system of manufacture by machinery.

The introduction of machinery and the application of the new discoveries of science first transformed the cotton industry. During the latter half of the eighteenth century English inventors perfected machines to spin the thread and to weave and to print cotton cloth, and applied the discoveries of chemistry to the process of bleaching the cloth. Because of the humidity of its climate and its nearness to the port of Liverpool, Lancashire continued to be the center for cotton manufactures.

About 1733 John Kay invented the first of the new machines, the fly shuttle. This device enabled a single workman to weave as wide a piece of cloth as he wished. By twitching a string he could throw the shuttle back and forth across the warp without the aid of an assistant. By 1760 the invention of Kay had come into general use in spite of much popular opposition. It created a demand for thread which the spinners, working with the antiquated spinning wheel, were entirely unable to supply.

This demand for more thread set many persons to experimenting with spinning machinery. Finally, about 1766, James Hargreaves invented a machine for spinning known as the "spinning jenny," which came into use about 1768 and which was patented in 1770. The new machines spun eight threads at once. As they were run by hand and could be used in the cottages, they rapidly came into general use. In 1769 Richard Arkwright patented a spinning machine known as the "water frame," which was the invention of other men. It drew out the carded cotton by carrying it through four successive pairs of rollers, each pair running faster than the preceding one, and spun the drawn-out "rovings" by a flyer adapted from the old-fashioned spinning wheel. The "spinning jenny" spun a finer thread; the "water frame" spun more rapidly. Consequently, in 1779 an ingenious weaver named Samuel Crompton combined the two machines into a single device, known as the "spinning mule," which possessed the good points of both the earlier machines. The machines of Hargreaves, Arkwright, and Crompton produced a revolution in the spinning of cotton.

The introduction of the "water frame" and the "spinning mule" led to the development of the factory system in the cotton-spinning industry. The new machines were heavy and costly and ill-adapted to use in simple cottages. Motive power of some sort was needed to run them. In consequence Arkwright began to establish spinning factories. In his first factory he used horse power to drive the spinning machines. In his second he utilized water. Finally, in 1783, he began to use steam power in his factories. The success of Arkwright led to the starting of many similar establishments. By 1788 there were 143 spinning factories in Great Britain. By 1790 mule spinning was also being carried on successfully in factories. Because of his pioneer work in establishing factories, Arkwright is known as the father of the factory system.

The adoption of the new spinning machines caused the weavers to lag behind the spinners. This situation created a demand for a power loom capable of using the output of the new spinning machinery. In response to this demand a clergyman, Edmund Cartwright, invented a cumbersome machine for automatic weaving. As he knew nothing about weaving, his first machine needed a great deal of improving, but by the opening of the nineteenth century his looms were beginning to come into general use.

The adoption of a number of other technical improvements completed the transformation of the cotton industry. Several persons invented mechanical carding machines for straightening out the cotton fibers preparatory to spinning. About 1785 cotton goods began to be printed by running them over cylindrical rollers like the printing presses for modern newspapers, instead of by the slow and primitive process of repeatedly applying to the surface of the cloth a small block of wood with a design carved on it. The application of the chemical discoveries of Scheele and Berthollet reduced from eight months to a few hours the time required for bleaching the cotton goods. In 1793 the invention of the cotton gin by Eli Whitney solved the problem of cleaning sufficient raw cotton to supply the demands of the new cotton industry.

Sooner or later all industries followed the example of the cotton manufacturers. First the woolen industry and later all divisions of the textile industry introduced the new machinery. In the end all branches of manufacture have gradually substituted machinery for hand power.

The adoption of textile machinery too heavy for operation by hand power created a demand for a more satisfactory motive power. Most of the early textile factories used water power to operate the new machinery. It did not prove to be altogether satisfactory. Water was often low at certain seasons of the year, and labor was often scarce at the points where the water power was to be found. The solution of the power problem proved to be the steam engine of James Watt.

Like most successful inventors, Watt merely perfected the work of many men. Three quarters of a century before the time of Watt, Savery had invented an engine capable of pumping water by the use of steam, and Papin, a French refugee, had produced an engine fitted with a piston and a safety valve. In 1705 Newcomen patented an engine that could pump water from mines. The pressure of the steam on the lower side of the piston first pushed up the mechanism operating the pump; then the pressure of the atmosphere forced the piston down into a vacuum that had been suddenly created by throwing jets of cold water into the cylinder containing the steam. After a valve gear, which automatically regulated the flow of steam into the cylinder, had been added in 1718, Newcomen's engine came into general use in the mines. In 1763 James Watt of Glasgow began to work at the problem of improving the steam engine of Newcomen. He completed his first engine in 1765 and patented his invention in 1769. He contributed to the development of the steam engine the separate condenser, the steam jacket which keeps the cylinder hot, the idea of closing the cylinder at both ends and applying the steam on each side of the piston, and the use of tallow and oil as a lubricant.

Watt soon found himself confronted with the problems of finding the capital with which to finance his experiments and workmen capable of embodying his ideas in iron and steel. He finally formed a partnership with Matthew Boulton, a wealthy manufacturer of Birmingham, who furnished without stint, during the trying years of experimentation and commercial introduction, capital, encouragement, and skilled workmen from his famous Soho factory, which manufactured ornamental metal work. The credit for making the modern steam engine a commercial success, therefore, belongs jointly to Boulton and Watt.

The adoption of the new textile machinery and the development of the steam engine had a vital connection with the iron and steel industry. The new machinery and the steam engine created a demand for iron and steel. The demand for iron and steel led to the development of better processes for refining the ore and for shaping the cast iron.

The first step in the transformation of the iron industry was the discovery of a new fuel. A family of ironmasters named Darby introduced coke as a substitute for charcoal in the smelting process. The second head of the family conducted a series of experiments with the new fuel between 1730 and 1735, and brought the family iron works to the pinnacle of success just after the middle of the century. The invention of a better blowing machine by John Smeaton in 1760 made the new fuel absolutely satisfactory. It made possible an increase of the draft in the furnaces used in smelting the ore.

English ironmasters next attacked the problem of converting the pig iron produced by the smelting furnaces into steel or wrought iron without increasing the amount of carbon in the metal. The reverberatory furnace and the art of puddling proved the solution of this problem. The new furnace reheated the metal without bringing it into direct contact with the fuel by passing heated gases over it instead. Puddling separated the scoria or cinder from the metal. Henry Cort first made a commercial success of the reverberatory furnace and of the process of puddling about 1784.

The ironmasters next developed machinery for shaping the refined product into rods and bars, and into sheet and structural iron. The development of sheet iron led to the construction of tanks and boilers. The discovery of structural steel made possible the building of skyscrapers and iron bridges.

A great development of mining followed the revolution in industry. The new steam engines and the new furnaces used great quantities of coal, and the new engines and machinery required a great deal of iron. Between 1750 and 1788 the production of the iron mines of England mounted from 18,000 to 68,000 tons of ore. In 1750 the coal mines of England produced almost no coal; by the end of the century they mined ten million tons of coal.

The Industrial Revolution also created a demand for better transportation facilities. In response to this demand came a period of canal-building. James Brindley first planned and supervised a canal to connect the mines of the Duke of Bridgewater with the city of Manchester. It cut in half the price of coal in that market. The new mine-owners and manufacturers, quickly seeing the advantages of the new means of transportation in broadening markets and in lowering the costs of carrying, promoted the construction of a network of waterways that furnished a cheap means of transportation to most parts of the country. The great improvements in roads and the invention of the railway and the steamboat came in the next century.

The Industrial Revolution had many economic results. Instead of doing a great variety of tasks as under the domestic system, the workers in charge of the new machinery confined themselves to a single step in the process of manufacture which they performed over and over again. Manufactured articles became the joint product of many workers. Both this division of labor and the introduction of machinery tended to increase production tremendously and to lower the costs of manufacture. The lowering of the cost of production not only led to a broadening of the domestic market for English goods, but enabled English manufacturers to undersell their competitors on the Continent. As a result of these conditions

English commerce steadily increased and the national capital grew by leaps and bounds. This remarkable growth of the national wealth as a result of the Industrial Revolution explains the ability of England to bear the tremendous financial strains of the wars of the French Revolution and of the Napoleonic period. In spite of the constant attacks of France on English commerce during these years, and the tremendous expenditures made by the English authorities as paymaster of the Powers opposed to France and Napoleon, England was wealthier at the close of the Napoleonic period than at the opening of the wars of the French Revolution.

The Industrial Revolution, likewise, led to important changes in the organization of English society. In the Middle Ages population was nearly stationary and to be found mainly in the south of England. From 1500 to 1750 it grew slowly. After 1750 it increased with great rapidity and shifted from Southern England to the Midlands and North of England. At the same time great industrial cities and towns like Manchester, Birmingham, and Sheffield in Northern England, and Glasgow in Scotland, arose at points where water power, iron, and coal were accessible, while the population of rural England remained stationary or declined. The Industrial Revolution, furthermore, produced two new classes of society: a small class of industrial capitalists and a large class of factory workers. Members of the gentry and the merchant class, who were lured by the hope of sudden profits, furnished some of the capital for the new factories, but artisans, petty manufacturers, yeomen, tenant farmers, and other persons of humble rank contributed by far the larger part of it. The factory laborers were recruited from the ranks of the declining yeomen, agricultural laborers, and workers in older industries, and among the poorer classes of Ireland and the mountaineers of Scotland and Wales. They were lured to the new factories by the higher wages paid in the new factories at the beginning. By the end of the eighteenth century the new class of industrial capitalists had begun to take a position of influence beside the landlords and merchant princes, but the ignorant and unorganized workers were largely at the mercy of their hard, unsympathetic employers until far into the nineteenth century.

The changes just described created many new social problems. The growth of factories brought the problems of the protection of the factory workers in respect to wages, hours of work, and working conditions, and of the employment of women and children. The development of great urban manufacturing centers confronted society with questions of housing, sanitation, and public health. The rise of the industrial capitalist and the factory laborer made the problem of capital and labor more acute.

In time the development of the new capitalist class and the shifting of population led to a demand for political reform. After the close of the Napoleonic period the manufacturers began to insist on a voice in political affairs along with the landlords and the merchants, and the new industrial centers, like Manchester, Birmingham, and Sheffield, objected to having no representation in Parliament when many depopulated towns of Southern England sent two representatives to the House of Commons. These demands finally led to the Reform Bill of 1832.

The Industrial Revolution has not been confined to the iron and textile industries or to England. These industries merely serve as typical examples of the revolution most industries have undergone since the eighteenth century. In the second quarter of the nineteenth century, in France, and in the third quarter, in Germany, industries began to be transformed by the adoption of machinery, the methods of science, and the steam engine. The United States, Japan, and most of the countries of Western Europe were sooner or later affected by the Industrial Revolution. It ranks in importance with the Renaissance, the Protestant Revolt, and the Commercial Revolution among the forces which have transformed the medieval into the modern world.

THE AGRICULTURAL REVOLUTION

Contemporary with the Industrial Revolution was the Agricultural Revolution. Unlike the movement in industry it was confined entirely to England. It came in response to a steady rise in the price of agricultural products after 1760, occasioned by the increase in the population and the wealth of England. The growth of manufacturing centers, in particular, created a demand for food which stimulated English landowners, in order to increase their profits, to adopt the methods of agricultural pioneers like Jethro Tull, Lord Townshend, and early stock-breeders like Robert Bakewell. The second half of the eighteenth century consequently saw much land enclosed and a widespread adoption of the new methods. While in the first six decades of the century English landlords enclosed only 337,877 acres, in the next five decades they enclosed 6,352,900 acres.

The large landowners were the only class of the population to profit from the enclosure movement. They alone possessed sufficient capital and credit to stand the expense of making the preliminary surveys, of pushing an act through Parliament, and of hedging the new enclosures, draining the land, and fertilizing the soil. In many cases the freeholder found his allotment too small to enclose. More often ignorance of the new methods and lack of capital hampered him in the development of the compact holding that had been given him in exchange for his arable strips and his rights in the meadow, the common pasture, and the woodland. In either case he surrendered his holding in the end and became a wage-earner. The cottager, who rented by the year a cottage to which valuable rights of common were attached, lost his rights without receiving any compensation. The squatters were brusquely evicted. This new class of landless men created by the enclosures became either workers in the new factories or agricultural laborers.

The crowding-out of the freeholders, the small tenant farmers, the cottagers, and the squatters concentrated the ownership of the land in the hands of a small class of capitalist landlords. The bulk of the rural population lost all rights in the land. The Agricultural Revolution left in England only the three classes of the present day: the landed proprietors, who own the land, the tenant farmers, who actually farm the land, and the agricultural laborers, who work on the land for wages.

THE WESLEYAN REVIVAL

The Wesleyan revival was part of a wider movement of reaction against the religious conditions prevailing in the Established Church of England in the early part of the eighteenth century. After the spiritual fervor of the Puritan Revolution, England had relapsed into religious formalism. Faith and enthusiasm in religion were perpetuated mainly by pious families here and there, and little religious societies organized for prayer, reading of the Scriptures, and Christian fellowship. Out of this unorganized reaction against the formalism of the State Church and its ministers grew the Methodist movement initiated and guided by John Wesley.

This important movement was greatly influenced by the experience and the personality of its founder. John Wesley was born in 1703 at Epworth, in Eastern England, in a family with strong Puritan traditions. He was educated at Oxford. In 1726 he was ordained a clergyman of the Church of England. Like Luther before him he early became troubled over the problem of sin and tried to work out his own salvation by good works. After a varied experience as a fellow at Oxford and a missionary in Georgia, he underwent in May, 1739, an evangelical conversion. This happened while he was listening, in a meeting of one of the little religious societies, that were so numerous at the time, to the reading of Luther's preface to the Epistle to the Romans.

Wesley immediately began to tell others of the possibility of salvation by conversion. At first he tried to preach in the Anglican churches, but the attitude of his religious superiors there soon closed the edifices of the state churches to him and forced him to preach in the open air. For fifty-two years he carried on a great revival movement in England, Ireland, and Scotland. He talked to men at every opportunity about religion — to his chance companions in the stage-coach, to fellow guests at the inns, to the great crowds that gathered to hear him on the streets and in the open fields. His activity was extraordinary. He traveled usually an average of 4500 miles a year, mostly on horseback, and preached two, three — occasionally even four — times a day, to crowds that often numbered 20,000 persons. In his fifty-two years of evangelistic work he is estimated to have preached over 40,000 sermons and to have traveled about 250,000 miles.

At first Wesley intended to work in and through the Church of England, but the hostility of the ecclesiastical authorities slowly compelled him to organize his movement into a separate church. The closing of parish churches to his meetings forced him to form religious societies for Christian fellowship and to build chapels as places of meeting. The opposition of the clergy, his need of helpers, and the eagerness of many of the new converts to assist him, compelled him to form a corps of lay preachers. The refusal of the Anglican clergy to administer the sacraments to many of the new Methodist converts forced him to authorize his assistants to dispense the sacraments in the Methodist chapels. The need of advising with his assistants led him to call together conferences of ministers and laymen. After the death of Wesley these bodies developed into the chief legislative and executive bodies of Methodists. The necessity of having some one to look after the business affairs of the little Methodist societies led to the creation of the office of stewards. Thus step by step under the compulsion of circumstances Wesley created and organized the Methodist Church.

The evangelical revival which swept England in the eighteenth century profoundly affected both England and the rest of the Empire. Wesley not only founded a powerful church which now has branches in nearly every country of the world, but he revived the sleeping consciences of men and transformed the lives of thousands of persons in the middle and lower classes of England. The Methodist movement aroused the consciences of the poor and the philanthropy of the rich; its methods are credited by some with having saved England from a social revolt similar to that which broke out in France in 1789.

ATTEMPTS TO MODIFY THE ENGLISH CONSTITUTION

In the latter half of the eighteenth century two attempts were made to modify the English Constitution that had emerged from the political struggles of the seventeenth century. George III attempted to reëstablish personal government in England, and a number of reformers tried to democratize Parliament.

George III was unwilling to permit Parliament to govern the country, as his immediate predecessors had done. He did not, like the Stuarts, aim to dispense entirely with Parliament, but he attempted to choose his own ministers, to influence their policies, and to maintain a majority in Parliament through bribery, pensions, and the use of patronage. The efforts of the King met with a large degree of success from the time of his accession in 1760 until the closing years of the American Revolution. His policy of personal rule could not survive the disaster of the loss of the thirteen colonies. In 1780 the House of Commons passed a resolution which declared that "the influence of the Crown has increased, is increasing, and ought to be diminished." In 1782, and again in 1783, it forced the King to accept ministers who were personally distasteful to him. After the disaster of the American Revolution George III never again became his own prime minister.

The attempt of George III to establish his personal rule, combined with the unrepresentative character of Parliament, gave rise after 1760 to a movement for a reform of the English Government. During the first years of the reform movement the agitation centered around the name and personality of a man of low moral and political principles named John Wilkes. For the sake of notoriety this man put himself into opposition to the King, the ministry, and the friends of the King in Parliament, and began in 1763 to attack them in a violent and abusive manner in a paper called the *North Briton*. In this way he won great popularity and the reputation of being an intrepid friend of the people. The Government replied to his attacks by prosecuting him for libel and expelling him from the House of Commons. His supporters, on the other hand, continued to elect him to Parliament. Finally in 1774 he was admitted without further opposition and in 1782 a motion was carried to expunge from the Journal of the House of Commons the record of his expulsion. The contest of Wilkes with the Government established two important principles: that warrants for arrest must specify the person to be arrested, and that no one could be excluded from the House of Commons who was not legally disqualified for membership. In addition, the whole struggle gave a tremendous impulse to public agitation and taught the Commons the lesson that the will of the electors could not be completely defied. As a result of the same general movement for reform, the House of Commons gave up in 1771 its efforts to punish individuals who were responsible for the publication of debates.

After the American Revolution the reformers centered their attacks mainly on the unrepresentative character of Parliament. In response to this agitation the younger Pitt brought in a bill in 1784 that was designed to abolish some of the more glaring inequalities in the representation. Too many members of Parliament, however, were interested in the maintenance of the existing political system, and the measure was defeated. The question remained a subject of agitation, nevertheless, until the excesses of the republicans in France caused the English governing classes to suppress all agitation for political reform and to postpone for forty years a settlement of the question. Finally in 1832 the forces of reform, reënforced by the new and rising class of industrial capitalists, pushed through a reluctant Parliament the first of the great reform bills.

THE AMERICAN REVOLUTION

The most important event in British imperial history between the Seven Years' War and the opening of the war with France in 1793 was the American Revolution. It began as a revolt of thirteen colonies against English rule. Before its close it broadened out into a world conflict between England on the one hand and France, Spain, the United Netherlands, and the thirteen colonies on the other. The intervention of these continental Powers transformed the war into a new European struggle for colonial and commercial supremacy.

The underlying cause of the revolt was the differences between the colonists and the inhabitants of the home country in origin, institutions, ideas, and interests. The people of England had accepted the monarchy and the Established Church. Many of the colonists had emigrated in response to a desire for greater political and religious freedom. In the new environment they had developed a different system of representation, a more democratic suffrage, different economic interests, and a spirit of resentment against all economic and political restraint. The development of this spirit of self-reliance gave rise to constant quarrels between the colonists and their English governors and to a general disregard of the English trade and navigation acts.

These acts were a product of the Anglo-Dutch rivalry of the seventeenth century. They breathed a spirit of mercantilism and aimed to destroy the commercial supremacy of the Dutch in the interest of British shipowners and merchants and to subordinate the interests of the colonies to those of the mother country. An ordinance of 1651 gave English and colonial shipowners and merchants a monopoly in the carrying of the products of Asia, Africa, and America to England and her colonies. As a result of this measure shipbuilding became the most important industry of New England. An act of 1660 reënacted the provisions of the ordinance of 1651 and gave English merchants a monopoly of the commerce and the markets of the colonies. This law required the colonists to send sugar, tobacco, cotton, and certain woods used in dyeing to England and excluded from England colonial products that were likely to compete with English goods. Later acts included in the list of commodities reserved for the English market naval stores (tar, pitch, turpentine, hemp, masts, and yards), rice, beaver skins, and several other products. This legislation seriously hurt the Carolina rice-growers. On the other hand, some of the colonists actually benefited by the policy of paying bounties on the production of naval stores.

An act of 1673 greatly interfered with intercolonial trade. Finally an act of 1733 menaced the trade of the colonists with the French, Danish, Dutch, and Spanish colonies in the West Indies by the imposition of prohibitive duties on the importation of sugar, molasses, and rum from foreign colonies. Parliamentary measures passed in 1699 and 1750 forbade the exportation of woolen and iron manufactures. Until 1763, however, these trade and navigation acts remained a threat rather than an actual obstacle to the growth of colonial trade and industry. English statesmen were too preoccupied with English domestic problems, or too wise, to insist on the rigid enforcement of this restrictive legislation.

The immediate cause of the American Revolution was a sudden determination of the English authorities to regulate colonial affairs more closely. The Seven Years' War had left England with its debt doubled and a great empire to defend. The English authorities determined to make the colonists in America at least share the burden of colonial defense. They decided to enforce the trade and navigation acts, to maintain an army of 10,000 men in America for the defense of the colonies, and to impose a stamp tax. They sent ships of war to patrol the American coast, gave strict instructions, and in 1764 revived and enlarged the act of 1733 that had been directed against the purchase of sugar, molasses, and rum in the Dutch and French West Indies. In the following year Parliament passed a stamp-tax act. The money derived from the strict enforcement of the trade and navigation acts and the stamp act was to be used in paying for the support of the troops that were sent to defend the colonies and of various colonial officials. These measures aroused the greatest resistance in America. The enforcement of the trade and navigation acts threatened the prosperity of the New England and Middle colonies by cutting off their lucrative, illicit trade with the Dutch and French West Indies, and the passage of the stamp-tax act threatened the political liberty of all the colonies by taking away from them the control of the purse. For the next decade the struggle continued. The English authorities showed a willingness to withdraw specific measures, but they stubbornly insisted on a recognition of the right of Parliament to tax the American colonists and to regulate their trade. The colonial leaders fought with equal determination against the policy of the English Government. The uncompromising attitude of both parties in the struggle led to a long series of incidents which inflamed colonial public opinion and finally precipitated in 1775 the armed resistance of the colonists.

From 1775 to 1778 the fighting was confined to the colonies. The first year of hostilities saw the defeat of the colonial expedition against Canada and the driving of the British garrison out of Boston. This latter success heartened the colonists to declare their independence on the Fourth of July, 1776. The entrance into the struggle of the Hessian troops raised in Europe, the loss of New York by the American colonies, the retreat of General Washington and his army across New Jersey, and the brilliant victories of the American army at Trenton and Princeton marked the second year of the war. This campaign shut the British up in New York. The third year of the war saw the capture of Philadelphia by the British and the defeat of Burgoyne at Saratoga with the consequent thwarting of the English attempt to capture the Hudson Valley and to cut off New England from the remaining colonies. The principal result of the first three years of fighting was to show the strength and vitality of the colonial resistance.

This strength finally caused France to intervene in 1778 in the hope of revenging the losses which had been incurred in the War of the Spanish Succession and the Seven Years' War. In 1779 Spain entered the war for the purpose of regaining Gibraltar, and in the following year the United Netherlands found itself impelled to join in the conflict. The entrance of France, Spain, and the Dutch both directly and indirectly aided the American colonists in their demand for independence. The money, men, and supplies contributed by France to the struggle in America and the coöperation of the French fleet materially helped the American colonists to carry on the war. The intervention of the three European Powers diverted the attention of the English to the maritime war and to the protection of England, Gibraltar, and the British West Indies; the war in America became secondary. England confined its efforts there to the holding of New York and to a campaign in the South where it hoped for a rising in behalf of England. The war in America ended with the disastrous surrender of Lord Cornwallis at Yorktown in 1781, while the fighting that had taken place in Europe, on the sea, and in the West Indies left the general situation unchanged.

Peace was finally concluded in 1783 by a new Treaty of Paris. The thirteen colonies gained from England a recognition of their independence, a share in the fisheries of Newfoundland, and all the territory from the Great Lakes to Florida and all from the Atlantic Ocean to the Mississippi River except the city of New Orleans. Spain regained Florida and the island of Minorca. The participation of France in the war practically bankrupted the French treasury and made inevitable the outbreak of the French Revolution.

THE EXTENSION OF THE EMPIRE IN THE FAR EAST

Even before the loss of her colonies in America had been consummated, England began to extend the frontiers of the Empire in the Far East. Before the end of the century, it had laid the foundations of British rule in India and made a beginning toward the settlement of Australia.

The rivalry with France had started the English authorities in the fateful policy of interfering in the native politics of India. After the defeat of the French the English continued the practice. A series of wars with the Hindu Confederacy of the Mahrattas in Central India and with the Moslem rulers of Mysore in Southern India followed the struggle for the control of Bengal and the famous victory of Clive at Plassey. These wars laid the territorial foundation for English rule in India. The British authorities retained direct control of part of the conquered territory and left some of it under the control of native rulers, who were carefully supervised by British agents. As a result of this policy of expansion all India had come under the direct or indirect control of England by the middle of the nineteenth century.

The extension of the imperial frontiers entailed a reorganization of the British administration in India. A number of unusual administrators contributed to the work. Using the methods of Dupleix, Robert Clive (1757-60, 1765-67) firmly established English rule in the provinces of Bengal, Behar, and Orissa. His military achievements in the Seven Years' War and his important contributions to the establishment of English rule in Bengal have caused him to be regarded as the founder of British rule in India. Warren Hastings (1772-85) reformed the system of collecting the revenue, established civil and criminal courts, and made large economies in the administration. Lord Cornwallis (1785-95) corrected many faults of the civil service and established a permanent system for the collection of the revenue in Bengal, Behar, and Orissa. During the same period the English Government took the first steps toward depriving the English East India Company of the independence that it had enjoyed in the government of India. By the Regulating Act of 1773 and the India Act of 1784 it subordinated the commercial company to the State.

The first settlements in Australia were among the results of the voyage of Captain James Cook to the Pacific Ocean in 1769. On the return voyage he rediscovered for the English both New Zealand and Australia. At the suggestion of one of the members of the expedition the English Government began in 1788 to send to Australia the criminals who were congesting English jails. The new settlers were by no means wholly undesirable. Many of the so-called convicts were merely political prisoners or persons guilty of very minor offenses. The first settlement was at Sydney, New South Wales.

Thus, in spite of the loss of the thirteen colonies in America, Great Britain continued to be the greatest of the colonial Powers. In the New World it possessed at the close of the eighteenth century Canada, Bermuda, the Bahamas, Jamaica, and smaller islands in the West Indies; in Africa, Gambia and the Gold Coast; in Europe, the British Isles and

Gibraltar; and in Asia a beginning had been made toward the establishment of British rule in India and the settlement of Australia.

During the latter half of the eighteenth century many distinct movements touched the British Empire and modified its organization. English history lost its former unity and simplicity. In England machinery and the steam engine transformed industry and profoundly affected the social and political organization; the enclosure of the land and the adoption of scientific methods in farming and stock breeding modernized agriculture and put the control of the land in the hands of a few great landowners; and the preaching of Wesley quickened the consciences of the middle and lower classes and led to the organization of the Methodist Episcopal Church. No important political changes, however, were effected during the period. Both the attempts of George III to increase the royal power and the efforts of the reformers to democratize the Constitution failed completely. In the Empire England lost thirteen of the English colonies in North America and extended British rule in India and Australia.

REFERENCES

ENGLAND ON THE EVE OF THE INDUSTRIAL REVOLUTION
    H. de B. Gibbins, *Industry in England*, chapter XX.
    H. T. Wood, *Industrial England in the Middle of the Eighteenth Century*.

CAUSES OF THE INDUSTRIAL REVOLUTION
    W. Bowden, *Industrial Society in England towards the End of the Eighteenth Century*, pp. 51–69.

THE NEW TEXTILE INVENTIONS
    E. P. Cheyney, *Industrial and Social History of England*, pp. 203–14.
    H. de B. Gibbins, *Industry in England*, chapter XXI.
    J. H. Robinson and C. A. Beard, *The Development of Modern Europe*, vol. II, pp. 30–38.
    A. P. Usher, *The Industrial History of England*, chapter XII.

THE REVOLUTION IN THE IRON INDUSTRY
    A. P. Usher, *The Industrial History of England*, chapter XIII.

THE STEAM ENGINE
    J. H. Robinson and C. A. Beard, *The Development of Modern Europe*, vol. II, pp. 39–44.

S. S. Smiles, *Lives of the Engineers, Boulton and Watt.*
R. H. Thurston, *The Growth of the Steam Engine.*
A. P. Usher, *The Industrial History of England*, pp. 324–29.

EFFECT OF THE INDUSTRIAL REVOLUTION
J. H. Robinson and C. A. Beard, *The Development of Modern Europe*, vol. II, pp. 45–49.

THE AGRICULTURAL REVOLUTION
F. A. Ogg, *Social Progress in Contemporary Europe*, chapter VI.
F. A. Ogg, *Economic Development of Modern Europe*, chapter VI.

THE FOUNDING OF METHODISM
W. H. Fitchett, *Wesley and his Century.*

THE CONSTITUTIONAL POLICY OF GEORGE III
A. L. Cross, *A Shorter History of England and Greater Britain*, pp. 506–10.

THE AMERICAN REVOLUTION
H. E. Bolton and T. M. Marshall, *The Colonization of North America, 1492–1783*, chapters XXIII–XXVII.
E. P. Cheyney, *A Short History of England*, chapter XVIII.
A. L. Cross, *A Shorter History of England and Greater Britain*, chapters XLII–XLIII.
A. Hassall, *European History, 1715–89*, chapter XII.
C. J. H. Hayes, *A Political and Social History of Modern Europe*, vol. I, chapter X.
H. Robinson, *The Development of the British Empire*, chapters VII–VIII.
W. H. Woodward, *The Expansion of the British Empire*, chapter VI.

EXTENSION OF THE BRITISH EMPIRE IN THE FAR EAST
W. H. Woodward, *The Expansion of the British Empire*, chapters VII, IX.

CHAPTER XV

FRANCE ON THE EVE OF THE FRENCH REVOLUTION

BETWEEN the close of the Middle Ages and the end of the reign of Louis XIV, medieval France gradually developed a civilization that is known now as the "*ancien régime*" because it preceded the French Revolution. As a result of this slow evolution its institutions were partly feudal and partly monarchical in origin. In less than a century after Louis XIV gave the institutions of the *ancien régime* their final form, the French Revolution profoundly modified all phases of French life. To understand the significance of this revolutionary movement, the organization of France under the absolute monarchy and the history of France between 1715 and 1789 must be studied.

THE ANCIEN RÉGIME — ECONOMIC CONDITIONS

In the eighteenth century French agriculture retained many of the features that had characterized it in 1500. The land was divided for the most part into large estates with open fields; the peasants lived in villages; and agriculture was carried on by the same antiquated methods, crude tools, and peasant coöperation. South of the Loire, olives and wine were the most important products. The peasants of this region practiced a biennial rotation of crops and followed the two-field system. North of the Loire, grain was the principal crop and the three-field system was in general use. Three centuries had made little difference in the habits of the great mass of the peasants.

Forces such as those at work in contemporary England, however, were initiating an agricultural revolution in France. The central government and the intendants were doing everything in their power to improve French agriculture. They encouraged the formation of societies and committees for the improvement of agriculture, the draining of swamps, and the cultivation of waste lands. Decrees issued in 1764 and 1766 authorized the division and enclosure of communal pasture, waste, and woodlands. A few of the great landlords in France were introducing on their estates the same scientific methods that were being used by the gentlemen farmers in England. On the whole, nevertheless, French farming was much more backward than English agriculture.

French industry in the eighteenth century still retained the form which Colbert, the great minister of Louis XIV, had given to it, but the progress of the doctrines of the economists had affected to some extent the administration of the regulations. Since the Government found it more convenient to tax the organizations of masters than scattered workmen, the craft gilds had persisted and had even extended their influence in the realm of small industry. As a result they kept even allied trades rigidly separated. Every gild watched most jealously to prevent other gilds from infringing on its rights. Lawsuits between gilds were frequent. In their efforts to protect their petty monopolies these organizations stood in the way of every invention and technical improvement and in the end, consequently, prevented industrial progress. Industry continued to be characterized also by a rigid inspection. The cloth industry well illustrates the situation in other industries. Colbert had fixed by law, for each kind of cloth, the length and breadth, the dimensions of the selvage, the number of threads in the warp, the quality of the raw materials, and the methods of manufacture. The instructions of Colbert for dyeing contained three hundred and seventeen articles. As a result of the watchfulness of the gilds and the inspectors the manufacturer constantly ran the risk of becoming involved in a protracted and expensive lawsuit, or of having his goods destroyed for some petty infraction of the rules laid down by the Government.

The jurisdiction of the gilds, however, did not extend over all French industry. Domestic industries had always existed in France just as in England. A law of 1762, which permitted every one to spin and weave in places where there were no

THE EVE OF THE FRENCH REVOLUTION

gilds, legalized and encouraged these industries. Some manufacturing on a large scale had also existed in France since the days of Henry IV. In the eighteenth century establishments for the production of textiles, hosiery, tapestries, paper, glassware, earthenware, and porcelain were more or less flourishing. Toward the latter part of the century forges and foundries increased in numbers. In contrast to England, however, French factories had not utilized to any great extent machinery and steam power.

Numerous obstacles still hampered internal commerce. French producers did not have the whole of France as a market, nor French consumers all of France as a source of supply. Internal customs lines, seigniorial tolls, and the *octrois* [1] levied by the municipalities hindered the free movement of commodities. In the north of France there was a region surrounded by the tariff line of 1664 in which internal trade was free. In the south of France there was a region subject to the tariff of 1667 in which the provinces retained their provincial tariff lines. Finally, in the east, there was a group of provinces which — commercially — were not in France.

SOCIAL ORGANIZATION

The social organization of France in the eighteenth century was in large part determined by this economic organization on which it rested. The population of rural France was unequally divided into seigniors and peasants, and of urban France into the upper and the lower bourgeoisie and artisans and domestics.

In 1500 the nobles held the great estates. In the eighteenth century they were visibly declining in wealth and prestige. By that time not more than a thousand of the eighty thousand noble families could boast of any great antiquity and not more than two or three hundred enjoyed any material prosperity. The remainder had obtained their rank by purchasing patents of nobility from the hard-pressed treasury or buying some of the four thousand offices that conferred noble

[1] Duties levied at the gates of French cities.

title. The impoverishment of the nobility arose from the development of the idea that certain professions were incompatible with noble rank, and that a gentleman should not directly administer his own property. As a result of these ideas the nobles leased their domains to commoners and refrained from commercial and industrial pursuits. Consequently they slowly gave ground before the adverse economic forces which were set in motion by the expansion of Europe overseas and the resulting commercial revolution. Their incomes from feudal dues declined in purchasing power and their fields and estates gradually came on the market and fell into the hands of members of the middle class who had prospered in industry and commerce. Thus by the end of the eighteenth century the majority of the estates in France were in the hands of the bourgeoisie or of nobles descended from that class.

The forces at work in France divided the nobles into a number of distinct groups. The policy initiated by Louis XIV grouped around the King the richest and most distinguished members of the nobility, who were known as the nobles of the court, while the mass of the provincial nobles vegetated and grew poorer on their own estates. Finally there were the nobles of the robe, recruited originally from the middle class and ennobled by the purchase of offices from the State.

The nobles of the court lived for a large part of the year in the royal palaces at Versailles, Trianon, Compiègne, and Fontainebleau and in the châteaux of members of the royal family. The richer members of the court nobility maintained at the same time great residences, or hôtels, at Paris and châteaux in the provinces. They made use of their position at court to procure sinecures, pensions, and gifts for themselves and their friends. The King gave them all the lucrative posts in the Church and in the army. They devoted a large part of their time to hunting, dancing, gambling, and the theater. Giving themselves up to amusements and idleness they cultivated fine manners and bad morals. Nevertheless, they were, on the whole, more broad-minded than the provincial nobles and provided many of the liberal leaders who played a dramatic part in the opening scenes of the French Revolution.

The majority of the nobles still resided in the provinces. Only a few of them lived in comfort. After serving the King in the army or navy for a few years, these retired to their estates and busied themselves with agriculture. Many of the provincial nobles were very poor; in some sections of France they could hardly be distinguished from the peasants. As a result of their poverty the poorer nobles clung all the more tenaciously to the privileges which marked them off from the peasantry.

In the eighteenth century the French seigniors retained only a small part of the rights which they had exercised over their tenants in medieval times. Even north of the Loire, the region which was peculiarly the home of the seigniorial dues, the rights of the lords of estates were limited to the collection of certain feudal dues and the naming of the judges for their patrimonial courts. They collected from their copyhold tenants [1] small sums of money as a kind of perpetual rent, but money as a result of the decline in its purchasing power was no longer equivalent to the feudal dues and services which it was supposed to represent. The lords, furthermore, continued to demand a fine of considerable size when the peasant sold his land, to enforce the old seigniorial *corvées*, to collect tolls, and to require payment for the use of the mill, the oven, and the winepress of the lord. The three thousand nobles who had the right of high justice hunted over the peasant's growing fields and kept flocks of pigeons that ate his grain. These nobles might still maintain gibbets and pillories, but they no longer exercised in person their former rights of jurisdiction. Those rights were delegated to persons versed in the law.

More serious for the lords than the loss of some of their rights was the loss of the influence that they had once exer-

---

[1] The copyhold was a piece of land granted by a seignior to a villein in consideration of the payment by the latter of rent and the performance of non-noble services.

cised over their tenants. Formerly the lord had come into intimate contact with his peasant tenants. He had aided them in time of distress, counseled and cared for them in times of perplexity, acted as witness at their marriages, and held their children at the baptismal font. The growth in the number of absentee landlords and the development of the nobles into collectors of dues and rents were creating an unbridgable gulf between the nobility and the peasantry. In the eighteenth century the old solidarity between the peasants and the seigniors was to be found only in a few of the more backward regions, like Brittany and the Vendée.

On the whole, the nobility was far from satisfied with the *ancien régime*. Though the nobles were loyal to the King, they detested the royal despotism and its agents. The provincial nobles wanted to live in comfort and envied the favored nobles of the court. Some of the younger members of the nobility wanted political liberties such as the English possessed. Practically the whole order desired a constitution. This discontent of the nobles was one of the factors that prepared the way for the upheaval of the French Revolution.

Below the nobles in rank was the middle class or bourgeoisie. This class constituted approximately one tenth of the nation. It included the judges of the thirteen parlements, holders of state bonds, farmers of the state taxes, capitalists engaged in industry and trade, financiers, lawyers, doctors, artists, and men of letters, the masters of the gilds, the petty shopkeepers, and the well-to-do farmers. The more prosperous members of the middle class were steadily buying titles from the royal treasury, estates from the impoverished nobility, and offices which conferred hereditary rank. The majority of the order, however, continued to live in the cities where they had been the dominant class since the rise of towns in the Middle Ages.

Like the nobles, the bourgeoisie as a class were dissatisfied with their position in society. They saw the faults and the decadence of the nobility and the upper clergy. They recognized their own superior wealth, talent, and significance to society. Yet at every turn they saw themselves subjected to humiliation. The regulations of the army excluded them from military rank and custom kept them out of high office in the Church. Rich and educated they were pushed aside for the benefit of men who had nothing save birth to recommend them. Consequently they readily adopted the theories of the French philosophers and later furnished most of the leaders of the French Revolution.

In the cities and towns the artisans formed the larger part of the population. They were divided into masters and journeymen. They lived in the drabber quarters where travelers and men of leisure seldom penetrated, and on streets and alleys that were dirty and unhealthy. A master usually occupied and often owned a whole house. A journeyman usually occupied a room or two and possessed only a few pieces of furniture. Wine, bread, and vegetables formed his ordinary fare. He worked from four or five o'clock in the morning to eight or nine at night. Excluded from the craft gilds by the masters, the journeymen organized illegal societies. As the eighteenth century progressed they grew more and more independent. They formed mobs on the streets, struck for higher wages, and put unpopular employers under a ban. In these economic struggles they developed the tactics which they later employed with tremendous effect in the political conflicts of the French Revolution.

In rural France the mass of the people were peasants. While a few of the rural population were serfs,[1] most of the French peasants were personally free. The free peasants were not all in the same position. A few of them were full proprietors of their small holdings. A few others leased farms of greater or less size. Most of them were copyholders or métayers. The copyholders held their land in consideration of the payment of a small rent. They were found especially north of the Loire. The métayers paid the seignior half the yield of their holdings. They were found mainly south of the Loire.

The peasants bore a heavy burden. They paid feudal dues

[1] Estimates vary from 140,000 to 1,000,000.

or part of the crop to the seignior, tithes to the Church, and taxes to the State. In addition to his yearly rent the copyholder was subject to tolls, seigniorial *corvées* (forced labor for his lord), and heavy fees for the use of the lord's mill, oven, and winepress. When he sold his land he was forced to pay the seignior a tax, known as *lods et ventes*, which often amounted to one sixth of the purchase price of the holding. If his lord possessed rights of high justice the peasant had to permit his growing grain to be eaten by the game and pigeons of the lord and his planted fields to be trampled over by the lord and his hunting companions. Both the Church and the State taxed the copyholders and the métayers. To the Church the peasants paid tithes and fees for the support of the clergy and contributed to the repair of the nave and tower of the parish church, and of the rectory for the priest. To the State they paid all the direct and indirect taxes. The French peasants thus had more reason to be discontented than any other class in France, but they were better off than most of the peasants on the continent of Europe. The French Revolution was a result of the diffusion of intelligence and of the weakness of the absolute monarchy. It did not spring from the exceptional misery of the French peasants.

RELIGIOUS CONDITIONS

Between 1500 and 1789 the Church in France lost many of its powers to the State. By the concordat of 1516 the King had obtained the right to appoint the bishops and archbishops of the French Church. In 1561 the French clergy had agreed to contribute to the support of the State, but had retained the right to vote their contribution in a general assembly of the Church, to call the tax a free gift, and to provide for its apportionment and collection. The jurisdiction of the Church courts in the meantime was gradually restricted to purely spiritual matters. Wills, contracts, and practical questions concerning marriage were restored to the secular courts. The courts of the State claimed cases concerning ecclesiastical benefices and tithes on the ground of public order. Consequently, by 1789 only minor offenses of the clergy were left to the Church courts and most people were unaware of their continued existence.

During the same period the French Government made an important declaration concerning the relations of the French Church to the Pope. In the course of a struggle between Louis XIV and the head of the Church over the right of the French monarchy to receive the income from vacant offices in the Church (the *regalia*), an assembly of the French clergy, summoned by the King, declared: That sovereigns were not subject to the Pope; that a general council was superior to the head of the Church; that the Pope was subject to the regulations and canons of the Church councils and might not decide anything contrary to the rules and constitutions of the French Church; and that his decisions were not irrevocable except by the consent of the universal Church. These resolutions, known as the "declaration of the Gallican liberties," became the law of the land and remained in force until they were abrogated by the religious legislation of the French Revolution.

In 1500 the son of a peasant might still occasionally rise to the highest offices in the Church. On the eve of the French Revolution the upper clergy of France were recruited almost exclusively among the nobility. In the great families the eldest son, if he were physically fit, was chosen to perpetuate and maintain the family name, while one or more of the younger sons was often forced into the Church to lighten the burden of the head of the family and to preserve the integrity of the family inheritance. While waiting for more lucrative posts the young nobles often served as grand vicars of the bishops and archbishops. These officials acted as companions rather than as assistants of the bishops and archbishops and helped to make life agreeable for the latter while they were detained by their ecclesiastical duties from the court and the world of fashionable society.

The power, revenues, and prestige enjoyed by the bishops and archbishops caused the nobles to seek these offices. The poorer bishoprics yielded, at least, comfortable incomes and the more important paid princely salaries. In many cases the bishops and archbishops also controlled the revenues of one or more monasteries. In spite of the encroachment of the State on the rights of the Church, many of the upper clergy exercised rights of high, middle, or low justice over the tenants of their ecclesiastical estates. A few of the bishops retained a part of the temporal power possessed by their predecessors in the Middle Ages. In the regions of Northern and Northwestern France acquired from the Holy Roman Empire the bishops and archbishops were veritable princes. The Prince-Bishop of Strassburg, for example, was at the same time Landgrave of Alsace. He controlled in the province estates fourteen leagues square and peopled by twenty-five thousand persons, from which he received an income of eight hundred thousand livres. In Baden he had jurisdiction over eighty cities, towns, and villages. The position of the upper clergy in France was thus a most lucrative and dignified one.

The duties of the higher clergy were not onerous. Many of them lived as did the great lords. They maintained princely establishments with large retinues of servants, gave receptions and entertainments, and kept open house for passing travelers of note and for the nobility of the neighborhood. They were often great builders — restoring, enlarging, and making over their feudal châteaux, or building modern palaces amid trees and gardens. They amused themselves by collecting great libraries, by hunting as did the secular nobles, and by bringing in musicians, dancers, and actors. Many abandoned their dioceses most of the year and lived at court. While it is true that only a minority lived in this fashion, their manner of living created a scandal that the lives of the more devout members of the upper clergy were entirely unable to counteract.

The position of the lower clergy was very different from that of the higher clergy. A large majority of the sixty thousand curés and vicars of France lived on insufficient and even miserable incomes. In the country districts the fees amounted to very little and the tithes, in many instances, had fallen into the hands of the neighboring nobles or monasteries. As a usual thing the lower clergy were not represented in either the political or the religious assemblies of France. The bishops, furthermore, used their power over the subordinate clergy in a most arbitrary manner. As a result of their miserable position in society the lower ranks of the secular clergy were recruited almost exclusively from the peasantry.

These differences in origin and position gave rise to a grave antagonism between the higher and the lower clergy. The higher clergy scorned their inferior brethren. The humble vicars and parish priests envied and hated their superiors and strove through organization to increase the minimum income allowed the inferior clergy by law. The enmity thus bred had an important influence on the course of the French Revolution.

In the latter part of the eighteenth century the numbers of the regular clergy tended to decline. In 1764 the Government suppressed the Jesuits in France and three years later it expelled them from the country on the general ground that the unlimited authority exercised by the head of the order was incompatible with the laws of France. Between 1774 and 1790 the number of monks declined from 26,674 to 17,500. In the latter year there were, all told, about 60,000 monks and nuns in the country.

The monastic communities differed greatly in respect to revenues, requirements for admission, and the life of the inmates. In a few cases convents had been turned into chapters for the support of daughters of the nobility. Such houses demanded several generations of noble ancestors for admission. The inmates followed the fashions of the day, received visits from their friends, traveled a great deal, and returned to secular life whenever they wished. In contrast to these the monks of La Trappe lived in bare cells, wore only a hood, robe, shoes, and stockings, rose twice during the night to attend religious services; and never spoke save to their confessors. Many orders continued to busy themselves with the education of the young and the care of the poor and the sick, but many others rendered no obvious service to society. Consequently the Physiocrats criticized them as a source of economic waste and the philosophers and their followers considered the monks idle and useless.

The heads of the monasteries and convents held a position similar to that of the bishops and the archbishops. Their ranks were recruited, in consequence, from among the nobility. The King appointed the heads of six hundred and seventy-eight convents and of more than a thousand monasteries. He gave these positions to bishops and archbishops, members of the nobility, or monks of noble birth who had been forced into the monasteries by their parents to assure the sons rich sinecures. Thus frequently the abbots were not members of the orders they governed. Such monastic administrators often left the monasteries in charge of a prior and spent their time in secular amusements or in scheming at court for ecclesiastical preferment.

The opportunity for advancement in the Church produced the class of French priests, called by courtesy in history and literature "little abbés." Being out of work they lived in garrets, haunted the houses of the rich and influential, and picked up a living as best they could. They made themselves agreeable to the great, sought employment as secretaries or as writers for the press, and, like the nobles, intrigued for ecclesiastical appointments. They could be recognized by their black clothes and small tonsures.

The idea of religious toleration developed slowly in the eighteenth century. It was cautiously advanced by a few distinguished thinkers in the last quarter of the seventeenth century and by most of the great French writers of the eighteenth century. About the middle of the latter century the persecution of the Protestants which started in the reign of Louis XIV began to abate. The last execution for heresy seems to have occurred in 1762. In 1770 the Government released from the galleys of Toulon the last persons imprisoned for conscience' sake. The Protestants, nevertheless, still suffered from many restrictions. Their marriages and the legitimacy of their children were not recognized by law until 1787. Until after the outbreak of the French Revolution, they had to meet secretly in barns and private houses for religious worship. At every step the French clergy opposed the movement for increased toleration, and in their general assemblies they regularly demanded the closing of the Protestant churches, the dispersion of their assemblies, the persecution of their pastors, and the application of the laws against heretics. In spite of the efforts of Turgot, the clergy prevented the elimination of the declaration against heretics from the coronation oath of Louis XVI. When the Government proposed to recognize the marriages and to legitimatize the children of the Protestants in 1787, great ladies of the court called on each councilor of the Parlement of Paris to remind him of his duty to the Catholic religion and the law of the land, and the Bishop of Dol told the King that he would be responsible to God and to man for the evils which the reëstablishment of Protestantism would bring on his kingdom.

New ideas encountered much the same sort of opposition. Scholars and thinkers, in the eighteenth century, seldom escaped the reproach of impiety or heresy. Both the Church and the secular authorities undertook to censor the press. The Church was quick to detect danger, but the Government was slower in enforcing the law when illegal writings had widespread public approval. Authors and publishers, accordingly, adopted all sorts of means to circumvent the ecclesiastical and governmental censors. They either published books at Paris with a foreign imprint on the title-page or printed them on the presses of Holland or Geneva. Authors framed passages in their works for the purpose of satisfying the censor and learned to satirize persons and institutions without naming them and to convey their meaning by hints rather than by plain statements.

POLITICAL CONDITIONS

As a result of the work of Henry IV, Richelieu, Mazarin, and Louis XIV in centralizing the Government, the French monarchy in the eighteenth century was a despotism tempered by the inertia of the royal officials, long-standing customs, and the privileges conceded to the clergy, the nobles, the cities, and the parlements. The subjects of the King had no political or civil rights. As individuals they had no guarantees such as those possessed by the English against arbitrary warrants of imprisonment (*lettres de cachet*) and arbitrary arrest. As owners of property they were unprotected against general confiscation, expropriation without indemnity, and excessive taxes. A multitude of regulations shackled labor, commerce, and industry. Liberty of conscience ceased with the revocation of the Edict of Nantes in 1685. Censorship of the press was exercised by the law courts, the University of Paris, the clergy, and the Council of State. The Government refused to permit freedom of association, assembly, or instruction. The King alone possessed political rights.

As a result of the policy of drawing the nobility around the King, the successors of Louis XIV were always surrounded by the court. This body was composed of the royal family, the nobles of the court, the functionaries of the central administration, and the civil and military households of the King. Although its members had no official position, the court played an important part in shaping the policy of the monarchy. By their intrigues, the nobles of the court caused the downfall of royal ministers, thwarted the most salutary reforms, and kept the King in ignorance of the real condition of his state. By their extravagance and opposition to measures of reform, they tended to bankrupt the State.

There was no political body corresponding to the English Parliament. From 1302 to 1614 France had had the beginnings of such an institution in the Estates General. It was composed of deputies representing the clergy, the nobles, and the commoners, or third estate, and deliberated on matters submitted to it by the King. In a final solemn session, the three houses or estates, composing the Estates General, laid their list of grievances (*cahiers*) before the King for his consideration. The failure to gain the right to consent to the levy of taxation during the Hundred Years' War (1337-1453) proved fatal to the development of a real parliament in France. The King obtained the right to levy a permanent tax, known as the "*taille*." With the loss of the control of the purse the Estates General lost the opportunity to acquire the right to legislate.

In eight of the outlying provinces, which had retained their independence longer than the rest, there existed provincial estates. Each was composed of representatives of the clergy, the nobles, and the third estate. In form they voted the taxes, apportioned and collected them through their agents, levied special contributions for the construction of public works, and exercised the right of remonstrance to the King. In reality the provinces with assemblies (the *pays d'états*) were almost as much under the control of the central government and the intendants as the other provinces of France (the *pays d'élection*).

The chief central organs of the monarchy were the Council of State and the ministry composed of the King's most important advisers. The Council was the chief deliberative body of the Government and was subdivided into five sections or councils, each of which had its own special work to perform. The Council did not act in its own name, but in that of the King. Through its general orders, however, it had a large share in shaping the legislation of the monarchical period. The ministry was the chief executive organ of the Government. Its members did not act as a unit as in the English cabinet. In theory, each minister was responsible to the King. In practice, the ministers were often responsible for the government of the country. The most important members of the ministry were the chancellor, the controller general of the finances, and the secretaries of state.

The central government made its powers felt in the provinces through the intendants. As a result of the administrative reforms of Richelieu, Mazarin, and Louis XIV, the noble officials of the Middle Ages and the early monarchy had been supplanted by docile members of the middle class, who owed everything to the central government and who could be depended upon to carry out the royal orders. The most important of the new officials were the thirty-three intendants in charge of the administrative districts known as "*généralités.*" They exercised powers of justice, police, and finance; and looked after the levying of the militia, the lodging and maintenance of soldiers, and enforcing the royal *corvées;* and supervised agriculture, industry, commerce, religious worship, poor-law relief, the administration of cities and rural communities, and the apportionment and collection of taxes. They were assisted by subordinates, known as "sub-delegates," in charge of districts, known as "*élections.*" Some of them, as Turgot, were most enlightened administrators.

French cities retained few rights of self-government. They were not permitted to incur any expense, prosecute suits in the courts, impose taxes on themselves, nor alienate or acquire property without the authorization of the intendant or the royal council. After the accession of Louis XIV the municipal offices had been alternately sold to the highest bidder in the interest of the royal treasury and bought back by the municipalities, until in 1771 they had passed permanently under the control of the King.

In the eighteenth century the rural communities had a slightly larger measure of self-government than the cities. Until 1787 the chief organs of rural government were the syndic and the local assembly. The syndic presided over the local assembly, received and expended the funds of the community, rendered an account of his handling of public funds to the sub-delegate and to the local assembly, maintained actions in the courts on behalf of the community, had the custody of its papers, levied taxes, recruited the militia and the royal troops, and kept the intendant informed of all the happenings of interest to the King. The office of syndic was poorly paid and little sought after. The assembly was composed, usually, of all heads of families. It voted expenditures; appointed the syndic, the schoolmaster, the herdsman, the keeper of the vineyards, the sergeant, and the collector of tithes and taxes; passed upon the sale, purchase, exchange, and location of communal land, and the repair of the church, the parsonage, roads, and public edifices. In 1787 the central government handed over most of these functions to a council of local notables, composed of the seignior, the parish priest, and six to nine other members elected by the local assembly.

A number of extraordinary courts and a hierarchy of ordinary courts administered justice. Most cases came under the jurisdiction of the municipal, seigniorial, and inferior royal (those of the *provosts* and *viguiers*) courts. Above these courts were the tribunals of bailiffs and seneschals. At the top of the judicial hierarchy were the thirteen parlements and the supreme councils of four of the outlying provinces. About one third of France was under the jurisdiction of the Parlement of Paris. The parlements were primarily courts of appeal, but by refusing to register royal decrees of which they disapproved they sometimes attempted to take a position in the State like that occupied by the English Parliament or by the higher courts in the United States when they pass on the constitutionality of a law.[1] Under weak sovereigns or ministers they sometimes managed to thwart the royal will. The members of the judiciary obtained their posts by purchase, but as a class the magistrates of the *ancien régime* were noted for integrity, industry, and learning.

The income of the Government was derived from the royal estates and from direct and indirect taxes. The most important of the direct taxes was the *taille*. In some parts of Southern France (Languedoc and Guienne) it was a tax on real property from which the lands of the nobles and certain Church lands were exempt. Elsewhere in France it was a personal tax paid by members of the third estate and based on income. Many of the larger towns either did not pay this tax or collected it in the form of an *octroi*. Every year, six months in advance, the total amount to be raised from each *généralité* of the region without provincial estates (*pays*

[1] The author owes this suggestion to Professor H. E. Bourne, of Western Reserve University.

d'élection) was determined by the King's Council. The intendant and his bureau of finance then apportioned the share of each *élection* of a *généralité* and the sub-delegate and his elected assistants the quota of each parish of the *élection*. Finally assessors and collectors, working under the direction of commissioners appointed by the intendant, determined the tax of each member of the parish. The *taille* was open to criticism for its variableness from year to year, for the inequalities between the amounts apportioned to districts and to individuals, and for the exemption of the nobles, the clergy, and much personal property from the tax.

The other important direct taxes were the royal *corvée*, the capitation tax, the "twentieths," and service in the militia. The royal *corvée* requisitioned the peasant and his cart twice a year for the building and maintenance of the public roads. The capitation tax was really only an addition to the *taille*. The "twentieths" was gradually added to until it took sixteen per cent of the income from landed property. Both the capitation and the "twentieths" in the form of a "tenth" became permanent during the War of the Spanish Succession. The royal *corvée* was open to criticism because the number of days of work demanded from the peasants and the distance they were required to go varied greatly. All the direct taxes put an unfair burden on the peasantry.

The chief indirect taxes of the *ancien régime* were the *aides*, the salt tax, and the customs duties. The *aides* were taxes on the sale and transportation of merchandise or objects of consumption — especially drinks. They were levied only in Central France in about two fifths of the kingdom. The salt tax was one of the most onerous, unequal, and vexatious taxes. As a result of the rates fixed by the Government the price of salt varied from two to sixty livres [1] per quintal. This inequality in the price of salt gave rise to a great deal of smuggling. In one year 2300 men, 1800 women, and 6600 children were arrested for trying to smuggle salt from one district to another. From the point of view of the

[1] An obsolete French coin.

customs duties, as has been explained, France was divided into three tariff zones. In twelve provinces of Central France Colbert's tariff of 1664 was effective. In most of the others the tariff of 1667 was applied. A few of the border provinces were treated as foreign territory. The customs duties and the taxes on salt and tobacco were collected by the farmers-general who paid the treasury a lump sum for the privilege of collecting the taxes and then made as much from the taxpayer as they could.

THE DECLINE OF THE ABSOLUTE MONARCHY

The death of Louis XIV in 1715 and the youth of his successor and grandson, Louis XV, made necessary the establishment of a regency. For the next eight years the Duke of Orleans, a nephew of the late king, controlled the Government of France as regent. He reversed the foreign policy of Louis XIV and broke down many of the accepted standards. In foreign affairs he allied France to England, the United Netherlands, and Austria, the Powers with which it had just been at war, in an effort to prevent Philip V of Spain from regaining the Kingdom of the Two Sicilies for Spain, from acquiring the Duchies of Parma, Piacenza, and Tuscany for the son of Elizabeth Farnese, his second wife, and, in case Louis XV should die, from establishing himself on the throne of France. The ambition of the Spanish Bourbons finally led to a short war which resulted, in 1720, in the cession of the island of Sicily by the Duke of Savoy to the Austrian Habsburgs in exchange for the poorer island of Sardinia and the title of King of Sardinia, and in the promise of the ultimate cession of Parma, Piacenza, and Tuscany to the son of Elizabeth Farnese. At home the period was one of excitement for contemporaries, but of little significance for future times. The Duke of Orleans lived in such a way as to make the period of the regency notorious for profligacy. The breakdown of the schemes of John Law [1] gave France its

---

[1] He founded a trading company and a national bank, which issued prodigious quantities of bank-notes. A panic, which followed the extraordinary speculation in the shares of his company, finally discredited Law in 1720.

first and most famous financial crisis. Forces were at work which were destined to destroy the respect that hitherto had hedged in the monarchy and the Church.

In 1723, the King became legally of age, but he made no effort to imitate Louis XIV by becoming his own first minister. After a short rule by the Duke of Bourbon, power fell into the hands of Cardinal Fleury, the tutor of the King. In the main his administration was a period of peace and recovery. The peace of the country was disturbed only by the brief struggle known as the War of the Polish Succession, which lasted from 1733 to 1735. The conflict was precipitated by the death of Augustus II, King of Poland and Elector of Saxony. Russia and Prussia supported the claims of his heir, Augustus III. The great majority of the Poles voted for Stanislas Leczinski, a former King of Poland and the father-in-law of Louis XV. Sardinia and Spain intervened in the struggle with a view to advancing their interests in Italy. Louis XV entered the war in the interest of his father-in-law. The fighting lasted for two years and the subsequent peace negotiations, for three years. In exchange for the Grand Duchy of Tuscany, Francis, the Duke of Lorraine (the son-in-law of the Emperor and the husband of Maria Theresa), ceded his hereditary lands to Stanislas Leczinski to compensate the latter for the loss of Poland. The King of Sardinia received two small provinces from the Austrian Duchy of Milan. Elizabeth Farnese obtained the Kingdom of the Two Sicilies for her son. The chief gain of France was a revival of prestige and the prospect of incorporating Lorraine into France upon the death of the father-in-law of Louis XV.

During the period from 1740 to 1763 the pacific policy followed by France since 1715 was abandoned. The War of the Austrian Succession and the Seven Years' War filled fifteen of the twenty-three years. The colonial Powers fought for colonial and commercial supremacy; the continental states, over the balance of power. France tried to play an important part in both the colonial and the continental struggles with disastrous results for its prestige, its finances, and its empire.

THE EVE OF THE FRENCH REVOLUTION

At the same time the Government continued to decline in popular respect. The King was intelligent, but indolent. He neglected the Government and devoted his time to personal amusement. After the death of Fleury in 1743, he allowed his mistresses to manage the gravest affairs of State. For many years Madame de Pompadour dictated appointments and decided on political and military plans. Her rule resulted in disastrous wars, the entrusting of the French armies to incompetent generals, and in changes of ministers for a mere whim. Everything went by favor. Nothing was done to check the growing disorder in the administration and the finances. By the time of the death of Louis XV in 1774, war and misgovernment had brought the monarchy to the verge of disaster. All looked to the young and well-intentioned Louis XVI to ward off the impending revolution by measures of reform.

The new ruler made an excellent start. He appointed Turgot, who was generally known as an excellent administrator and a warm sympathizer with the doctrines of the French philosophers, as his chief adviser. The new minister initiated a number of important reforms. He introduced greater economy into various branches of the administration, removed the different restrictions on the sale and importation of grain, substituted for the royal *corvée* an addition to the "twentieths," and abolished the monopoly of the craft gilds. To friends of reform France seemed to be on the threshold of a new era.

The reform policies of Turgot, however, soon encountered determined opposition. His proposals ran against the private interests of many and the profound ignorance of the majority. The Queen, the courtiers, the upper clergy, the magistrates, the financiers, and the master artisans combined against him and finally caused his resignation in May, 1776. The most promising attempt at reform in eighteenth-century France failed because of the tactlessness of Turgot, who was too frank and outspoken to be a good courtier, the opposition of the privileged classes, and the failure of the King to support his minister.

A succession of ministers followed Turgot in office. Each encountered the same problems and the same obstacles as Turgot. A few months after the resignation of Turgot the King entrusted the management of the French finances to Necker, a wealthy banker, who had made a considerable reputation for himself both as a financier and as a publicist. He found the task of financing the French intervention in the War of the American Revolution confronting him. Instead of increasing taxation as had his English opponents, a policy which would have made him unpopular, he resorted to a series of loans that proved most profitable to investors, but exceedingly costly to the State and paid the interest on his earlier loans with money received from succeeding loans. Among the unthinking, Necker's feat of financing three years of war with England without adding to the burden of taxation aroused the greatest admiration. In 1781 he increased popular confidence in the stability of France by publishing his famous *Compte Rendu au Roi*, a work in which he pretended to set forth the details of the finances of the State. Unfortunately he misled the general public by omitting from his figures the extraordinary expenditures of the treasury for war and other purposes. Trusting in his general popularity, he finally felt strong enough to demand the rank of minister which had been refused him because he was a Protestant. Upon his request being denied through the jealousy of some of the ministers, Necker resigned (1781).

After two years the King placed Calonne, an experienced administrator and a man of great versatility, in charge of the finances. Convinced that the resources of the State were really unbounded, he deliberately adopted an air of prosperity. He paid the debts of the King's brothers, bought the château of Rambouillet for the King and the estate of Saint-Cloud for the Queen, and showered gifts and pensions on the court. For a time his policy met with success. The public eagerly subscribed to the loans of the State, and the Government borrowed in all 800,000,000 livres. The increasing criticism of his policies, however, convinced Calonne that he could not go on indefinitely with his extravagant expenditures. Consequently, he suddenly proposed to the King a resumption of the reforms of Turgot. In an effort to win immediate public support for his plans Calonne summoned an Assembly of Notables in 1787. Upon encountering stiff opposition to all his proposals among the members of this body, Calonne resigned his office.

By this time the financial situation of the Government was desperate. The expenditures of the Government greatly exceeded its revenues. The financiers would not lend the State any more money. The parlements refused to register decrees providing for new taxes. The peasants could not, and the privileged classes would not, pay any more taxes. In his perplexity the King summoned the Estates General to aid the incompetent absolute monarchy in extricating itself from its financial difficulties. The summons of the Estates General to meet in May, 1789, after a lapse of one hundred and seventy-five years, was the first step in the French Revolution.

A survey of conditions on the eve of the French Revolution discloses many defects in the institutions of France. Agriculture was backward. The gild restrictions hampered labor and industry. Tolls and interior customs lines interfered with domestic commerce. The population was composed of privileged and unprivileged classes separated from each other by almost impassable barriers. The upper clergy enjoyed great revenues, but lacked spirituality; the lower ministered to the parishes with fidelity, but lived in great misery. Many of the monks were idle and careless in the observance of their duties. The Church as a whole was intolerant. The monarchy was a despotism. Individuals had no political or civil rights. The court kept the King in ignorance of the needs of his people. Arbitrary officials administered the Government. Taxation was unjust. Worst of all the French sovereigns failed to take any effective steps to remedy conditions.

REFERENCES

THE KING AND THE ADMINISTRATION
  E. J. Lowell, *The Eve of the French Revolution*, chapter I.
  S. Mathews, *The French Revolution*, chapter I.

THE FRENCH COURT
  E. J. Lowell, *The Eve of the French Revolution*, chapter II.
  Histoire de France, vol. IX, pt. I, pp. 131–43.

THE CLERGY
  E. J. Lowell, *The Eve of the French Revolution*, chapter III.
  S. Mathews, *The French Revolution*, chapter V.
  Histoire de France, vol. IX, pt. I, pp. 144–74.

THE NOBILITY
  E. J. Lowell, *The Eve of the French Revolution*, chapter VI.
  S. Mathews, *The French Revolution*, chapter III.

THE COURTS OF LAW
  E. J. Lowell, *The Eve of the French Revolution*, chapter VIII.
  Histoire de France, vol. IX, pt. I, pp. 186–202.

CITY LIFE
  E. J. Lowell, *The Eve of the French Revolution*, chapters XI–XII.

FRENCH RURAL LIFE
  E. J. Lowell, *The Eve of the French Revolution*, chapter XIII.
  Histoire de France, vol. IX, pt. I, pp. 246–60.

FRENCH TAXATION
  Cambridge Modern History, vol. VIII, pp. 72–78.
  E. J. Lowell, *The Eve of the French Revolution*, chapter XIV.
  S. Mathews, *The French Revolution*, chapter II.
  A. Tilley, *Modern France*, pp. 291–322.

FRENCH FINANCE
  Cambridge Modern History, vol. VIII, pp. 72–78.
  E. J. Lowell, *The Eve of the French Revolution*, chapter XV.
  Histoire de France, vol. IX, pt. I, pp. 405–09.

THE REIGN OF LOUIS XV
  G. B. Adams, *The Growth of the French Nation*, pp. 234–50.
  A. J. Grant, *The French Monarchy, 1483–1789*, vol. II, chapters XVI–XX.
  W. H. Hudson, *France*, bk. IV, chapters VIII–IX.
  G. W. Kitchin, *A History of France*, vol. III, pp. 360–475.
  J. R. Moreton Macdonald, *History of France*, vol. II, chapter XXVII.
  J. B. Perkins, *France under Louis XV*.
  Histoire générale, vol. VII, chapter VII.

THE REIGN OF LOUIS XVI
  G. B. Adams, *The Growth of the French Nation*, pp. 250–57.
  Cambridge Modern History, vol. VIII, chapter IV.
  A. J. Grant, *The French Monarchy, 1483–1789*, vol. II, chapter XXI.

A. Hassall, *European History, 1715-89*, chapter XIV.
W. H. Hudson, *France*, bk. IV, chapter X.
G. W. Kitchin, *History of France*, vol. III, pp. 476-94.
J. R. Moreton Macdonald, *History of France*, vol. II, chapter XVI.
Histoire de France, vol. IX, pt. I, pp. 1-90.
Histoire générale, vol. VII, chapter XII.

TURGOT
Leon Say, *Turgot*.

MAPS
France in 1789, W. R. Shepherd, *Historical Atlas*, pp. 146-47.

CHAPTER XVI

THE FRENCH REVOLUTION

THE STRUGGLE FOR CONTROL OF THE GOVERNMENT

The Estates General, which had been summoned to extricate the absolute monarchy from its difficulties, met on May 5, 1789. In accordance with past custom each of the three classes in the nation elected its own representatives, but the Government permitted the third estate to send twice as many deputies as either of the two privileged orders. This innovation was a concession to the increased importance of the third estate. Consequently, the 130,000 members of the clergy had about three hundred representatives; the 80,000 noble families about the same number; and the third estate, constituting something like ninety-eight per cent of the whole nation, slightly over six hundred. Most of the representatives of the latter class belonged to the bourgeoisie. The Estates General, therefore, drew its membership almost exclusively from the ranks of the privileged, the well-to-do, and the educated.

The twelve hundred members of the Estates General were divided into two opposing groups. Some ninety of the more liberal nobles, about two hundred parish priests, and all the representatives of the third estate desired a thoroughgoing reform of the *ancien régime*. The great majority of the nobles and most of the clergy of noble origin stood for the maintenance of privilege. Those in favor of reform had the support of the mass of the nation; those in favor of privilege, that of the court, the upper clergy, and the majority of the nobles.

Immediately after the formal opening of the Estates General a serious and protracted struggle broke out between the two parties [1] over the question of how that body should be organized. The party of privilege demanded that the clergy,

[1] These groups should not be thought of as modern political parties.

the nobles, and the third estate should organize as three houses and vote by order. This method of organization would put the two privileged orders in a position to veto measures of reform. The party of reform stood for the union of the representatives of the three social classes into a single chamber and for individual voting. This organization would give the party of reform control of the Estates General. Under the influence of the party of privilege the clergy and the nobles verified their own credentials and organized as separate houses. The deputies of the third estate refused to organize themselves until they were joined by the deputies of the other two orders. In spite of frequent negotiations the deadlock continued through May and the early part of June. Finally on June 11th, after issuing a last invitation to the members of the two privileged orders to join them, the deputies of the third estate announced their intention of effecting an organization. On June 17th, they assumed the title of the National Assembly, took an oath to proceed with the task of reforming France, decreed illegal all taxes not approved by the nation, and declared against any relief of the treasury by bankruptcy. On June 19th the new National Assembly established a committee to provide a food supply for Paris. The declaration against bankruptcy assured the bold deputies of the support of the powerful financiers of Paris. The creation of a committee charged with the supervision of subsistence assured the National Assembly of the good will of the turbulent lower classes. The whole policy of the deputies of the third estate aimed at the destruction of the old division of the nation into three orders and at the creation of a political power independent of the King.

The reply of the party of privilege to these daring measures of the newly established National Assembly was the royal session of June 23d. When the deputies of the third estate assembled on June 20th they found their place of meeting closed and the entrance guarded by troops in order to permit preparation for a royal session. The King had not done them the courtesy of warning them in advance of his proposed action. Angered and alarmed at this discourteous treatment, the deputies retired to a large building in the neighborhood used as an indoor tennis court, and in one of the most dramatic scenes of the French Revolution they took an oath with upstretched arms never to separate until they had given France a constitution. This is known as the "Tennis Court Oath." Three days later the royal session took place. At the instigation of the Queen, the courtiers, the upper clergy, and the whole party of privilege, the King solemnly ordered the deputies of the Estates General to organize in three houses and, with a few unimportant exceptions, to vote by order. The royal party, the nobles, and most of the clergy then withdrew. The deputies of the third estate, many of the parish priests, and a few of the liberal nobles hesitated. To leave the hall meant the abandonment of the cause of reform; to remain meant defiance of the royal authority. The master of ceremonies said to the wavering deputies, "Gentlemen, you have heard the King's orders." His words brought the crisis to an issue. At these words the great Mirabeau, the ablest man in the third estate, rose and thundered to the dazed official, "Go tell those that sent you that we shall not leave here but at the point of the bayonet."[1] Encouraged by this declaration the deputies of the third estate held their ground. Two days after the royal session (June 25th) a majority of the clergy joined the National Assembly. On the following day (June 26th) forty-seven of the liberal nobles followed their example. Judging further resistance futile, the King reversed himself and ordered the clergy and the nobles to join with the deputies of the National Assembly. The effort to command the obedience of the third estate had failed.

The party of privilege next tried to coerce the recalcitrant deputies. Early in July considerable bodies of troops, composed mainly of foreign mercenaries and brought from the frontiers of France, began to arrive at Paris and Versailles. On July 11th the King, at the instigation of the reactionary group around him, dismissed the popular Necker and three of his colleagues in the ministry. Unprotected as it was the

[1] The words used by Mirabeau have been variously reported.

National Assembly seemed in grave danger of being dispersed by military force.

The reply of the party of reform to the threat of force was a great popular uprising at Paris. The news of Necker's dismissal reached the city at noon on July 12th. The whole population took alarm. The bourgeoisie foresaw the bankruptcy of the State and the ruin of their own personal fortunes. The lower classes feared the defeat of the revolution. Crowds began to assemble at the Palais Royal, a popular meeting-place, and in the streets. Orators began to harangue the people. Collisions occurred between the crowds and the military. The mobs started a search for arms. On July 13th the first steps were taken toward the establishment of a popular city government to replace the old royal government and a National Guard to protect life and property against the mob. On July 14th the people of Paris, aided by some of the royal troops, obtained possession of the fortress of the Bastille after a dramatic struggle with its feeble garrison. Built originally to overawe the city, this edifice had long been used as a prison of State and had become a symbol for all the tyranny of the *ancien régime*. The anniversary of its capture has always been celebrated as the national holiday by republican governments in France.

The fall of the Bastille had a number of important immediate consequences. On the following day (July 15th) the King appeared unexpectedly before the National Assembly and announced the withdrawal of the troops from Versailles and the environs of Paris. Two days after the fall of the fortress the younger brother of the King and many of the clergy, nobles, and members of the parlements emigrated from the country, becoming known as *émigrés* because of their flight. Three days after the capture of the Bastille the King went to Paris and formally approved of the changes which had been made. In recognition of the restoration of harmony between the King and his people the white of the flag of the Bourbons and the red and blue from the arms of the city of Paris were united in a new national standard, the tricolor of France.

The revolution at the capital caused similar movements in the cities and the country districts of France. The larger cities had been violently agitated at the report of the dismissal of Necker. The news of the victory of the people of Paris set all the French municipalities in motion. Mobs burned the municipal toll offices at the city gates and pillaged the houses of the rich, the city magistrates, and the royal representatives. The bourgeoisie, threatened simultaneously with aristocratic reaction and popular anarchy, set up armed forces similar to the National Guard established at Paris and pushed aside or reorganized the old municipal oligarchies. The royal authority vanished and the municipalities assumed all the powers of government.

In rural France the revolution at Paris provoked one of the strangest movements of history. A great unreasoning fear of brigands seized the peasants. To ward off the danger they armed themselves and assembled in mobs. Gradually the fear of the brigands became transformed in the simple minds of the country folk into rage against the aristocrats, who had oppressed them for centuries. Impatient at the slowness of the National Assembly in giving them relief from their burdens, the peasants made war on the châteaux of the seigniors, burned the records of the feudal dues, and attacked the seigniors and their families. In this way feudalism was practically, though not legally, abolished.

The reaction of the National Assembly to the news of the disturbances occurring throughout rural France was dramatic. On August 4th the committee on the state of the nation made a report concerning the "war on the châteaux." The reading of the report created a warm discussion. Late in the evening one of the liberal nobles rushed to the platform of the assembly, declared that the causes of the disorder must be removed, and proposed the abolition of the heavy burden of the seigniorial dues. Instantly, the greatest feudal lord in France, next to the King, seconded the motion. The members of the privileged orders quickly saw the futility of continuing the struggle to retain the privileges that they had enjoyed during the *ancien régime* and vied with each other in a veritable frenzy of renunciation. Amid scenes of the wildest enthusiasm which continued throughout the night, the nobles surrendered the remnants of their feudal privileges; the clergy abandoned their tithes; and the cities and the provinces with provincial estates gave up their special privileges.

The decree of August 11th, which was supposed to embody the results of the night of August 4th, did not entirely abolish the remaining vestiges of feudalism. It suppressed dues representing real or personal servitude without indemnity, but declared all other seigniorial dues merely redeemable. The decree also suppressed the exclusive right of the nobles possessing high justice to keep pigeons and maintain warrens, to hunt over the lands of the peasants, and to have manorial courts, abolished tithes on condition that some other method for the support of the clergy and the maintenance of divine worship should be devised, discontinued the sale of judicial offices, did away with the privileged position of the nobles and the clergy in respect to taxation, declared all French citizens eligible to political office, and finally inaugurated a reform of some of the worst features in the Church. These provisions made the decree of August 11th one of the great charters of French liberty.

A second of the great fundamental documents of French liberty was the "Declaration of the Rights of Man and of Citizen." Since July the National Assembly had been discussing the advisability of drawing up such a document. Finally on August 26th the report of the committee in charge of the question was brought to a vote. The document declared that "Men are born and remain equal in rights." "The natural and imprescriptible rights of man are liberty, property, security, and resistance to oppression." "All sovereignty resides in the nation." "Law is the expression of the general will." "No person shall be accused, arrested, or imprisoned except in the cases and according to the forms prescribed by law." "The law shall provide for such punishments only as are strictly and obviously necessary." "No one shall be disquieted on account of his opinions, including his religious views, provided their manifestation does not disturb the public order established by law." "Every citizen may speak, write, and print with freedom, but shall be responsible for such abuses of this freedom as shall be defined by law." Taxes "should be equally distributed among all the citizens in proportion to their means." "All citizens have a right to decide personally or by their representatives, as to the necessity of the public contribution, to grant this freely, to know to what uses it is put, and to fix the proportion, the mode of assessment and collection, and the duration of taxes." "Property is an inviolable and sacred right." The declaration omitted the rights of assembly, association, and petition, inadequately guarded freedom of the press, and granted only religious toleration instead of religious freedom. Nevertheless, for the first time in their history the French had most of the elementary rights of free men.

Meanwhile the ground was being prepared for a new uprising of the people of Paris. Frequent elections, dissatisfaction with the attitude of the court and the National Assembly, the constant agitation of the new Parisian press, the increasing misery of the lower classes, the shortage of food, rising prices, and the growth of unemployment were creating a dangerous effervescence among the lower classes of the capital. At any minute the people of Paris might break into open revolt.

The impetus needed to start a new revolutionary movement was furnished by the indiscreet conduct of the officers of the troops guarding the palace at Versailles. At a banquet given by the officers of the royal bodyguard to the recently arrived Flanders regiment, the drunken banqueters trampled the new national tricolors under foot. The Queen sanctioned the proceedings by her presence. The episode caused a mob of six thousand women to march from Paris to Versailles on October 5th. The rabble of Paris and the National Guard, which was under the command of Lafayette, followed them. The crowd demanded bread, the ratification of the decrees passed by the National Assembly during August, and the removal of the King to Paris. After scenes of wild disorder the

King accepted the decrees of the National Assembly and on October 6th allowed himself and his family to be taken back to Paris by the mob. After considerable debate the National Assembly decided to follow the King. The insurrection of October 5th and 6th thus placed both the King and the National Assembly under the control of Paris and completed the work begun by the revolution of July.

THE REFORMS OF THE NATIONAL ASSEMBLY [1]

The victory of the people of Paris gave the National Assembly an opportunity to set to work at the task of reforming France. During the two years following the march of the women of Paris to Versailles it drew up a series of great reform measures, crowning its work finally by drawing up the Constitution of 1791, the first written constitution of France.

Some of the measures of the National Assembly tended to establish the ideal of civil equality. The division of French society into three social classes, serfdom, religious intolerance, and slavery were the chief obstacles to its establishment. The decrees of August 11, 1789, swept away serfdom and the special privileges of the nobles. A decree of June, 1790, abolished titles of nobility. The Protestants obtained religious toleration through the "Declaration of the Rights of Man." A decree of December, 1789, declared them eligible to civil and military offices. A decree of the following year returned to the heirs the property confiscated from Protestants at the time of the revocation of the Edict of Nantes, which had not passed out of the hands of the State. So by the end of 1790 Protestants had acquired religious toleration and all the civil and political rights of Frenchmen. The Jews encountered greater opposition in their efforts to obtain their freedom. The Jews of Southern France, indeed, received full rights of citizenship as early as 1790, but those of Alsace and Lorraine, long regarded as little better than serfs, did not obtain a similar status until 1791. As a result of the resistance and power of the French planters, however, the National Assembly did not abolish slavery in the colonies of France.

[1] Also known as the National Constituent Assembly.

The National Assembly also made a great deal of progress toward the establishment of civil liberty. As early as October, 1789, it instituted a commission for the reform of criminal jurisprudence and began to suppress some of the more crying abuses of the criminal procedure of the *ancien régime*. In criminal cases it copied from England trial by jury and oral procedure. The penal code of 1791 substituted for the savage punishments of the *ancien régime* a code that adjusted the punishment to the crime, and abolished torture, the pillory, branding with a hot iron, and public confession of guilt (*amende honorable*), but retained irons and the death penalty. It established liberty of the press in fact, but not in law. Finally the Constitution of 1791 guaranteed the freedom of citizens to assemble peaceably without arms and to petition the constituted authorities. On the other hand, the National Assembly frowned on freedom of association, abolished the craft gilds, and forbade the organization of both masters and workers.

In the sphere of agriculture the two great achievements of the French Revolution were the freeing of the land of the peasants from feudal restrictions and the transfer of the lands of the Church, the nobles, and the King to new owners. The National Assembly made important contributions to both movements. In March, 1790, it passed an important decree designed to carry out in detail the resolutions adopted on August 11th. This measure abolished without indemnity personal servitude, feudal *corvées*, seigniorial justice, and compulsory use of the lord's mill, oven, and winepress; and made redeemable dues paid in money or in produce, taxes levied at the time of the sale of land (*lods et ventes*), and perpetual rents. The peasant could redeem his land at any time by paying the seignior twenty-five times the value of the dues paid in produce and twenty times the value of those paid in money. This legislation aroused violent protests among the peasants. Only a few of them availed themselves of the opportunity to redeem their lands. Most of them awaited developments and many of them even refused to pay their ordinary feudal dues.

Landed property of the Church, the Crown, and the *émigrés* was put on sale early in 1791.[1] The greater part of it fell into the hands of the well-to-do peasants, farmers on a large scale, rich proprietors, and members of the bourgeoisie. Those who were already landholders increased their holdings. To the great disappointment of the National Assembly the number of landholders was not increased as much as had been expected.

The legislation of the National Assembly affected industry comparatively little. The only legislation of any importance dealt with the craft gilds and patents. A decree of February, 1791, suppressed the craft gilds, which had become such an obstacle to freedom of work and industrial progress. Decrees passed in 1790 and 1791 granted inventors the privilege of exploiting their inventions.

Considerably more was done to free commerce from the restrictions of the *ancien régime*. The National Assembly abolished the limitations on the grain trade within the borders of France, suppressed the provincial tariff lines, moved the customs lines to the frontiers of the kingdom, and freed both commerce and industry from *aides* and municipal tolls (*octrois*). These measures gave the domestic commerce of France complete freedom.

In the realm of finance the National Assembly aimed to pay off the national debt, to balance the budget, and to establish a new system of taxation. The law of April 17, 1790, authorized the State to issue paper money (*assignats*) on the security of the property confiscated from the Church. In itself the measure was sound, but it opened the way for a reckless issuing of paper money. As has happened repeatedly in other countries the people of France refused to tax themselves as long as the easy way of printing paper money was open to them. The Government printed quantities of *assignats*, which gradually declined in value, good money disappeared, and prices rose. Debtors, the purchasers of national property, and leaseholders paid off their obligations in

---

[1] The National Assembly decided, in November, 1789, to relieve the financial situation by confiscating the lands of the Church.

depreciated money, while persons living on salaries and fixed incomes suffered greatly from the decline in the purchasing power of money. The financial policy of the National Assembly, therefore, was in the main an unsuccessful one.

Reforms of great importance were effected in taxation. Most of the taxes of the *ancien régime* were abolished. In place of the old system of taxation, with its inequalities between persons and between places and its inquisitorial methods, the National Assembly devised a new system consisting of a land tax, a personal property tax, a tax upon industrial and mercantile establishments (the *patente*), and a tariff on imports and exports. The tariff was to be collected solely at the frontiers of the country.

Politically the final result of the deliberations of the National Assembly was to establish a constitutional monarchy in which the powers of the King were strictly limited. By the new Constitution the sovereign of France became "King of the French" instead of "King of France and Navarre." In place of being able to draw on the royal treasury at will, he was assigned a definite civil list. The Constitution granted him the right to appoint ambassadors, ministers, and a part of the officers in the army and navy, but deprived him of the power to declare war and to conclude peace. All royal orders had to be countersigned by ministers, who were responsible to the legislative branch of the Government. Finally the Constitution granted him only a suspensive veto. Through this the King could delay the enactment of laws desired by a majority of the legislative assembly during a period of two years.

In theory the Constitution of 1791 transferred to the people of France the sovereignty formerly exercised by the King. In practice it vested sovereignty in the "active" citizens. This class included all male citizens twenty-five years of age, who paid annually a direct tax equivalent to three days' wages. Servants, being in the pay of other persons and accordingly not considered as free agents, debtors, bankrupts, and persons not paying the required tax were excluded from the suffrage, and were known as "passive" citizens. Not even the active citizens, however, exercised directly the sovereignty vested in them by the Constitution. They merely voted for electors, who in turn chose the members of the legislative assembly and the judges of the royal courts. As they had to be persons who paid annually a direct tax equivalent to 150 to 200 days' wages, only about 43,000 persons in France were eligible to be electors. Thus by the new Constitution, political rights were made the monopoly of the propertied classes.

The Constitution entrusted the legislative power to a single chamber, known as the "Legislative Assembly," composed of 745 members elected for a term of two years, and endowed with extensive authority. War and peace, taxation and expenditure, the ratification of treaties, and the determination of the nature of legislation were under its control, and the ministers of the King were made responsible to it. As a consequence of these powers the Legislative Assembly became the dominant body under the new Constitution.

The Constitution of 1791 entirely reorganized the judiciary system of France. It did away completely with the parlements, the tribunals of the bailiffs and seneschals, and the seigniorial courts. In their place it established a new hierarchy of civil and criminal courts, in which the judges of the new courts obtained their positions by election instead of by purchase as under the old régime.

The system of local government was also transformed. The old irregular and overlapping military, political, and historical divisions of France were replaced by a new system of administrative districts. The country was divided into eighty-three departments nearly equal in size, named after rivers, mountains, and other physical features. Each department was divided into a number of districts; each district, into a number of cantons; and each canton, into a number of communes. Both the departments and the districts had administrators and councils charged with the double task of managing local affairs and acting as agents of the national Government. The cantons, serving only as electoral units, needed no organs of government. The life of the new system of local government centered in the 44,000 communes of France. These units varied in size from the largest French cities to the smallest rural parishes. The new organization left the central government no effective means of coercing indolent, ignorant, or refractory local administrators into doing their duty.

In many ways the most revolutionary and the most important of the legislative enactments of the National Assembly were those dealing with religion. The decree of November 2, 1789, confiscated the property of the Church in order to relieve the finances of the State. This legislation created the problem of the support of the regular clergy. In February, 1790, the National Assembly solved the problem by suppressing monastic vows entirely and abolishing the orders requiring such vows from their members. It gave the inmates of the monasteries and convents a choice between reëntering civil life with a pension from the State or retiring to one of the establishments provided for the shelter of the old, the sick, and the religious. The scale of pensions took into consideration both the age of the monks and nuns and the order to which they belonged, the old receiving more than the young and the monks larger pensions than the friars. The majority of the monks did not leave the monasteries until the end of 1791. They became professors, librarians, priests, vicars, administrators, and even national guards. Most of the nuns continued to follow their accustomed mode of life until 1792.

The National Assembly likewise attempted to alter profoundly the organization of the secular clergy by the Civil Constitution of the Clergy adopted in July, 1790. This measure reduced the number of dioceses from 135 to 83, each department becoming a diocese. Parish lines, also, were to be run again in order to make them conform to modern conditions. Henceforth the bishops and parish priests were to be elected as were the secular officials. They were to be paid also from the state treasury instead of by tithes, fees, and the income from ecclesiastical property. The new salary scale greatly reduced the income of most of the bishops and materially increased that of the parish priests. After their election the bishops were merely to write to the Pope a letter in recognition of his position as head of the Church. The whole tendency of the Civil Constitution of the Clergy was to make the Church in France simply a department of the political government and to destroy the jurisdiction of the Pope.

During the two years it was in session at Paris the National Assembly carried out a work of reform more extensive than that ever accomplished by any similar body. It transformed the absolute monarchy into a limited monarchy, and transferred sovereignty from the King to the nation. It made great progress toward the establishment of civil equality and civil liberty. It freed property from feudal obligations, and transferred much of the soil of France from the Church, the Crown, and the nobles to new owners, belonging to the nonprivileged classes. It freed labor by the suppression of the craft gilds, delivered industry and commerce from innumerable restrictions, and greatly favored them by the adoption of a high tariff. It lightened the public burdens by the abolition of exemptions from taxation and by the levying of taxes in proportion to incomes. The reforms of the National Assembly were of incalculable advantage to the bourgeoisie and the rich peasants. They made the middle class the dominant class in the State as a result of the revolution. The poorer peasants and the artisans of the cities gained almost nothing.

DECLINE AND FALL OF THE MONARCHY

To insure its success the new Constitution needed the whole-hearted support of both the King and the nation. Long before the Constitution was completed, however, the *émigrés*, the clergy, and the King had shown unmistakable signs of their hostility. Their hostility led ultimately to the creation of a party opposed to the King and in the end to the downfall of the monarchy.

The *émigrés* had shown their attitude toward the movement for reform by leaving the country. Immediately after the fall of the Bastille nobles, army officers, and members of the upper clergy and the parlements had begun to emigrate from France. The "war on the châteaux," the destruction of the feudal dues, and the abolition of titles of nobility steadily increased the number of these *émigrés*. They gathered in Piedmont, in Belgium, and especially in the petty German states on the northern border of France, organized little armies, intrigued in the hope of enlisting the aid of the monarchs of Europe, and dreamed of returning to France in triumph. By their activity they exasperated and alarmed the patriots, discredited and embarrassed the King, and helped to embroil the states of Europe in a war with revolutionary France which lasted twenty-two years.

The opposition aroused by the adoption and enforcement of the Civil Constitution of the Clergy was much more serious. The provisions of the law dealing with the Pope and providing for the election of the bishops and the parish priests as secular officials effected a veritable revolution in the organization of the French Church. Influenced by the loss of the property of the Church, their privileges, and their honors, as well as by their religious convictions, the bishops, with four exceptions, declared against the new law. After considerable hesitation the Pope followed the lead of the bishops. The action of the Pope and the bishops made the prescribed oath of fidelity to the Civil Constitution of the Clergy a question of conscience. Consequently, nearly half of the French clergy refused to take the required oath in spite of the larger salaries and other advantages which the new Civil Constitution offered to them. Their action divided the French clergy into the juring or constitutional clergy and the non-juring or refractory priests. In reply the State filled the places of the refractory clergy with former monks and other priests. This action of the French Government introduced religious discord into most of the cities and villages of France and drove thousands of the lower clergy and millions of their parishioners into opposition to the revolution. In some districts, as Brittany, Anjou, and the Vendée, the peasants rose against the newly elected, constitutional clergy and drove them out of the pulpits. When the National Guard tried to coerce the peasants into obedience, they flew to arms and began a civil war that embarrassed the revolutionary government for years. In the end this Catholic movement of the peasants became merged with the royalist movement of the *émigrés*.

The Civil Constitution of the Clergy was also the determining factor in turning the King against the revolution. A sincere Catholic, the new Constitution wounded him in his conscience and endangered the salvation of his soul. The King had no sooner signed it than he began to plan his escape from Paris to the royal troops stationed on the northeastern frontier. Surrounded by armed troops on whom he could rely, he could again feel himself a king and return to Paris master of the situation. In accordance with plans which had been carefully worked out, the members of the royal family fled from Paris during the night of June 20, 1791, and made their way toward the northern border of France. At the little village of Varennes, however, the King and Queen were recognized, arrested, and turned over to three commissioners of the National Assembly to be taken back to the capital. Thus the attempt of the royal family to escape completely failed.

The flight to Varennes had serious consequences for the French monarchy. The King had shown his real feeling in regard to the revolution and the people had learned that the King was not indispensable. The immediate result of the flight was the temporary suspension of the King from his royal functions. The ultimate effect was to create a republican party. Feeling that the King was not in sympathy with the new Constitution, some of the leaders of the people of Paris began to agitate for his abdication. During a popular demonstration against the monarchy, held July 17th on the Champ-de-Mars, the National Guard shot down some fifty members of the crowd gathered on the field. The flight of the King and the massacre of the Champ-de-Mars were decisive events. They tended to divide the patriotic party into a radical and a moderate wing. The radical wing soon developed into a republican party.

The nation, however, was not yet ready for an experiment in republican government. Under the influence of the moderates the new Constitution was completed and the King was permitted to take the oath of fidelity to the Constitution and to reassume his place in the Government. Accordingly, the National Assembly disbanded on September 30, 1791, having completely fulfilled the promise made over two years earlier never to separate until they had given France a constitution. On the following day the Legislative Assembly, elected in accordance with the Constitution of 1791, took over the work of government.

In spite of the temporary victory of the moderate wing of the patriotic party in replacing Louis XVI on the throne of France after his flight to Varennes, the influence of the more radical leaders, as Marat, Danton, and Robespierre, was becoming dominant in the nation. This change in public opinion was due to a variety of causes. The majority of Frenchmen erroneously supposed that the victory over absolutism had been won and began to neglect their political duties. The control over public opinion then fell into the hands of a determined minority composed of the lower classes and managed by the press and the radical political clubs. The fiery denunciations of revolutionary journalists such as Marat and Camille Desmoulin, the friend of Danton, contributed powerfully toward the shaping of public opinion. Political clubs like that of the Cordeliers gave this opinion organization and direction. This club derived its name from the former monastery in which it met. It was composed of representatives of the lower classes. Under the leadership of Danton it became, in time, the nucleus of the republican party in France. The watchwords and the ideas of both the orators and the journalists of the party came from the works of Rousseau.

A more famous club was that of the Jacobins. Like the Cordeliers, the Jacobins received their name from the former monastery in which they met. The society was organized originally by some deputies of the Estates General under the name of the "Friends of the Constitution." At first the

Jacobin Club included men of very moderate opinions. In time it added to its membership both at Paris and in the provinces until Jacobin Clubs existed in over two thousand villages and cities of France. Through these affiliated societies the club at Paris seemed at times to dominate public opinion and the term "Jacobin" became synonymous with radicalism. In reality the society followed rather than led public opinion.

In time the influence of the revolutionary extremists made itself felt in the speech, the dress, and the manners of the people. The French officially abolished the expressions "Sire" and "Your Majesty" previously used in addressing the King, adopted the term "citizen" (*citoyen*) instead of the title "Monsieur," and abandoned the silk stockings, the knee-breeches, and the powdered hair of the *ancien régime* for the red caps (*bonnets rouges*), the long beards, and the long pantaloons of the working class. The new sovereigns of France, the members of the Parisian mob, began to crowd into the hall of the Legislative Assembly and to show their disapproval of legislative proposals by hooting and stamping in the galleries. Later they dictated to the deputies exactly what they should do.

The Legislative Assembly was more moderate in opinion than the radical elements in Paris. The electors had been chosen by the active citizens before the flight to Varennes and the new deputies that they selected represented in the main the bourgeoisie. Owing to a quixotic proposal of Robespierre the new assembly included none of the members of the National Assembly. The deputies quickly divided into loosely organized parties and groups. On the right of the new legislature sat some two hundred and fifty constitutional monarchists who favored the Constitution of 1791. From the monastery in which they met to discuss political questions they were sometimes called "Feuillants." In the center were two hundred and fifty to three hundred independents, who showed a tendency to vote with the deputies on the right. On the extreme left were about one hundred and thirty Jacobins who favored radical changes in the

Constitution. Questions of policy finally divided the latter into the groups later known as the "Girondins" and the "Mountain."

The Legislative Assembly immediately set to work at the tasks confronting it. One of the most important of its problems was the *émigrés*. A decree of November, 1791, declared the *émigrés* mustered beyond the frontiers of France suspects for conspiracy against their country. If they were still in arms on January 1, 1792, they were to be declared guilty of conspiracy and punished by death. The French princes and the civil and ecclesiastical officials absent from France at the same date were to be treated in the same manner. The King greatly widened the gap separating him from his people by vetoing this decree.

A second problem was the non-juring or refractory priests. For a time after the adoption of the Civil Constitution of the Clergy the National Assembly followed a tolerant policy toward the clergy who refused to take the prescribed oath, but gradually the policy of the French Government changed. In May, 1791, the Legislative Assembly forbade the refractory clergy to say mass. In November of the same year it passed a law requiring them to take an oath of loyalty within a week. If they refused to obey they were to be considered suspicious characters, to lose their incomes from the State, and to be subject to the close supervision of the Government. The royal veto of this measure further inflamed public opinion against the monarchy.

A third pressing problem was the question of foreign relations. There was a natural antagonism between revolutionary France and feudal Europe. The democrats of France, imbued with the missionary spirit, wished to spread their principles to neighboring peoples. At first the rivals of France welcomed the signs of its weakening power, but later they began to feel menaced by the revolutionary principles. Specific causes of conflict increased the natural antagonism. The German princes on the northern border of France sheltered the *émigrés* and permitted them to plot against the security of France. The French Government, on the other hand, disregarded the rights of some of the German princes over certain possessions retained by them in Alsace after the Peace of Westphalia by abolishing all feudal dues in the province. In 1791 France complicated matters still more by annexing the Papal territories of Avignon and the County of Venaissin. The treatment accorded the King and the royal family after the flight to Varennes convinced the sovereigns of Europe finally that the revolution menaced them as well as Louis XVI, and caused Prussia and Austria to draw together in an alliance against its subversive doctrines. The formation of this alliance brought the European Powers to the verge of war.

Unfortunately for Europe the question of war had got into French politics. The King, the constitutional monarchists, and the Girondins all desired war, but for different reasons. The King hoped to be extricated from his humiliating position by a victory of the Powers. The constitutional monarchists believed that a successful war would popularize the monarchy. The Girondins thought that a war would rouse the French nation, unmask the disloyalty of the King, and compel him to follow the lead of the French people. Only Marat, Danton, and Robespierre and a handful of their followers among the members of the Mountain had the foresight to oppose the war. The situation became more serious still as a result of the succession of the young and bellicose Francis II on March 1, 1792, to the throne of the pacific and hesitant Leopold II of Austria. The new ruler of the Habsburg lands renewed the alliance which his predecessor had concluded with Prussia, and demanded the reëstablishment of the German princes with treaty rights in Alsace in the enjoyment of their feudal dues and the restitution to the Pope of the Papal territories of Avignon and the County of Venaissin. With almost the unanimous approval of the French people, therefore, Louis XVI, at the instigation of his ministers, proposed to the Legislative Assembly on April 20, 1792, a declaration of war on Austria. The French ministers had attempted to confine the conflict to the Habsburg Power, but Frederick William II of Prussia took the attitude that a declaration of war against his ally involved his kingdom as well. France thus found herself at war with both Austria and Prussia. The war begun so light-heartedly continued, with one slight interruption, for a period of twenty-two years.

The opening events of the conflict quickly demonstrated the unpreparedness of France for the struggle. The army was not up to war strength, discipline had been undermined by the revolutionary effervescence, military equipment was lacking, and two thirds of the officers of the French army had resigned and emigrated. As a result of these conditions the war opened with a series of reverses. In the first engagements the French troops threw away their arms and retreated in wild disorder. Only the unpreparedness of Austria and Prussia for an offensive campaign saved France from an immediate invasion.

Threatened at the same time by foreign invasion from the troops of Austria and Prussia and from civil war by the nonjuring priests and their parishioners, the Legislative Assembly passed two decrees designed to destroy every possibility of counter-revolution and to finish with the refractory priests. One ordered the deportation of all the refractory or nonjuring priests to the penal colony. The other provided for an army of twenty thousand men drawn from the patriots of the provinces to protect Paris and to overawe the King and the aristocrats. The King promptly vetoed both measures. The reply of the radical party at Paris was the demonstration of June 20, 1792, the anniversary of the flight to Varennes. A mob of several thousand men, wearing red caps, armed with pikes, and drawn from the working quarters of the capital, marched to the hall of the Legislative Assembly and demanded that the King should cease to betray the country. After leaving the Legislative Assembly the motley throng broke into the palace of the Tuileries and for three hours filed past the King, demanding that he should sign the decrees. The demonstration was a clear sign of the imminence of the fall of the monarchy. Only some unusual event was needed to crystallize public opinion and precipitate the overthrow of the King.

THE FRENCH REVOLUTION

The manifesto (July 25, 1792) of the Duke of Brunswick, the general in command of the Austrian and Prussian armies, furnished the needed impetus. The proclamation was inspired by the *émigrés* and was issued just as the allies were on the point of invading France. The document ordered the French people to restore Louis XVI to full freedom of action, to obey the sovereigns of Austria and Prussia, and to abstain from every form of opposition to the invading armies. It threatened severe punishment for resistance on the part of the National Guards or administrative officers, and menaced Paris with ruin if the slightest insult was offered to the King or his palace was invaded again by a Parisian mob. The declaration was therefore a challenge to the whole French nation.

The people of Paris replied to the manifesto of the Duke of Brunswick by overthrowing the monarchy. Their leaders began to plan almost openly a popular uprising. At midnight on August 9, 1792, they gave the signal for the insurrection. On the following day the mob forced the royal family to flee to the hesitant Legislative Assembly for protection, captured and sacked the royal palace, and needlessly caused the death of eight hundred of the Swiss mercenaries guarding the Tuileries and of three hundred and seventy-six members of the mob attacking the palace. As a result of these stirring events the Legislative Assembly suspended the King, imprisoned the royal family in the Temple, installed a municipal government representing the Jacobins and the Parisian mob in the place of the moderate municipal government set up after the fall of the Bastille, and created a provisional government, which managed the State until the assembly on September 21st of the Convention elected to draw up a constitution to take the place of the one that had just broken down.

THE NATIONAL CONVENTION

No political body was ever confronted with more varied or graver tasks than was the National Convention which took over control of the government of France on September 21,

1792. It had to decide on the fate of Louis XVI, defend the country from foreign and domestic foes, draw up a new constitution, and give France a stable government while the new constitution was being framed. How the National Convention solved these problems was determined in large measure by political conditions at Paris, in the Convention, and in the provinces, and by the course of the foreign war.

During the three years the revolution had been in progress the political situation in France had steadily grown more complicated. In the provinces conditions had remained comparatively simple. People were still divided into aristocrats and patriots. But at Paris the patriots had split up into an ever-increasing number of factions and political power had shifted gradually toward the left. After the fall of the Bastille in 1789, the capital had been under the control of constitutional monarchists drawn mainly from the ranks of the bourgeoisie. After the suspension of the King, the city had fallen under the control of the middle-class leaders of the working classes. Prior to that date the latter had been only passive citizens, but soon after the insurrection of August 10, 1792, they had been given universal suffrage. As a result of this addition to the electorate Paris sent a delegation of radicals as its representatives in the National Convention. The new masters of Paris were united in their hatred of the aristocrats, but during the period of the Convention they gradually separated into three groups, popularly but erroneously known as the parties of Danton, Robespierre, and Hébert. Danton never had a real party behind him, and an obscure priest, Jacques Roux, not Hébert, was the moving spirit among the so-called Hébertists or "*Enragés*." The latter group, the most radical one in Paris, was interested primarily in economic questions.

The chief political organ of the popular party at Paris was the municipal government (commune) of the city. The victory of the working classes over the monarchy had greatly increased its importance. From the time of the suspension of the King on August 10, 1792, until the assembling of the National Convention, it had been the controlling force behind the provisional government. The power of the municipal government rested on the support of the assemblies of the forty-eight sections or electoral districts of Paris. After the establishment of universal manhood suffrage in August, 1792, as a result of the popular insurrection, these assemblies became political clubs. It was to these turbulent, vigorous bodies that the municipal government learned to appeal for the armed forces needed to overawe its opponents.

The legislative branch of the Government had likewise become more radical since 1789. One half of the membership of the National Assembly had been composed of representatives of the privileged orders. The party of reform in the National Assembly, however, became the relatively conservative constitutional monarchists of the Legislative Assembly. In the Convention again only the left of the preceding legislative body was represented. The 749 deputies of the Convention were divided into three equal groups: the Girondins, the center, and the Mountain.[1] The latter party derived its name from the high seats which its members chanced to occupy. The Girondins passed for federalists. In reality they were liberals. They wished to govern France in a democratic manner as if circumstances were normal. They feared the dictatorship of Paris, hated Marat, Danton, and Robespierre and their followers in the Mountain, and wished to reduce Paris to the level of the other departments of France. The leaders of the Mountain did not plan a personal dictatorship, but they believed in a strong centralization of the government for the purpose of national defense. They were ready to submit to the dictatorship of Paris during the crisis. The work of the Convention was hampered for months by the quarrels of the two factions.

One of the pressing problems facing the National Convention was the question of the future form of the government of France. The new constitution depended largely on the solution of this question. An unexpected vote taken just at the close of the first day's session settled the question.

[1] In continental Europe legislative bodies sit in semi-circular amphitheaters, the more conservative members on the right, the more radical on the left.

On the motion of one of its members the Convention voted the abolition of the monarchy, but made no mention of a republic. The crowds demonstrating in the streets first used this word. In this almost accidental fashion France became a republic.

The abolition of the monarchy made the question of the fate of the King more acute. After considerable deliberation the committee appointed by the Convention to consider the matter decided early in November that Louis XVI should be brought to trial. Investigation of the royal palace after the insurrection of August 10th had revealed the existence of some exceedingly compromising documents. When he was confronted with the damaging evidence, Louis XVI did not make a good impression. His method of defense was to deny, to say that he did not recall, or to fail to recognize the documents shown to him. At the end of the trial the deputies of the National Convention voted unanimously that the King was guilty of conspiracy against the State and of an attack on its security. By a small majority they decided in favor of the penalty of death. In accordance with this decision Louis XVI was executed on January 21, 1793, in the presence of an immense concourse of people.

During the months that followed the execution of the King the situation of the National Convention grew steadily worse. Food was scarce; prices were rising; and the problem of feeding Paris and the larger cities of France was becoming a serious one. The authorities were having difficulty in maintaining order. The news from the front was alarming. The French armies were being beaten and four new states were entering the war. Many of the provinces were in open revolt against a decree of February 21, 1793, providing for the conscription of 300,000 men for the army. In Normandy, in Brittany, in some of the departments of the East, in the valley of the Lower Rhone, and in the Vendée, a maritime province lying just south of the mouth of the Loire River, there was determined resistance to the carrying-out of the law. Mobs gathered; officers were prevented from designating the conscripts; and bands of peasants rose in revolt. The rising in the Vendée was the most serious one. The whole region rose in insurrection. The peasants did not regret the abolition of the *ancien régime*, but they were opposed to the constitutional clergy who had been forced on them, and to the conscription of their sons for the army. These conditions placed the Convention in a most serious situation.

The Government was ill-prepared to cope with the problems confronting it. The Constitution of 1791, in a modified form, was still in force. Its decentralized form of government was a tremendous obstacle to national unity and national defense. To meet the difficult situation facing it the National Convention created a number of extraordinary institutions. A central executive body, known as the Committee of Public Safety, a Revolutionary Army[1] to cow the aristocrats and to enforce the decrees of the agents of the National Government, Revolutionary Committees of Surveillance, and an extraordinary criminal court, known as the Revolutionary Tribunal, were established. For some time, however, the new institutions did not function satisfactorily. Their activity was paralyzed by the bitter quarrels of the Girondins and the Mountain.

Since the opening of the Convention the leaders of the Girondins and the Mountain had opposed each other on nearly every question which had arisen. Menaces and insults were interchanged daily between them. The Girondins aimed to retain control of the Convention and the newly created extraordinary institutions and to use the latter with moderation. They failed, however, to show the slightest capacity to bring success to the French arms or order to the State. The leaders of the Mountain believed that extraordinary measures were necessary. They identified the Girondins with the aristocrats and demanded the arrest of their leaders. They wished to nerve France to great deeds by ruthlessly striking down every obstacle to success. The Girondins depended on their legal majority in the Convention. The Mountain depended on the support of the people of Paris. The quarrels of the two parties reached their cul-

[1] The Revolutionary Army was not established until the fall of 1793.

mination in the *coup d'état* of June 2d. The assemblies of the radical sections of Paris began to agitate for the arrest of the Girondin leaders. A revolutionary committee composed of representatives of the forty-eight sections of Paris assumed power and associated itself with the municipal authorities. An insurrection was then organized. Thousands of revolutionists armed with artillery surrounded the hall of the Convention. Cowed by the demonstration the Convention tamely voted the expulsion of twenty-nine of its Girondin members and the arrest of the expelled deputies and two Girondin ministers. This *coup d'état* of June 2d threw political power for over a year into the hands of the party of the Mountain.

The immediate result of the victory of the Mountain over the Girondins was a rising of the provinces against the capital. For the first time since the opening of the Revolution the provinces did not follow the leadership of Paris. Until the *coup d'état* of June 2, 1793, the people of the provinces had been divided into aristocrats and patriots. The action of the leaders of the Mountain ranged patriot against patriot. Most of the departments rose in revolt against the dictatorship of Paris. The cities of Bordeaux, Lyons, Marseilles, and Toulon, and the department of the Vendée offered a particularly determined resistance. The revolts, in most instances, started as republican movements. The monarchists were quick to turn the uprisings into monarchist channels, and many of them evolved into movements for the restoration of the monarchy. The leaders of the Mountain, therefore, were compelled to face at the same time a great coalition of foreign Powers and a revolt of a large part of France.

The resolute, determined band of leaders in control of Paris never flinched in the face of this terrible situation. They pursued and executed the Girondin leaders, galvanized the Committee of Public Safety into vigorous activity, voted a long list of important reforms, tracked down the enemies of the republic by the revolutionary committees and the revolutionary armies, turned raw levies into capable armies, cast the church bells into cannon, manufactured thousands of muskets, swords, and bayonets, rapidly increased the supply of powder, found new military leaders, and evolved new tactics and strategy. By the end of the year 1793 the Government had practically suppressed the domestic revolt and stemmed the tide of foreign invasion.

The leaders of the Mountain obtained these successes in large part by the complete sacrifice of political liberty. The activity of the Convention practically ceased after the proscription of the Girondins. The Girondins had been expelled; many members of the Mountain were absent on mission, and others prudently ceased to attend. As a result of this situation not more than two hundred and thirty deputies on an average were present at the sessions. There were no more important political debates and measures were often put through by one hundred or even fifty votes. All authority was still invested theoretically in the Convention, but it was delegated in practice to the extraordinary institutions created to supplement the inadequate governmental machinery provided by the Constitution of 1791.

The most important of these special institutions was the Committee of Public Safety. It was organized by a decree of April 6, 1793, for the purpose of supervising the executive council and putting unity in the direction of military and diplomatic affairs. At first the committee was composed of nine members and was dominated by Danton. After July it was reorganized with a membership of twelve and came under the influence of Robespierre. It deliberated behind closed doors and disposed of secret funds. The only check on its power was the necessity of reporting fully and regularly to the Convention concerning its executive and administrative measures. The power and authority of the committee was greatly increased by the decree of December 4, 1793. By this measure the departmental governments were practically destroyed and were replaced by national agents strictly subordinated to the Committee of Public Safety. In personnel the committee was composed of honest, patriotic men of more than usual ability, who devoted themselves body and soul to the task of saving France. Besides using the national agents just mentioned, the committee made its power felt in the departments through the representatives on mission, the revolutionary armies, and the revolutionary committees.

The representatives on mission were veritable itinerant intendants. Like the Committee of Public Safety they were created to meet a special emergency. They were first sent in March, 1793, to every department of France to assist in raising the 300,000 conscripts which had just been voted by the Convention. Later they were sent both to the armies and to the departments. They were on the alert to detect treason and inefficiency. They demanded nothing less than victory from the officers of the French armies. More than one revolutionary general was guillotined for the crime of having lost a battle. This merciless policy, in the end, brought results. The French armies for a combination of reasons became wellnigh irresistible. In the departments the representatives on mission had full power to dismiss and replace provisionally local officials and to arrest and execute persons suspected of hostility to the republic. The revolutionary armies were created to carry out the orders of the representatives on mission and the other revolutionary authorities. They were frequently guilty of the worst excesses and were finally abolished both in the provinces and at Paris.

The revolutionary committees owed their origin to a decree of March, 1793, which ordered the establishment in each commune or section of a committee of twelve citizens elected by popular vote. Their function at first was to watch over foreigners, to receive their declarations, and to designate those that should be expelled. They were called at first committees of surveillance. Those at Paris did not delay long in extending their functions. Their conscious purpose soon became the stimulation of the revolution. A decree of September, 1793, charged them with the duty of disarming and arresting persons suspected of conspiracy against the State. By a later decree suspects were defined so as to include all those who had sought to promote the reëstablishment of royalty, to betray the republic, to cause a scarcity of food at

Paris, to second the projects of the enemies of France, to deceive or to discourage the people, or who were related in any way to *émigrés*, refractory priests, or conspirators against the republic. The committees at Paris in particular exercised their powers with terrible results.

In September, 1793, the Convention reorganized a second extraordinary committee. This Committee of General Security was charged with the general police power throughout France. It controlled the arrest of persons suspected of conspiracy, supervised prisons, and designated the individuals to be brought before the terrible Revolutionary Tribunal. These powers made the Committee of General Security one of the most dreaded institutions of the period known as the "Terror."

The Committee of General Security acted through various criminal courts. In the departments there were the ordinary criminal courts, the special courts instituted in some of the cities in imitation of the Revolutionary Tribunal at Paris, and the special courts organized in the regions in revolt against the Government. At Paris the Convention created the extraordinary criminal court known as the "Revolutionary Tribunal." Its jurisdiction extended over the whole area of France. Toward the end of the period of the Terror it became the sole revolutionary tribunal.

The period during which the Committee of Public Safety, the representatives on mission, the revolutionary armies, the revolutionary committees, the Committee of General Security, and the Revolutionary Tribunal were most active is known as the Terror. It lasted from the *coup d'état* of June 2, 1793, to the overthrow of Robespierre on July 27, 1794. As its name would indicate the period has a bad reputation on account of the losses of life which occurred both at Paris and in the provinces.

The Revolutionary Tribunal at Paris took the lives of some 2627 persons. From June, 1793, to June, 1794, the number of executions steadily mounted. At first the Girondins were the principal persons to suffer. In December, 1793, 69 individuals were executed; in January, 1794, 71; in February, 73;

in March, 127; in April, 257; and in May, 352. From March, 1793, to June, 1794, 1251 persons were condemned by the Revolutionary Tribunal and executed by the guillotine, not three a day. During the months of June and July, 1794, the number of victims mounted by leaps and bounds. From June 10th to July 27th, 1376 persons were executed, an average of nearly thirty a day. During this period Robespierre was using the Terror to establish his ideal state. The victims included persons of all ages and conditions: humble domestics, the richest nobles, *émigrés*, refractory priests, former farmers of the taxes, forgers of *assignats*, officials of the *ancien régime*, unsuccessful generals of the republican armies, and members of the vanquished parties. The list includes many of the most famous names in French history.

In the provinces the number of victims of the Terror probably numbered 16,000 to 18,000. In the Vendée veritable hecatombs of prisoners were executed repeatedly. On two different occasions several hundred victims were shot down in cold blood. At Nantes a representative on mission, named Carrier, applying to the letter the theories of the revolutionary extremists, shot and drowned in batches between 2800 and 4600 individuals. After the capture of Lyons by the troops of the National Convention that body took a terrible vengeance on the rebellious city. It decreed the destruction of the houses of the rich and the suppression of the very name of the city. The persons convicted of complicity in the revolt were shot down in masses. At Toulon a tribunal, formed of republicans who had been imprisoned during the revolt of the city against the Convention, tried those taken with arms in their hands. Such incidents as these, however, should not be considered as typical of the period of the Terror. In reality many periods in history have been more terrible.

With the suppression of domestic revolt and the rolling back of the tide of foreign invasion dissensions began to appear in the ranks of the Terrorists. Two factions disapproved of the policies of Robespierre. Danton and his friends considered the Terror as merely a tool to be used during the crisis and then abandoned. Hébert and the *Enragés* wished to proceed to even more extreme measures. Robespierre declared both enemies of the republic and persuaded the two great committees of the revolutionary government to decree their arrest. In March, 1794, Hébert and several of his associates were condemned and guillotined. Early in the following month Danton and a number of his friends met the same fate. Danton had compromised himself by association with profiteers and by the accumulation of a considerable fortune. The Hébertists, supported by the club of the Cordeliers and the working-class quarters, were a real menace to the plans of Robespierre for the establishment of an ideal state.

Robespierre did not long survive his two famous victims. The number of his enemies steadily grew. The Girondins, the friends of Danton, and the associates of Hébert were hostile to him. The Committee of General Security resented the establishment of a bureau of police attached to the Committee of Public Safety. The latter committee was itself divided into two hostile factions. One of the factions ridiculed the plans of Robespierre for establishing the worship of the Supreme Being and an ideal state based on the ideas of Rousseau. His vague suggestions of the need of still further purification of the Convention alarmed moderates and extremists alike. Both the members of the Convention and the people of Paris were beginning to turn against him. Out of these heterogeneous elements grew a coalition for the overthrow of Robespierre. On July 26, 1794, his opponents openly opposed him in the Convention, while he was attempting to force the passage of a decree against his enemies. On the following day, amid scenes of a most dramatic character, the Convention voted for the arrest of Robespierre. At that point the municipal government of Paris attempted an insurrection in his behalf. Its agents broke into his prison and bore him to the city hall of Paris. The people of Paris, however, did not rise in his defense with the enthusiasm and the unanimity they had shown in storming the Bastille or in causing the suspension of the King. While they hesitated, the

Convention acted. Armed forces were assembled and Robespierre was outlawed as a rebel on account of the popular rising in his behalf, and recaptured. On July 28th he was guillotined along with twenty of his associates. During the next two days eighty-three more of his friends were executed.

The elections for the Convention had put the Girondins in power. The *coup d'état* of June 2, 1793, put the Mountain in control of the convention. The overthrow of Robespierre put power into the hands of the moderates of the center. They made use of their control of the Convention to modify the severity of the Terror. They freed the Convention from the dictatorship of the Committees of Public Safety and General Security, reorganized the Revolutionary Tribunal, and set free many of the prisoners who had been incarcerated during the period of the Terror. The guillotine slackened its activity. The moderates grew bolder and attacked the Jacobins in the streets. The surviving Girondins were readmitted to the Convention. The club of the Jacobins was closed. Carrier was executed for his crimes at Nantes. The public prosecutor of the Revolutionary Tribunal was similarly punished. The departmental governments recovered their power. A constitutional commission was set up. In retaliation the Jacobins were subjected to a veritable reign of terror in many of the provinces. The military forces of the Convention defeated and disarmed the working-class quarters. The Revolutionary Tribunal disappeared. Men regained the protection of the law. Before the Convention finished its task of giving France a constitution, the last vestiges of the institutions of the Terror had disappeared.

The reëstablishment of normal political conditions gave the National Convention an opportunity to take up at last the task of drawing up a constitution. The inadequate sketch of a constitution adopted by the Convention while the Mountain was in power did not satisfy the new masters of that body. Accordingly it drew up a new constitutional instrument. This document replaced universal suffrage by a franchise based on property. Taught by the experiences of France with a single chamber the Convention created a legislature of two houses. The Council of Elders was composed of two hundred and fifty members, who were required to be married or widowers and at least forty years of age. The lower chamber, known as the Council of Five Hundred, was to consist of men at least thirty years of age. Fearing the establishment of another dictator like Robespierre the new constitution entrusted the executive power to a Directory of five members elected by the councils. One new Director came into office each year. Directors were required to be at least forty years of age. The Constitution of 1795 was thus a reaction against the extreme democracy of the Convention. It restored the bourgeoisie to power. In order to make sure that the government did not fall into hostile hands the Convention voted that two thirds of each of the legislative councils should be chosen from among the members of the Convention.

The people of the departments accepted the new constitution by overwhelming majorities, but the people of Paris rejected it. The decrees providing for the continuance of the power of the Convention looked to many like a barefaced attempt of men who knew they were discredited to continue in office. Under the leadership of the royalists a new insurrection was organized at Paris. For a time the Convention appeared to be in serious danger. The vigorous measures taken by a young general named Napoleon Bonaparte to defend the Convention soon averted this danger. Three weeks later (October 26, 1795) the Convention quietly made way for the government which was to succeed it.

REFORMS OF THE LEGISLATIVE ASSEMBLY AND THE NATIONAL CONVENTION, 1792–95

The National Convention devoted more attention to the subject of religion than to any other question. The Civil Constitution of the Clergy adopted by the National Assembly in 1790 caused a break between the revolution and the ancient Church of France. The insurrection in behalf of the Girondins discredited the Constitutional Church, created to take the place of the older religious organization, because many of the constitutional clergy sympathized with the Girondins. Thereupon the Mountain began to make war on the constitutional clergy and to substitute worship of the State for the ancient religion of France. The new religion also had its traditions, its symbols, its rites, and its hymns. With the men of the Mountain the trees of liberty and the tricolor cockades, the Constitution and the rights of man, the busts of dead patriots like Marat,[1] and the national holidays took the place, in a way, of the symbols, the sacred books, the statues of the saints, and the religious fête days of the Catholic Church. In October, 1793, the Convention forbade the wearing of religious costumes and the observance of religious ceremonies outside of the churches. Many priests resigned their ecclesiastical functions. In November the Constitutional Bishop of Paris, together with a number of his clergy, resigned from office. The so-called Hébertists seized the Cathedral of Notre Dame and with elaborate ceremonies worshiped Liberty in the person of a handsome actress. Similar parodies on religion, accompanied by the closure of churches and the seizure of sacred vessels, occurred during November and December (1793) in various parts of the country.

The State never approved of the follies of the worship of Liberty, but, upon the initiative of Robespierre, the Convention established in May, 1794, the worship of the Supreme Being as the official religion of France. By decree the French people recognized the existence of God and the immortality of the soul. The Convention created four national holidays commemorating the fall of the Bastille (July 14, 1789), the suspension of the King (August 10, 1792), the execution of the King (January 21, 1793), and the beginning of the *coup d'état* which overthrew the Girondins (May 31, 1793). Every tenth day was set aside for the worship of the Supreme Being. In June, 1794, the fête of the Supreme Being was observed with Robespierre himself acting as high pontiff, assisted by men, women, and children from the electoral districts of Paris and members of the Convention. The words and

[1] He had been assassinated by Charlotte Corday in 1793.

music of the hymns, the work of eminent artists, and the pageantry of the spectacle seem to have made a lasting impression on all who saw the ceremonies.

Of more permanent importance was the separation of Church and State in the closing months of the Convention. Suspicion of the loyalty of the constitutional priests prepared the way for the complete separation of Church and State. In September, 1794, the Convention decreed, partly as a measure of economy, that the French Republic no longer should pay the salaries or expenses of any sect. In February of the following year the Convention issued a decree declaring that the State should furnish neither a salary nor a church nor a rectory and forbidding the observance of religious ceremonies outside the churches, all signs of worship, the use of church bells, and the wearing of ecclesiastical costumes. As the churches had been nationalized, religious services had to be held elsewhere. As a measure of pacification in Brittany and the Vendée the Government permitted the reopening of the churches in case the priests made formal submission to the laws of the republic. Seeing the anomaly of granting privileges to persons recently in revolt denied to citizens of proved loyalty, the Government finally extended in May, 1795, the same privilege to all French citizens. This decree threw the churches open to refractory priests, constitutional clergy, Protestant ministers, and Jewish rabbis. Some of the constitutional clergy took advantage of the decree to reconstitute their church as an independent religious body. Others retracted their oaths and reëntered the Roman Church. After the close of the Reign of Terror the churches were reopened nearly everywhere. Finally by a general law of September, 1795, the separation of Church and State was thoroughly established and freedom of worship guaranteed to all faiths.

The National Convention also gave much of its time to the problem of establishing a comprehensive system of public education. The creation of such a system had been one of the demands repeatedly made in the statements of grievances (*cahiers*) sent in 1789 by the clergy, nobles, and third estate to the Estates General. The leaders of the revolution appreciated from the first the necessity of establishing a system of general education for the people. They realized that political equality was not possible without equality of opportunity. Various plans and projects were presented to the Convention, the most important being those of Talleyrand and Condorcet. The plan of Condorcet called for a system of lower and higher primary schools, secondary schools, and professional schools, and a national society of arts and sciences. By this scheme education was to be gratuitous and open to all ages and to both sexes. The actual legislation of the Convention lagged far behind the noble idealism of Condorcet. The decree concerning primary education finally enacted by the Convention provided schools for the teaching of reading, writing, simple arithmetic, and the elements of republican morals in each canton in France. The teachers were to receive lodgings from the State and fees from the parents of the pupils, though one fourth of the pupils might be exempted from the payment of fees on account of the indigence of their parents. Each school was divided into a section for boys and one for girls. Secondary schools were created at Paris and in the departments. Provision was also made for the establishment of ten special schools for the teaching of astronomy, geometry and mechanics, natural history, medicine, veterinary science, rural economy, antiquities, political science, painting, sculpture, and architecture, and music. Special schools for instruction in military science, civil and military engineering, the art of teaching, medicine, mining, and navigation, and for construction of roads and bridges, were also actually created. The system of general education thus nobly planned and imperfectly executed was one of the greatest achievements of the National Convention. To France belongs the honor of having inaugurated the first general system of public education.

Many of the famous scientific establishments of modern France owe their origin or their present form to the National Convention. A School of Oriental Languages for the study of Persian, Malay, Arabic, Turkish, Tartar, and other languages in commerce and politics was established. The royal gardens were transformed into public botanical gardens (*Jardins des Plantes*), which have served ever since as a vast laboratory of natural history. The royal library was changed in a similar manner into the National Library (*Bibliothèque Nationale*). Libraries were likewise established at the chief places of each department. Both the national and the departmental libraries were enriched by the books and the manuscripts confiscated from the monasteries. National and departmental archives were established for the deposit and protection of documents dispersed in the thousands of convents, châteaux, and cities. For the development of industry and the instruction of the public a great museum of the arts and sciences (*Conservatoire des artes et métiers*) was created for the housing of models and examples of useful machines and apparatus. To save from destruction and preserve the innumerable pictures, statues, memorials of antiquity, and examples of architecture scattered by the sack of palaces and churches a National Museum was created at the palace of the Louvre. The crown of the scholarly and scientific edifice erected by the Convention was the Institute. It took the place of the royal academies which had been suppressed. Composed of resident and associate members its task was to advance the arts and sciences by the promotion of research, the publication of scientific discoveries, and correspondence with other learned societies.

During the military crisis science more than repaid its debt to the State. The men of science devised a system for the rapid signaling of messages from Paris to the frontiers, made a beginning toward military aeronautics, and discovered shorter methods for the manufacture of steel and powder, and the tanning of leather. These discoveries made possible the arming of the French levies or troops.

Another of the legacies of the Convention to mankind was the metric system of weights and measures. Standard units of length, area, volume, and mass were established. Each unit was a decimal part of the units above and some multiple of ten of the units below it. Most of the countries of the continent of Europe and men of science everywhere have since adopted this rational system.

An equally interesting but less important creation of the Convention was the republican calendar. Time was dated from the establishment of the republic. The year was divided into twelve months, each thirty days in length, and five complementary days. Each month was divided into three equal periods of ten days called "decades." The day was divided into ten hours. The months were named after natural phenomena and the days of the lengthened weeks were simply numbered. The new calendar caused great confusion at first, but remained in force until the close of 1805. It was an incident in the general movement to dechristianize and rationalize France.

In line with this general secularizing tendency were a number of laws dealing with marriage, divorce, and the registration of vital statistics. Under the *ancien régime* the registration of births, marriages, and deaths had been in the hands of the parish priest. Marriage had been a sacrament. Divorce had been against the laws of the Church. The legislation of the Legislative Assembly and the National Convention established civil marriage and divorce, and entrusted the registration of births, marriages, and deaths to civil officials.

In July, 1793, the Convention finally completed the task of transforming the peasant into a free proprietor. A decree of the Convention suppressed all the former seigniorial dues without any further payment of indemnity to the seigniors. By stubborn resistance the peasants had won the battle for freedom of the soil begun on the night of August 4th.

Upon coming to power the National Convention faced a task of almost incredible difficulty. During the three years it was in power in France foreign invasion, anarchy, and domestic revolt were defeated and a series of notable reforms put through. In spite of the blot of the Terror, the National Convention made a record of achievement second only to that of the National Assembly.

The French Revolution was an attempt to remedy the

evils of the *ancien régime* in France. It profoundly modified the political, social, religious, and economic organization of France. It reëstablished self-government in the towns and cities, abolished feudalism, guaranteed personal liberty in fundamental, constitutional documents, made the peasants full owners of their lands, transferred the lands of the royal family, of the Church, and of many of the nobles to new masters, did away with the gilds, and relieved domestic commerce from tolls, customs dues, and other restrictions. It introduced a more just system of taxation, and replaced the old, arbitrary, extravagant absolutism first by a limited monarchy and later by a republican form of government. It first reformed and then disestablished the intolerant State Church. It laid the foundations for a great national system of education. By thus modernizing their institutions the French people prepared themselves for the great achievements which they performed under the leadership of Napoleon.

REFERENCES

GENERAL ACCOUNTS OF THE FRENCH REVOLUTION
  H. Belloc, *The French Revolution*.
  H. E. Bourne, *The Revolutionary Period in Europe*, chapters VII-XIV.
  C. J. H. Hayes, *The Social and Political History of Europe*, vol. I, chapter XV.
  C. D. Hazen, *The French Revolution and Napoleon*, chapters II-V.
  L. R. Holt and A. W. Chilton, *European History, 1789-1815*, chapters III-V.
  R. M. Johnston, *The French Revolution*.
  L. Madelin, *The French Revolution*.
  J. A. R. Marriott, *The Remaking of Modern Europe*, chapters II-VI.
  S. Mathews, *The French Revolution*.
  J. H. Rose, *The Revolutionary and Napoleonic Era*, chapters III-V.
  H. M. Stephens, *A History of the French Revolution*.
  Histoire générale, vol. VIII.
  Histoire de France contemporaine, vols. I-II.

THE REFORMS OF THE NATIONAL ASSEMBLY
  H. E. Bourne, *The Revolutionary Period in Europe*, chapters VIII-IX.
  S. Mathews, *The French Revolution*, chapter XIII.
  H. M. Stephens, *The French Revolution*, vol. I, chapters IX-X, XII.
  Histoire de France contemporaine, vol. I, pp. 111-96.

THE TERROR
  H. E. Bourne, *The Revolutionary Period in Europe*, chapter XIII.

S. Mathews, *The French Revolution*, chapters XVIII–XIX.
Cambridge Modern History, vol. VIII, chapter XII.
Histoire générale, vol. VIII, pp. 189–215.
Histoire de France contemporaine, vol. II, pp. 165–234.

DANTON
H. Belloc, *Danton*.

ROBESPIERRE
H. Belloc, *Robespierre*.

SOURCES ON THE FRENCH REVOLUTION
F. M. Anderson, *Constitutions and Documents: France*, pp. 1–253.
J. H. Robinson, *Readings in European History*, vol. II, chapters XXXV–XXXVI.
J. H. Robinson and C. A. Beard, *Readings in Modern European History*, vol. I, chapters XII–XIII.
Translations and Reprints, vol. I, no. V; vol. IV, no. V.

DECREE ABOLISHING THE FEUDAL SYSTEM
F. M. Anderson, *Constitutions and Documents: France*, pp. 11–14.
J. H. Robinson and C. A. Beard, *Readings in Modern European History*, vol. I, pp. 256–59.
Translations and Reprints, vol. I, no. V, pp. 2–5.

DECLARATION OF THE RIGHTS OF MAN
F. M. Anderson, *Constitutions and Documents: France*, pp. 59–61.
J. H. Robinson and C. A. Beard, *Readings in Modern European History*, vol. I, pp. 259–62.
Translations and Reprints, vol. I, no. V, pp. 6–8.

CHAPTER XVII

CONSOLIDATION AND EXTENSION OF THE FRENCH REVOLUTION

THE French Revolution freed France from the *ancien régime*, but involved it in protracted wars with the Powers of Europe. These struggles led to the establishment of the military dictatorship of Napoleon Bonaparte, the most successful general of the revolution. His domestic policy tended to consolidate many of the reforms of the revolutionary period in France. His ambition for world dominion resulted in a series of wars which extended to a greater or less extent the reforms and institutions of Napoleonic France to the states and countries which fell for a time under the political sway of Napoleon Bonaparte.

EUROPE ON THE EVE OF THE WARS OF THE FRENCH REVOLUTION

The leaders of the French Revolution and Napoleon Bonaparte owed much of their astonishing success to the political, social, and economic situation in Europe. On the south Spain and Portugal seemed half lifeless. Across the Alps the petty states of Italy invited foreign invasion. On the northern border of France neither the Austrian Netherlands nor the moribund Holy Roman Empire, with its three hundred and sixty-four states, could offer any great resistance to a skillful, determined invader. Poland was on the verge of disappearing entirely from the map of Europe. Both Prussia and Austria were more concerned with the fate of the various provinces of the Polish kingdom than with that of Louis XVI. Holland had been declining for many years. England, though rich in movable wealth and mistress of the seas, had no army of any importance. Turkey still ruled feebly over her Christian subjects in the Balkans. The remaining states of Europe, with the exception of Russia, counted for little in the politics of the time.

In nearly all the states of the Continent outside of France the *ancien régime* reigned supreme. With the exception of those of England, the Swiss cantons, and the United Netherlands all the European governments were arbitrary and most of them were inefficient. In all of the states a privileged class existed. The state churches were intolerant. Mediæval land arrangements and methods of cultivation hindered the development of agriculture everywhere in Europe. The privileges of the craft gilds hampered industry on the Continent. Innumerable tolls and interior customs lines interfered with trade. The states with such an antiquated organization proved to be no match for the liberated people of France.

THE WAR OF THE FIRST COALITION

Neither France nor the alliance formed by Austria and Prussia was ready for the war which began on April 20, 1792. The question of the future of Poland distracted the attention of the two German allies. Their armies had made little or no progress since the close of the Seven Years' War. Political agitation and the emigration of two thirds of its officers had disorganized the French army. In consequence the first forward movement of the French ended in a fiasco and in the battle of Valmy (September 20, 1792) the French checked the half-hearted advance begun by the Prussians toward the end of July. This victory at Valmy heartened the French out of all proportion to the importance of the battle.

Upon the retreat of the Prussians the French began a general advance across the frontiers. Tempted by the enthusiasm aroused in neighboring states by the "Rights of Man," two French armies entered Savoy and Nice; a third pushed into the Valley of the Rhine and seized the cities of Speyer, Worms, Mainz, and Frankfort; and a fourth overran the Austrian Netherlands after overwhelming its Austrian defenders at Jemappes (November 6, 1792) by enthusiasm and weight of numbers. Under the protection of the French armies Savoy and Nice voted for union with France; a convention of democrats from the occupied regions in the Rhine

Valley proclaimed at Mainz the reunion of the left bank of the Rhine with France; and the inhabitants of the Austrian Netherlands announced the fall of the Habsburgs. Stirred by these victories the National Convention voted to give assistance and fraternity to all peoples who wished for liberty.

The generous war of propaganda, however, soon became a selfish war of conquest. The representatives of the Convention levied requisitions on the people of wealth in the Austrian Netherlands and in the Rhenish provinces. In December, 1792, the Convention itself voted that the "liberated" regions should pay the cost of their liberation. In all the conquered provinces the French confiscated the ecclesiastical lands, replaced the aristocratic authorities with democrats, abolished feudal rights, and introduced the French system of government. When the inhabitants of the Austrian Netherlands voted for the independence of their country the representatives of the Convention tried to force them to unite with France.

The policies of the Convention and its representatives soon caused a reaction among the Powers of Europe. England objected to the conquest of the Austrian Netherlands and to the opening of the Scheldt River to navigation. The United Netherlands feared a democratic revolution and a French invasion. In the Kingdom of Naples Queen Caroline, a sister of Marie Antoinette, urged her pusillanimous husband on toward war. The offers of liberty to oppressed peoples and the execution of Louis XVI arrayed all of the Governments of Europe against the Republic of France. Most of them broke diplomatic relations with the French state, and France declared war against England and the United Netherlands on February 1, 1793, and against Spain in the following March. By the end of 1793 only Denmark, Sweden, Turkey, Venice, and Switzerland remained neutral.

A series of disasters followed the broadening of the conflict. The allies forced the French armies on the Rhine and in the Austrian Netherlands back into France. After failing in an attempt to lead his army against the Convention, Dumouriez, a trusted French leader, deserted his army and rode across the frontier. Two of the fortresses on the northeastern frontier of France designed by Vauban, the celebrated military engineer of Louis XIV, fell into the hands of the enemy. Five hostile armies pushed their way into France. The English fleet blockaded the French coast. The allies began to plan the dismemberment of France. More than half of the French provinces rose in revolt against the policies of the radicals in control of Paris. These events placed France in a desperate situation.

To the astonishment of Europe the French triumphed in their struggle with foreign invaders, domestic revolt, and political anarchy. The divisions among its enemies, the energy of the Convention, and the organization of a powerful army saved France. In Northern Europe Prussia and Austria intrigued for shares of Poland. In Northern France the allies halted their advance on Paris in order to divide the spoils. At Paris the leaders of the party of the Mountain, to meet the emergency, spurred into feverish activity the extraordinary instruments of government that had been created by the Convention, and put the whole French nation under martial law. The Convention placed first 300,000 men and later the whole nation (*levée en masse*) at the disposal of the State. The Government established forges, foundries, and powder works. The men of science gave their knowledge and their services. As a result of this extraordinary effort France finally trained and equipped nearly a million men.

These measures prepared the way for the sweeping French successes of 1793, 1794, and 1795. During the campaign of 1793 French armies cleared Alsace and Northern France of Austrian and Prussian troops and drove the forces of the King of Sardinia beyond the Alps. In June of the following year (1794) the French gained the stunning victory of Fleurus in the Austrian Netherlands. At home this splendid success convinced the majority of the French people that France no longer needed the "Terror." Abroad it opened the way for the French conquest of the United Netherlands (1794-95) and the left bank of the Rhine. In the meantime other French forces had driven the Spanish forces out of

Southern France and had penetrated into Northern Spain. These French victories led to the negotiation of treaties of peace with Spain, Prussia, Tuscany, and the United Netherlands.

The withdrawal of Prussia from the war greatly modified the political situation in Central Europe. In the Treaty of Basel (April 5, 1795) France agreed to evacuate the Prussian territories on the right bank of the Rhine, but postponed definitive territorial arrangements concerning the left bank of the Rhine until the conclusion of peace between France and the Holy Roman Empire. In a subsequent convention Prussia promised not to oppose the acquisition of the left bank of the Rhine by the French at the conclusion of peace between France and the Holy Roman Empire, and France guaranteed to Prussia a territorial indemnity on the right bank of the Rhine for its losses on the left bank of that river. Thus Prussia agreed to the dismemberment of the Empire which it was supposed to defend.

The conquest of the United Netherlands made the Dutch republic a satellite of France. In the Treaty of The Hague (May 16, 1795) the Dutch agreed to establish a defensive and offensive alliance with the French Republic, to cede to France certain territories south of the Rhine, to permit French troops to occupy the country for the duration of the war, and to furnish Dutch troops and ships for French military and naval operations. These provisions practically destroyed Dutch independence.

As a result of the elimination of so many states from the ranks of its enemies the French centered their attention in the campaign of 1796 on the forces of Austria and Sardinia. The French plans called for the advance of two French armies through Germany in the direction of Vienna and the march of a third and smaller army into Italy. The campaign in Germany failed completely, but the military genius of Napoleon Bonaparte, who had been appointed the commander of the army in Italy, in part as a reward for his defense of the Convention in 1795, when it was attacked by hostile National Guards from the conservative quarters of

Paris, turned the minor Italian campaign into one of the most brilliant military operations of history. Napoleon took charge of an army of thirty thousand ragged, unpaid men, and occupied the passes of the Maritime Alps and some of the cities of the Italian Riviera. Fifty thousand Austrians and Sardinians blocked the path into the Valley of the Po. The strategy of Napoleon cut the forces opposed to him in two, compelled the demoralized Sardinians to withdraw from the war and to surrender their most important fortresses, and forced the Austrians to abandon Lombardy[1] and to fall back on Mantua. Napoleon defeated four separate attempts to relieve the Austrian garrisons which were shut up in Mantua and compelled the Austrian forces in Italy to surrender. The subsequent march of Napoleon toward Vienna decided the Austrians to sue for peace. Their request for terms led first to a cessation of hostilities, then to the preliminary Treaty of Leoben, and finally to the Treaty of Campo Formio (October 17, 1797).

The first Italian campaign of Napoleon stirred the Italian people from their lethargy. For two centuries all ideas of change had encountered the two insuperable obstacles of the determined resistance of the privileged classes and the indifference of the ignorant and superstitious lower classes. Only the comparatively small middle class had been open to new ideas. To these inert masses Napoleon came with the promise of liberty, equality, and the constitution of an Italian state with a capital at Milan. His promises awakened democratic and nationalist aspirations in the breasts of the Italian people.

Later his onerous and vexatious demands turned their gratitude into hatred. From Lombardy Napoleon demanded two heavy war contributions, examples of its most beautiful works of art, and repeated requisitions for the army. From Modena, the Pope, Bologna, and Venice he required — and received — similar contributions. By these measures he fed, clothed, and paid the army of Italy, refilled the French treasury, and enriched the Louvre. He thus transferred over one

[1] By skillful maneuvers and the battle of Lodi.

hundred and fifty of the world's most famous paintings and many manuscripts and works of art from the public and private collections of Italy to the national collections at Paris. The plundering of their art collections and libraries, the arbitrary measures of Napoleon, and his disregard for their rights finally forced the Italians to interest themselves in public affairs.

The victories of Napoleon also profoundly modified the old political map of Northern Italy. By a treaty signed at Paris (May 15, 1796) Sardinia ceded Nice and Savoy to France. By the Treaty of Tolentino (February 17, 1797) the Pope transferred Avignon and the County of Venaissin to France and renounced his rights to the three legations of Bologna, Ferrara, and Ravenna. By the Treaty of Campo Formio (October 17, 1797) Austria lost the province of Lombardy. The Duchy of Modena and the Republic of Venice disappeared entirely. From the Duchy of Modena, the province of Lombardy, the three legations seized from the Pope, and the portion of Venetia west of the Adige River Napoleon formed the Cisalpine Republic, a state of 3,200,000 inhabitants with a capital at Milan. He retained the Ionian Isles of Venice for France and handed the remaining territories of the Venetian Republic over to Austria to compensate it for the loss of the Austrian Netherlands.

The first Italian campaign of Napoleon also brought two of the states of Northern Italy into a position of political vassalage to France. Napoleon abolished the feudal dues and the system of primogeniture in the Cisalpine Republic, and provided the new state with a constitution modeled after the directory at Paris, a tricolor flag (green, white, and red), and a national guard composed of Italian patriots; but he gave the new republic no real freedom. In January, 1798, the French Government summoned the Directors of the Cisalpine Republic to Paris and forced them to sign a defensive and offensive alliance entirely to the advantage of France. By this treaty the Italian state agreed to support a French army of occupation of twenty-five thousand men, to give France command of the country's military forces, and to permit France to enjoy special commercial privileges in its territories. In the preceding year the French had brought about the transformation of the independent oligarchical Republic of Genoa into the docile, democratic Ligurian Republic. These arrangements put the two Italian states into a position similar to that held by the Dutch Republic.

The Treaty of Campo Formio had an equally important influence on the political situation in Central Europe. In secret articles attached to that treaty Austria consented to the acquisition by the French of the Austrian Netherlands and pledged its assistance in obtaining from the Empire the formal cession of the left bank of the Rhine for France. France, on the other hand, promised to use its good offices to obtain for the Habsburg Power the archbishopric of Salzburg and part of Bavaria as an indemnity for its losses on the left bank of the Rhine. Since Prussia and Austria were predominant in Germany the treaties of Basel and Campo Formio really decided the fate of the German territories on the left bank of the Rhine.

THE STRUGGLE WITH ENGLAND

The elimination of Austria and Sardinia from the war left England to carry on the conflict alone. Neither France nor England could directly attack her opponent. France was supreme on land, but weak at sea. England was mistress of the seas, but without an army. During the early years of the war England had fought the French by blockading the coasts of France and the United Netherlands, by attacking the French colonies in the West Indies, and by paying the states of Europe to maintain armies in the field. During the same period the French had made a number of unsuccessful attempts to strike at England by sending expeditionary forces into Ireland to incite the Irish against their English conquerors. Upon his return from his victorious campaign in Italy, Napoleon Bonaparte persuaded the French Directors to permit him to seize Egypt and thus threaten the hold of England on India. He realized that inaction would dim the glamour of his recent exploits. The Directors understood

EXTENSION OF THE FRENCH REVOLUTION

well enough that the conquest of Egypt could have little effect on the fate of India, but they grasped at the opportunity to rid themselves of the troublesome general. The Egyptian campaign of Napoleon Bonaparte was the result of this situation.

The campaign started brilliantly. With an army of thirty-five thousand veteran troops and a well-equipped fleet Napoleon captured the strategic island of Malta from the decaying military order of the Knights of Saint John and reached Egypt in safety before the English fleet on duty in the Mediterranean learned of the real destination of the French expedition in preparation at Toulon. The conquest of Egypt quickly followed. In the celebrated battle of the Pyramids, near the city of Cairo, the French defeated and dispersed the forces of the military caste known as the Mamelukes, who really ruled the country. At this point, however, disasters began to overtake the French expedition. The English destroyed the French fleet at anchor in Aboukir Bay and cut off the French army in Egypt from France. In the following year (1799) the Turkish Government declared war on the French for their invasion of the Turkish province of Egypt, and the forces of the Pasha, aided by the English fleet and by Turkish reënforcements, repulsed the army of Napoleon before Acre in Syria and forced its retreat into Egypt. As a result of these disasters Egypt seemed to offer the young general nothing but ultimate defeat and surrender, while the news from Europe seemed to promise him opportunities for new triumphs. He decided to return to France. He accordingly abandoned his army and, accompanied by a few trusted companions, reached France after a succession of extraordinary adventures.

In spite of its failure the Egyptian expedition had important and interesting results. Immediately after his conquest of the country Napoleon reorganized its government. He conciliated the Moslems by appearing at the great mosque of Cairo dressed in Oriental costume and reciting Moslem litanies. He established municipal governments in the principal cities, assessed the taxed land more fairly, and consulted the natives concerning reforms. From these measures Napoleon gained additional administrative experience.

The scientific work of the expedition produced more lasting results. In the train of his army Napoleon had brought over a hundred distinguished scientists, archæologists, painters, and architects. They studied the sphinxes, the obelisks, the temple ruins, the climate, the soil, and the inundations of the Nile, and made a beginning toward the decipherment of the Egyptian hieroglyphs. They recorded the results of their scientific work in a monumental work of ten volumes. By their achievements these scientists laid the foundations of Egyptology and pushed back the beginnings of human history thousands of years.

THE DIRECTORY, 1795-99

From 1795 to 1799 the government finally established by the Convention ruled France. At home this corrupt government, known as the Directory, failed to solve the most pressing domestic problems. Abroad it lost the territories which had been conquered by General Bonaparte in the first Italian campaign. By its political and military failures the Directory prepared the way for the establishment of the dictatorship of Napoleon Bonaparte.

The first elections held under the Constitution of 1795 put the moderates in power. They were opposed on the left by the remnants of the party of the Mountain, which had been discredited by the Terror, and on the right by a small party of royalists. Although their club had been closed, the radical opponents of the Government were known as the Jacobins. They were opposed to the rule of property and were inclined as a matter of tactics or of conviction to a socialistic régime. The royalists masked themselves as conservative republicans, while conspiring in secret against the Directory. Some of them desired the restoration of the *ancien régime;* others, a return to the Constitution of 1791. The first group aimed at the restoration of the brother of Louis XVI as Louis XVIII; the second group planned to establish the Orleanist family on the throne. The dominant constitutional majority opposed a return to either monarchy or the Terror. The party life of the period of the Directory, however, was largely factitious and was carried on apart from the mass of the people. The nation generally had lost interest in everything but its most pressing needs.

The Constitution of 1795 entrusted political power to five Directors elected by the legislative branch of the Government. Under the National and Legislative Assemblies political authority had been vested in the legislature. Under the Convention it had been delegated most of the time to the Committee of Public Safety. Under the Directory it was lodged for the first time in the executive branch of the government. The Directors appointed the commanders of the armies, chose the ministers and diplomatic agents of the Government, and through commissioners controlled the administration of the departments and the communes. As a result of the powers concentrated in their hands the French people held the Directors accountable for the successes and failures of the Government.

The Directors faced a situation of extreme difficulty. In the fall of 1795 France was still at war with Austria, Sardinia, and England; the poor were suffering terribly from depreciated *assignats* and scarcity of food; the national finances were in disorder; and the pressing problems of the *émigrés*, the refractory priests, and the insurrection in the Vendèe were still unsettled. The permanence of the new Government was to depend on the solution of these problems.

In the face of this perplexing situation the Directors shortsightedly thought only of maintaining themselves in power. As a result of the wretchedness of the people, the practical bankruptcy of the Government, the extravagant display of army contractors and speculators in *assignats* and national property, the continuation of the war, and the failure to establish religious freedom and genuine constitutional government, public opinion in France began to run against the Directors. The election of 1797 put their party in an actual minority in the Council of the Elders and the Council of Five Hundred. Scarcely a dozen of the two hundred and sixteen ex-members of the National Convention who stood for office were reëlected and the newly elected Director was hostile to his colleagues. To save their power the old Directors planned to purge the legislative councils and the Directory itself of their conservative and royalist opponents. The three Directors who represented the party formerly in power caused the arrest of the editors and proprietors of opposition newspapers, of hostile legislators, and of the newly elected Director. Purged of the conservative and royalist deputies of the opposition, the legislative councils then condemned to deportation fifty-three deputies and the editors or proprietors of forty-two journals, annulled the elections in forty-nine departments, subjected the press to police control, and renewed the laws against the *émigrés* and the refractory priests. In the following year the Directors, by the use of similar methods, annulled the election of sixty-four Jacobin deputies. In the elections of 1799, however, the discredited Directors did not dare to thwart the will of the voters by a third *coup d'état*, and political power passed into the hands of their opponents.

The new men in control of the Government gave no better satisfaction than had their predecessors. To relieve the treasury they resorted to a forced loan levied on the rich. In order to stop the reign of assassination and pillage which was being carried on by the royalists, they passed a terrible law of hostages which made the relatives of the *émigrés* and the former nobles responsible for the maintenance of order in their departments and subject to deportation or fine. Brigands were everywhere; France was on the verge of financial ruin; and commerce and industry were practically destroyed. As a solution for this desperate situation a group of French politicians headed by Sieyès, a popular figure of the Revolutionary period, was planning to overthrow the Directory by a *coup d'état*. They were in search of a popular general who could give them military support when, suddenly, the return of Napoleon Bonaparte from Egypt was announced in France.

In the meantime the Directory had been equally unfortunate in its conduct of foreign affairs. The seizure of Malta had offended the half-mad Tsar Paul of Russia (1796–1801), who had been paid the empty honor of election to the Grand Mastership of the Order of the Knights of Saint John. The transformation of the United Netherlands into the Batavian Republic (1798), the Swiss Cantons into the Helvetian Republic (1798), and the Papal States into the Roman Republic (1798), the annexation of Geneva to France, and the dethronement (1798) of the King of Sardinia (on the Continent) alarmed all the Powers of Europe and aroused Austria into active hostility against France. England was already at war with the Directory. These conditions led to the formation of the second coalition in December, 1798, and to a renewal of the general European war in 1799. The aim of the allied Powers was to deprive France of its conquests and vassal states and to restore the French monarchy. Allied armies moved toward the Batavian Republic, Northern France, the Helvetian Republic, and Northern Italy. The French warded off the attacks on the Batavian and Helvetian Republics but lost the fruits of the Italian campaign of 1796. This was the military situation at the moment Napoleon Bonaparte landed in France after his secret return from Egypt.

THE ESTABLISHMENT OF NAPOLEON BONAPARTE IN POWER

For the next fifteen years the history of France was colored and modified by the remarkable personality of the young general, Napoleon Bonaparte, known later as Napoleon. This man was born in Corsica and was educated at the French Military Academy of Brienne. At fifteen he entered the army as a lieutenant of artillery. Handicapped by his Italian origin and comparatively humble birth he would probably never have been heard of under the old régime. The Revolution gave him a chance to display his remarkable military and administrative talents and to rise to important commands. His brilliant campaign in Northern Italy in 1796 made him the most distinguished soldier in

France. The reports of his spectacular victories in Egypt had enhanced his reputation. Sieyès and his group decided that his coöperation was indispensable.

After some hesitation Napoleon Bonaparte agreed to coöperate with the conspirators. As early as his first Italian campaign he had planned to make himself chief of the French Republic. Because he realized that the French were not yet ready to acclaim him as head of their state he had undertaken the expedition to Egypt. He saw in the plot of his fellow conspirators an opportunity for the realization of his personal ambitions.

The plans for the proposed *coup d'état* called for the appointment of three provisional consuls (Sieyès, Bonaparte, and Ducos) to carry on the administration and of two legislative commissions, one from each house, to draw up a new constitution for France. The Council of Elders was to decree the transfer of both legislative councils to Saint-Cloud, where they would be out of reach of the Jacobins of Paris. Sieyès and one of his colleagues in the Directory were to resign voluntarily. A third Director was to be intimidated into following their example. The three resignations would thus paralyze the executive power of the old government. Napoleon Bonaparte was to be entrusted with the command of the troops of Paris. Then by a judicious mixture of military force and parliamentary maneuvering the conspirators hoped to push their proposed measures through the legislative councils. They set November 9 (18th Brumaire) as the date for their *coup d'état*.

The conspirators carried through their plans with little regard for constitutional forms. They obtained without much difficulty the necessary decrees for the transfer of the legislative councils to Saint-Cloud and for the appointment of Napoleon Bonaparte to command of the troops, but on the following day at Saint-Cloud the legislators began to ask troublesome questions about the alleged Jacobin conspiracy which had been used as a pretext for the removal of the legislative councils. The conspirators had to scatter their opponents by the use of the troops and to put through late the following night, by a friendly minority of the dispersed legislators, the decrees appointing the three provisional consuls and the two legislative commissions.

By his dominating personality Napoleon Bonaparte quickly relegated his two colleagues into the background. The constitution which was finally worked out only slightly resembled the elaborate schemes of Sieyès for a balanced constitution. It really entrusted the executive power to Napoleon Bonaparte, as First Consul, but it camouflaged his real position in the Government by associating two other men with him in the consulship. By the new Constitution the First Consul appointed most of the agents of the consular Government and initiated legislation through a Council of State of his own selection. He had final decision in all matters of administration. At the suggestion of Sieyès the Constitution provided a cumbersome system of four assemblies: a Council of State, appointed by the First Consul, to propose the laws, a tribunate to discuss them, a legislative body to vote on them, and a conservative Senate to pass on their constitutionality. In practice the Council of State proved to be the most important of the four assemblies. The voters designated those eligible to office, but did not appoint the agents of the Government. They chose one tenth of their number as a communal list from which the central government was to select the communal officials. Those on the communal lists designated one tenth of their number for the departmental list. Finally those on the departmental lists picked one tenth of their number to make a national list of about six thousand names. In practice this elaborate scheme for appointing officials was scarcely used. The Constitution thus gave the Consuls more power than the Directors had ever exercised.

Napoleon Bonaparte realized that his maintenance in power in France depended on his ability to bring the European war to a speedy and honorable conclusion. Russia had already withdrawn from the war because of the treatment her troops had received at the hands of Austria, but England and Austria remained to be eliminated. As his navy was very inferior to that of England, Napoleon Bonaparte decided to strike the Habsburg Power a decisive blow in Upper Italy, the scene of his first Italian campaign. With great daring he led an army across the Alps by the Great Saint Bernard Pass, united his troops with reënforcements which had crossed the mountains by the way of the Saint Gotthard Pass, captured arms and supplies left by the Austrians at Milan, and cut off the main Austrian army from its base of supplies. The Austrians then had to fight or fall back on Genoa. The decisive battle of the campaign took place at Marengo near Alessandria. Though the French were outnumbered two to one, brilliant charges by the fresh troops of Desaix and the wearied dragoons of Kellermann turned defeat into victory just at the end of the battle. On the following day the Austrian commander signed a truce by which he agreed to retire into Venetia. By one brilliant stroke Napoleon Bonaparte had regained all that had been lost in Italy. By his victory at Hohenlinden (December 3, 1800), north of the Alps, Moreau completed the task of defeating Austria.

The two smashing victories of Marengo and Hohenlinden led to the negotiation of the Treaty of Lunéville (February 9, 1801). This agreement followed in the main the lines laid out in the Treaty of Campo Formio. It provided that the boundaries in Italy should be the same as those stipulated in the Treaty of Campo Formio, with the exception that the Grand Duchy of Tuscany should be handed over to France to be formed into the Kingdom of Etruria; that the Austrian Netherlands and the left bank of the Rhine should be ceded to France; and that only the hereditary princes of the Holy Roman Empire should be compensated with territory on the right bank of the Rhine for territorial losses on the left bank of that river.[1] The negotiation of this successful treaty gave Napoleon Bonaparte an indisputable hold on France.

The withdrawal of Austria from the war led to the negotiation of the treaty of Amiens (March 27, 1802) with England. Both countries felt the need of peace. English shipping had suffered severely from the depredations of French privateers,

[1] See the discussion of the Treaty of Campo Formio on pages 397-98.

EXTENSION OF THE FRENCH REVOLUTION

and the financial burdens of England were staggering. The French had lost their own colonies, most of the Dutch colonial possessions, and one or two Spanish colonies. By the terms of the Treaty of Amiens England kept only the former Dutch colony of Ceylon and the former Spanish island of Trinidad, and promised to restore Egypt to the Turkish Sultan and Malta to the Knights of Saint John. The treaty stipulated nothing about the situation on the Continent or about commerce. As a result of the Treaties of Lunéville and Amiens, France was at peace with all her neighbors for the first time in eleven years.

THE BENEFICENT DICTATORSHIP

Napoleon Bonaparte needed the period of peace given him by the Treaties of Lunéville and Amiens. He aimed to establish around France as a center a European confederacy under his own rule. His plans called for a France strong, rich, and powerful. Accordingly he devoted this time of quiet to introducing a series of beneficent reforms, and to consolidating his position in France and in Europe.

Immediately after it assumed power the consular Government adopted a number of measures calculated to reconcile public opinion to the new Government. Three days after the *coup d'état* the consuls abrogated the obnoxious law of hostages. A little later they made a beginning toward the repatriation of the *émigrés* and the refractory priests. The consular Government also substituted a regular war tax for the forced loan of the Directory. These measures tended to gain for the new Government the favor of the royalists, the Catholics, and the financiers.

The first major reform of the consular Government was the reorganization of the administrative system. The new law carried farther the centralizing tendencies of the Terror and the Directory. For administrative purposes it divided France into departments, arrondissements, and communes. At the head of each department was a prefect. He was assisted by a council of prefecture which considered questions arising between the administration and the citizen, and by a general council of the department which supervised the assessment of taxes and the expenditure of revenues. In each arrondissement, subordinate to the prefect, was a subprefect, who was assisted likewise by a council. Finally in each commune was a mayor and a communal council. The First Consul appointed the prefects, the subprefects, and the mayors of the larger cities. Although the prefects and subprefects resembled the intendants and subdelegates of the *ancien régime*, the new system of administration gave general satisfaction. Politicians of all parties found employment in the new administrative posts, and the really able men appointed to the more important offices soon brought order out of the general chaos. In its broad outlines the system of local government established by the First Consul has persisted until the present day.

The most pressing problem of the Government of the consulate was the lack of money. The Revolution had destroyed the unjust financial system of the *ancien régime*. The decade of civil disorder and foreign war had prevented the establishment of a successful system in its place. At the time of his accession to power the First Consul found the treasury practically empty, the army and the officials of the Government unpaid, taxes several years in arrears, and the Government living on the contributions of its vassal states and trying to pay its debts in paper that had no value except in payment of taxes. The First Consul sought to teach the people of France that the payment of taxes was a public duty. He appointed officials charged with the task of collecting taxes, collected arrears of taxes, made up the new tax lists, and replaced extravagance and corruption with economy and rigid inspection. After the battle of Marengo the Government began to pay certain classes of its creditors in coin. The financial policy of the First Consul resulted in a slight surplus for the year 1801–02.

The religious situation was also exceedingly confused. The vast majority of the French people were Catholics, but they were divided in allegiance between the Roman and the constitutional churches. In old France there were over half a million Calvinists and in Alsace 200,000 Lutherans. In the new departments on the left bank of the Rhine there were 370,000 Calvinists and Lutherans. Since the separation of Church and State and the reopening of the churches the religious bodies of France had been gradually solving the problems of maintaining religious worship under a régime of religious freedom. Two courses were open to the First Consul in regard to religion: a continuance of the policy of religious liberty and the adoption of the policy of state intervention. The autocratic instincts of Napoleon Bonaparte caused him to make the choice of state intervention. The result of this decision was the negotiation with the Pope of the Concordat of 1801.

The Concordat liquidated the past and regulated the future relations of Church and State. The past had left many troublesome problems. In the interest of peace and unity the Pope undertook to deprive the refractory bishops of their dioceses, agreed that the clergy should take an oath of submission to the State, and that they should pray publicly for the safety of the Republic and its consuls, and promised never to disturb the purchasers of confiscated Church property. The French Government, on the other hand, agreed to pay the clergy a stipend and to place at the disposal of the Church all the churches which had not been sold by the State. Both the Pope and the First Consul, therefore, made important concessions in an effort to settle the problems inherited from the past.

The future relations of Church and State offered less difficulty. The Concordat provided for a new circumscription of the dioceses and the parishes of France, for the nomination of bishops by the First Consul and their canonical institution in office by the Pope, for the appointment of parish priests by the bishops, and for the payment of a suitable stipend to the French clergy by the Government. The Church in general obtained the important right to receive pious bequests and the bishops the right to maintain cathedral chapters and seminaries for the education of priests. The Concordat made no mention of the status of the regular clergy. The French Government merely recognized the Catholic religion as the religion of the majority of the French people and guaranteed its free exercise. The agreement subjected the Church, however, to such police regulations as the Government deemed necessary for the public tranquillity.

In negotiating the Concordat the First Consul, according to his custom, looked mainly at the present; the Papal authorities looked mainly to the future. The document satisfied Napoleon Bonaparte because it solved three of his immediate problems. It restored to the French people the normal exercise of their old religion and confirmed their titles to the Church lands which were purchased during the Revolution. The refractory priests and their adherents also ceased to oppose the Government and became supporters of the new political régime. On the other hand, by reuniting Church and State the Concordat prepared the way for future trouble. A quarrel soon arose between Bonaparte and the Pope which ended in the excommunication of Bonaparte and the imprisonment of the Pope. Throughout the nineteenth century the problem of the relations of Church and State continued to be a source of danger and irritation. Some historians consider the negotiation of the Concordat one of the worst blunders in the career of Napoleon Bonaparte.

The new Concordat encountered much opposition. The First Consul forced it through the various assemblies only after five months of struggle. In order to make the agreement more acceptable to its opponents, he incorporated with it at the time of its publication as the law of France (April 8, 1802) seventy-seven Organic Articles for the Catholic Church drawn up in the spirit of the Declaration of Gallican Liberties of 1682. In a number of points these Organic Articles annulled or modified the Concordat which had just been negotiated. So from the beginning the agreement with the Pope failed to establish harmony between Church and State.

At the same time that the Concordat was promulgated as the law of France the First Consul issued Organic Articles for the Protestant sects. The tendency of the regulations was to put Catholics, Calvinists, and Lutherans on the same footing. This official recognition gave great satisfaction to the Protestants.

In the same year (1801) the Government began to permit large numbers of *émigrés* to return to France. The first list contained about fifty thousand names and included persons that in no real sense were opposed to the Revolution. In the following year the Government allowed most of the remaining royalists to reënter France. In case their lands had not been sold it restored to them their estates. Only about one thousand militant royalists remained excluded from the country.

During the consulate, likewise, the Government made a substantial beginning on the long-delayed task of codifying the laws of France. In medieval times Roman law had predominated in Southern France and many local customs in Northern France. During the modern period a mass of royal ordinances had been superimposed on these medieval foundations. This situation resulted in a confusing maze of legal rules that were known only to the initiated few. The reform of French law had, therefore, been one of the insistent demands of the *cahiers* that were forwarded to the Estates General in 1789. Owing to the foreign war and to domestic disorders the legislative bodies of the Revolutionary period never completed the task of codifying the laws of France. Within two years after the inauguration of the Consulate, however, the Government appointed commissions for drawing up a civil code, a criminal code, a commercial code, a rural code, and a code of civil procedure. Only the first completed its task during the Consulate. The civil code was the work of a group of able lawyers, but was modified in particular points by the orders of the First Consul. It was a compromise between the Revolution and the *ancien régime*. It guaranteed civil equality and civil liberty, but consecrated the régime of property in France. All its provisions were drawn up in the interest of the propertied classes. The influence of the civil code has been tremendous. Under its later name of Code Napoléon it was introduced into all the regions annexed by Napoleon to France and into several of the vassal states. It is still the law in Belgium, Geneva, and Luxemburg. It was utilized in codifying the laws of Italy, Romance Switzerland, Rumania, Egypt, Canada, Louisiana, Bolivia, Haiti, and Japan.

In 1802 a combination of forces led to the establishment of the Consulate for life. The First Consul wished to make his power monarchical. Personal interest caused many persons in France to hope for the maintenance of his rule. Frenchmen in general felt profoundly grateful to him for his beneficent dictatorship and the establishment of peace with Austria and England. His friends planned to persuade the Senate to elect Napoleon Bonaparte as Consul for life. The majority in that body, however, tried to head off the proposal by reëlecting him First Consul for a second term of ten years. Thwarted by the Senate, Napoleon Bonaparte caused the question of the consulship for life to be submitted to a popular referendum (*plébiscite*). The people ratified the proposed amendment to the Constitution by an almost unanimous vote. By this vote the French really abdicated in favor of Napoleon Bonaparte the position of sovereignty that they had assumed in 1789.

The First Consul took advantage of the overwhelming vote on his behalf to increase his power. Without any authorization at all he proceeded to modify the Constitution of 1799. He assumed the right to designate his successor and to ratify treaties, and secured control of the Senate through assumption of the right to appoint additional members, and of officials by acquiring the right to select his subordinates from the names proposed by newly established electoral assemblies. The new Constitution thus made the First Consul practically a monarch.

A return to monarchical manners quickly followed the change in the Constitution. In 1802 the French celebrated the birthday of Napoleon Bonaparte as if he had been one of their old line of monarchs. His civil list or salary was increased from 500,000 to 6,000,000 francs. A royal court was gradually reconstructed at the Tuileries Palace, at which were to be found the returned nobles of the *ancien régime* and the notables who had distinguished themselves in the service of the First Consul. The titles "monsieur" and "madame" reappeared. The creation of a Legion of Honor with distinctions and grades of honor gave France a partial substitute for its old nobility. The celebration of the old holidays in the old ways consecrated by custom was renewed. Paris resumed its position as the center of fashion.

The monarchy which was thus gradually restored in fact was reëstablished in name by a decree of the Senate that was adopted in 1804. As a result of this measure France became an Empire, the First Consul, the Emperor, and Napoleon Bonaparte, Napoleon I.

CONSULAR IMPERIALISM

At the same time that he was improving French institutions the First Consul was extending his influence far beyond the borders of France. During this period he sent his agents into the Near and Far East in the interests of France, brought the Batavian, Helvetian, Cisalpine, and Ligurian Republics into more complete subjection, reorganized Germany in such a manner as to advance French interests, obtained control of the foreign policy of Spain and made a beginning toward the reëstablishment of France as a colonial power. These encroachments of the First Consul alarmed the other states of Europe and led to the formation of the third coalition against France.

In September, 1802, Napoleon sent Sebastiani, under the guise of a commercial agent, into the Levant with instructions to note with care the condition of the ports and the state of the arsenals, and to offer the good offices of the First Consul to the chiefs of Egypt and Syria. The report of Sebastiani was published in the *Moniteur*, the official newspaper of France. His statement that six thousand French troops would be sufficient to reconquer Egypt convinced every one that at the first favorable opportunity Napoleon would make an attempt to reconquer that country.

The first Consul desired to make the circle of vassal republics on the continent of Europe more responsive to his will. Modeling the governments of the vassal states after that of France, the Directory had set up directories in the Batavian,[1] Cisalpine, and Ligurian Republics. With his absolutist tendencies, Napoleon Bonaparte desired to mould these states in the direction of monarchies. In the Batavian Republic the new Constitution imposed by him diminished the power of the legislative assemblies, weakened the influence of the people over their government, and concentrated political power in the hands of a regency dominated by the First Consul of France. At Genoa Bonaparte augmented the power of the executive and nominated one of his creatures to the office of Doge. Upon the death of its old duke, the First Consul annexed the Duchy of Parma to France. He also divided the Sardinian province of Piedmont into six departments, and incorporated it into France, deprived the Kingdom of Etruria of the island of Elba, and gave the Canton of Valais, which dominated the important Simplon Pass, a constitution patterned after that of the Consulate. In the Cisalpine Republic Napoleon Bonaparte was made president of the Republic, and the name of the state was changed to the Italian Republic. The First Consul likewise intervened between the federal and unitarian factions of Switzerland and imposed a constitution on the Helvetian Republic.[2]

The Treaties of Basel, Campo Formio, and Lunéville made the reorganization of Germany necessary. The military prestige of France gave its ruler the deciding voice in the redistribution of German territory. The reorganization of Germany was nominally the work of a committee of the Empire known as the Imperial Deputation. In reality the First Consul or Talleyrand, his minister of foreign affairs, made all the important decisions. In an effort to win the good will of the latter, the representatives of the German princes filled his anterooms, patted his poodle dog, played

---

[1] The Republic of the United Netherlands had been renamed the Batavian Republic in 1798.
[2] The Swiss cantons had received this name in 1798.

drop the handkerchief with his favorite niece, and made presents of jeweled snuffboxes filled with coin of the realm to the minister himself. The final results of the long negotiations were embodied in a document known as the Principal Decree of the Imperial Deputation (February 25, 1803).[1]

This measure greatly simplified the map of Germany. Ninety-seven German states disappeared from the left bank of the Rhine, and one hundred and twelve from the right bank. The ecclesiastical states, the free cities, and the petty states were the chief sufferers. The archbishopric of Mainz, which was transferred to Regensburg on the Danube River, was the only ecclesiastical state to survive. All the city states except Bremen, Hamburg, Lübeck, Frankfort-on-the-Main, Nuremberg, and Augsburg disappeared. Prussia, Austria, and the substantial states of Southern Germany, as Bavaria, Württemberg, Baden, Hesse-Darmstadt, and Hesse-Cassel, were the chief states to benefit from the exchanges of territory. In reorganizing Germany Napoleon Bonaparte aimed to cement good relations with Prussia and to reduce the hundreds of petty, inconsequential political divisions to a few moderate-sized, easily managed states. In carrying out this plan, however, he unwittingly laid the foundations for the later unification of Germany.

The significance of this territorial reorganization is well illustrated by the State of Bavaria. In 1799 the Elector of Bavaria was ruler, nominally at least, of a compact group of territories in the valley of the Upper Danube and of several detached territories in the valley of the Rhine. The compact group of territories included Upper and Lower Bavaria, Neuburg, Sulzbach, and the Upper Palatinate. The more important of the detached possessions of the Elector of Bavaria were the Rhine Palatinate and the Duchies of Zweibrücken, Julich, and Berg. By the Treaty of Lunéville the Elector lost to France the larger part of the Rhine Palatinate, the Duchies of Julich and Zweibrücken, and several small lordships. By the Principal Decree of the Imperial Deputation he ceded the remainder of the Rhine Palatinate to Baden,

[1] This body was a committee representing the Holy Roman Empire.

Hesse-Darmstadt, and Nassau-Ussingen, and several bits of detached territory to the rulers of the lands in which they were enclaved. As a compensation for these territorial losses Bavaria received all, or important parts, of five former bishoprics, seventeen former free imperial cities and towns, twelve abbeys, and the provostship of Kempten. These exchanges of territory gave Bavaria, in place of its former scattered domains, an enlarged state composed of contiguous territories.

The Principal Decree of the Imperial Deputation also transferred to the Catholic states of Germany much of the power that was formerly exercised by the bishops and an immense amount of ecclesiastical property. It put at the disposal of the sovereigns of Germany all of the property of the cathedral and collegiate chapters, the abbeys, and the endowed monasteries and convents, together with all their rights, capital, and revenues, and gave these rulers the privilege of suppressing or preserving them as they chose. In most instances the secular rulers grasped at the opportunity to seize the accumulated wealth of the Church. In the single State of Bavaria the property of sixty-six monastic institutions came into the possession of the Elector. As in France, however, the Bavarian Government made provision for the pensioning of the administrators and conventuals of the chapters, abbeys, monasteries, and convents, and encouraged them to resume a normal life in the world as teachers or parish priests, but established central houses for the care of the old, the sick, and the religiously minded.

At the same time the power of the bishops to oppose the secular authorities in the weaker states was practically destroyed. Prior to the Napoleonic period the bishops ordered or made in person visitations of their dioceses, and judged in their courts the criminal cases of the clergy and cases concerning the wills of the clergy. Any invasion of these rights created an outcry which brought Austria to the assistance of the "oppressed" prelates. The Principal Decree of the Imperial Deputation deprived the bishops of their power, while leaving them their rank and personal dignity.

EXTENSION OF THE FRENCH REVOLUTION

The intervention of France in the reorganization of the Holy Roman Empire therefore extended many of the changes of the French Revolution to Germany and solved in the interest of the State many problems of long standing. It simplified the map, subjected the bishops and the clergy to the jurisdiction of the State, and stopped the steady accumulation of property in the hands of the Church. As a result of its reorganization Germany took a long step toward transforming the *ancien régime* into modern Germany.

The story of Spanish diplomacy during this period is a complicated one. Early in 1793 Spain had become involved in the general European war with France, but like Prussia and several other of the European Powers it had made peace with France in 1795, losing Spanish San Domingo to France as a result of its participation in the war. In the following year the treatment received by Spain at the hands of England drove it into a military alliance with France. Its experiences, however, as an ally of France were far from happy. In 1800, as a result of the threats of Napoleon Bonaparte, it secretly receded Louisiana to France in return for the enlargement of the domains of the Duke of Parma. In the same year the First Consul compelled Spain to go to war with Portugal in order to force that country to break its alliance with England. Finally by the treaty of peace signed at the time of the Treaty of Amiens Spain lost the island of Trinidad to England.

The First Consul planned also to make France a colonial power again. With this object in view he bullied Spain, as has been explained, into ceding the province of Louisiana to France, and sent a military expedition to bring into subjection the practically independent republic which had been set up in the island of San Domingo. He never carried out his plans. Yellow fever destroyed the expedition to the West Indies, and the reopening of the war with England cut short his plans concerning Louisiana. To prevent this latter territory from falling into the hands of England, the First Consul sold it to the United States in 1803 for $15,000,000. The sale of Louisiana to the United States was one of the most important political acts of the whole career of Napoleon Bonaparte.

REFERENCES

GENERAL ACCOUNTS OF THE NAPOLEONIC PERIOD
  H. E. Bourne, *The Revolutionary Period in Europe*, chapters XV–XXVI.
  C. A. Fyffe, *A History of Modern Europe*, vol. I.
  C. J. H. Hayes, *A Political and Social History of Modern Europe*, vol. I, pp. 512–81.
  C. D. Hazen, *The French Revolution and Napoleon*, chapters VI–X.
  L. H. Holt and A. W. Chilton, *European History, 1789–1815*, chapters VI–XIV.
  J. A. R. Marriott, *The Remaking of Modern Europe*, chapters IV–X.
  J. H. Robinson and C. Beard, *The Development of Modern Europe*, vol. I, chapters XIV, XV.
  J. H. Rose, *The Revolutionary and Napoleonic Era*, chapters VI–X.
  E. R. Turner, *Europe since 1789*, chapter III.
  Histoire générale, vol. IX.
  Histoire de France contemporaine, vol. III.

BIOGRAPHIES OF NAPOLEON
  A. M. Broadley, *Napoleon in Caricature, 1795–1821*.
  The Corsican.
  H. A. L. Fisher, *Napoleon*.
  A. Fournier, *Napoleon the First*.
  R. M. Johnston, *Napoleon*.
  J. C. Ropes, *The First Napoleon*.
  J. H. Rose, *The Life of Napoleon I*.
  W. M. Sloane, *Napoleon*.

EUROPE ON THE EVE OF THE NAPOLEONIC PERIOD
  L. H. Holt and A. W. Chilton, *History of Europe, 1789–1815*, chapter VI.

THE FIRST ITALIAN CAMPAIGN
  H. E. Bourne, *The Revolutionary Period in Europe*, pp. 237–47.
  Cambridge Modern History, vol. VIII, chapter XVIII.
  H. A. L. Fisher, *Napoleon*, chapter II.
  A. Fournier, *Napoleon the First*, chapter V.
  C. A. Fyffe, *History of Modern Europe*, vol. I, chapter III.
  R. M. Johnston, *Napoleon*, pp. 27–44.
  J. H. Rose, *Life of Napoleon I*, vol. I, chapters V–VII.

OVERTHROW OF THE DIRECTORY AND ESTABLISHMENT OF THE CONSULATE
  Cambridge Modern History, vol. X, chapter XXII.
  A. Fournier, *Napoleon the First*, chapter VII.
  C. A. Fyffe, *History of Modern Europe*, vol. II, pp. 189–203.
  R. M. Johnston, *Napoleon*, pp. 59–78.
  J. H. Rose, *The Life of Napoleon I*, vol. I, chapter X.

THE BENEFICENT DICTATORSHIP
  H. E. Bourne, *The Revolutionary Period in Europe*, chapter XVII.
  Cambridge Modern History, vol. IX, chapters V–VII.
  H. A. L. Fisher, *Napoleon*, chapter IV.
  A. Fournier, *Napoleon the First*, chapter IX.
  R. M. Johnston, *Napoleon*, chapter VII.
  J. H. Rose, *Life of Napoleon I*, vol. I, chapter XII.

CHAPTER XVIII
NAPOLEONIC EUROPE

NAPOLEON rose to power on the shoulders of the patriotic nationalists of revolutionary France. As time went on he forgot more and more the true interests of France and used the French nation merely as a tool for carrying out his world ambitions. After his elevation to the imperial dignity he brought the South Germans, Southern Italy, Central Germany, Prussia, and finally Poland under his sway. Only England offered steady and unyielding opposition to his plans. For a time he seemed to change at will the boundaries and institutions of the states of the Continent. In the end the slow, steady pressure of the English fleet and the subsidies paid to the continental Powers from the English treasury combined with the growing resentment at his tyranny and the rising tide of national patriotism among the peoples of Europe to hurl Napoleon from his position of dominance.

ENGLAND DURING THE REVOLUTIONARY PERIOD

At first the English showed great sympathy for the ideas of the French reformers. They believed that the French were going to set up a constitutional system like their own and hoped that the similarity in their governments would draw the two countries closer together. The prime minister, William Pitt the Younger, looked with friendly eyes on the movement, and Fox, one of his chief Whig opponents, thought the French Revolution the greatest thing that had happened in the history of the world. In the larger towns people formed clubs to spread the revolutionary principles. A few extremists wished to remodel the English Government after the French.

In time, however, the excesses of the French Revolution began to frighten the English. Thoughtful conservatives came to the conclusion that the movement tended to upset states rather than to reform them. Late in 1790 Edmund Burke embodied this point of view in his famous pamphlet *Reflections on the French Revolution*. In this work he pointed out the great differences between the spirit of the French reformers and the leaders of the English Revolution of 1688. The English had limited themselves to correcting the abuses in their old constitution. The French had attempted to alter all their institutions. In the end the great majority of Englishmen followed Burke.

Even Pitt finally came round to Burke's way of thinking. In spite of his old liberal leanings he initiated a policy of repression. He ceased to support the movement for parliamentary reform on the ground that it was not a time for hazardous experiments. He suspended the Habeas Corpus Act, put down even lawful agitation, caused an Alien Act to be passed which gave the Government power to remove suspected foreigners from the country, and put in prison many leaders of the revolutionary clubs. Finally at Pitt's instigation Parliament passed a law which made uttering words against the authority of the King treason and exciting hatred against the Government or the Constitution a misdemeanor.

From 1793 to 1802 England was continuously at war with France. In opposing the Revolution Pitt showed no special capacity. He joined the great coalitions against France, spent vast sums in subsidizing his continental allies, and frittered away the resources of the country in aiding royalist plots and risings against the revolutionary governments of France. In the end he had little to show for his great expenditures.

At home the policy of Pitt threw the country into financial difficulties. The subsidies paid to foreign Powers drew much of the gold and silver out of the country. Perfectly solvent merchants could not meet their debts because of the scarcity of money. To save them Parliament had to authorize the Bank of England to suspend cash payments. For the next twenty years England depended on bank notes for currency.

The peace signed at Amiens in 1802 proved little more than a truce. The consular imperialism contributed greatly to the renewal of the war between England and France. The French tariffs followed the advance of French political influence and excluded English goods from Holland and Italy as well as from France. The merchants and manufacturers of England found the peace more ruinous than the war. This situation finally created a war party in England. The First Consul aggravated conditions by publishing a report[1] in the French official newspaper which seemed to threaten a new attack on Egypt. Under these circumstances England hesitated to evacuate the island of Malta in accordance with the terms of the Treaty of Amiens and thereby greatly angered the First Consul. The English demand for the indemnification of the King of Sardinia and for the evacuation of Holland and Switzerland finally precipitated the war.

Since he could not strike at England directly, the First Consul resorted to a variety of indirect measures. Within two weeks after the reopening of hostilities twenty thousand French troops invaded Hanover. Almost simultaneously fifteen thousand French troops marched into the Kingdom of Naples to insure its neutrality. In the Iberian Peninsula the First Consul compelled both Spain and Portugal to unite with France against England on the most humiliating terms. Along the English Channel he gathered fleets of small boats and a vast army composed of contingents furnished by France and its vassal states with the avowed object of invading England. The proposed invasion kept England in alarm, drained her resources by compelling her to resort to extraordinary measures of defense, and furnished the First Consul an excellent excuse for maintaining a large army ready to strike quickly if, as he secretly desired, war should break out on the Continent.

Napoleon seems to have gradually realized, as time passed, that he must conquer the English fleets blockading the French coasts. He forced his ally, Charles IV of Spain, to build a great navy and made repeated efforts to unite the French and Spanish naval contingents that were shut up by the English fleet in the various French and Spanish ports.

[1] Of Sebastiani.

The decisive naval battle of the war did not occur until October, 1805, shortly after the renewal of the war on the Continent. After failing to unite his naval detachments in one great fleet, Napoleon ordered Villeneuve, in command of the fleet at Cadiz, to attack the English under the command of the celebrated admiral, Lord Nelson. The fleets met off Cape Trafalgar. The battle resulted in a decisive victory for the English. This great victory gave them undisputed command of the sea for the remaining nine years of the war and put an end to their fear of a French invasion of England.

THE WAR OF THE THIRD COALITION AND ITS RESULTS

In the meantime England had been working toward the formation of another great alliance against France. After considerable delay Russia joined the alliance on condition that it should receive a large subsidy, but the Habsburg Power held back until the annexation of the Ligurian Republic and the coronation of Napoleon as King of Italy [1] seemed to threaten Austria with the loss of the province of Venetia. The three allied Powers declared for the reëstablishment of the balance of power, the freeing of Holland, Italy, and Switzerland from French control, and the return of Piedmont to the King of Sardinia. Prussia, however, continued the policy of neutrality which it had consistently followed since the signing of the Treaty of Basel.

The first concern of both Austria and Napoleon was to gain the alliance of the South German states, which had benefited so much by the Principal Decree of the Imperial Deputation. In a vain effort to intimidate them into an alliance, Austria rashly advanced an army of eighty thousand men toward Ulm on the western confines of Bavaria, instead of waiting for the advancing Russians. After agonizing moments of doubt the German princes decided for Napoleon. Meanwhile the French divisions were closing in on the Austrians at Ulm like the fingers of a great hand. Before the incapable Austrian commander was aware of their presence, the French had surrounded him and cut off his retreat. After the failure

[1] The former Italian Republic became the Kingdom of Italy in 1805.

of a half-hearted effort to cut his way out, he, with sixty thousand of his troops, surrendered unconditionally to Napoleon. As a result of the battle of Ulm the French occupied Vienna and the Austrian court, and a handful of Austrian troops joined the oncoming Russians.

Napoleon was now in a distinctly critical position. His army was far from its base of supplies and inferior in numbers to the advancing Russians. Neutral Prussia for a moment held the fate of Europe in its hands. In this crisis Napoleon rose to supreme heights. He spun out the diplomatic negotiations with Prussia and to all appearances offered the Russians battle on their own terms. His policy resulted in the victory of Austerlitz (December 2, 1805). This great victory left him in a position to dictate his own terms to both Prussia and Austria.

Prussia paid dearly for its failure to seize the favorable opportunity presented to it before Austerlitz. Napoleon half tempted, half bullied it into an alliance with France, and forced it to cede to France the Prussian territories of Cleves, Neuchatel, Ansbach, and Bayreuth and to close its ports to English commerce. For these concessions it received the long-desired territory of Hanover. Prussia paid for the French alliance by a war with England which caused the loss of four hundred Prussian vessels.

Austria was forced to sign the Treaty of Pressburg (December 26, 1805). By this agreement she ceded Venetia, Dalmatia, and Istria, with the exception of Trieste, to the new Kingdom of Italy; Tyrol, Vorarlberg, and the former bishoprics of Brixen, Trent, Passau, and Augsburg to Bavaria; and smaller possessions to Württemberg and Baden; recognized the new titles assumed with the permission of Napoleon by the Kings of Bavaria and Württemberg and the Grand Duke of Baden and their independence of the Holy Roman Empire. As a slight compensation for these enormous losses Austria received the former archbishopric of Salzburg. The treaty cost Austria three million of her subjects and one sixth of her revenues.

The battle of Austerlitz resulted likewise in the dethronement of the Italian Bourbons. French troops entered Naples, and the Neapolitan court fled to Sicily, where it remained during the rest of the Napoleonic period. In March, 1806, Napoleon proclaimed his oldest brother, Joseph Bonaparte, King of Naples with the title of King of the Two Sicilies.

This was but an incident in Napoleon's general policy of rewarding the members of his family and his faithful lieutenants. In June, 1806, he appointed his brother Louis ruler of the former Batavian Republic with the title of King of Holland. He made two of his sisters princesses of small Italian principalities. He made his brother-in-law, Murat, Grand Duke of Berg, a Rhenish principality which had been ceded to Napoleon by Bavaria. Berthier, his trusted friend and chief of staff, became Prince of Neuchatel. Napoleon also married three members of his family to members of the reigning families of Bavaria, Württemberg, and Baden.

The victory of Austerlitz resulted further in the establishment of the Confederation of the Rhine and the disruption of the Holy Roman Empire. By the final treaty of organization (July 12, 1806) Bavaria, Württemberg, Baden, Hesse-Darmstadt, Nassau, and several smaller states of Germany were organized in a confederation, with Napoleon as Protector. On August 1st they formally announced to the Imperial Diet their withdrawal from the Empire. A few days later the Emperor, who had assumed the title of Emperor of Austria two years before (1804) in anticipation of the dissolution of the Empire, laid down the imperial crown and brought to an end an Empire that dated back to Charlemagne, with traditions and pretensions which linked it to that of Augustus. By the terms of the new agreement the sixteen states of the Confederation of the Rhine entered into a defensive and offensive alliance with France and agreed to furnish Napoleon 63,000 troops in case of war. Before the end of the Napoleonic period all the states of Germany except Prussia and Austria had joined the Confederation.

THE WAR OF THE FOURTH COALITION (1806-07) AND ITS RESULTS

In the meantime the war spirit had been rising in Prussia. The formation of the Confederation of the Rhine had given umbrage to many Prussians. The discovery that Napoleon, with entire disregard of the claims of Prussia, had offered to restore to England the territory of Hanover, which Prussia had just bought at the price of important cessions of territory to Napoleon and of a war with England involving the loss of four hundred Prussian ships, decided even the wavering Frederick William III of Prussia for war. Early in August, 1806, the King ordered the mobilization of the Prussian army, appealed to the Tsar for aid, and strove to get in touch with the English Government. These measures aroused the upper classes of Prussia to the highest pitch of enthusiasm. In answer to these preparations Napoleon mobilized the French army.

The military campaign which followed was short and decisive. The battles of Jena and Auerstadt quickly decided the fate of Prussia. The French veterans proved their superiority to the Prussian troops and drove them in wild disorder from the field. Within six weeks after the battle the pursuing French troops had captured every fortified city west of the Oder River except a few in Silesia.

Napoleon made excellent use of his astounding victory over Prussia. From the old capital of Frederick the Great he issued the Berlin Decree, which inaugurated the "Continental System," designed to bring England to terms. He also sent French forces into Hesse-Cassel, Brunswick, and Hanover in Central Germany and toward Warsaw in Poland. Immediately upon his arrival at Berlin he had sent agents into Prussian and Russian Poland in the hope of using their national enthusiasm to advance his own political and military schemes. His occupation of Central Germany prepared the way for the creation of the Napoleonic Kingdom of Westphalia. His intrigues with the Poles and his advance into Poland led to the raising of a Polish national guard of sixty thousand men by voluntary enlistment, the defeat of Russia in the campaign of 1807, and the establishment of the Duchy of Warsaw.

Two more battles had to be fought to complete the discouragement of Russia. While attempting to surprise the Prussian court at Koenigsberg during the winter of 1807, one of the French generals brought on the bloody but indecisive battle of Eylau. In the following June Napoleon drove the Russians across the Niemen River in the greatest disorder as a result of the battle of Friedland. This great victory led to the establishment of peace, the dismemberment of Prussia, and the creation of the Duchy of Warsaw and the Kingdom of Westphalia.

The peace negotiations began at a famous interview between Tsar Alexander of Prussia and Napoleon which took place on a raft in the Niemen River near Tilsit in East Prussia. The negotiations resulted in the Treaty of Tilsit (July 7, 1789). By this agreement France gained the permission of Russia to occupy most of the ports in Northern and Western Germany, its recognition of the new vassal states created by Napoleon, and its promise to coöperate in enforcing against England the "Continental System" inaugurated by the Berlin Decree. Napoleon and the Tsar also agreed to coerce Sweden, Denmark, and Portugal into closing their ports to English commerce and into declaring war on England. Prussia fared far worse than Russia in the treaty. Napoleon forced Prussia to cede practically all of its former provinces on the left bank of the Elbe to the new Kingdom of Westphalia or to the Grand Duchy of Berg and the provinces obtained by the first and second partitions of Poland to the Grand Duchy of Warsaw, to renounce possession of the city of Danzig, and to agree to coöperate in enforcing the "Continental System" of Napoleon by closing the ports of Prussia to English commerce. Russia emerged from the war of the fourth coalition with its territory and its dignity intact; Prussia came out of the struggle humiliated by the studied insults of Napoleon at Tilsit and mutilated by the loss of half of its provinces.

From the former German states of Brunswick and Hesse-

Cassel and most of the Prussian provinces on the left bank of the Elbe Napoleon created the artificial Kingdom of Westphalia. The new state had no natural boundaries and its population of two millions had no unity of feeling. Napoleon intrusted to the superficial talents of his brother Jerome the almost superhuman task of welding these discordant German elements into a state with French institutions.

From the Polish territory taken from Prussia by the Treaty of Tilsit Napoleon formed the Duchy of Warsaw, a state of 2,300,000 inhabitants. The Duchy was but a fragment of the Poland of 1772. From fear of offending the Tsar Napoleon did not use the name Poland to designate the new state. He offered the title of Duke of Warsaw to the new King of Saxony. The pleasant memories retained by the Poles of the rule of the Saxon royal house over Poland in the eighteenth century made the choice of Napoleon a particularly happy one.

THE CONTINENTAL SYSTEM

The Treaty of Tilsit marks the nadir of the fortunes of the states that were opposed to Napoleon. On the morrow of Tilsit began the reaction of the people of Europe against the "Continental System," the national uprising in Spain, and the movement for the regeneration of Prussia. These were three of the most important factors in bringing about the final overthrow of Napoleon.

In promulgating the Berlin Decree against Great Britain Napoleon applied an old French policy on a wider scale. The idea of compelling the surrender of England by isolating it commercially had early laid hold of the minds of French statesmen. They argued that English prosperity was based on commerce. If Europe could be closed to English wares, Great Britain could be starved into submission. With this object in view both the National Convention and the Directory had passed measures that were designed to operate against the importation of English goods. The decrees issued by Napoleon for the same purpose are usually known as the "Continental System." The first measure of Napoleon was the decree issued from Berlin. This decree declared the British Isles in a state of blockade and prohibited all commerce and communication with them and all trade in British goods. The kingdoms of Spain, Holland, Etruria, and Italy were also expected to apply the system. By the Treaty of Tilsit Prussia and Russia [1] promised to enforce the system in their dominions. These measures legally debarred English trade from the greater part of the continent of Europe.

England replied to the challenge of Napoleon by a series of orders in council. An order of January, 1807, forbade trade between ports from which British ships were excluded. Orders in council issued in November of the same year declared all ports in a state of blockade from which British ships were excluded, declared trade with countries excluding British ships or trade in the products of such countries to be unlawful, and required neutral ships wishing to trade with the Continent to stop at a British port and to pay certain duties. Napoleon replied to these English orders in council in the Milan Decree of 1807, which made a lawful prize of war any neutral ship that stopped at an English port or that paid the required tax.

The decrees of Napoleon and the British orders in council put neutrals in a difficult position. Up to this point neutral shipping had made enormous profits, and the trade of neutral countries had grown by leaps and bounds. The English orders in council now permitted neutral trade with the Continent only on terms which subjected neutral shipping to the danger of capture and confiscation by the agents of Napoleon. The United States was the chief sufferer from the Continental System. The danger to American shipping and the inability of the United States to compel the respect of its rights led President Jefferson to recommend the Embargo Act of 1807, which was designed to keep American ships in port. The immediate effect of the act was to destroy the foreign commerce of the United States and to cause the American people much economic suffering. Its ultimate effect was to divert American capital from shipping to manufactures.

The effort of Napoleon to exclude English goods from the

[1] If England refused to make peace.

markets of Europe was the signal for the rise of gigantic smuggling operations. Illegal centers for the distribution of English manufactures and colonial goods sprang up at Heligoland, Jersey, Sardinia, Sicily, and Malta. From these points the contraband goods reached European consumers through the craft of traders or the connivance of continental officials. In Spain, Holland, Etruria, and the Papal States the administration of the decrees of Napoleon against English goods was particularly ineffective. This leakage of British wares into Europe threatened to nullify the whole Continental System.

Both Napoleon and the English permitted evasions of their publicly announced policies. The English granted licenses to many Prussian, Russian, and Swedish ships to continue their commercial activity. In spite of his decrees to the contrary, Napoleon issued licenses permitting the entry of most English goods, with the exception of English cottons. In time his license system assumed large proportions.

In his efforts to insure the strict administration of the "Continental System" Napoleon resorted to many harsh and arbitrary measures. He confiscated and burned quantities of English wares, forced Denmark (1807), Austria (1809), and finally Sweden (1810) into the system, occupied Portugal with French troops, forced the Spanish royal family to abdicate in 1808 in favor of his brother, Joseph Bonaparte, and finally incorporated into France Etruria (1807), the Papal States (1809), Holland (1810), and the whole western coast of Germany as far as Lübeck. These measures had much to do with arousing the irresistible storm of national feeling that at last swept Napoleon from his throne.

The economic system of Napoleon worked great hardship on the vassal states of the developing Napoleonic empire. They suffered all the disadvantages of the "Continental System" without sharing any of the advantages of union with France. The "Continental System" made many colonial and manufactured products scarce, raised prices, and interfered with the normal flow of commerce. The tariff policy of Napoleon subordinated the commercial and industrial interests of the vassal states to those of France. The suffering and deprivations entailed by these economic policies gradually undermined the loyalty of the vassal states to the Napoleonic political system.

THE NATIONAL UPRISING IN SPAIN

In spite of the apparent submissiveness of Spain to all his demands Napoleon had no confidence in the Spanish Bourbons. Upon learning through his agents of the mobilization of the Spanish army just prior to the battle of Jena, and through the Prussian archives of Spanish plots against French control, Napoleon determined to punish those in authority in Madrid. He made the mistake of using indirect methods for carrying out his purpose. Under the pretext of sending soldiers to coerce Portugal into adopting the "Continental System," he introduced French troops into the principal towns of Northern Spain. Then, taking advantage of a violent quarrel between the Spanish King Charles IV and his heir Ferdinand, he cajoled the members of the royal family into coming to Bayonne and laying their quarrel before him. Next, by threats of personal violence he intimidated the Spanish King and his son into surrendering their rights to the Spanish throne. His next move was to induce a handful of Spanish notables to come to Bayonne and ask him for the appointment of his brother Joseph, King of Naples, as ruler of Spain.

At this point the Spanish people intervened. In a memorable uprising on May 2, 1808, a date which the Spanish people have celebrated ever since as the national holiday, the whole populace of Madrid flung itself on the French garrison. At the news of the events at Bayonne popular movements of extreme violence broke out at many points in Spain. Within a few weeks 150,000 untrained, ill-armed men had volunteered for the national uprising. Opposed to them were very raw forces made up for the most part of Swiss, German, and Italian conscripts. Three disasters quickly overtook the French. At Baylen in Southern Spain the Spanish compelled a force of 20,000 French troops to surrender. In August of the same year (1808) this capitulation led to the retreat of King Joseph from his capital. In Portugal an expeditionary force sent out by the British cabinet in response to appeals from the Spanish insurgents for aid compelled the capitulation at Cintra of the French forces that were occupying Portugal. For the first time in his career Napoleon found himself confronted by a whole people.

The capitulations at Baylen and at Cintra revealed to Napoleon the seriousness of the situation in Spain. Rushing experienced troops into the peninsula he took command of the situation in person. By 1811 his troops had overrun most of the country, but they had not succeeded in winning the hearts of the people. Supported by the English under Wellington, aided by the political and military errors of the French, and inflamed by religious zeal and patriotism, the Spanish people kept up an heroic guerilla warfare that wearied the French army of occupation and drained the resources of Napoleon. In 1811 Wellington drove the French out of Portugal; in the campaign of the following year he forced them out of Southern Spain; and in 1813 he pushed them out of the peninsula.[1]

The French occupation of the Iberian Peninsula had a number of important results. It shook the Spanish people out of their torpor, and drove the Portuguese dynasty overseas, where it founded the Empire of Brazil. The example of the Spanish people heartened other peoples in Europe to resist the tyranny of Napoleon. Finally, the efforts of Napoleon to quell the national uprising in Spain drained France of troops that were badly needed elsewhere and disordered its finances.

THE WAR OF 1809 WITH AUSTRIA AND ITS RESULTS

The Treaty of Pressburg had mutilated Austria without destroying it. The despoiling of Prussia, the creating of new states at the expense of long-established kingdoms, the annexation of Etruria and the Papal States to France, the highhanded proceedings of Napoleon in Spain, and his promise of the Danubian provinces (Wallachia and Moldavia) to Russia

[1] The fighting in Spain is known as the Peninsular War.

seemed to menace the Habsburg state with complete destruction. Angered by her dismemberment in the past, fearful of extinction in the near future, and encouraged by the success of the Spanish people in their rising against Napoleon and by the promise of English subsidies, Austria prepared for a renewal of her struggle with Napoleon.

The campaign of 1809 began with an advance of the Austrians into Bavaria. For a moment they had a decided advantage over the French forces opposed to them. Tactical blunders, however, soon forced their retreat along the northern bank of the Danube and led to the loss of Vienna. The decisive battle of the war took place at Wagram (July 6, 1809). Although the victory was not so decisive as the victories won at Marengo and Austerlitz, the defeat of his troops made the Austrian Emperor decide to sue for peace.

The subsequent peace negotiations resulted in the Treaty of Schönbrunn (July 12, 1809) or Vienna. By this agreement Austria lost fifty thousand additional square miles of territory and four million more subjects. The territory around the head of the Adriatic was handed over to Napoleon and was united with Dalmatia to form the Illyrian provinces. Another slice of Austria proper was ceded to Bavaria. Western Galicia was handed over to the Grand Duchy of Warsaw.[1] A much smaller portion of the province of Galicia was transferred to the Tsar. In addition the Austrian Emperor was required to reduce his army to 150,000 men and to pay a large war indemnity. The Treaty of Schönbrunn cut off Austria from the sea and reduced it to the rank of a second-rate power.

An heroic incident of the war of 1809 was the rising in the Tyrol. The Tyrolean peasants objected to the innovations introduced by their new Bavarian masters and clung to their old sovereign and their old customs. Aided by their mountain fastnesses they drove the Bavarian garrisons out of the province, and, before they were finally overwhelmed by the superior numbers of their opponents, they defeated several times the Bavarian and French armies that were sent to sub-

[1] The Duchy of Warsaw became a Grand Duchy in 1809.

due them. The chief political result of the insurrection was the division of the Tyrol between the Kingdom of Italy and the Kingdom of Bavaria.

THE PARTIAL REORGANIZATION OF PRUSSIA

The trials of the Prussians did not end with the signing of the Treaty of Tilsit. They still had to get the French out of the country. With almost inconceivable carelessness one of the Prussian generals signed a convention making the withdrawal of the French army contingent on the payment of a war contribution of indefinite amount. Napoleon pushed to the utmost the advantage which this blunder gave him. He forced the Prussian Government to run for months on the revenues to be obtained from the single province of East Prussia, while the remaining provinces of the monarchy were compelled to support 160,000 French troops and to submit to requisitions of all sorts. Finally, in September, 1808, a treaty was signed between France and Prussia which provided for the occupation of a number of Prussian fortresses by French troops, the reduction of the Prussian army to 42,000 men, the contribution by Prussia of a contingent of 16,000 men in case of war with Austria, and the payment of a war contribution of 140,000,000 francs from the luckless Prussian state.

The disasters suffered by Prussia after the opening of the fourth coalition convinced even the most stubborn Prussian reactionaries that some concessions must be made to the spirit of the age. During the six years following the Treaty of Tilsit, in consequence, important administrative, military, and social reforms were introduced in Prussia. The work of reform was begun by recalling Stein to office, a man personally distasteful to the King of Prussia because of his strong character and energetic methods.

The first important reform measure authorized by Stein was the edict emancipating the Prussian serfs. Up to 1807 two thirds of the people of Prussia were still without freedom, unable to leave the lands to which they were bound, and compelled to perform personal and often menial services for their masters. Land was still divided into noble, burgher, and peasant land, and occupations were fixed by birth. The Edict of Emancipation was designed to remedy these evils. It did away with the old distinctions between noble, burgher, and peasant land, and threw open all occupations to Prussian citizens. It likewise abolished serfdom. Since the measure did not touch the feudal dues, it left the Prussian peasants in the position in which the Revolution had found the majority of the French peasants.

The second important measure of Stein was the Prussian municipal ordinance of 1808. This decree restored to the towns of Prussia the right of self-government, and gave a uniform system of administration to all towns with a population of over eight hundred. The chief matters reserved for the decision of the central government were the naming of burgomasters and the control of the police. This ordinance of Stein still forms the basis of Prussian municipal government.

Stein did not stay in office long enough to put into effect his plans for the central administration. Under his successors the system of governing boards or colleges, with their faults of divided authority, endless reports, and official red tape, and the system of ministers in charge of provinces instead of governmental departments, was replaced by modern ministers in charge of interior affairs, justice, foreign affairs, and war. The special privileges of the different provinces disappeared. The ancient territorial divisions were rearranged. The chambers of war, domains, and finances were relieved of their judicial functions. The various treasuries were consolidated. The plans of Stein for provincial and national consultative assemblies, however, were not realized for half a century.

The reorganization of the army was also begun under the ministry of Stein. The war had demonstrated that the military system of Frederick the Great must be abandoned. The armies of vagabonds recruited from all over Europe proved no match for the military levies conscripted from a whole nation. Serious drills and target practice replaced the tricks of the parade ground. The captains ceased to own and exploit their companies. The French system of requisitions on the surrounding country was lightened, and promotion in rank was thrown open to all citizens of the state. The limitation of the army to 42,000 men led to the adoption of the "krumper" system, by which recruits were given intensive training for a short time and were then given leave of absence. By this system some 150,000 men were partially trained for military service before the opening of the War of Liberation.

In 1808 Stein was dismissed from the ministry, because of pressure from Napoleon after having been in office only a little more than a year. After two discouraging years for Prussian patriots he was followed in office by Hardenberg, the second great reforming minister of the period. In his edict of 1810 on the finances of the State the latter promised that all inhabitants should be subjected to the same tax burdens, but the promise remained a dead letter from the start. An ordinance of 1811 freed the peasants with hereditary rights in their holdings from the payment of all feudal dues on the condition of their abandoning one third of their holdings to the noble proprietors. Peasants without hereditary rights in their lands were required to abandon one half of their holdings to escape the payment of feudal dues. Hardenberg unfortunately did not execute the ordinance rigorously, and the work was hardly begun when it was interrupted by the opening of the War of Liberation in 1813 and the reaction against all measures of reform which followed it. In 1812 the Jews of Prussia obtained civil but not political equality.

One of the most important of the new institutions of Prussia was the University of Berlin, founded in 1810. The new university soon became the center of intellectual activity in Northern Germany. From the first it numbered illustrious names on its faculty. Its instructors played a noble part in arousing the patriotism of the Prussian people and made a place for themselves by the side of the soldiers and the statesmen of Prussia.

The motives of Stein and Hardenberg and their co-workers

Napoleonic Empire at its Height

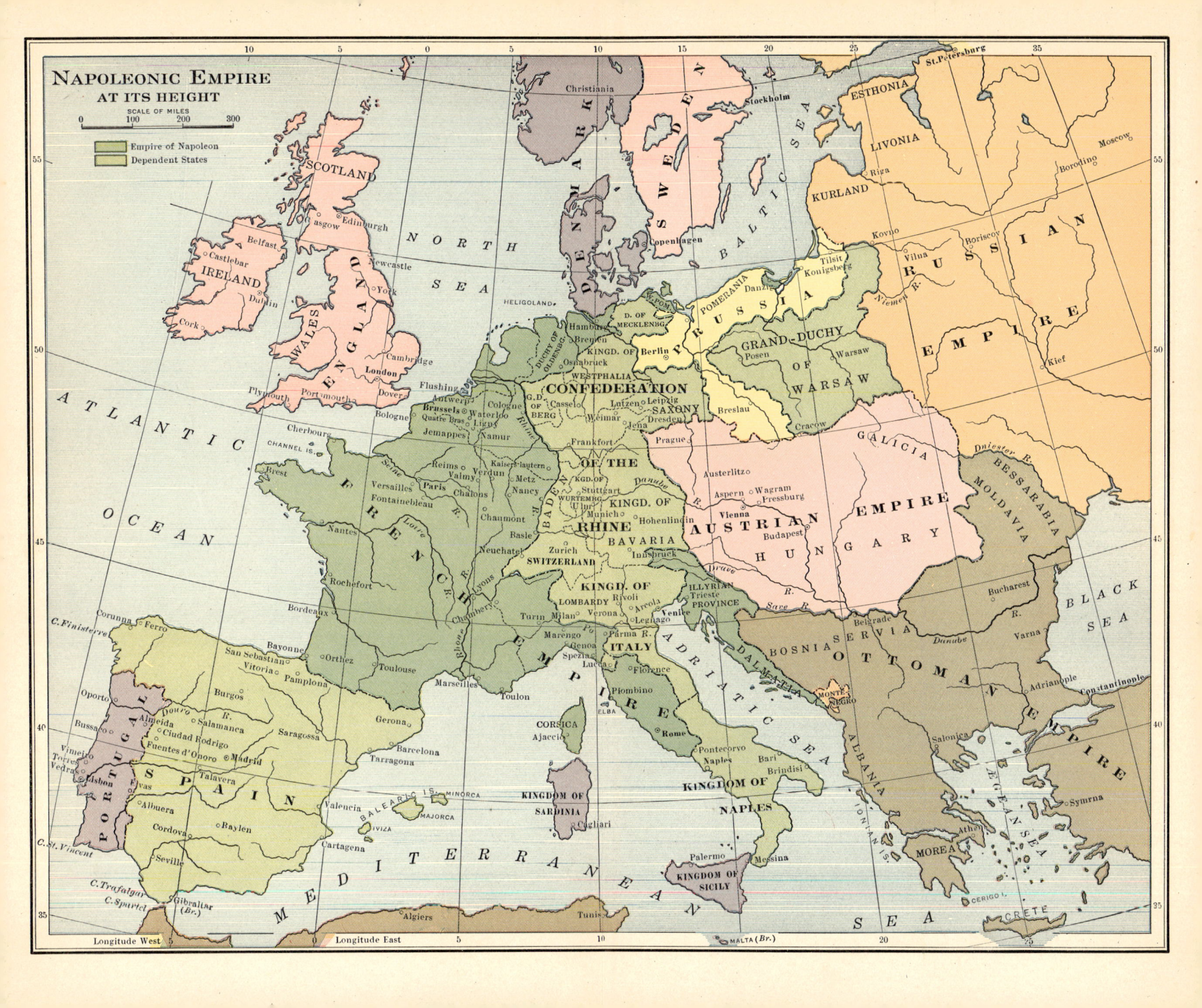

were far different from those which had actuated the statesmen of Revolutionary France. In Prussia the leaders were attached to the *ancien régime* and were interested only in the efficiency of the State. In France they had broken with the past and had a generous passion for the rights of the common man. The ideals of the Prussian statesman made a thoroughgoing reorganization of Prussia impossible.

EXTENSION OF FRENCH INFLUENCE IN EUROPE

In 1812 Napoleon became involved in war with Russia. From that date until his abdication in 1814 his entire attention was absorbed by military affairs. By 1812, therefore, his constructive work in Europe and in France was done. At this point, in consequence, a survey of the extension of French influence to Europe and of the work of Napoleon for France can appropriately be made.

The life and institutions of Italy were probably modified by French influence to a greater degree during the Napoleonic period than those of any other country. As finally organized by Napoleon the peninsula of Italy was divided into French Italy, the Kingdom of Italy, and the Kingdom of Naples. Before the end of the Napoleonic period a third of the peninsula had been annexed to France. At its greatest extent French Italy included Piedmont, Genoa, Tuscany, Parma, and the greater part of the Papal States. French Italy enjoyed the same laws and the same administration as the older portions of France. Its inhabitants profited from the abolition of feudal dues, the introduction of civil equality, the expansion of French commerce and industry, the construction of important public works, the opening of public careers to men of talent, the improvement in the administration of justice, and the promotion of well-being and intellectual culture. In common with all the peoples under the sway of Napoleon they suffered from the military conscription, the increased burden of taxation, and loss of political liberty.

As finally constituted the Kingdom of Italy included the original Cisalpine Republic, Venetia, Guastalla, part of the

Papal States, and the Italian Tyrol, and possessed a population of six and one half millions. After the coronation of Napoleon as King of Italy, the government of the kingdom was practically a despotism under the immediate rule of the viceroy, Eugène Beauharnais, the stepson of Napoleon. Under the viceroy's administration conscription was introduced in the face of determined opposition from the Italian people; an army of eighty thousand men was developed; schools for the education of officers were established; the revenues of the state were doubled and its budget balanced; and most of the religious, legal, social, and economic reforms of the French Revolution were introduced. The greatest contribution of Napoleon to the Italian people was the revival of the ideal of a free and united Italy.

French rule began in Southern Italy in 1806. Under the administration of Joseph Bonaparte (1806–08), the oldest brother of Napoleon, the feudal system with all its fiscal and social inequalities was abolished; the French civil code was introduced; primary schools were established in each commune; and a general reform of taxation was undertaken. Under Murat (1808–15) conscription was established; the army was completely reorganized; the number of free proprietors was increased by several hundred thousands through the division of fiefs and ecclesiastical lands; the monasteries were suppressed; and important public works were completed. With the introduction of French influence a new life seemed to commence for the Kingdom of Naples.

Next to Italy Germany was most affected by the extension of French influences. Napoleonic Germany included the German territories annexed to France, the new states created by Napoleon, and the old states subject to his will. In 1795 the left bank of the Rhine had been annexed to France. This region shared with France and French Italy all the benefits and the disadvantages of French rule. In 1810 the seacoast from the Kingdom of Holland to the city of Lübeck was annexed. This region was incorporated into France too late for a thorough absorption of French institutions.

Napoleon created two new states in Germany: the Grand Duchy of Berg and the Kingdom of Westphalia. As finally organized the Grand Duchy of Berg included the territory of Berg, ceded by Bavaria in 1805, and a number of districts taken from Prussia in 1807, and possessed a population of about 900,000. Into both the Grand Duchy of Berg and the Kingdom of Westphalia the reforms of the Revolution, as modified by Napoleon, were transferred almost bodily.

The influence of France on the rest of Napoleonic Germany was indirect. In the Duchies of Thuringia and the two Mecklenburgs the domination of France caused the rulers of these states to cling with tenacity, by a strange twist of patriotism, to everything inherited from the past. In Saxony the only important reform was the establishment of Lutherans and Catholics on the same footing. In the states of Southern Germany France had a more positive influence. There the old feudal estates were suppressed; tithes were abolished; the seigniorial *corvées* were reduced; innumerable tolls and customs lines were done away with; the feudal system was modified somewhat in the interest of the peasants; and the central and local administrations were modernized. In the Catholic states the political power of the Church was broken; the property of the Church was secularized; many monasteries and convents were suppressed; and Catholics, Lutherans, and Calvinists were put on the same footing. The equality of citizens, however, was still not recognized by law, and custom lagged far behind the law.

Spain, Holland, Switzerland, the Grand Duchy of Warsaw, and the Illyrian Provinces were also penetrated more or less by French influences during the Napoleonic period. In Spain decrees were issued by the Government of King Joseph abolishing the Inquisition, the feudal dues, provincial tariff lines, and two thirds of the monasteries and convents, but the national uprising of the Spanish people prevented the thorough execution of those decrees. Finally in 1810 Holland was annexed to France, and was subjected to both French law and French administration. In the Grand Duchy of Warsaw the people received from Napoleon a constitution, religious toleration, the French civil code, and the principle, at least, of the freedom of the peasant from serfdom. In the Illyrian Provinces Napoleon reorganized justice and administration on French models, abolished the manorial courts, serfdom, and seigniorial *corvées*, suppressed the gilds, and constructed a network of admirable roads. In nearly every country of Europe the Napoleonic period saw the ideals of the French Revolution implanted more or less firmly.

FRANCE UNDER THE EMPIRE

After Napoleon assumed the imperial dignity life at the Tuileries began to show signs of the new principle upon which the State was organized. The trappings of power replaced the former republican simplicity. A court, marked by careful organization and rigid etiquette, made its appearance. Ségur, once minister of Louis XVI to Russia, perfected and supervised the new ceremonial. Madame Campan, a former lady-in-waiting to Marie Antoinette, lent her assistance. The great officers of the State assumed high-sounding titles borrowed from ancient France and the Empire of Charlemagne. The leading generals became marshals of the new Napoleonic Empire. Many returned *émigrés* filled minor posts in the new court.

The work of Napoleon for France during the period of the Empire was largely a continuation of the reforms that had been begun under the Consulate. He displayed the same energy and efficiency in government under the Empire as during the Consulate, but he introduced few reforms. His struggles with the states of Europe absorbed most of his time.

The work of the commissions charged with the task of codifying the laws of France, which was begun under the Consulate, was not completed until just before the close of the Empire. In 1806 the new code of civil procedure was adopted. It was practically the code of 1667 with a few slight amendments. In the following year the new commercial code was completed. It showed little advance over the commercial ordinances of the *ancien régime*, and the adoption of new commercial methods soon made it antiquated. In 1811 the code of criminal procedure and the new penal code were put into effect. The distinctive features of the new code of criminal procedure was the retention of trial by jury and the adoption of the principle that an accused person is innocent until he is proved guilty. The new penal code was a distinct step backward. It made more crimes punishable by death and reintroduced the branding and mutilation of the criminal.

Napoleon sought to use the schools of the Empire to bolster up his political system. All public and private schools of France were finally organized into the University of France, and became subject to the inspection and orders of the State. Promotion depended on the favor of the Imperial Government. The curriculum was influenced by the current demand for practical subjects.

Napoleon's quarrel with the Pope frustrated his plan of making the Church as well as the schools of France a prop of the imperial régime. The quarrel had many causes. The Pope resented the issuing of the Organic Articles for the Catholic religion, the introduction of the French civil code into Italy, and the treatment which he received at the hands of Napoleon at the time of the coronation of the latter as Emperor.[1] Napoleon resented the refusal of the Pope to enforce the Continental System and to enter the Napoleonic system as an ally. The quarrel finally led to the annexation of the Papal States and the arrest of the Pope by Napoleon, and to the excommunication of Napoleon and the refusal by the Pope to fill vacant bishoprics.

For France the Napoleonic period was a time of prosperity till about 1810. The peasants slowly freed themselves from the practices of the past, and made more use of artificial grasses, rotation of crops, fertilizers, and vegetables. Commerce and industry benefited from the period of internal peace, the extension of the French tariff lines in such a way as to include new markets, and the partial exclusion of Eng-

[1] After inviting the Pope to Paris to participate in the ceremony, Napoleon put the crown on his head with his own hands.

lish goods from competition. The expansion of business, however, led to inflation and its attendant ills. Credit was overstrained and money became scarce. As a result France suffered from a terrible panic in 1810.

Napoleon had no sympathy with the ideals of freedom of thought and freedom of the press. He established a rigorous censorship of literature and the press. His agents scanned plays for lines of ambiguous meaning, persecuted writers, and suppressed many newspapers. Printers were rigorously restricted and their publications strictly censored. Napoleon's policy stifled the free development of the intellectual life of France.

THE DEFEAT OF NAPOLEON

In the meantime Russia and France had been drifting toward war. The conflict with England which the adoption of the Continental System had inflicted on Russia, had interfered seriously with the Russian export trade in wheat, timber, and naval stores. Consequently, by 1810, Russia had a large deficit, and the Russian ruble had fallen to one fourth of its face value. The Grand Duchy of Warsaw was a constant source of uneasiness to the administrators of Russia, who feared the effect of Napoleon's reforms in the Grand Duchy on the Polish provinces of Russia. The efforts of Napoleon's agents to prolong the war between Russia and Turkey was a cause of irritation. Napoleon's annexation in 1810, in the interest of the Continental System, of the maritime state of Oldenburg, which was ruled by a near relative of the Tsar, was considered an insult by Alexander of Russia. The Tsar, on his side, established a tariff in 1810 which either levied high duties on many French articles or prohibited their importation while at the same time it facilitated the commerce of neutral Powers. Steps were taken looking toward a reëstablishment of the Kingdom of Poland under the protection of Russia. Finally, early in 1811, the Tsar began to move troops toward the frontier of the Grand Duchy of Warsaw. As a result of these measures relations between Napoleon and Alexander became strained to the breaking point, and in the spring of 1812 both Powers began to prepare for war.

The Russian campaign which followed began in June, 1812. Napoleon crossed the Niemen River with a motley army of 450,000 French, South-German, Italian, Austrian, and Prussian troops, and started on the six-hundred-mile march toward Moscow. In this campaign he faced new conditions, and from the first the expedition began to go wrong. In spite of Napoleon's strong efforts to prevent it, the Turks made peace with the Tsar and freed a large Russian army for the campaign of 1812 against the French Emperor. The Spanish national uprising with English assistance immobilized three hundred thousand troops in Spain. The Poles of Russian Poland made no move in behalf of Napoleon. The steady retreat of the Russians into the interior of their country increased his difficulties in proportion as he drew away from his base of supplies. In sparsely settled Russia the usual French system of requisitions could not be depended on, and the transport system of the army broke down under the strain of feeding a half-million men. Before a month had elapsed, fatigue, disease, and starvation began to do their work, and men and horses perished in great numbers. By the end of July a third of the invading army had disappeared. When he reached Moscow Napoleon found the city practically deserted by its Russian population. The very day the French entered the Russian capital fires broke out which destroyed the greater part of the city.

The burning of Moscow left Napoleon in a precarious situation. He had failed to bring the campaign to a decision. His army, as a result of the fire, was without winter quarters. The terrible Russian winter was not far off. After lingering amid the smoldering ruins of Moscow for five precious weeks in the hope that the Tsar would consent to make terms of peace, Napoleon began in the middle of October his retreat toward Poland. The military situation compelled the French army to retrace its steps through the region which had just been devasted by the passage of two armies, and the forces of Napoleon suffered terribly. The Russian soldiers and peasants gave the French no peace night or day, and the oncoming winter proved to be the deadliest foe of all. As a result of its terrible sufferings, the army of Napoleon reached the Niemen River with hardly a shadow of organization. The immediate results of the disastrous Russian campaign were the desertion of General York with the Prussian contingent to the side of the Tsar, the withdrawal of Austria from the war and its resumption of an independent position, a dangerous popular agitation against Napoleon in Prussia, Italy, and Southern Germany, and a feverish activity on the part of the French leader to repair the losses of the campaign.

During the following winter events steadily pushed the hesitating Frederick William III of Prussia toward war with France. On the last day of 1812 General York had deserted with his Prussian contingent to the side of the Tsar after receiving the express assurance of Alexander that Russia would not lay down her arms until she had procured for Prussia an aggrandizement of territory such as to enable her to resume the place among the Powers which she had held before the war of 1806. The Prussian army and the Prussian people also demanded a war of independence. At length the wavering King came to an understanding with the Tsar (Treaty of Kalisch, February 28, 1813) and in March Prussia declared war against France (March 16, 1813). A veritable crusading spirit swept over Northern Germany. The whole nation threw its energies into the War of Liberation, and Prussia reaped the first rewards of reorganization.

The campaign of 1813, which followed the entrance of Prussia into the struggle, was really a continuation of the campaign of 1812. At the opening of the struggle the contending forces faced each other along the line of the Elbe River. The campaign began with two victories for Napoleon, which his lack of cavalry prevented him from making decisive. At this point his failure to meet the demands of Austria caused that Power to join the coalition. Austria's entrance into the conflict made the defeat of Napoleon practically certain. Three great allied armies, which greatly outnumbered the forces of France, began to push the French out of Germany. Only incredible blunders on the part of his enemies could have saved Napoleon from defeat. The campaign reached its culminating point at the great battle of Leipzig, which ended in the defeat of the Emperor. This defeat led to the defection of the German vassal states, the collapse of Berg and Westphalia as independent states, the retreat of Napoleon's depleted and exhausted army across the Rhine, and the defection of the King of Naples (Murat) from the French alliance in the hope of saving his crown.

The campaign of 1814 was a short one. While Eugène Beauharnais was making an effort to hold Northern Italy, Napoleon himself attempted to save France with an army that never numbered more than ninety thousand men. The efforts of Napoleon were made in vain. In spite of his brilliant strategy and the division of counsel among his opponents, he was defeated and his capital occupied. The civil authorities at Paris began to negotiate with the coalition. The marshals of Napoleon refused to continue the struggle. His troops were deserting him. He had no alternative but to abdicate his throne (April 4, 1814) in the hope of saving it for his young heir, the King of Rome.

SUMMARY

In 1792 the natural antagonism between the Revolution and the *ancien régime*, combined with the undiplomatic methods of the revolutionary leaders, involved France in war with most of the Governments of Europe. The exigencies of this struggle led to the gradual militarization of the state, the expansion of the boundaries of France, the adoption of a policy of imperialism, and the final establishment of one of the most successful generals of the Revolution, Napoleon Bonaparte, as military dictator of France. The ambition of Napoleon led him to continue the war with Europe in the hope of creating a federation of states under his imperial sway to take the place of the old balance of power. For a time his plans met with extraordinary success. The Treaties of Lunéville, of Pressburg, and of Tilsit enabled him to overthrow old dynasties, to shift long-established boundary lines, to create new states, and to introduce new institutions in France, Italy, Spain, and Central Europe, seemingly at will. His arbitrary rule, his disregard of the rights and prejudices of other peoples, and the hardships entailed by his "Continental System," a device for bringing the English nation to terms, in the end aroused forces which even Napoleon could not control. After 1808 the Spanish national uprising steadily drained his resources and his treasury. The Russian campaign of 1812 destroyed the largest army Europe had ever seen, and shattered the prestige of Napoleon. The national rising of Prussia and the general defection of his allies in Central Europe drove him back of the Rhine. His stubborn refusal to give up his grandiose designs for world dominion led to the invasion of France in the early months of 1814 and to his final downfall.

REFERENCES

NAPOLEONIC STATES
  Cambridge Modern History, vol. IX, chapter IV.
  H. A. L. Fisher, *Studies in Napoleonic Statesmanship: Germany*.
  A. Fournier, *Napoleon the First*, pp. 325-55.

THE CONTINENTAL SYSTEM
  H. E. Bourne, *The Revolutionary Period in Europe*, chapter XXI.
  Cambridge Modern History, vol. IX, chapter XIII.
  J. H. Rose, *The Life of Napoleon I*, vol. II, chapter XXVI.

THE FRENCH CODES
  Cambridge Modern History, vol. IX, chapter VI.

THE REORGANIZATION OF PRUSSIA
  H. E. Bourne, *The Revolutionary Period in Europe*, chapter XXII.
  G. S. Ford, *Stein and the Era of Reform in Prussia, 1807-15*.
  E. F. Henderson, *A Short History of Germany*, vol. II, chapters VI-VII.
  F. Schevill, *The Making of Modern Germany*, chapter III.
  J. R. Seeley, *The Life and Times of Stein*.

SOURCES ON THE NAPOLEONIC PERIOD
  F. M. Anderson, *Constitutions and Documents: France*, pp. 208-451.
  J. H. Robinson, *Readings in European History*, vol. II, chapters XXXVII-XXXVIII.
  J. H. Robinson and C. A. Beard, *Readings in Modern European History*, vol. I, chapters XIV-XV.
  Translations and Reprints, vol. II, no. II.

MAPS

The Napoleonic Campaign in Egypt, W. R. Shepherd, *Historical Atlas*, p. 150.
The Napoleonic Campaigns in Italy, *ibid.*, p. 150.
Principal Seats of the War, 1788–1815, *ibid.*, p. 153.
Treaty Adjustments, 1801–1812, *ibid.*, p. 152.
Central Europe in 1812, *ibid.*, pp. 154–55.

CHAPTER XIX

THE RECONSTRUCTION OF EUROPE

THE French Revolution swept away the abuses of the *ancien régime* in France, overthrew the ruling family under which they had arisen, and extended the French boundaries even beyond the limits of which Richelieu and Louis XIV had dreamed. The wars of the French Revolution and the Napoleonic period overthrew old dynasties, changed political boundary lines, swept away ancient states, extended the reforms of the French Revolution to a large part of Europe, and ingrained in the minds and hearts of a whole generation in Southern and Central Europe new ideas and fresh ideals. The overthrow of the Napoleonic system naturally necessitated a certain amount of reconstruction of Europe. The character and traditions of the victorious governments made some reaction from the Napoleonic régime certain. But the new forces introduced into Europe during the French Revolution and the Napoleonic period made a complete restoration of the *ancien régime* impossible.

RESTORATION AND REACTION

One of the first dethroned sovereigns to regain his crown was Ferdinand, the son of Charles IV of Spain. As a result of the French defeats in the peninsula, Napoleon concluded, in December, 1813, a treaty with the imprisoned Spanish prince and recognized his title to the Spanish throne. In the following March he permitted him to return to Spain.

During the six years of Ferdinand's enforced absence from the country Spain had been ruled by a provisional government of more liberal tendencies than those of the nation. In 1810 the self-constituted leaders of the Spanish Revolution had summoned an irregular Cortes, which assumed the rôle of a constitutional assembly. The result of its deliberation was the famous Spanish Constitution of 1812, which holds such a singular position in the annals of the revolutionary movements of the nineteenth century. This document declared that sovereignty resided in the people, entrusted the legislative power to a National Cortes, put executive authority into the hands of ministers responsible to the Cortes, granted the suffrage to all male Spaniards over twenty-five years of age, safeguarded the fundamental rights of the Spanish people, made judges irremovable, and suppressed the Inquisition. The Catholic religion, however, was declared the religion of Spain and all other forms of worship were prohibited.

Ferdinand was entirely out of sympathy with this Constitution of 1812. Encouraged by the attitude of the nobility, the clergy, some of the generals, and the ignorant populace, the King, early in May, 1814, declared null and void both the Constitution of 1812 and the liberal decrees of the Cortes created under its authority. A few days later the captain-general of New Castile arrested the chiefs of the liberal party. As a result of these measures Ferdinand entered Madrid in the middle of May an absolute king.

The return of Ferdinand to his capital was the signal for a furious reaction. The antiquated political machinery of the *ancien régime* was restored. The Inquisition was revived. The Jesuits reëntered the peninsula. The monasteries and convents were reopened and their property was restored; and the purchasers of ecclesiastical property were despoiled without indemnity. The prisons were filled with liberal deputies. The press was gagged and individual liberty was shamelessly violated. At the end of May all Spaniards who had sworn allegiance to Joseph Bonaparte were banished from the kingdom. Everything possible was done to stamp out the influence of the French occupation.

In Italy the Governments of 1798 were never all restored, but the peninsula suffered from a wave of reaction second in intensity only to that which Spain experienced. For a year after the first abdication of Napoleon, Murat retained his hold on the Kingdom of Naples. In Northern Italy it looked for a time as if the Kingdom of Italy might survive under the rule of Eugène Beauharnais, the viceroy and stepson of

Napoleon. After the military defeat of the French in the campaign of 1814, however, a revolution at Milan overthrew the old government of the Kingdom of Italy; but it failed to put a successful government in its place. In consequence the Austrians finally occupied both Venetia and Lombardy, and the French withdrew beyond the Alps.

The defeat of the French in Northern Italy as a result of the campaign of 1814 initiated a period of restoration and reaction. Out of the provinces of Lombardy and Venetia Austria created the Lombardo-Venetian Kingdom. In this new state Austria retained the conscription, the taxation, and the police system that had been introduced by Napoleon. The French civil code, trial by jury, and civil marriage were abolished. Neither the clergy nor the nobility regained their special privileges. In the province of Piedmont, the King, upon his return in May, 1814, from the island of Sardinia, where he had lived since the occupation of his continental provinces by the French, abolished at one stroke all French laws and institutions and restored the privileges of the nobility, feudal rights, tithes, primogeniture, and the domains and special tribunals of the Church. The King even wanted to close the road over Mont Cenis and the bridge across the Po at Turin because they had been built by the French. In Central Italy the papal authorities adopted a similar policy. For a time they even abandoned street-lighting in Rome because it had been introduced by the French.

The Grand Duchy of Warsaw did not survive the campaign of 1812. After the retreat of the French armies from the country the Poles found themselves powerless to prevent the occupation of the Duchy by the Russians. Just as the hopes of Polish national independence seemed destroyed by the defeat of Napoleon, however, the Tsar, to the astonishment of the Polish nation generally, began to hold out hopes for a revival of Poland as a constitutional monarchy under his own protection. The settlement of the problem of the future of the Grand Duchy had to be left to the diplomats representing the four Powers of the coalition.

In Germany less of the work of Napoleon was undone than

in Spain and Italy. After the collapse of the Napoleonic states of Westphalia and Berg, the old governments were restored in Hanover, Brunswick, Hesse-Cassel, Oldenburg, Bremen, Hamburg, and Lübeck, but no effort was made to revive the hundreds of petty secular and ecclesiastical states which had been suppressed during the Napoleonic period, or to return to the laws and institutions of the *ancien régime*. In October, 1814, Bavaria deserted Napoleon, signing an agreement with Austria by which the Tyrol and certain other Austrian provinces were surrendered to that Power in return for a guarantee of Bavarian independence and an indemnity to be determined. In November of the same year the sovereigns of Württemberg, Hesse-Darmstadt, Baden, and Nassau followed the example of Bavaria. The King of Saxony waited too long before deserting Napoleon and was put under arrest and threatened with the loss of his kingdom for his stubborn fidelity to his former benefactor.

In France the abdication of Napoleon immediately raised the problems of the future status of the Emperor and the future government of France. The first problem was regulated finally by the Treaty of Fontainebleau (April 11, 1814). By the terms of this agreement Napoleon was to receive an annual revenue from France of two million francs for himself and an additional two and a half million for the various members of his family; the Duchies of Parma, Piacenza, and Guastalla were assigned to the Empress Maria Louisa; and the island of Elba and the title of Emperor were to be retained by Napoleon himself.

The problem of the future government of France was solved by recalling the Bourbons. Their recall was largely the work of Talleyrand. Convinced that France could obtain better terms from the Powers of the coalition if the Bourbons were on the throne of France, Talleyrand skillfully manipulated both the Tsar and the constituted authorities at Paris and brought about the restoration of Louis XVIII as king. He first induced the Tsar and his royal colleagues to announce that they would make no peace with Napoleon or with members of his family. Then he persuaded the pliant

French Senate to establish a provisional government and to decree the abdication of Napoleon. The French people thereupon accepted the Bourbons as the most feasible solution of the situation. As a guarantee for the future, however, the Senate stipulated the adhesion of the Bourbons to a constitutional charter, drawn up by the Senate, which preserved for the French people most of the important gains of the French Revolution. Louis XVIII rejected the charter of the Senate on the ground of the signs of haste in its composition, but in a declaration issued from Saint-Ouen he signified his assent to its more important principles. On June 4, 1814, he promulgated a charter of his own which provided for a chamber of hereditary peers to be chosen by the king, a chamber of deputies to be elected by an extremely limited suffrage, a definite civil list for the crown, freedom of worship for all creeds, protection for the purchasers of national property, retention of the jury system, and the independence of the judiciary.

After the installation of the Bourbons the allied Powers negotiated a treaty of peace with France (May 30, 1814). This Treaty of Paris assured to France the French frontier of 1792 with the addition of part of Savoy and certain enclaved territories like Avignon. The treaty also made a start toward the reconstruction of the rest of Europe. The Powers agreed that Holland should be restored to the House of Orange with an increase of territory, that the states of Germany should be independent and united by a federative bond, that Switzerland should continue to govern itself as an independent state, that the provinces of Lombardy and Venetia should be given to Austria, that the province of Piedmont should be restored to the Kingdom of Sardinia, that the rest of Italy should be composed of independent states, that the island of Malta should belong to Great Britain, that the former colonies of France, with the exception of the islands of Tobago and Santa Lucia in the West Indies and the Isle de France off the eastern coast of Africa, should be returned to France, and that the portion of San Domingo that was ceded to France in 1795 should be restored to Spain. The disposal of the remaining territories taken from Napoleon and the reëstablishment of a balance of power in Europe were to be regulated in accordance with principles determined by the allied Powers among themselves at a congress to be held at Vienna.

THE CONGRESS OF VIENNA

Europe looked forward with high hopes to the proposed congress. The liberals confidently expected that the territory in Italy, Germany, and Poland reconquered from Napoleon would be distributed in accordance with principles, that would insure a real and permanent equilibrium among the states of Europe, and they hoped for the establishment of an effective and permanent international court, the ultimate disarmament of Europe, the encouragement of representative institutions, the abolition of the African slave trade, the suppression of piracy in the Mediterranean, the independence of the American colonies of Spain, and freedom of the seas.

Of the sovereigns, aristocratic diplomats, and representatives of the two hundred and eight states, organizations, and former sovereigns that were officially represented at the Congress of Vienna and interested in its settlements few shared these hopes. Upon their arrival in Vienna in September, 1814, they began to work and to intrigue for definite objects of immediate practical advantage to the interests which they represented. They thought in terms of population, revenues, strategic boundary lines, the acquisition of new provinces, and the restoration of former states, and had little interest or faith in the larger interests of humanity.

The four allied Powers, Russia, Prussia, England, and Austria, which had been responsible for the defeat of Napoleon, planned to arrogate to themselves the disposition of the territories at their disposal and to dictate the terms of the settlement. Their plans soon encountered two obstacles: the clash of their own conflicting claims and the remarkable diplomacy of Talleyrand, the representative of France at the Congress. The first obstacle prevented the Congress from making progress in the reconstruction of Europe. The second interfered with the plans of the four Powers to dictate the rearrangement of Europe.

The most serious difference of opinion between the Powers developed over the question of the indemnification of Russia and Prussia for their sacrifices during the war against Napoleon. The Tsar demanded the Grand Duchy of Warsaw as his share of the Napoleonic spoils and planned to reëstablish the Kingdom of Poland with himself as its constitutional king. Prussia wished to be restored geographically, statistically, and financially to the rank which it held before the disaster of Jena (except for Hanover). As the Tsar desired for his proposed Kingdom of Poland the territories which Prussia had acquired in the second and third partitions of Poland, Prussia had centered its attention on the acquisition of the territories of the imprisoned King of Saxony. Since the two problems were inseparably linked, the King of Prussia and the Tsar supported each other's claims. Austria and England opposed the plans of the two Northern Powers. Both feared to see Russia advance its borders to the Oder River. Austria, in addition, had no wish to surrender its claims to Galicia. This so-called Polish-Saxon question absorbed the attention of the Congress for several months.

Upon his arrival at Vienna Talleyrand found himself socially and politically isolated. The story of how he restored France to a place in the councils of Europe is one of the most interesting chapters in the history of the Congress of Vienna. With consummate skill he first convinced the most skeptical that France asked nothing for itself and merely stood for the principles of the public law of Europe. This policy coincided exactly with the aims of the smaller states and of the dethroned sovereigns. Next he forced the representatives of the four great Powers to admit France to a voice in their councils. The final stage in the rehabilitation of France came in January, 1815, with the admission of France, on terms of equality, to an alliance with England and Austria which was designed to prevent the consummation of the plans of Russia and Prussia with regard to Poland and Saxony.

The Congress really never met and never organized. The diplomats of the four principal Powers of the coalition began by arrogating to themselves the power to dictate the solution of the questions before the Congress. These self-constituted directors of Europe decided that German questions should be settled by a committee representing the German states of Austria, Prussia, Bavaria, Hanover, and Württemberg, and that the German, Italian, and Polish territories in the hands of the allies should be distributed by the committee composed of the representatives of the four great Powers. The remarkable skill of Talleyrand forced the expansion of the committee of four so as to include the representatives of France and Spain (the committee of six). Upon the presentation of the demands of Sweden and Portugal, the other two signers of the Treaty of Paris, for admission to the directing committee the representatives of the eight Powers, after much discussion, finally constituted themselves the preliminary committee of eight. No formal opening of the Congress ever took place. Metternich and Gentz, two of the representatives of Austria, acted as president and secretary of the directing committee of eight. The real work of the Congress was done by committees of the Powers. Upon receiving the reports of its military and political experts each Power decided on the line of action that it would take in regard to a particular problem under discussion. The question was then fought out in the special committee having jurisdiction over the question. The decision of this committee was then ratified by the directing committee. Lastly it was embodied in formal treaties. The famous figures on the directing committee put their trust in the knowledge of their expert subordinates and passed judgment on many questions about which they knew little or nothing.

The clash of interests seemed destined to extend interminably the negotiations of the Congress when the news of the return of Napoleon from the island of Elba electrified the diplomats into feverish activity. On March 13, 1815, the representatives of the eight directing Powers formally outlawed Napoleon and promised their support to the King of

France and the French nation against the usurper. Two weeks later, England, Russia, Austria, and Prussia renewed their alliance against the Emperor. In the meantime the diplomats accelerated the work of the Congress and rapidly settled the outstanding problems. The results of their work were finally embodied in special treaties and in the document known as the Final Act of the Congress of Vienna (June 9, 1815).

As a result of the decisions of the Congress, the Italian people became a divided nationality ruled by a number of petty governments under the suzerainty of Austria. Austria received the Italian provinces of Lombardy and Venetia, which it had already occupied. In Piedmont, Modena, Tuscany, the Papal States, and, after some delay, Naples, the former rulers were restored. Parma was given to the Empress Maria Louisa, and Genoa, against its will, was handed over to the King of Sardinia. Modena, Parma, and Tuscany were practically ruled by Austria, and Naples pledged itself to make no separate alliance and to grant to its subjects no liberties not also enjoyed by the inhabitants of the Lombardo-Venetian Kingdom. Sardinia was the only one of the ten states in the peninsula which dared to follow an independent policy.

In Germany the liberals hoped for a union of the German states into a strong whole and for the establishment of civil and political liberty. The princes desired to be masters of their states and to suffer no check to the exercise of their sovereignty either within or without their dominions. The future of Germany was settled in accordance with the wishes of the princes. The thirty-four sovereign princes and the four free cities of Germany formed a confederation of equals, under the presidency of Austria, known as the German Confederation. The new union was the old Holy Roman Empire under a new name. The liberals of Germany had to wait fifty years for a real national state and a century for democratic government.

As a compensation for the loss of its former Polish provinces Prussia gained most of the territory in Germany at the

EUROPE IN 1815

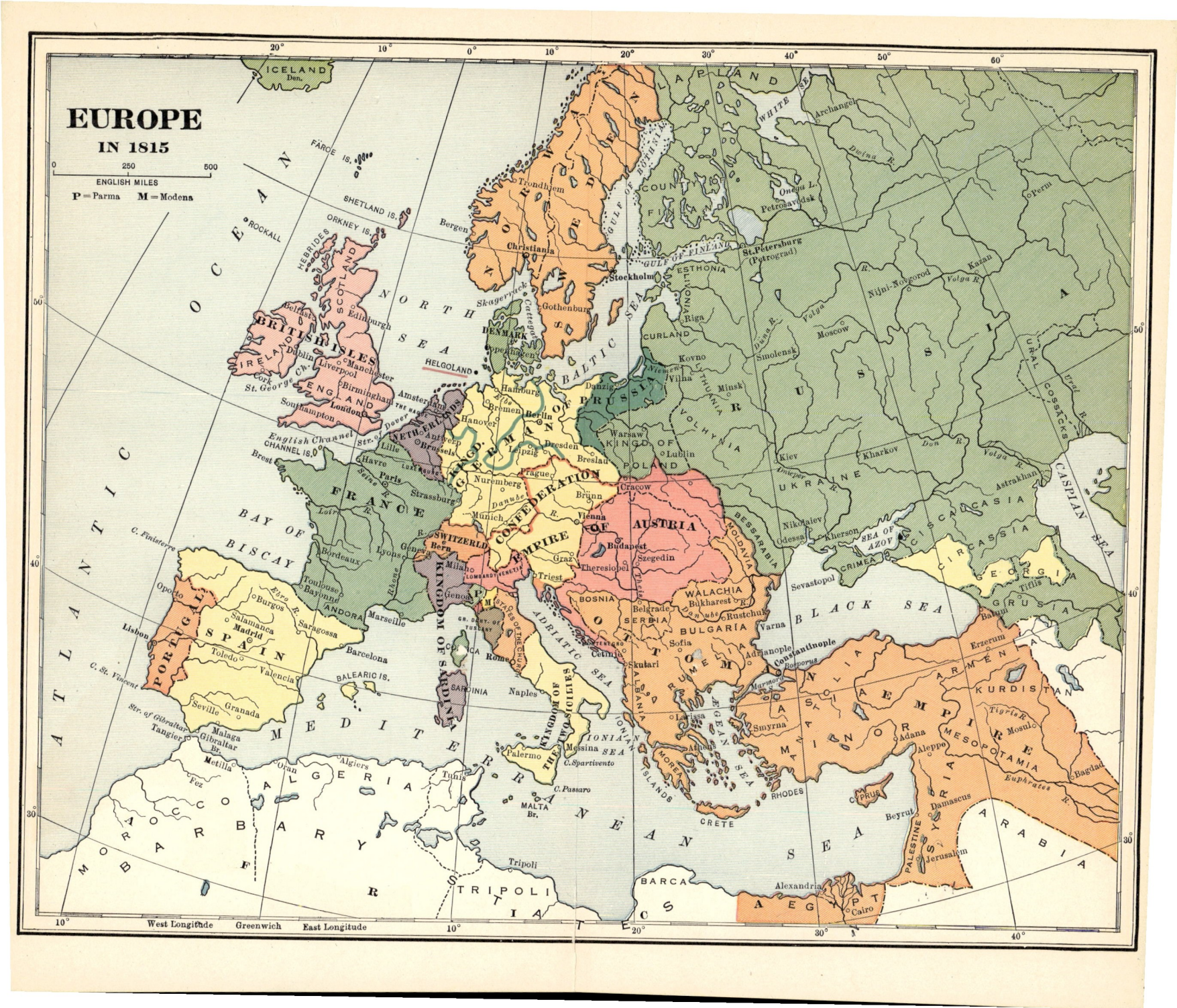

disposal of the allies. It received most of the territory which it had possessed at the end of 1803 (all except Ansbach, Bayreuth, and the greater part of the territory gained by Prussia in the second and third partitions of Poland) two fifths of Saxony, and a large area in Westphalia and on the left bank of the Rhine. The territorial gains of Prussia gave it a barrier against possible French aggression and left it divided into two unequal parts. The remaining three fifths of Saxony was restored to its former ruler. Hanover regained the provinces lost in 1803 and a number of small contiguous districts. Bavaria received Wurzburg and Aschaffenburg in the valley of the Main and the present Bavarian Palatinate on the left bank of the Rhine.

The Tsar had to sacrifice some of his plans for Poland. Of the territories the Tsar had hoped to acquire, Prussia regained the province of Posen and the fortress of Thorn, and Austria recovered a large part of the province of Galicia. With the remaining portions of the Grand Duchy of Warsaw the Tsar carried out his original plan of establishing a constitutional monarchy under his own sovereignty.

The former Kingdom of Holland was reëstablished as the Kingdom of The Netherlands under the sovereignty of the House of Orange. In order to strengthen the restored kingdom and to make it a real buffer against possible aggression by France, the former Austrian Netherlands were incorporated in the new kingdom.

The problem of the future of Switzerland gave comparatively little trouble. The Congress recognized the Swiss cantons as free and equal and agreed never to invade their neutrality by sending troops through their territory. The cantons were then allowed to draw up a constitution of their own, which bound them together into a federal union.

Changes of much importance were effected by the decisions of the Congress concerning Northern Europe. Denmark lost Norway as a result of its fidelity to Napoleon. Sweden — under the former French Marshal Bernadotte, by this time safely King of Sweden — surrendered its claims on Finland to Russia and possession of Swedish Pomerania to Prussia and received in exchange the Kingdom of Norway.

England indemnified itself with colonies conquered from the French and the Dutch. The most important of its acquisitions were the Cape of Good Hope and the island of Ceylon off the coast of India. The immediate importance of the latter colony was its position on the road to India.

This total disregard of those principles of democracy and nationality to which the French Revolution and the Napoleonic period had given such a tremendous impetus was the greatest weakness of the Congress of Vienna. People and provinces were handed around with entire disregard of their own wishes in the matter. In the Belgian Netherlands a people strongly attached to the Catholic Church and to local traditions was passed over to the rule of Dutch and Protestant neighbors on the north. Parts of the proud Polish nation were left under the control of Prussia and Austria. The Italian people were parceled out among ten different despots. In Germany the hopes raised during the War of Liberation were thwarted by the intrigues of Austria and the particularism of the smaller states. In Norway the people were transferred from Denmark to Sweden. In the Balkans no attention was paid to the nascent spirit of nationality animating the Christian subjects of the Sultan. Europe was to pay a heavy price during the next hundred years for this disregard of the principles of democracy and nationality.

THE HUNDRED DAYS

While the allies were wrangling over the division of the spoils that had been taken from Napoleon, the Bourbons and their supporters in France were turning the greater part of the French nation against the restored monarchy. The state of the French finances made necessary a rigorous reduction of the military forces of the country. Twelve thousand officers were put on half pay and ten thousand were retired entirely. With nothing to do they spent their time creating public sentiment against the Bourbons. The appointment of *émigrés* as officers in the army, the disrespect shown for the Legion of Honor, and the organization at great expense of a new corps of royal bodyguards composed of *émigrés* and old royalists increased the bitterness of the old soldiers. French industry suffered from lack of protection against the machine-made goods of England. The *émigrés* began to agitate in favor of depriving of their property the new owners of the lands which had been confiscated from the Church and the émigrés. The old nobility patronized the nobility of Napoleon as upstarts. The Bourbons interfered with old habits by their efforts to introduce into France the quiet of an English Sunday. These things help to explain the remarkable reception accorded to Napoleon upon his return to France from the island of Elba.

Of the course of events both at Vienna and in France Napoleon had been kept informed by his secret agents. Through them he learned of the discord between the allies over the Polish-Saxon question and of the discontent of the French nation with the policy of the Bourbons. Inspired by the reports from these sources and irritated by the failure of the Bourbons to pay the allowance stipulated in the Treaty of Fontainebleau, Napoleon laid his plans for an attempt to regain his throne. Setting sail from the island of Elba with eleven hundred men of his guard he landed on March 1, 1815, at a little bay near Nice.

The march of Napoleon to Paris was the happiest experience of his life. Hastening through the royalist regions around Marseilles the Emperor made his way by mountain paths toward the friendlier population around Grenoble. The troops sent out from the latter city to effect his capture received him with cries of "*Vive l'Empereur!*" From Grenoble to Paris his march was a continuous ovation. His old soldiers flocked to his standard, the peasants and workingmen received him with enthusiasm, and the cities opened their gates. As the Bourbons slipped out of Paris and across the frontier to the protection of the allied armies, Napoleon entered the city and installed himself in the Tuileries Palace without having fired a shot or shed a drop of blood.

He experienced little difficulty in forming a government. At the news of his arrival many of his old officials pressed around him and offered their services. After a brief resistance to the new government in Southern France and in the Vendée all active opposition to Napoleon vanished in France. He strove from the first to reassure the French nation of his good intentions. His first message promised liberty and peace, and as a pledge of his sincerity he issued a new constitution known as the "Acte Additionnel," which provided for a parliament of two houses, responsibility of ministers, and freedom of the press.

Napoleon's fate, however, depended on the allies rather than on the French people. He made every effort to assure the Powers of Europe of his pacific intentions, but they refused to receive his messengers. The Powers were determined that he should be overthrown. Their attitude made a renewal of the war inevitable. Napoleon decided to strike at the allied armies in Belgium commanded by Wellington and Blücher in the hope of solidifying his position by a victory and of gaining the line of the Rhine as a barrier against the advancing Austrians and Russians. The result of this maneuver was the decisive battle of Waterloo (June 18, 1815) in Belgium, in which the French army was completely routed.

The defeat of Napoleon at Waterloo led to his second abdication and to the second restoration of the Bourbons. The deputies who had been elected under the authority of the "Acte Additionnel" decided against any further sacrifice in behalf of Napoleon and demanded his resignation. A few days later they warned him of their inability to protect him from the allies. Unable to elude the watchful British fleet, Napoleon threw himself on the generosity of the English Government. After some discussion, the allies resolved that his liberty should be restricted in the interest of the peace of Europe and caused his transportation to the isolated island of Saint Helena in the South Atlantic, where he passed the remaining six years of his life.

France did not suffer for its desertion of the Bourbons as much as might have been expected. The second Treaty of Paris (November 20, 1815) deprived the country of only a few border fortresses and some square miles of territory and forced her to pay an indemnity of 700,000,000 francs within five years, to submit to the military occupation of her northern departments at French expense, and to accept the joint advice of the ambassadors of the four great allied Powers even on matters of domestic politics. This was much better than Prussia had fared at Tilsit, or Austria at Pressburg and Schönbrunn.

An incident of the return of Napoleon from Elba was the rising of Murat against the allies. In an effort to put himself at the head of a united Italy he left Naples in the middle of March, 1815, and moved rapidly northward. His rising resulted in his decisive defeat by the Austrians and the restoration of the Italian Bourbons to the throne of Naples.

PERMANENT RESULTS OF THE FRENCH REVOLUTION AND THE NAPOLEONIC PERIOD

In spite of the reaction which followed the overthrow of Napoleon the *ancien régime* was by no means entirely restored in Europe. In France the most important political and social gains of the Revolution were retained in the charter which had been granted by Louis XVIII to his subjects. Poland received a relatively liberal constitution from Tsar Alexander. Prussia and the South-German states retained their improved political and administrative machinery. In the rest of Napoleonic Europe the political conditions of the *ancien régime* were in general restored. In France and Southern Germany the Protestants made notable progress toward religious toleration and the State gained the upper hand over the Church. In Naples, France, and Southern Germany there was no general restoration of ecclesiastical property to the Church. The special privileges of the clergy and the Church remained abolished almost everywhere. The feudal dues were restored only in Piedmont, the States of the Church, and a few other places. The gilds were practically destroyed in France and were weakened in other places by the growth of big business enterprises not under their control. Commerce and agriculture retained all the gains they had made since 1789. The peasants kept the lands they had acquired. The enclosure movement made notable progress in France and

Southern Germany. Serfdom was not restored in France, Germany, or Poland. Likewise there was no attempt to reëstablish interior tariff lines or tolls.

REFERENCES

RESTORATION AND REACTION IN SPAIN
   C. J. H. Hayes, *A Political and Social History of Modern Europe*, vol. II, pp. 20–26.
   C. D. Hazen, *Europe since 1815*, pp. 36–40.

RESTORATION AND REACTION IN ITALY
   C. D. Hazen, *Europe since 1815*, pp. 40–45.

RESTORATION AND REACTION IN GERMANY
   C. D. Hazen, *Europe since 1815*, pp. 22–35.

RESTORATION IN FRANCE
   H. E. Bourne, *The Revolutionary Period in Europe*, pp. 446–52.
   C. J. H. Hayes, *A Political and Social History of Modern Europe*, vol. II, pp. 15–20.
   L. H. Holt and A. W. Chilton, *European History, 1789–1815*, pp. 324–28.
   Histoire générale, vol. IX, chapter XXVII.
   Histoire de France contemporaine, vol. IV, pp. 1–43.

THE CONGRESS OF VIENNA
   H. E. Bourne, *The Revolutionary Period in Europe*, pp. 452–56.
   C. J. H. Hayes, *A Political and Social History of Modern Europe*, vol. II, pp. 5–14.
   C. D. Hazen, *Europe since 1815*, chapter I.
   L. M. Holt and A. W. Chilton, *European History, 1789–1815*, pp. 328–35.
   J. S. Shapiro, *Modern and Contemporary European History*, pp. 17–20.
   Histoire générale, vol. X, chapter I.

THE HUNDRED DAYS
   H. E. Bourne, *The Revolutionary Period in Europe*, pp. 456–64.
   A. Fournier, *Napoleon the First*, pp. 685–720.
   L. M. Holt and A. W. Chilton, *European History, 1789–1815*, pp. 336–46.
   J. A. R. Marriott, *The Remaking of Modern Europe*, pp. 121–26.
   Histoire générale, vol. IX, chapter XXVIII.
   Histoire de France contemporaine, vol. IV, pp. 42–64.

THE FINAL ACT OF THE CONGRESS OF VIENNA
   J. H. Robinson and C. A. Beard, *Readings in Modern European History*, vol. I, pp. 381–84.

THE FRENCH CHARTER OF 1814
   F. M. Anderson, *Constitutions and Documents: France*, pp. 457–65.
   J. H. Robinson and C. A. Beard, *Readings in Modern European History*, vol. II, pp. 2–5.

MAPS
   Treaty adjustments, 1814–1815, W. R. Shepherd, *Historical Atlas*, p. 157.

CHAPTER XX
EUROPE IN 1815

The first chapter of the present work gave a survey of the main features in the economic, social, ecclesiastical, and political organization of Europe in the year 1500. The rest of the book has traced the outstanding movements of modern history during the three centuries which intervened between the opening of the modern era of history and the close of the Napoleonic period. The aim of the present chapter is to summarize the effects of these three hundred years of history on the organization of Europe.

POLITICAL ORGANIZATION

By 1815 the weak, backward Grand Duchy of Muscovy had developed into the most powerful state of Europe. Its dominant position was due to the extent and resources of the Russian Empire, the autocratic power wielded by the Tsar of Russia, and the leading part taken by the Russian armies in the overthrow of Napoleon.

The great area of the Empire was the result of three hundred years of steady expansion. The activities of Russian pioneers carried its limits across Siberia to the Pacific Ocean on the east. The victory of Peter the Great over the Swedes gave Russia an outlet on the Baltic. The policies of Catherine II extended the boundaries of the Russian state to the Black Sea on the south and across the Grand Duchy of Lithuania on the west. The alliance of Tsar Alexander with Napoleon resulted in the acquisition of Finland. The war with Turkey during the Napoleonic period gave Russia Bessarabia and extended the limits of the Empire to the Pruth. These conquests made the rulers of Russia sovereigns of nearly half of Europe and of almost one seventh of the land surface of the earth.

As a result of this extension of its boundaries the Russian Empire included a great mixture of peoples. The earlier conquests of the Grand Dukes of Muscovy had brought into the Empire the Great Russians, the Little Russians, and the White Russians; the acquisition of the steppes of Southern Russia and the vast areas of Siberia, many varieties of Turco-Tartars; the victories of Peter the Great, Esthonians, Letts, Lithuanians, and a sprinkling of Germans; the partitions of Poland, large numbers of Lithuanians, White Russians, and Jews; the seizure of Finland in 1809, the Finns; and the treaty of peace with Turkey in 1812, the Rumanians, Little Russians, and the Jews of Bessarabia. In the territories along the Baltic Sea that belonged to the Teutonic Knights, the Germans dominated. They owned the great estates, conducted the business of the region, and filled the honorable professions. German was the language of the universities and of the educated classes. In Finland the Swedes held a somewhat similar position. In the rest of the Empire the Great Russians were predominant.

This great mixture of peoples was held together by the autocratic government of the Empire. The Tsar had practically unlimited authority over his subjects. The nobles, in turn, had almost unlimited power over their serfs and enforced their will by the use of the knout and the threat of banishment to Siberia. As in other countries of the *ancien régime* the members of the nobility were given most of the offices in the army and in the administration and were exempted from paying many of the ordinary taxes. Corruption was rife in all branches of the government.

In spite of its great political and military prestige the Empire was extremely backward economically, socially, and intellectually. Agriculture was still the principal occupation of the people and the large estate the chief agricultural unit. The chief exports were wheat, timber, furs, and naval stores. The population of the Empire, numbering about 45,000,000, was divided into landlords and peasants. The latter class, comprising nine tenths of the population, were mainly serfs. The 140,000 families of the landlord class had made considerable progress along the lines of western culture. The peasants were still incredibly ignorant, drunken, and brutalized. Built upon such a social and economic foundation the Russian state found itself increasingly handicapped in its rivalry with the great Powers of Western Europe as the nineteenth century progressed.

United to Russia in a personal union was Poland. Congress Poland, as it is known, contained only three million inhabitants and included less than one sixth of the kingdom partitioned by Austria, Prussia, and Russia. The new state possessed a Diet of two houses with power to legislate and to examine the budget, a fairly liberal suffrage, religious toleration, and freedom of the press. Unlike Russia, Poland was a land of Western culture.

Next to Russia, England was probably the most important state in Europe in 1815. By reason of its victories over the Spaniards, the Dutch, and the French in the struggle for colonies and commerce, it was the first naval and colonial power in the world. Industrially, commercially, and financially, it had outstripped its neighbors on the continent of Europe. During the wars of the French Revolution and the Napoleonic period it had proved the one steadfast enemy of France and Napoleon, and its subsidies had been the foundation on which every coalition against them had been built. The prestige derived from its colonies, its navy, its industry, its commerce, and its wealth gave England an important place in the councils of Europe.

Its colonial empire was the result of three centuries of history. Religious persecution and the desire for commercial profits had driven the first merchants to India and the first settlers to America. The Anglo-Dutch wars and the English trade and navigation laws of the seventeenth century had caused the transfer of the colony of New York to England and destroyed a considerable portion of Dutch commerce. The struggle with France in the eighteenth century for colonies and commerce gave England possession of the greater part of North America and an opportunity to conquer the native states of India. The years following the close of the Seven Years' War (1763) had witnessed the loss of the thirteen American colonies, the expansion of British rule in

India, and the beginnings of British exploration and settlement in Australasia. The Napoleonic conflict had resulted in the acquisition of Ceylon, the Cape of Good Hope, and three small islands that formerly belonged to France. Hand in hand with the growth of the British Empire had gone the development of the British navy and the increase of British commerce.

In the three centuries between 1500 and 1815 England experienced many remarkable economic changes. The population of the kingdom had probably quadrupled. The Industrial Revolution shifted the center of population northward and westward. The growth of commerce and manufactures had caused the development of great commercial and industrial cities. Agriculture slowly gave place to commerce, industry, and banking. The merchant and the manufacturer were thrusting themselves into a position of power. In the cities a commercial class of tremendous potential power was developing. In rural England the Agricultural Revolution had thrown the land into the hands of a few and transformed the mass of the population into landless agricultural and industrial workers. These changes made England a land of great economic power and profound social misery.

As a result of the reaction of the ruling class in England to the excesses of the French Revolution, the government was run in the interest of the upper classes. Parliament and the administration were under the control of a small oligarchy. Not more than one man in ten had the right of suffrage. Parliament legislated in the interest of the landlord, the merchant, and the manufacturer. The penal code was barbarous. The judges belonged to the governing oligarchy. Trial by jury and the Habeas Corpus Act had been suspended repeatedly. The government sorely needed to be democratized. Nevertheless, the new society, which was springing up as a result of the Industrial Revolution, was destined to change many of the features that were characteristic of England in 1815.

In Central Europe by 1815 the place of the Holy Roman

Empire had been taken by the German Confederation. In some ways nothing had changed in the course of three hundred years. Austria held the presidency of the Confederation. The Diet was still composed of representatives of the states of the Confederation. The executive still lacked real authority. The Diet was kept inactive by the refusal of the states composing the Confederation to delegate any real authority to the central government. The Confederation still had no army, no flag, no administrative organs of government. Real progress toward the unification of Germany had been made, however, during the Napoleonic period. As a result of the policies of Napoleon the number of states had been reduced from three hundred and sixty-four to thirty-eight, and in the hearts of a few professors, students, lawyers, editors, and writers had been planted the seed from which was destined to grow a movement of ever-increasing strength for the unification and democratization of Germany.

After the Thirty Years' War, Germany was naturally sterile in literature, but at about the same time that Rousseau was bursting the conventional barriers in France a group of vigorous young poets and essayists was reviving German literature. The two great names of this era of "Storm and Stress" were two poets and dramatists: Schiller (1759–1805), with his appeal to the sense of patriotism and Goethe (1749–1832), whose deeper nature sought rather the universality of the antique thought and combined it with an almost prophetic appreciation of modern science. Both Schiller and Goethe lived through the romanticism of their youth into a calm and exalted mood of tempered idealism. Their influence upon their contemporaries in this regard was paralleled by a remarkable development in the field of philosophy. The outstanding figure in this field was Emmanuel Kant (1724–1804) a professor in the University of Königsberg, who throughout these troubled times lived a quiet, secluded life in an academic environment, almost untouched by the transient march of armies or the passing of ancient societies. In his *Critique of Pure Reason* and other works of profound analysis of the character of thought itself, he inaugurated a new era in philosophy. Man's place in the universe received a justification, not only by his capacity as the builder of thoughts which are real in themselves, but also through the recognition of the imperative moral duties and the moral worth of the individual which are the inevitable consequences of freedom of judgment. So vast a system of philosophy as that of Kant cannot well be described here; but a practical effect was soon given to it by a professor at Berlin, Fichte (1762-1814), whose philosophical works concern us less than his *Addresses to the German Nation*, which were delivered in 1807-08 in the midst of the period of greatest political disaster for Prussia. This proved to be a clarion call to his discouraged fellow citizens, and has ever since remained a source of inspiration for German patriotism. Less effective in moving the impulses of the people than Fichte, but exercising a wider and more lasting influence, was his younger contemporary, the leading philosopher of the next generation, Hegel (1770-1831), who is remembered chiefly for his contributions to the philosophy of history, an interpretation of the successive ages, empires, or civilizations as a progressive revelation of that divine purpose of which different aspects are emphasized by various peoples. The culmination was naturally to be found in the modern Teutonic world. This Germany of idealism long battled with the material Germany for supremacy and never quite lost its hold on German thought.

Prussia came out of the ordeal of the Napoleonic wars a transformed state. From the original margraviate of Brandenburg, it had grown into a powerful kingdom of eight provinces inhabited by a population of twelve millions, mainly Germans. Its territories lay in two groups separated by the Kingdom of Hanover. In Northern and Eastern Germany Prussia possessed Brandenburg, Pomerania, Silesia, Prussia proper, Posen, and Saxony. In Western Germany it had acquired Westphalia and the Rhine Province. Only in Posen and West Prussia were the Germans in a minority. The thoroughly Germanic character of its population and its position on the border of France marked Prussia out as the future defender of the German Confederation and the leader in any movement for the unification of Germany.

The eastern portion of the kingdom differed greatly from the western. The east remained a region of the *ancien régime*. The land was divided into great estates and was inhabited by *Junkers* and peasants. The former lived in manorial style, exercised judicial and police powers over the peasants, and enjoyed rights of patronage over the Lutheran parish churches. The peasants lived in small, wretched villages and eked out a miserable existence from the products of their petty holdings and the wages paid them by the landlords for their labors. The western provinces had been democratized as a result of the French occupation. The nobles had lost their special privileges and shared social leadership with the manufacturers, merchants, and lawyers. The two western provinces also retained the French municipal organization in the cities, the French codes of law, public trials, and trial by jury.

The kingdom was still governed by an absolute monarchy. The weak and timorous King was swayed by conflicting influences. He failed to give the kingdom the representative assembly promised on the eve of the battle of Waterloo. The reform measures of Stein and Hardenberg were pushed feebly or neglected entirely. Court intrigue took the place of party struggles. The ministers and administrative officers were responsible only to the King. The government was infused with the spirit of the *ancien régime*.

The most distinctive feature of the Prussian state was the army. By a decree of 1814 the principle of universal military service was made permanent. The middle class was not permitted to buy substitutes as in other countries, but young men who gave evidence of certain educational attainments were let off with one year of army training, on condition that they supplied their own support and equipment. Other recruits were required to give three years' service to the army. From active service recruits passed first into the reserve and then into the *Landwehr*. Both of these divisions of the army had some military training annually with the standing army.

This system gave the Government at a minimum expense the service of all the country's man power in time of war. In time the system was adopted by all the principal countries of Europe.

During the three centuries that intervened between the opening of the modern period of history and the close of the Napoleonic period the Austrian Habsburgs made extensive acquisitions of territory. The Bohemian crown and its dependencies and a small part of Hungary were acquired in 1526 as a result of the marriage and diplomacy of Ferdinand, the brother of Charles V. By the end of the seventeenth century the Turks had been driven out of Hungary, Transylvania, and Croatia. The Italian province of Lombardy had been annexed as a result of the War of the Spanish Succession. Through the first partition of Poland, Galicia had been obtained. By cajolery and the threat of force the province of Bukowina had been acquired shortly afterwards from the Turks. During the Napoleonic period the Habsburgs had received Venetia and the eastern coast of the Adriatic Sea in exchange for their outlying possessions in Germany and The Netherlands. As a result of Francis's assumption of the title of Emperor of Austria in 1804 the heterogeneous states of the head of the Habsburgs received for the first time the common name of Austria.

This extension of their dominions made the Habsburgs sovereigns of a great mixture of peoples. The Slavs formed a submissive and unorganized majority in the population of twenty-eight or twenty-nine millions. They were separated by the Germans and the Magyars of the Empire into a northern and southern group, each subdivided into several races. In Western Galicia both the landlords and the peasants were Poles. In Eastern Galicia the landlords were Poles and the peasants mainly little Russians or Ruthenians, kinsmen of the inhabitants of Southern Russia. In Bohemia and its dependencies the Czechs formed the majority of the population, but the Germans predominated in the cities and in the regions adjoining Germany. The latter were likewise in a majority in Austria, Styria, Carinthia, and Carniola. In

Italy and the cities around the Adriatic the inhabitants were Italians. In the provinces around the Adriatic and in Southern Hungary the peasants were Southern Slavs and were subdivided into Slovenes, Croats, and Serbs. In Transylvania and Bukowina the peasants were mainly Rumanians. In Northern Hungary the peasants were largely Slovaks and akin to the Czechs of Bohemia. In the rest of Hungary the Hungarians and the Germans predominated. In the Empire as a whole the Germans were the dominant race. The Emperor, his family, and the court were German. Vienna, the capital of the Empire, was a German city. German was the language of the Government, the army, and the educated classes.

The great problem of the Austrian Government in 1815 was to hold this conglomeration of peoples together. The inhabitants of the Empire were not a nation; their only bond of union was their common allegiance to the Emperor. In such a state the doctrines of nationality and representative institutions might work havoc with the unity of the state and destroy the power of the central government. Five or six nationalities might arise which would refuse to work together. In consequence of this situation the great aim of the Austrian Government came to be to keep things as they were. The censor became all powerful. Every form of association was forbidden. The theater, newspapers, and books were censored. The lectures of university professors and even private conversations were subject to denunciation by spies of the Government. Everything was under surveillance.

In foreign affairs Austria held a position of importance. In Italy it dominated the peninsula through its possession of Lombardy and Venetia and its arrangements with most of the minor Italian states. In Germany it controlled political action through the German Confederation and by playing on the particularist fears of the minor German states. Abroad as at home Austria was the protagonist of counter-revolution.

France in 1815 held a most humiliating position. The excesses of the French Revolution had first made France an object of aversion to the rest of Europe. Its later military victories had then made it an object of fear. Finally the overthrow of Napoleon had reduced it to the boundaries of 1792 and caused its occupation by the troops of the coalition. The great task of the restored Bourbons was to establish their own rule solidly in France and to rehabilitate their country in the eyes of Europe.

The remaining states of Europe were of second and third rank. In 1815 Switzerland had been neutralized by the Powers. Sweden and Denmark were out of the main current of European politics. The Kingdom of The Netherlands was of importance only by reason of its colonial empire and its position on the northern border of France. Spain and Portugal had lost most of their colonies and had sunk to an unimportant position among the states of Europe. The states of Italy were too small to count for much in European politics. Only the Kingdom of Sardinia seemed to have a premonition of the part it was destined to play in the unification of Italy. The declining Ottoman Empire was on the verge of losing the Serbs, the Rumanians of Moldavia and Wallachia, and the Greeks of the Greek peninsula.

CULTURAL CONDITIONS

The chief change in the intellectual life of Europe between 1500 and 1815 was the transition from the scholastic to the scientific way of looking at things. At the beginning of the modern period even the leaders of thought based their thinking on authority. The statements of Aristotle, the Church fathers, and medieval theologians far outweighed the most careful human observations. At the close of three hundred years of modern history the intellectual leaders of the race were beginning to base their thinking on the results of patient observation, careful experimentation, and the use of instruments of precision. The slow methods of science were taking the place of ingenuous deductions from sacred texts. The old methods, however, still held sway over the minds of ordinary men.

Parallel with the growth of the physical sciences, new light began to be cast upon the origin and history of human society and institutions, due largely to a more careful criticism of the sources of our knowledge of the past. We have already seen how Voltaire and the philosophers of the eighteenth century questioned orthodox beliefs in the most thoroughgoing and fearless manner. But alongside this tendency of philosophic doubt, historical scholars were at work preparing great collections of the documents of history, after having established systematic and almost infallible tests for determining their authenticity. The same kind of criticism applied to the poems of Homer by the German scholar Wolf, in a volume published in 1795, raised substantial doubts as to the authorship and unity of the great Greek epics, while the historian Niebuhr, a Dane by birth, but a Prussian official living in Berlin, employed it to disprove the legendary history of early Rome. A still more important application of it to the Bible, in what is called "the higher criticism," opened up almost inexhaustible fields of religious and historical controversy. The nineteenth century took up this heritage of historical scholarship and remade the perspective of the past; reaching even beyond the confines of the written texts by means of the science of archæology. The result was something more than a mere enlargement of knowledge; the sense of historical development of the slow but ever-changing movement of institutions and society tended to color speculative thought as well. But, while the foundations of "scientific history" were already laid by the opening of the nineteenth century, one cannot yet say that it is generally appreciated or that its rules are observed in popular narrative.

The philosophers of the eighteenth century were even more directly responsible for the rise of the new science of political economy than for the transformation of history. We have already seen how the French Physiocrats had advanced the theory that the real source of wealth was in the products of the soil, and that they consequently were opposed to the narrow "mercantilism" of their day, which was based upon the idea that a nation's wealth largely depended on its ability to take advantage of another by the use of high tariffs and trade restrictions. The newer school of thinkers rejected the over-regulation of industry and commerce by the gilds, and especially opposed the paternalism of government prevalent in the old régime. Their motto was the French phrase: "*Laissez faire; laissez aller,*" — "Leave people to do as they please; let them go their own way," meaning that business people know better than government officials what is good for them. In the realm of commerce this called for a reduction or abolition of national customs tariffs. The greatest single contribution to this idea of "free trade" — or rather "freer trade" since some restrictions were admitted — came from a Scottish professor, Adam Smith, whose *Wealth of Nations*, published in 1776, is one of the world's great books. By a vast survey of economic facts he proved, at least to most British statesmen and thinkers throughout the whole nineteenth century and to many on the Continent as well, that the wealth of one's own country is conditioned more upon the maintenance of the prosperity of others than upon merely getting the better of them in a bargain or by trade restrictions. A prosperous market brings prosperity to the producer. Thus the economic doctrine of Adam Smith proved to be a liberating influence in politics as well. So far did this reach that the opening era of the nineteenth century has not unfittingly been called "The Era of Laissez Faire."

RELIGIOUS AND ECCLESIASTICAL CONDITIONS

Between 1500 and 1815 many changes took place in the religious and ecclesiastical organization of Europe. The Protestant Revolt split the people of Western Europe into Protestants and Catholics. The states steadily restricted the sphere of the Church and weakened its political power. In France, the French Revolution led to the confiscation of the property of the Church, the suppression of tithes and monastic orders, the abolition of the control of the Church over marriage, divorce, and the parish register, and the adoption of the policy of religious toleration. The Napoleonic period caused the extension of these reforms to Southern Germany, to Italy, and, to a slight extent, to Spain. The Catholic

Reformation, on the other hand, remedied the points wherein the Church was most open to criticism in the sixteenth century and put it in a position to strike vigorous blows in its own defense.

The religious map of Europe changed little after 1600. By that date the Protestant movement seemed to have spent its force. In France the Catholics even gained some ground as a result of the policy of persecution inaugurated by Louis XIV. In England the Protestants divided into many different sects, the religious fermentation of the seventeenth century producing the Presbyterians, the Congregationalists, the Baptists, and the Friends. The Wesleyan movement in the eighteenth century led to the organization of the Methodist denomination. The boundaries of Islam and the Eastern Church changed but little during the whole period of modern history.

In 1500 the Church still performed a wide variety of the functions that are now exercised by the State. In Protestant countries the Protestant Revolt deprived the Church of its special privileges and powers and subordinated it to the temporal authorities. In Catholic countries the victory of the State over the Church came later and more gradually. By 1815 the states in Napoleonic Europe had deprived the Church of most of its political privileges and powers. The Catholic sovereigns had increased the royal control over ecclesiastical appointments. The clergy and laity were taxed alike. The Church courts had become merely the disciplinary organs of the Church. The right of the Pope to interfere in the domestic affairs of Catholic states was no longer recognized. Large amounts of ecclesiastical property had been confiscated; many schools had been transferred to lay control; and in many of the states of Napoleonic Europe the clergy had been deprived of control of marriage, divorce, and the parish registers.

In 1500 the principle of religious toleration had no adherents. The ideal of the Protestant leaders during their struggle against the Church was independence rather than toleration. The principle of religious toleration was the product of political expediency, the humanitarian movement, and religious indifferentism. Toleration was extended to the English Dissenters as a reward for their fidelity to the Parliamentary cause in the struggle of the nation with James II. On the Continent men did not become tolerant until a deep interest in humanity began to take the place of a profound concern for personal salvation. By the end of the Napoleonic period Protestants had gained religious toleration in France, Southern Germany, and Poland; and Catholics in Prussia and Saxony. The Jews by the same date had obtained a much more limited degree of toleration.

SOCIAL ORGANIZATION

The first three centuries of modern history also effected many changes in the organization of European society. The Commercial Revolution swelled the numbers of the middle class in Europe and increased its wealth and power. The Industrial Revolution added still more to the numbers and wealth of the middle class and created a great class of factory workers. The Agricultural Revolution separated the mass of Englishmen from the land. The French Revolution destroyed the privileges of the nobles and the clergy and the feudal burdens of the peasants in France. The wars of the French Revolution and the Napoleonic period extended the reforms of the French Revolution to Napoleonic Europe. By 1815 the forces set in action by these great movements had implanted in the minds of the lower classes of Europe the ideals of political freedom and social equality and had begun in countries like France, England, and Western Germany to put the merchant and the manufacturer, the banker and the professional man in the position of power that was once held by the clergy and the nobility.

THE CITIES: INDUSTRY AND COMMERCE

By the close of the Napoleonic period the cities were beginning to dominate European society. In the course of three hundred years many mere villages had grown into great commercial and industrial centers and many old medieval towns had spread their suburbs far beyond their ancient ramparts. In most instances walls had been pulled down and moats filled up to provide broad boulevards for the circulation and recreation of the inhabitants. The castle no longer either overawed or defended the citizens. The belfry had become an artistic relic of antiquity. The faithful endowed schools and hospitals instead of rearing great cathedrals. Old streets had been straightened and widened, and broad, commodious avenues had been laid out in the newer quarters of the towns. Street-lighting and paving were becoming general. The various sections of the cities were being differentiated into residence sections, working-class quarters, commercial and manufacturing districts, and retail centers.

Both trade and industry were being conducted on an increasingly large scale. The capitalists were beginning to employ hundreds of workers in place of a handful of journeymen and apprentices. The factory and the warehouse were fast supplanting the tiny shop at the front of the master's dwelling. The fields outside the city walls, once tilled by the citizens, had long been built up. The great rural estates were beginning to be run for profit. Farmer and townsman alike were beginning to sell all that they produced and to buy all that they consumed. There was a lively exchange of products, therefore, between town and country, district and district, state and state, and continent and continent. The weekly market, the annual fair, and the wandering trader no longer met the needs of the people. Their places had been taken by the retail merchant and the wholesaler. With the rise of trade most of the obstacles to commerce gradually disappeared. The robber baron, countless tolls, and barbarous commercial laws were displaced by a social system which put the interest of the merchant and the manufacturer first.

By 1815 the independence and the special privileges of the cities were disappearing everywhere in Europe. With the four exceptions of Bremen, Hamburg, Lübeck, and Frankfort the independent city-state had disappeared in Italy and in Germany. In France, Germany, and The Netherlands, the cities had lost their special privileges. The State regulated by general laws the political organization of the urban centers. The representatives of the central government penetrated at will the limits of the cities. The gilds were losing their significance. The common man was slowly acquiring power at the expense of the old municipal oligarchies.

On the whole, life was possibly less joyous for the mass of the urban dwellers in 1815 than in 1500. The working quarters were still dirty, unsanitary, and malodorous. Life was more monotonous. The pageants and saints' days were disappearing. The Commercial and Industrial Revolutions brought wealth, power, education, and luxury into the hands of the few; they subjected the many to a wretched existence and the galling discipline of the factory.

RURAL ORGANIZATION

Great estates were still prevalent in most parts of Europe. In many instances in France and Western Germany they had been broken up, but in England and Eastern Germany they had grown at the expense of the small holdings. In most parts of Europe the peasants lived much as they had lived three hundred years before. The village was still a characteristic feature of the landscape. The peasant often shared his roof with his cattle and poultry. Glass windows and floors were more common than formerly, but the courtyard retained much of its medieval appearance.

The enclosure movement was spreading rapidly. In France, in Southern Germany, and in England the medieval strips were being exchanged and the arable fields, the common pastures, the meadows, and the woodlands divided into parcels under individual ownership. Artificial grasses were being introduced. The common pasture, the waste land, and the common woodland were in the process of disappearing. Hedges were becoming a characteristic feature of the English landscape.

In England, in France, and in Southern and Western Germany the primitive agricultural methods were giving way to more scientific methods of farming. The crude medieval tools were still in use everywhere, but the more enterprising landowners and farmers managed their estates and farms as they saw fit. The practice of leaving one third of the land to lie fallow was dying out. In the light of new knowledge crops were being rotated more scientifically and fertilizers more widely used. Europe was on the eve of a greater agricultural revolution.

In England, France, Germany, and The Netherlands the relation of the villagers to the owners of the great estates was changing. In England and the eastern provinces of Prussia the peasants were becoming landless agricultural laborers. In France, the Belgian Netherlands, Westphalia, and on the left bank of the Rhine the peasant had become a free landholder. He owned his cottage and one or more parcels of land. His holdings were no longer widely scattered. He was losing his rights in the pasture land, the common fields, and the woodland of the village. He no longer owed either services or payments to the neighboring lord, or shared with him the profits of his commercial transactions. The lord, on the other hand, no longer seized the peasant's best beast, forced him to pay for the use of the seigniorial mill, oven, or winepress, or hunted over his growing fields. In Southern and Eastern Germany serfdom, at least, had been abolished. In France, the Belgian Netherlands, Westphalia, and the Rhine Province the lords had lost the right to judge their peasants.

Consequently, for the more favored villagers on the continent of Europe life in 1815 seemed to hold out a promise of better things. Though they continued to suffer from the forces of nature, from sickness, and from ignorance and superstition, the peasants of France, The Netherlands, and Southern and Western Germany were beginning to see signs of a brighter day. The French Revolution and the Napoleonic period had made them masters of their own land, and agricultural science, public education, and manhood suffrage were thrusting into their clumsy, unskillful hands the tools with which they might learn to work out their political, economic, and spiritual salvation.

INDEX

Absolutism, tendency toward, in France, 146; under Louis XIV, 196; undermined in England, 287; on eve of French Revolution, 337 ff.; decline in France, 343-47, 363-71; in Prussia, 469.
Academy, Calvin's, at Geneva, 99.
Act of Settlement, the, 184.
Africa, struggle of the Powers in, 221; English colonies in, 322.
Agricultural Revolution, the, 312-14.
Agriculture, at opening of sixteenth century, 1 ff.; England in 1750, 301 ff.; legislation in France, 358. *See also* Economic conditions, and Rural conditions.
Aix-la-Chapelle, Treaty of, 226 ff.; 244.
Alba, Duke of, in The Netherlands, 128 ff.
Albert of Brandenburg, 76, 214.
Albuquerque, Portuguese administrator in the East, 53.
America, discovery and exploration, 51; Jesuit missionaries in, 123; struggle of the Powers in, 221 ff.; wars between England and France, 225 ff.
American Revolution, the, 317-21.
Amiens, Treaty of, 406, 421.
Anabaptist revolt, the, 83-85.
Ancien Régime, in France, 325-27.
Anglican revolt, the, 103-10.
Archbishop, at opening of sixteenth century, 14.
Architecture, under Louis XIV, 195, 198.
Arkwright, Richard, 306.
Armada, Spanish (1588), 132.
Art, medieval, 27.
Attrition, to accompany the act of penance, 67.
Auerstadt, battle of, 426.
Augsburg, League of, 193 ff.
Augsburg, Peace of, 151.
Augsburg Confession, the, 77.
Augustus II, of Poland, 211 ff.
Austerlitz battle of, 424 ff.
Australia, first settlements in, 322.
Austria, in 1740, 235-36; alliances with France and Russia, 246; war with France, 370, 392; on eve of wars of French Revolution, 391; war with France, 423 ff., 432-34; at Congress of Vienna, 455; at opening of nineteenth century, 470 ff.
Austria and Prussia in the eighteenth century, 235-57; Austria in 1740, 235; Prussia under Frederick William I, 236; the wars of Frederick the Great, 241; Frederick the Great as an enlightened despot, 249; Joseph II as an enlightened despot, 254.
Austrian Succession, War of, 225, 236, 242.
Authority, intellectual revolt against, 274-300; the medieval world scheme, 274; the new astronomy, 276; progress in the other sciences, 280; progress in philosophy, 284; development of skepticism, 286; development of political theory, 287; the French philosophers, 290.

Bacon, Francis, 285.
Bacon, Roger, 27.
Baden, Treaty of, 194.
Baptism, 18.
Barwalde, Treaty of, 157.
Basel, Treaty of, 395.
Bastille, fall of, 353.
Bavaria, gains of Jesuits, 121; under Napoleon, 415.
Baylen, French capitulation at, 431.
Beccaria, 298.
Berg, Grand Duchy of, 439.
Berlin Decree, the, 426 ff.
Bible, Luther's translation of, 71; King James version, 169.
Bill of Rights, the, 183.
Bishop, at opening of sixteenth century, 13.
Black, Joseph, 283.
Blenheim, battle of, 194.
Boerhave, 283.
Bohemia, at opening of sixteenth century, 40; religious and political conditions at opening of seventeenth century, 151 ff.
Bohemian Brethren, the, 151.
Bonaparte, Joseph, 431, 438.
Bonaparte, Louis, 425.
Bonaparte, Napoleon. *See* Napoleon.
Boris Gudunov, 205 ff.
Boulton, Matthew, 309.

INDEX

Bourgeoisie. *See* Middle class.
Boyle, Robert, 282.
Brahe, Tycho, 276.
Brandenburg, Mark of, 214 ff.
Brazil, discovery of, 54; Portuguese dynasty founds empire in, 432.
Breda, Declaration of, 177.
Breitenfeld, battle of, 158 ff.
British Empire in the last half of the eighteenth century, 301-24; England in 1750, 301; the industrial revolution, 304; the agricultural revolution, 312; the Wesleyan revival, 314; attempts to modify the English constitution, 316; the American Revolution, 317; the extension of the Empire in the Far East, 321; at opening of nineteenth century, 465 ff.
Brumaire, Eighteenth, coup d'état of, 404 ff.
Bruno, Giordano, 284.
Buffon, 283.
Bunyan, John, 179.
Burgundian State, at opening of sixteenth century, 31 ff.
Burke, Edmund, 421.

Cabot, John, 54.
Calixtines, the, 151.
Calonne, 346.
Calvin, John, 93 ff.
Calvinist revolt, the, 93-103.
Cambrai, Treaty of, 79.
Campo Formio, Treaty of, 396 ff.
Canada, English victories in, 230.
Capuchins, the, 115.
Cardinals, at opening of sixteenth century, 14.
Carolina, founding of, 180.
Cartier, 54.
Cartwright, Edmund, 307.
Cateau-Cambrésis, Treaty of, 82, 135.
Cathedral, at opening of sixteenth century, 13.
Catherine II, 248; as an enlightened despot, 259-61.
Catholic church, split into Eastern Church and Roman Catholic Church, 21. *See also* Religious conditions.
Catholic league, in France, 135.
Catholic Reformation and the Ascendancy of Spain under Philip II, 115-39; the Catholic Reformation, 115; Philip II, 124; the revolt of The Netherlands, 127; the war between England and Spain, 131; the wars of religion in France, 132; position of Spain at the close of the sixteenth century, 136.
Catholics, in Thirty Years' War, 151-66; tolerant policy of James I, 170; interests advanced by James II, 181 ff. *See also* Religious situation.
Cavendish, 283.
Censoring books, rise of the idea, 120.
Chancellor, English explorer, 205.
Charles I, 171 ff.
Charles II, restored to English throne, 177; secretly in pay of Louis XIV, 180; court dominated by Louis XIV, 198.
Charles IV, of Spain, 431.
Charles V, 70, 79 ff.; abdication of, 124.
Charles VI, of Austria, 236.
Charles XII of Sweden, 210 ff.
Chemistry and physics, 282 ff.
Church, organization at opening of sixteenth century, 12-18; 21-22; purposes, doctrines and services, 18-19; criticisms, 19-21; in eastern Europe, 21-22; assumes many political functions, 28; experiments with taxation, 64; result of Protestant revolt, 110; reorganization under French Constitution of 1791, 362 ff.; discredited during French Revolution, 383. *See also* Religious conditions.
Church and State, relations under Concordat of 1801, 409; separation during French Revolution, 385.
Cintra, French capitulation at, 432.
Cisalpine Republic, the, 397.
Cities, at opening of sixteenth century, 5-9; government in France, on eve of French Revolution, 340; at opening of nineteenth century, 476-78.
Civil Constitution of the Clergy, in France, 364.
Classes, social, at opening of sixteenth century, 10. *See also* Social conditions.
Clergy, on eve of French Revolution, 333-35. *See also* Church, and Religious conditions.
Clive, Robert, 231, 322.
Coalitions, wars of the. *See* French Revolution.
Codification of laws of France, 411.
Colbert, 143, 186 ff.
Coligny, Admiral, 133.
Colonial and commercial supremacy, 140-67; the period of Dutch colonial and commercial supremacy, 140; Henry IV and Richelieu, 144; the Thirty Years' War, 151; Mazarin and the war with Spain, 164; in the eighteenth century, 220-34; the colonial situation in 1689, 220; the

INDEX

early struggles of the English, French, and Spanish, 221; the work of Dupleix, 226; the Seven Years' War, 229.
Columbus, Christopher, 51.
Comfort, increase in, 59.
Commerce, widening of area of, 56; new agencies of, 57; Dutch supremacy in, 140–44.
Commerce and industries, at opening of sixteenth century, 5–9; at opening of nineteenth century, 476–78. *See also* Economic conditions.
Committee of General Security, during French Revolution, 379 ff.
Committee of Public Safety, during French Revolution, 375 ff.
Commonwealth, in England, 175 ff.
Commune, Paris, 372 ff.
Companies, commercial, rise of, 57.
Concordat of 1801, the, 409 ff.
Condé, French general, 165 ff., 186.
Condorcet, 386.
Confirmation, 18.
Congress of Vienna, the, 453–58.
Congress of Westphalia, 160.
Constantinople, captured by Turks, 269.
Constitution of 1791, French, 345.
Constitution of 1795, French, 383, 400 ff.
Constitution, English, attempts to modify during eighteenth century, 316–17.
Consular imperialism, under Napoleon, 413–18.
Consulate, life, establishment of, 412.
Consuls, provisional, appointment in France, 404.
Continental System, the, 426 ff., 428–31.
Contrition, to accompany the act of penance, 67.
Conventicle Act (1664), 179.
Convention Parliament, the, 183.
Cook, James, voyages of, 322.
Copernicus, Nicolaus, 275 ff.
Corday, Charlotte, 384.
Coronado, 52.
Cort, Henry, 309.
Cortez, 52.
Cossacks, history of, 202.
Cotton-spinning, in England, 307 ff.
Council of Elders, during French Revolution, 383.
Council of Five Hundred, during French Revolution, 383.
Council of State, in France, 339.
Council of Trent, the, 119 ff.
Council of Troubles ("Council of Blood"), 128, ff.

Coup d'État, of 18th Brumaire, 404 ff.
Court of Louis XIV, 195.
Crompton, Samuel, 306.
Cromwell, Oliver, 165, 174 ff.
Cromwell, Richard, 177.
Culture, European, at opening of nineteenth century, 472–74.

Da Gama, Vasco, 50, 56.
Danton, 366 ff., 377 ff.
De Medici family, the, 24; Catherine, 133; Marie, 147 ff.
Declaration of Indulgence, the, 181.
Declaration of Rights, the, 183.
D'Étaples, Lefèvre, 92.
De Soto, 52.
Deists, English, 287.
Demarcation, line of, 51.
Denmark, at opening of sixteenth century, 44; intervention on behalf of Protestants of Germany, 154 ff.; effect of Congress of Vienna, 457; at opening of nineteenth century, 472.
Descartes, 285.
Desmoulin, Camille, 366.
Devolution, War of, 188 ff.
Dictatorship, under Napoleon, 407–13.
Diderot, 298.
Diet of Holy Roman Empire, 30.
Diet of Nuremberg, 80.
Diet of Speyer, 80.
Diet of Worms, Luther at, 70.
Diplomatic revolution, the, 246.
Directory, French (1795–99), 383, 400–03.
Divine right of kings, the, 169 ff. *See also* Absolutism.
Doctrines, church, results of Protestant revolt, 111.
Dumouriez, 393.
Dupleix, French governor in India, 226 ff., 322.
Dutch East India Company, 141 ff.
Dutch West India Company, 142.

East Prussia, Duchy of, 214 ff.
Eastern Europe, religious organization of, 21–22.
Ecclesiastical and religious conditions, at opening of sixteenth century, 11 ff.; at opening of nineteenth century, 474–76. *See also* Religious conditions.
Economic conditions, 1–11; 140–67; 220–33; in France, 146; under Colbert, 187 ff.; England at middle of eighteenth century, 303 ff.; effect of Industrial Revolution, 310; on eve of French Revolution, 325–37; under French National Assembly,

357 ff.; England at opening of nineteenth century, 466. *See also* Reforms.
Edict of Nantes, 135, 144; Revocation of, 190.
Education, system under French National Convention, 385.
Edward VI, Protestantism in reign of, 106.
Egypt, Napoleon's campaign in, 398.
Eighteenth century, struggle for colonial and commercial supremacy, 220–33; Austria and Prussia in, 235–56; the British Empire in latter years, 301–23.
Elba, Napoleon exiled to, 451; return from, 455.
Electors, of Holy Roman Empire, 30.
Elizabeth, Protestantism, in reign of, 108.
Emigration, to America, 59; Huguenot, 190 ff.; German, 199; Puritan, 171, 172.
Émigrés, French, 353 ff.; under Concordat of 1801, 411.
Emperor of Holy Roman Empire, 30.
Empire, British. *See* British Empire.
Empire, French, 440 ff.
Enclosure movement, in England, 313, 478.
Encyclopedia, French, 290 ff., 298 ff.
England, Calvinism in, 103; efforts of Jesuits, 122; war with Spain, 131–32; war with Netherlands, 143, 175 ff., 180; development of parliamentary government in, 168–84; expansion into British Empire, 171; colonial possessions in eighteenth century, 220 ff.; war with France, 221 ff.; war with Spain, 222 ff.; war with France, 229 ff.; war with Spain, 232; alliance with Prussia, 246; at middle of eighteenth century, 301–04; American Revolution, 317–23; on eve of wars of French Revolution, 391; war with France, 393, 398–400; during Revolutionary period, 420–22; war with France, 423 ff.; effect of Congress of Vienna, 458; at opening of nineteenth century, 465.
England, Scotland, and Ireland, at opening of sixteenth century, 39–40.
English East India Company, 171, 322.
Episcopal Church, in America, 109.
Equality, under French National Assembly, 357 ff.
Erasmus, 25; breach with Luther, 72.
Established Church of England, 109.

Estates, at opening of the sixteenth century, 1–5.
Estates General, in France, 338 ff.; meeting of 1789, 350.
Eucharist, the, 18.
Eustachia, 281.
Expansion, overseas, beginnings of, 47–63; commerce in the later Middle Ages, 47; the Portuguese explorations, 50; Spanish explorations, 53; the results of overseas expansion, 54.
Extreme unction, 18.
Eylau, battle of, 427.

Fabricius, 281.
Factory system, introduction of, 307.
Far East, medieval trade with, 47; extension of British Empire in, 321–23.
Farnese, Alexander, duke of Parma, 130.
Fehrbellin, battle of, 218.
Ferdinand, regains throne of Spain, 448.
Feudalism, survival of, 9–11; 28.
Fichte, 468.
Finland, conquered by Sweden, 44.
First Coalition, war of, 392–98.
Fleurus, battle of, 394.
Florence, under the Medici, 24; at opening of sixteenth century, 35.
Fontainebleau, Treaty of, 451.
Fourth Coalition, war of, 426–28.
Fox, Charles James, 420.
France, at opening of sixteenth century, 35–37; explorations in North America, 54; war with Charles V, 79 ff.; Calvinism in, 100; wars of religion in, 132–36; war with Netherlands, 143; accessions of territory, under Henry IV, 147; in Thirty Years' War, 151 ff.; war with Spain, 159, 164–66; war with Netherlands, 188; ascendancy under Louis XIV, 186–200; the work of Colbert, 186; the war of Devolution, 188; the Dutch war, 188; the revocation of the Edict of Nantes, 190; the "Reunions," 190; the war of the League of Augsburg, 193; the war of the Spanish Succession, 193; the results of the reign of Louis XIV, 194; colonies lost, 195; colonial possessions in eighteenth century, 220 ff.; war with England, 221 ff., 229 ff.; alliance with Austria, 246; intervenes in American Revolution, 320; the eve of the French Revolution, 325–49; the *Ancien Régime*, 325; economic conditions, 325; social organization,

INDEX

327; religious conditions, 332; political conditions, 337; the decline of the Absolute Monarchy, 343; war with Austria and Prussia, 370, 392; war with England and Netherlands, 393, 398–400; war with Turkey, 399; war with Third Coalition, 423 ff.; war with Fourth Coalition, 426 ff.; war with Austria, 432–34; war with Russia, 437; the First Empire, 440–42; war with Prussia, 444; at Congress of Vienna, 454; at opening of nineteenth century, 471. *See also* French Revolution.
Francis I, 79 ff.
Franklin, Benjamin, 283.
Frederick the Great, wars of, 241–49; as enlightened despot, 249–56.
Frederick William I, 215 ff., 236 ff.
Frederick III, 218 ff.
French Revolution, the eve of, 325–46; the struggle for the control of the government, 350; the reforms of the National Assembly, 357; decline and fall of the monarchy, 363; the National Convention, 371; reforms of the Legislative Assembly and the National Convention, 383; consolidation and extension of, 391–419; Europe on the eve of the wars of the French Revolution, 391; the war of the First Coalition, 392; the struggle with England, 398; the Directory, 400; the establishment of Napoleon Bonaparte in power, 403; the beneficent dictatorship, 407; consular imperialism, 413; permanent results of, 461.
Friars, at opening of sixteenth century, 17.
Friedland, battle of, 427.
Fronde, the, 164 ff.

Galileo, 277 ff.
Généralitiés, in France, 340.
Geneva, Calvin at, 96 ff.
Genoa, trade with Far East, 47.
Gentz, at Congress of Vienna, 455.
George III, personal rule of, 316 ff.
German Confederation, formation of, 456; at opening of nineteenth century, 467.
Germany, the Protestant Revolt in, 64–78; Calvinism in, 100; in Thirty Years' War, 152 ff.; ravaged by Louis XIV, 199; reorganization under Napoleon, 414 ff.; French influence in, 438; work of Napoleon undone, 450; effect of Congress of Vienna, 456.
Gibraltar, gained by England, 194.

Gilds, in cities at opening of sixteenth century, 7.
Girondins, the, 368 ff.
Goethe, 467.
Gold, discovered in Mexico and Peru, 58.
Government. *See* French Revolution, Political conditions, and Reforms.
Grand Remonstrance, the, 173.
Great Elector, the, 215 ff.
Gustavus Adolphus, intervention in Thirty Years' War, 156 ff.
Gutenberg, John, 27.

Habeas Corpus Act, 179.
Habsburg State, at opening of sixteenth century, 31 ff.; creation of modern state of Austria, 235.
Habsburg and Burgundian states, the, at opening of sixteenth century, 31–33.
Hague, The, Treaty of, 395.
Hampton Court, conference of Puritans and Anglicans, 169.
Hardenburg, reforms of, 436 ff.
Hargreaves, James, 306.
Harrington, James, 288.
Harvey, William, 281.
Hastings, Warren, 322.
Hébert, 372, 381.
Hegel, 468.
Helmont, van, Jan, 282.
Henry of Navarre (Henry IV), 135 ff.; and Richelieu, 144–51.
Henry VIII, revolt against the Church, 104 ff.
Henry the Navigator, Prince, 50.
Heriot, right of, 5, 73.
Hoffman, Melchior, 84.
Hohenlinden, battle of, 406.
Hohenzollerns, rise of the, 214 ff.
Holy orders, 18.
Holy Roman Empire, the, 29–30.
Hubertusburg, Treaty of, 248.
Hudson, Henry, 142.
Huguenots, in France, 133 ff.; treatment by Richelieu, 148 ff.; exodus from France, 191 ff.
Humanism, the rise of, 24.
Hundred Days, the, 458–61.
Hungary, at opening of sixteenth century, 40–41; Calvinism in, 103.
Huss, John, 151.
Huygens, 282.

Imperialism, consular, of Napoleon, 413 ff.
Independence, American, war of, 317–21.
India, struggle of the Powers in, 221 ff.;

INDEX

England and France in, 225 ff.; foundations of English rule in, 321.
Indulgences, history of, 67; sale of, 88.
Industrial Revolution, the, 284, 304-12.
Industries and commerce, at opening of sixteenth century, 5-9; at opening of nineteenth century, 476-78. *See also* Economic conditions, and Reforms.
Inquisition, given new lease of life in Spain by rise of Protestantism, 116; abolished in Spain, 439; revival in Spain, 449.
Instrument of Government, Cromwell's, 175.
Intellectual activity, stimulated by expansion of Europe, 61.
Intendants, in France, 339.
International rivalries, 79-83. *See also* Colonial and Commercial Supremacy, and names of various countries.
Ireland, at opening of sixteenth century, 39 ff.; events during reign of Charles I, 173; rising of Catholics in, 221.
Iron industry, transformation of, 309.
Islam. *See* Mohammedanism.
Italy, at opening of sixteenth century, 33-35; war between France and Spain, 79 ff.; struggle for control of, 242; on eve of wars of French Revolution, 391; extension of French influence, 437; reaction in, 449; effect of Congress of Vienna, 456.
Ivan the Terrible, 202.

Jacobin club, the, 366 ff.
James I, 168 ff.
James II, 181 ff.
Jamestown, English colony, 171.
Jemappes, battle of, 392.
Jena, battle of, 426.
Jenkins's Ear, War of, 224.
Jesuits, founding of the order, 117; lead attack on Protestantism, 121. *See also* Catholics, and Religious situation.
John (Ivan) III, 202.
John (Ivan) IV, 202 ff.
John of Oldenbarnevelt, 130.
John Sobieski, King of Poland, 272.
Joseph, King of Naples, 431 ff.
Joseph II as an enlightened despot, 254-56.
Justice, administration on eve of French Revolution, 341; system reorganized under French Constitution of 1791, 361. *See also* Social conditions.

Kalisch, Treaty of, 444.
Kalmar, Union of, 44.
Kant, Emmanuel, 467.
Kay, John, 306.
Kepler, mathematician, 277.
King George's War, 225.
King William's War, 193, 221.
Knox, John, 101 ff.
Koran, the, 22.
Kunersdorf, battle of, 248.
Kutchuk-Kainardji, Treaty of, 266.

La Rochelle, revolt of Protestants, 148.
Laissez faire, doctrine of, 474.
Laud, Archbishop, 172 ff.
Lavoissier, 283.
Law, John, 343.
League of Augsburg, 193; war of, 221.
Legislative Assembly and National Convention, reforms in France, 383 ff.
Legislative power, under French Constitution of 1791, 361.
Leoben, Treaty of, 396.
Liberty, civil, in France under National Assembly, 357.
Liberty, worship of, during French Revolution, 384.
Line of Demarcation, the, 51.
Linnæus, 283.
Literature and art, under Louis XIV, 197.
Local government, system reorganized under French Constitution of 1791, 361. *See also* Cities.
Locke, John, 286, 289 ff.
Lodi, battle of, 396.
Long Parliament, the, 173.
Louis XIV, alliance with Charles II, 180; ascendancy of France under, 186-99.
Louis XV, 344.
Louis XVI, 345 ff.; execution of, 374.
Louis XVIII, restoration of, 451 ff.
Louisiana, sale to United States, 417.
Loyola, Ignatius, 117 ff.
Lübeck, Treaty of, 155.
Luneville, Treaty of, 406.
Luther, Martin, 65 ff.
Lutheran Revolt, the, 64-78.
Lutheranism, spreads into various countries of Europe, 75.

Machinery, textile, invention of, 306.
Magellan, Ferdinand, 51.
Maintenon, de, Madame, 190.
Malta, Knights of, 17.
Manifesto (July 25, 1792), of Duke of Brunswick, 371.
Manors, in England, 1.

INDEX

Manufacturing. *See* Economic conditions.
Marat, 366.
Marengo, battle of, 406.
Maria Theresa, 242 ff.
Mark, or march, the, 214.
Marlborough, English general, 194.
Marston Moor, battle of, 174.
Mary Stuart, 132.
Mary Tudor, Protestantism in reign of, 107.
Mass, central ceremony of the Church, 19.
Mathematics and astronomy, 274–81.
Maurice of Nassau, 130.
Maurice of Saxony, 81.
Mazarin, Cardinal, 144, 164–66.
Melanchthon, draws up the Augsburg Confession, 77.
Merchantilism, developed as new economic theory, 59.
Methodist Church, created by Wesley, 315.
Metternich, at Congress of Vienna, 455.
Mexico, conquest of, 52.
Middle class, rise to political predominance, 60; effect of Protestant revolt, 112; on eve of French Revolution, 330–31. *See also* Social conditions.
Milan, duchy of, at opening of sixteenth century, 34.
Military orders, semi-religious, at opening of sixteenth century, 17.
Milton, John, 287.
Mining, development in England, 310.
Missionaries, Catholic, in America, 123; the French in America, 223; the Spanish in America, 224. *See also* Jesuits.
Mohács, battle of, 236.
Mohammedanism, at opening of sixteenth century, 21. *See also* Ottoman Empire, and Turks.
Monarchies, national, rise of, 60.
Monarchy, decline and fall during French Revolution, 343–47, 363–71.
Monastic institutions, at opening of sixteenth century, 16; dissolution in England, 106.
Money, used as regular basis of exchange, 58.
Monk, English general, 177.
Monks, at opening of sixteenth century, 15; on eve of French Revolution, 335–36.
Montesquieu, 290 ff.
Moriscos, revolt of, 126.
Moro, Lazzaro, 283.

Moscow, campaign by Napoleon, against, 443.
Mountain, the, 368 ff.
Mühlberg, triumph of Charles V, at, 81.
Murat, made Grand Duke of Berg, 425; rule in Italy, 438; rising against allies, 461.
Muscovy, Grand Duchy of, at opening of sixteenth century, 43–44, 201 ff.; expansion of, 463.
Muscovy Company, the, 205.

Naples, kingdom of, at opening of sixteenth century, 34.
Napoleon Bonaparte, 383, 395 ff.; established in power, 403–07, 420; the Hundred Days, 458–61.
Napoleonic Europe, 420–47; England during the Revolutionary Period, 420; the war of the Third Coalition and its results, 423; the war of the Fourth Coalition and its results, 426; the Continental System, 428; the national uprising in Spain, 431; the War of 1809 with Austria and its results, 432; the partial reorganization of Prussia, 434; extension of French influence in Europe, 437; France under the Empire, 440; the defeat of Napoleon, 442.
Naseby, battle of, 174.
National Assembly, in France, 351 ff.; reforms during French Revolution, 357–63.
National Convention, during French Revolution, 371–89.
Navarre, 37, 38.
Navigation Ordinance, English, 175 ff.; disregarded by English colonies in America, 318 ff.
Necker, 346 ff.
Nelson, Lord, 423.
Netherlands, The, succeeds Portuguese as dominant commercial and colonial power of Europe, 54; Calvin's gains in, 101; revolt of, 127–31; period of colonial and commercial supremacy, 140–44; war with France, 142; war with England, 143; independence recognized, 161; war with England, 175 ff., 180; war with France, 188; colonial possessions in eighteenth century, 220; war with England, 320; on eve of wars of French Revolution, 391; war with France, 393; French influence in, 439; reëstablishment as kingdom, 457; at opening of nineteenth century, 472.
New Netherland, surrendered to English, 180.

Newcomen, 308.
Newton, Sir Isaac, 280 ff.
Nile, the, battle of, 399.
Nineteenth century, opening of, 463-79; political organization, 463; cultural conditions, 472; religious and ecclesiastical conditions, 474; social organization, 476; the cities: industry and commerce, 476; rural organization, 478.
Nobles, French, crushed by Richelieu, 149; on eve of French Revolution, 327-30.
Nördlingen, battle of, 159.
Norway, effect of Congress of Vienna, 457.
Nuremberg, Diet of, 80.

Oldenburg, Napoleon's annexation of, 442.
Orders in Council, British, 429.
Orellana, 52.
Ottoman Empire, at opening of sixteenth century, 41-42; at opening of nineteenth century, 472. *See also* Turkey.
Ottoman Turks, the, 268-72.

Palatinate, Upper and Lower, in Thirty Years' War, 154.
Papal Curia, at opening of sixteenth century, 14.
Papal States, at opening of sixteenth century, 35.
Paraguay, Jesuit colonies in, 123.
Paris, treaty of 1763, 232; treaty of 1783, 321; treaty of 1796, 397; treaty of 1814, 452; treaty of 1815, 460.
Parish, at opening of sixteenth century, 12.
Parlement of Paris, protest against taxes, 164.
Parlements, French, restrictions of freedom under Henry IV, 147.
Parliament, English, conflict with James I, 170 ff.; struggle with Charles I, 171.
Parliamentary Government, the development in England, 168-85; the quarrels of the early Stuarts with their Parliaments, 168; the period of personal rule, 171; the Long Parliament, 173; the Civil War, 173; the Commonwealth and the Protectorate, 175; the Restoration, 177; the Revolution of 1688, 182; the results of the Revolution, 183; at middle of eighteenth century, 304.
Parma, Duke of, 130.
Parties, political, growth of, 179 ff.
Partition of Poland, the, 264-68.

Pascal, 282.
Passau, Treaty of, 82.
Pavia, battle of, 79.
Peasants, at opening of sixteenth century, 1-5; Russian, 203 ff.; on eve of French Revolution, 331-32; at opening of nineteenth century, 479. *See also* Social organization.
Peasants' Revolt, the, 72.
Penance, the act of, 18, 67.
Peninsular War, the, 432.
Penn, William, 179.
Pennsylvania, founding of, 179.
Perez, Antonio, 127.
Persia, campaign of Peter the Great, 212.
Peru, conquest of, 52.
Peter III, 248.
Peter the Great, 206 ff.; immediate successors of, 258-59.
Petition of Rights, the, 172.
Philip of Hesse, 80.
Philip II, 124 ff.; ascendancy of Spain, 115-37.
Philosophers, the, 284 ff.
Physiocrats, the, 298.
Physiology, 281.
Pitt, William, 229.
Pitt, William, the younger, 420 ff.
Pizarro, 52.
Plassey, battle of, 231.
Plymouth, English colony, 171.
Poland, at opening of sixteenth century, 42 ff.; Calvinism in, 103; on eve of first partition, 261-64; the partition, 264-68; on eve of wars of French Revolution, 391; personal union with Russia, 465.
Polish Succession, War of, 344 ff.
Political conditions, at opening of sixteenth century, 28-29; in England, 168-84; France on eve of French Revolution, 337-43; countries of Europe at opening of nineteenth century, 463-72.
Poltava, battle of, 211.
Pompadour, de, Madame, 345.
Pope, at opening of sixteenth century, 14; relations with French church, 333; Concordat of 1801, 409; Napoleon's quarrel with, 441. *See also* Religious situation.
Portugal, at opening of sixteenth century, 37 ff.; pioneer explorers, 50; supremacy in the East, 53; united with Spain under Philip II, 54; annexation by Spain, 126, 141; independence regained, 164; colonial possessions in eighteenth century, 220; on eve of wars of French Revolution, 391; Wellington's Campaign

INDEX

in, 432; at opening of nineteenth century, 472.
Pragmatic Sanction, the, 236, 242.
Prague, assembly of Protestant nobles at, 152.
Prague, Peace of, 159.
Pressburg, Treaty of, 424, 432.
Priestley, 283.
Principal Decree of the Imperial Deputation, 415 ff.
Printing, invention of movable types, 27.
Protestant Revolt, in Germany, 64-86; the Lutheran revolt, 64; international rivalries, 79; the Anabaptist revolt, 83; in other lands, 87-113; the work of Zwingli, 87; the Calvinist revolt, 92; the Anglican revolt, 103; results of the Protestant Revolt, 110.
Protestant Union, in France, 135.
Protestants, growth of strength, 74; in Thirty Years' War, 151-66; treatment by Louis XIV, 189 ff.; persecution in France, 336-37; in France, under Concordat of 1801, 410.
Protestants. See also Religious conditions.
Prussia, rise of, 214-19, 236-41; alliance with England, 246; war with France, 370; on eve of wars of French Revolution, 391; war with France, 392; alliance with France, 424 ff.; partial reorganization of, 434-37; war with France, 444; effect of Congress of Vienna, 456; transformed by Napoleonic wars, 468.
Puritans, growth of party in England, 168.
Pyramids, battle of, 399.

Queen Anne's War, 222.

Races, mixture in Russian Empire, 464; in territories controlled by Austria, 470 ff.
Rastadt, Treaty of, 194.
Reaction, after defeat of Napoleon, 448 ff.
Reconstruction of Europe, the, 448-62; restoration and reaction, 448; the Congress of Vienna, 453; the Hundred Days, 458; permanent result of the French Revolution and the Napoleonic Period, 461.
Reformation, Catholic, 115-24.
Reforms, Peter the Great, 206 ff.; Frederick William, the Great Elector, 216 ff.; Frederick William I of Prussia, 238 ff.; Maria Theresa, 244 ff., Frederick the Great, 249 ff.; Joseph II, 254 ff.; Catherine II, 259 ff.; Turgot, 345; the National Assembly, during French Revolution, 357-63; the Legislative Assembly and the National Convention (1792-93), 383-89; consular government under Napoleon, 407 ff.; Stein, 434 ff.; Hardenberg, 436 ff.; Napoleon, 440 ff.
Regensburg, Diet of, 156.
Religious and ecclesiastical conditions, at opening of sixteenth century, 11 ff.; organization of Eastern Europe, 21-22; effect of expansion of Europe, 61; the Protestant Revolt, 64-78, 87-103, 110-13; the Anabaptist Revolt, 83-85; the Anglican Revolt, 103-110; Catholic Reformation, 115-24; wars in France, 132-37; the Thirty Years' War, 151-63; problems in England, 168 ff.; problem after English civil war, 178 ff.; France under Louis XIV, 189 ff.; skeptical attitude, 286; the Wesleyan revival, 314 ff.; France on eve of French Revolution, 332-37; at opening of nineteenth century, 474-76. See also Church, and Ecclesiastical conditions.
Restitution, edict of, 155.
Restoration, reaction in favor of sovereigns after Napoleonic period, 448-53.
Restoration, Stuart, 177.
Reunions, a policy of Louis XIV, 190.
Revolution of 1688, English, 183 ff., 288 ff.
Revolutionary Tribunal, in France, 375 ff.
Richelieu and Henry IV, 144-51.
Rights of Man, French Declaration of, 355 ff.
Robespierre, 366 ff., 377.
Roman Catholic Church, effect of Protestant revolt, 110 ff. See also Catholics, Pope, and Religious conditions.
Rousseau, Jean Jacques, 294 ff.
Roux, Jacques, 372.
Rural conditions, 1-5; government in France, on eve of French Revolution, 340; organization, at opening of nineteenth century, 476-78.
Russia, rise of, 201-13; the early modern period, 201; the work of Peter the Great, 206; alliance with Austria, 246; change of policy, 248; intervention in Seven Years' War, 258; war with Turkey, 266 ff.; on eve

of wars of French Revolution, 391;
war with France, 423 ff., 437; at
Congress of Vienna, 454; effect of
Congress of Vienna, 457; expansion
of, 463 ff.
Russian church, the, 209.
Rutherford, 283.

Sacraments, church, at opening of sixteenth century, 18.
St. Bartholomew, Massacre of, 133.
St. Helena, Napoleon exiled to, 460.
Sardinia, war with France, 395; at opening of nineteenth century, 472.
Saxony, alliance with Austria, 246.
Schiller, 467.
Scholarship, at opening of nineteenth century, 473.
Scholasticism, a cultural heritage from the Middle Ages, 22.
Schönbrunn, Treaty of, 433.
Science, revival of study, 26 ff.; in sixteenth century, 274 ff.; societies for advancement of, 282 ff.; establishment of organizations for study during French Revolution, 386.
Scotland, at opening of sixteenth century, 39 ff.; Calvinism in, 101; armed revolt in, 172.
Sea beggars, the, 129.
Sebastiani, 413.
Secular clergy, at opening of sixteenth century, 15.
Self-government, city, at opening of sixteenth century, 8. *See also* Local government.
Selim I, 270.
Services, church, results of Protestant revolt, 112.
Seven Years' War, the, 229, 247 ff.
Seventeenth century, opening decades of, 140; development of Parliamentary Government in England, 168–85; ascendancy of France under Louis XIV, 186–99; rise of Russia and Prussia, 201–19; modern science and philosophy, 282 ff. *See also* Colonial and commercial supremacy, and Expansion, overseas.
Siberia, conquest of, 203.
Sicily, at opening of sixteenth century, 35.
Sieyès, 297, 402 ff.
Silesia, Prussian occupation of, 242 ff.
Silver, discovered in Mexico and Peru, 58.
Sixteenth century, the opening of, 1–46; the great estates, 1; the cities: industry and commerce, 5; social organization, 9; religious and ecclesiastical conditions, 11; the cultural heritage from the Middle Ages, 22; political conditions, 28; the Holy Roman Empire, 29; the Habsburg and Burgundian States, 31; Italy, 33; France, 35; Spain and Portugal, 37; England, Scotland, and Ireland, 39; Bohemia, 40; Hungary, 40; the Ottoman Empire, 41; the Teutonic Knights, Poland, and the Grand Duchy of Muscovy, 42; other States, 44; position of Spain at close of, 136.
Slavic Europe and the Ottoman Empire, in the eighteenth century, 258–73; the immediate successors of Peter the Great, 258; Catherine II as an enlightened despot, 259; Poland on the eve of the First Partition, 261; the Partition of Poland and the dismemberment of Turkey, 264; the southern Slavs and the Ottoman Turks, 268.
Smeaton, John, 309.
Smith, Adam, 298, 474.
Social organization, at opening of sixteenth century, 1 ff.; at opening of sixteenth century, 9–11; effect of expansion of Europe on different classes, 59; England at middle of eighteenth century, 301 ff.; effect of Industrial Revolution, 311; France on eve of French Revolution, 327–32; Prussia, 469; at opening of nineteenth century, 476. *See also* Reforms.
Society of Jesus, the, 117. *See also* Jesuits.
Solyman the Magnificent, 270.
South America, Dutch attempts at colonization, 143. *See also* Portugal and Spain.
Sovereignty, transferred from King to people, by French Constitution of 1791, 360.
Spain, at opening of sixteenth century, 37–39; exploration of North and South America, 51; rivalry with France, 79 ff.; ascendancy under Philip II, 115–37; Inquisition established in dominions, 116, 126; Protestants suppressed in, 125; commerce raided by Hawkins and Drake, 131; war with England, 131–32; position at close of sixteenth century, 136; commerce raided by Dutch, 142; war with France, 159; revolt of Catalonia and Portugal, 160; war with France, 164–66; colonies lost, 195; colonial possessions in eighteenth century, 220 ff.; war

INDEX

with England, 222, 224, 232, 320; on eve of wars of French Revolution, 391; diplomacy during Napoleon's consulship, 417; national uprising in, 431–32; French influence in, 439; Ferdinand regains throne, 448; at opening of nineteenth century, 472.
Spanish Constitution of 1812, 448.
Spanish Succession, War of the, 194 ff., 222.
Speyer, Diet of, 80.
Stanislas Leczinski, 344.
State, worship of, during French Revolution, 384.
Steam engine, invention of, 308.
Steel, first made, 309.
Stein, reforms of, 434 ff.
Strassburg, Calvin at, 96.
Sully, Duke of, 145.
Sweden, at opening of sixteenth century, 44; intervention in Thirty Years' War, 156 ff.; attacked by Russia, 210; alliance with Austria, 246; at opening of nineteenth century, 472.
Switzerland, cantons, at opening of sixteenth century, 44; Protestant revolt in, 87–92; independence recognized, 161; French influence in, 439; effect of Congress of Vienna, 457; at opening of nineteenth century, 472.

Talleyrand, 386, 414; recalls Bourbons to French throne, 451.
Taxation, reform in France, 145; abuses under Louis XIV, 196; as a cause of American Revolution, 319; on eve of French Revolution, 331, 341 ff. *See also* Reforms.
Tennis Court Oath, the, 352.
Terror, the, during French Revolution, 380.
Test Act (1673), the, 183.
Teutonic Knights, the, 17, 42–43.
Textile machinery, 307 ff.
Theatines, the, 116.
Third Coalition, war of, 423–25.
Thirty Years' War, the, 151–64, 215 ff.
Tilsit, Treaty of, 427, 434.
Tolentino, Treaty of, 397.
Toleration, religious, growth of, 475.
Toleration Act, the, 183.
Torricelli, 282.
Trade, medieval, 47; changing of routes, 56. *See also* Commerce and industries.
Trafalgar, battle of, 423.
Transportation, development of facilities, 310.
Trent, Council of, 119 ff.

Tsar, Russian, powers of, 464.
Turenne, French general, 186.
Turgot, 298, 345.
Turkey, the dismemberment of, 264–68; intervention in behalf of Poland, 265; war with Russia, 266 ff.; on eve of wars of French Revolution, 391; war with France, 399. *See also* Ottoman Empire.
Turks, attack territories of Charles V, 79; invasion of Hungary, 236.
Turks, Ottoman, 268–72.
Tyrol, rising in, 433.

Ulster, Scotch-Irish settlements in, 171; Irish rebellion in, 173.
Union of Arras, 130.
Union of Kalmar, the, 44.
Union of Utrecht, 130.
United Netherlands, new republic established, 130.
United States, purchase of Louisiana, 417; suffers under the Continental System, and orders in Council, 429. *See also* American Revolution.
Utrecht, Treaty of, 194, 222 ff.

Valmy, battle of, 392.
Varennes, flight of Louis XVI, 365.
Vauban, French military engineer, 186.
Venice, at opening of sixteenth century, 34; trade with Far East, 47.
Verrazano, 54.
Versailles, march of the women to, 357.
Vervins, Treaty of, 144.
Vesalius, 281.
Vienna, Congress of, 453–58.
Villagers, at opening of sixteenth century, 4.
Voltaire, 292 ff.

Wagram, battle of, 433.
Wallenstein, 155 ff.
Wandewash, battle of, 232.
Warsaw, Duchy of, 428, 433, 439, 450.
Washington, George, 320.
Waterloo, battle of, 460.
Watt, James, 308.
Wesley, John, 314 ff.
Wesleyan revival, the, 314–16.
West Indies, English colonies in, 322.
West Prussia, acquired by Frederick the Great, 253.
Westphalia, Kingdom of, 439.
Westphalia, Peace of, 160 ff., 215.
White Mountain, battle of, 153.

Whitney, Eli, 308.
Wilkes, John, 316.
William of Orange, 129 ff., 182, 189.
William and Mary, 182 ff.
Willoughby, English explorer, 205.
Wittenberg, Luther at, 66.
Woolen industry, in England, 303 ff.

Worms, Diet of, 70.

Xavier, Francis, 122.

Zurich, Great Council of, 89.
Zwingli, Ulrich, 88 ff.
Zwinglian revolt, the, 87–93.